PREHISTORIC CUMBRIA

DAVID BARROWCLOUGH

For Mary Chester-Kadwell

First published 2010

The History Press
The Mill, Brimscombe Port
Stroud, Gloucestershire, GL5 2QG
www.thehistorypress.co.uk

British Library Cataloguing in Publication Data.
A catalogue record for this book is available from the British Library.

ISBN 978 0 7524 5087 2

Typesetting and origination by The History Press
Printed in Great Britain
Manufacturing managed by Jellyfish Print Solutions Ltd

CONTENTS

ACKNOWLEDGEMENTS

I have only been able to write this book through the help of many people and organisations. The research was begun whilst studying for my PhD at the Department of Archaeology, University of Cambridge and the book largely written whilst I held a Fellowship at Wolfson College, also at Cambridge, and my thanks go to Graeme Barker and the staff and members of the department, and to Gordon Johnson and the Fellows of Wolfson College. Much of the fieldwork that underpins the research was undertaken in collaboration with other people, in particular Mary Chester-Kadwell and Alan and Gillian Barrowclough.

The methodological and theoretical approaches to prehistory adopted in the book derive from my time at Cambridge from my undergraduate days onwards. My thanks go to Richard Bradley, a frequent visitor to the department, always with new insights into British archaeology; Charles French, who renewed my interest in physical geography; Cornelius Holtorf, who always reminds me to think outside the box; Andrew Jones, who first made me aware of the significance of colour; Martin Jones, for his strictures on methodology; Colin Renfrew, for his insights into art and cognition; Pamela Jane Smith, for her encyclopaedic knowledge of departmental history; and Marie Louis Sørensen, my Director of Studies and later doctoral supervisor. Informal, yet also significant, were the conversations and debates with fellow students and members of the Archaeological Field Club and *Archaeological Review from Cambridge*.

In addition, many people have made this project easier and much more enjoyable by showing me their sites, collections and records, answering my questions, discussing their ideas and commenting on my interpretations. My thanks are due to the following: Craig Asquith, Robert Bewley, Clive Bonsall, Roger Broadie, Peter Cherry, Nick Dooley, Ann Hallam, Rachel Newman and her staff at Oxford Archaeology North, Tim Padley and the staff at Tullie House Museum and Art Gallery in Carlisle, and the curators and staff at: The Dock Museum at Barrow-in-Furness, Kendal Museum, Keswick Museum and Art Gallery, Lancaster City Museum and Penrith and Eden Museum. I would like to thank English Heritage for permission to reproduce site plans of Mayburgh henge and the associated landscape; Robert Bewley, Clive Bonsall, Roger Broadie, Peter Cherry, Ann Hallam and Pamela Jane Smith for permission to reproduce their illustrations and photographs; Craig Asquith for producing the base map of Cumbria and Nick Dooley for the reconstructions of Shap Stone Avenue and Oddendale circle. Unless marked otherwise the remaining photographs and illustrations are my own. Mary Chester-Kadwell read all the text and suggested many improvements. I am extremely grateful to them all.

CHAPTER 1

INTRODUCTION

The searchers after antiquity find much more to recreate their minds, and satisfy their curiosity, in these northern countries than in those farther south, which are more populous and better inhabited, because the remains of ancient things have met with less injury here, where there are not so many people, or so many buildings, or alterations, enclosings and plantings, as in other places.

Daniel Defoe, 1727

This study attempts to provide a synthesis of the prehistoric archaeology of Cumbria. I, like many before, have been frustrated that there was no up-to-date account of the county's archaeology. This concerned me for it has meant an over reliance on such texts that do exist, which, because of their age, lack discussion of more recent excavations. This has led to the proliferation of misconceptions about the region's archaeology; in particular, that it was in some way a 'black hole' in prehistory. This book therefore takes the opportunity to publish, often for the first time, details of excavations that have in some cases only been hinted at in previous works, and in other cases not known of at all. Regionality and ritual are the twin themes that have interested me for some time and I am pleased to say these themes are becoming increasingly important in studies of prehistory in Britain and beyond (Barrowclough 2008; Barrowclough and Malone 2007). Building on the work of archaeologists, past and present, that have been active in the county it has been possible to begin to develop a narrative that stands for the past. Focusing on the question which first brought me to the study of archaeology, 'what was life like in Cumbria in the past?', the answer begins to reveal something of the ritual and belief that underpinned prehistoric society in Cumbria.

Prehistoric Cumbria spans the period from the end of the last ice age to the arrival of the Romans, a span of over 8000 years. For convenience and ease of comparison, the traditional terms for the divisions of the prehistoric period – Mesolithic, Neolithic, Bronze and Iron Age – have been adopted with the addition of sub-divisions, such as Early Bronze Age, used to further refine the chronology. The discussion is, however, led by the archaeology, rather than terminology, thus the discussion of the 'hillforts', defended hilltop enclosures, spans the whole of the later prehistoric period from Late Bronze Age to Early Iron Age (Chapter 8). It is felt that this retains clarity whilst also addressing the complexity of the archaeological record.

Within these broad period divisions it is possible to further sub-divide the period into numerous phases (Burgess 1979; 1980; 1988; Needham 1996; Needham *et al.* 1997; Gibson and Kinnes 1997; Garwood 1999). Although the different systems of phases are numerous and sometimes contradictory, it is possible to distinguish between those chronologies based on metalwork assemblages and the Grave Series based on ceramic evidence. In each case several attempts have been made at defining different phases and the results are subject to ongoing debate. For the

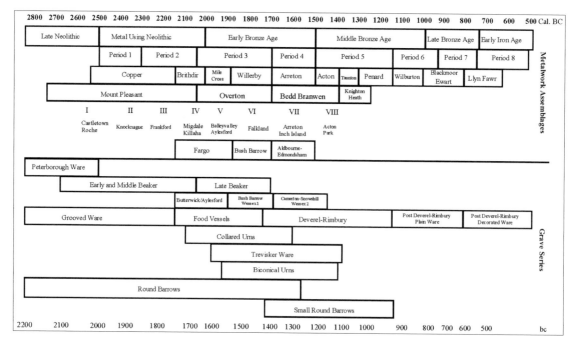

1 A simplified chronological chart of concordances of major periodisations for metalwork assemblages and major burial traditions in England and Wales from the Late Neolithic to Early Bronze Age. *Burgess 1979, 1980, 1988; Needham et al 1997; Gibson and Kinnes 1997; Garwood 1999*

purposes of the current discussion a concordance has been produced (*1*), which reconciles the different sequences with each other and with a timeline marked in years cal BC and bc.

The order of the chapters is basically chronological, with one exception: before dealing with the prehistory I have devoted a chapter to consideration of the history of archaeological research in Cumbria, Chapter 2. In the absence of a published history I felt it necessary to set what follows in some sort of historic and theoretical framework. Cumbria has a long tradition of archaeological research, beginning with the antiquarian study of the county's stone circles and early collections of polished stone axes, and as a consequence has been at the forefront of national debates concerning the origins of the Neolithic since the nineteenth century. More recently, in the twentieth century, the county's upland bogs and lowland mosses provided the preserved remains that made pioneering palynological studies possible. Chapter 2 aims to provide an historic account of the significant role played by Cumbrian archaeology which, as well as being of interest to historians of archaeology, will also set the chapters which follow in historical context.

Chapter 3 deals with the post-glacial colonisation and Mesolithic exploitation of Cumbria. Evidence for the Late Upper Palaeolithic is scarce in northern Britain because the ice sheets took longer to retreat than they did further south. Nonetheless Kirkhead Cave in the south of the county has produced a number of interesting Late Upper Palaeolithic (11,000-10,000 BC) remains, including 21 flint blades and antlers (see discussion in Salisbury 1997). In addition, Upper Palaeolithic blades have been found nearby at Lindale Low Cave (Salisbury 1988). Together these finds were remarkable because they represent the most northerly recorded

Palaeolithic sites in Britain (Hodgkinson *et al* 2000, 33). During the Mesolithic the activities of mobile hunter–gatherer communities can be discerned from the many flints found by Peter and John Cherry. Over a 40-year period father and son undertook two extensive surveys, the first concentrated on the south-west coastal strip between St Bees and Haverigg and the second on the limestone uplands of eastern Cumbria between Shap and Kirkby Stephen (summarised in Cherry and Cherry 2002). Most finds consist of stray flints, collected rather than excavated, from surface scatters. Almost all the coastal assemblages found by the Cherrys were the result of plough action, whereas the finds in the uplands came in significant proportion from mole hills and erosion scars (Cherry and Cherry 2002, 1). What is needed to develop our understanding of the way that these hunters lived their lives can only be provided by an archaeological context.

Turning to the Neolithic, *c.*4500-2350 cal BC, recent research has done much to develop our understanding of occupation, for example a recent study of the Neolithic and Bronze Age landscape of the Furness Peninsula completed by Helen Evans (2008). In Cumbria, as in many parts of western Britain, the most visible aspect of the Neolithic are the stone circles and henge monuments. Many of these, notably Long Meg and her Daughters, King Arthur's Round Table and Castlerigg Stone Circle, have been known about for almost 500 years. The Cumbrian monuments have been comprehensively catalogued by Tom Clare in *Prehistoric Monuments of the Lake District* (2007). As with stone circles and henge monuments elsewhere in Britain, notably Stonehenge, research continues to reveal new insights into their possible use and significance to the prehistoric population (Darvill 2007). What is most distinctive about the Neolithic period in Cumbria are the stone axe 'factories' of the Langdales, discussed in Chapter 4. The stone used to fashion many of the polished stone axes found throughout Britain originates from these quarry sites. The Langdales have been the subject of considerable research (e.g. Bradley and Edmonds 1993) and the focus here will be on the ritual aspects of axe production, distribution and deposition. The focus in Chapter 5 will be on new interpretations of the Cumbrian sites as centres of ritual and ceremony associated with calendrical festivals. Against a backdrop of new insights gained from ongoing studies of Stonehenge (Darvill 2007) and following recent research in Cumbria by Steven Hood (2004) the approach is to consider the known sites, in the context of the surrounding landscape. The aim is to use modern scientific observations to identify possible solar and lunar alignments common to the sites from which something may be inferred about a pre-Christian calendar and its associated festivals.

Overall, the evidence for the Neolithic has striking similarities with that of the Mesolithic, which suggests that the population remained relatively mobile. This sense of continuity in the face of technological innovation is a theme I have previously identified in Lancashire (Barrowclough 2008) and it continues into the Early Bronze Age, *c.*2350-1400 cal BC, in Cumbria and is the subject of Chapter 6. The earthworks and monuments are the most visible testament to the prehistoric occupation of Cumbria and are widely spread across the county. Many barrows were destroyed at the end of the nineteenth century and the early part of the twentieth, and the literature has often bemoaned the lack of scientific excavation. I have therefore taken this chapter as an opportunity to combine the details of more recent excavations of Early Bronze Age cemeteries with a review of the older excavations, analysing the records and museum collections for information on the details of the burials, funerary urns and grave goods. These data underpin a renewed analysis of the period, which includes consideration of the regional chronology, grave good assemblages, and demography in the context of what we know about settlement and domestic activity during this period. One result of this analysis is a reaffirmation of the continuity between Neolithic and Early Bronze Age ritual beliefs and practices. This is demonstrated by a study of the prehistoric ritual sequence undertaken at Oddendale, Shap (Turnbull and Walsh 1997). Excavations show that the site was a focus for ritual and burial in both the Neolithic and Early Bronze Ages, during which it was constructed and reconstructed four times, suggesting to the excavators a four-phase sequence of ceremonial activity over a long period of time (cf. Bradley 2005, 103-4).

Chapter 7 progresses to the Middle and Late Bronze Ages, and focuses on the deposition of metalwork. The break between Early and Late Bronze Ages is one of the more obvious disjunctures in the archaeological record. It is still not at all clear why the long-standing Early Bronze Age burial practices came to an end, although suggestions that it may have something to do with a deteriorating climate are supported by the local environmental evidence. The advent of popular metal detecting combined with more consistent reporting, thanks in part to the Portable Antiquities Scheme, has led to an increase in the number of finds of this period (see below). Using all the available evidence it has been possible to discern a distinct regional flavour to metalwork deposits in Cumbria. Moving beyond simplistic observations about the absence of large hoards, and an almost total absence of certain weapon types, such as swords, it has been possible to identify particular local associations between certain types and certain modes of deposition.

Chapter 8 is concerned with the Late Bronze Age and pre-Roman Iron Age, with a particular focus on the evidence for ritual burial. Historically, evidence for the Late Bronze Age and Iron Age of north-west England has been poor, partly because of the difficulty associated with site identification in areas dominated by pasture and partly because of an intellectual focus on Roman remains rather than prehistoric activity. In recent years this has begun to change with significant new sites emerging in Lancashire (see Barrowclough 2008). Developments in Cumbria have lagged a little behind those to the immediate south, but nonetheless research in recent years has led to the identification of a number of new sites, for example in Matterdale (Hoaen and Loney 2003, 2004). The relationship between the later prehistoric settlement sites studied by Hoaen and Loney in Matterdale and earlier Neolithic and Bronze Age burial sites is striking and reinforces the sense that ritual beliefs and practices guided the actions of the prehistoric inhabitants of Cumbria over many hundreds of years. Despite the recent advances made in our understanding of later prehistoric settlement patterns, perhaps the best known evidence for this period remains that of the bog bodies of the lowland mires. This chapter presents a new analysis of the bog burials from the lowland mosses of Cumbria, based on the re-analysis of two bog bodies found at Seascale Moss in 1845 and 1834 (Turner 1988; 1989). The discussion sets them in the ritual context of other finds from north-west England, Ireland and Scandinavia. Attention is also directed towards comparison with other contemporary burial practices drawing on the recent excavation of a Late Iron Age inhumation cemetery at Levens (courtesy of Oxford Archaeology North).

The book concludes with an assessment of our understanding of social reproduction in Cumbria, Chapter 9. Using the evidence from studies of stone axes, monuments, burials and metalwork deposition, it is possible to begin to develop an understanding of the difference between local and non-local identity, which highlights the importance of regionality in the later prehistoric period. The reality of a community firmly rooted in a specific environment, and the ensuing sense of belonging, seems to have been at odds with another reality, that of participation in long-distance, supra-regional, exchange networks which linked Cumbria with Ireland in the west and Yorkshire in the east. These were not just about the inhabitants of other regions acquiring access to Cumbrian stone axes, for example, but also about sharing cultural knowledge of the supra-regionally acknowledged categories of polished stone axe.

The Physical Landscape: Reconstructing the Prehistoric Environment

Before considering the archaeological evidence for prehistory in Cumbria I first need to say something about the physical environment of the county. To do so is more than to set the scene, as the physical environment shapes and has been shaped by human activity in a complex series of interactions through the millennia. The changing environment is one important connecting thread between the people that inhabit it in different periods. Particularly in non-industrial, non-literate societies, inhabiting a landscape requires an engagement with the properties of that environment, and the constraints and opportunities that it presents. Those properties transcend the boundaries of world view, language and culture that may separate the inhabitants of that landscape of one period from those that inhabited the same place in another. The physical environment is therefore an enduring, but not unchanging, frame of reference and holds considerable promise as a platform of shared understanding across time (Barrowclough 2005, 39-54; Barrowclough 2007).

During the last two decades there has been a growing recognition that the way that the landscape is perceived by past societies may be highly culture specific. Different ways of thinking about the landscape result in very different ways of organising it physically. This realisation led to a shift away from the generalising models of spatial organisation that had been sought in the 1970s. The new challenge has been how to retrieve these idiosyncratic cognitive elements from the material record. Christopher Tilley, Richard Bradley and Colin Renfrew have all suggested alternative approaches to the problem. I have previously adopted a contextual approach that is multi-scalar and draws upon elements of these different approaches in order to construct an interpretation that, whilst grounded in empirical research, remains flexible enough to account for individual perception (Barrowclough 2007).

Many of the issues and questions that may be raised about ritual (defined as the observance of actions or procedures in a set, ordered and ceremonial way) beliefs in prehistoric times are, to a large extent, tied to the relationship between the county's prehistoric inhabitants and this environment. A useful point to begin addressing these questions is to consider the key characteristics of the physical environment, and the processes that have changed it over time. A sound grasp of these processes is useful for two reasons. First, the physical environment defined the constraints and opportunities that faced its prehistoric inhabitants. An understanding of

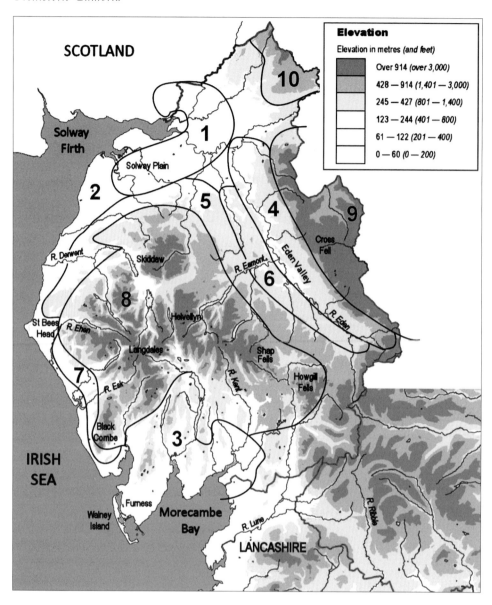

2 Cumbria's topography. Topographically, Cumbria may be divided into 10 sub-regions:

1 The Carlisle and Solway Plains
2 The West Cumbria Coastal Plain
3 Lancashire North of the Sands
4 The Eden Valley
5 Central Lakeland limestone escarpment
6 The Lazonby Fells
7 South West Cumbrian Fells
8 Central Mountainous Zone
9 The Pennines
10 Bewcastle Fells

the processes that altered the environment over time, and the timescales over which they took place, will make it clearer which elements of the environment may have been different from the conditions that may be observed today, and which elements have remained largely unchanged. A second reason is that the dynamics of the physical environment, through human as well as natural agencies, may also determine which parts of the prehistoric material record are destroyed or preserved, as well as the circumstances in which they are discovered. This may in turn determine when patterns in the known evidence may be representative of the original patterns, and when they may be misleading artefacts of selective preservation or discovery.

Cumbria lies on the west side of Britain in the north-west of England, 490km north-west of London (London to Keswick) and 215km south of Glasgow (Glasgow to Keswick). The focus is on the county of Cumbria, which comprised the historic counties of Cumberland, Westmorland and Lancashire North of the Sands, covering an area of 6768 square kilometres. The natural boundaries formed by the waterways of the Irish Sea to the west, the Solway to the north, the sands of Morecambe Bay to the south and the upper Lune Valley to the east, have always tended to give Cumbria a regional character which distinguishes it from those parts of England and Scotland with which it comes into contact. It is, however, sometimes necessary to consider areas beyond these boundaries as the prehistoric occupants of the region also occupied parts of adjoining counties, in particular the Carlisle Plain, which extends into Dumfriesshire, and Morecambe Bay, which extends into North Lancashire.

Topographically, Cumbria comes within the Highland Region of Britain (Fox 1932), with the highest mountains in England at one extreme and the extensive lowland plains of Carlisle, the west coast and Furness on another (*2*). The topography and superficial geology combine to create a number of natural sub-regions into which Cumbria may be divided. These may be grouped into four: the low lying areas of the Carlisle Plain, the West Cumbrian Coastal Plain, Lancashire North of the Sands and the Eden Valley. These form a ring within which sits the central Lakeland limestone escarpment, Lazonby Fells and the south-west Cumbrian Fells. These, in turn, ring the mountainous zone which sits at the core of Cumbria. To the east of the Eden Valley lie the Pennines and to the north the Bewcastle Fells, marking the border of Cumbria with Northumbria and Scotland (Hogg 1972).

The Carlisle and Solway Plains

This extensive area of low-lying ground extends from the central Lakeland outcrop of Carboniferous rocks northwards over the northern boundary of Cumbria and continues deep into Dumfriesshire. The landscape is dominated by a series of low ridges forming a gently undulating terrain, typical of a boulder clay landscape, giving way to the Solway Firth, comprising sand dunes, intertidal mudflats, estuarine and lagoonal complexes, and saltwater marshes. Inland from these are considerable expanses of wetland followed by an area covered by boulder clay and numerous drumlins, which have an average thickness of 8m (25ft) in the Carlisle area. The natural vegetation of these heavy clay soils was a mixed oak forest with dense wet undergrowth, which discouraged settlement. Prehistoric activity seems to have been confined to the wetlands of Solway (Bewley 1993; 1994) and to the vicinity of Carlisle, where the Eden valley, a principal prehistoric routeway, crosses the Carlisle Plain. In this area a number of Early Bronze Age cemetery sites have been found at Garlands, Carlisle; Waterloo Hill, Aglionby; and How Hill, Thursby. They are located on glacial eskers, lobated spreads of bedded sands deposited on basal clays by melt waters as the last ice sheets retreated, which rise above the boulder clay, as demonstrated by the How Hill esker at Thursby. Their sandy soils are drier than those of the boulder clays making them more sparsely wooded. The presence of eskers can be problematic for our understanding of the county's archaeology as these natural features may be confused with prehistoric burial monuments. For example, near Dalston Hall are two mounds, one each side of the road, which were marked on the 6in OS map as 'tumuli' but are in fact gravel knolls, the extremities of a long, winding ribbon-like esker. The same applies to the 'tumulus' at Lanercost Bridge, and to many in the area around Brampton. Some of the Brampton eskers were opened by General Pitt Rivers and Lord Carlisle, but nothing but gravel was found. Other areas where there are large numbers of eskers that may be confused with cairns are the following: between Great Orton and Carlisle; between Abbey Town and Allonby; between Black Snib peat moss and Brackenhill Tower at Kirklinton; south of Arthuret Church; and between the Heather Burn and the Longtown and Brampton Road, where in the vicinity of Horsegills farmhouse a series of circular mounds similar in appearance to cairns may be found, of which Torkin on the north side of Crofton Park is the most conspicuous.

The West Cumbria Coastal Plain

The narrow coastal plain of West Cumbria, stretching from Haverigg on the Duddon estuary to St Bees Head, is of considerable archaeological interest because it was utilised from the Mesolithic onwards as both a routeway and settlement zone. The plain is composed of raised beaches, the result of post-glacial sea-level change (see below), which create a well-drained fringe no more than 7km wide around the coast, ideal for human exploitation. In later times the terraces were enveloped by extensive deposits of blown sand which are well developed between Silloth and Allonby, and also south of the cliffs at St Bees Head, masking the archaeological evidence for the exploitation of the coast. Further to the south in the Drigg Peninsula, south of St Bees Head, where there has been a migration inland of the shoreline dune belt, Mesolithic and later occupation levels are being re-exposed, and heavily sand-blasted flint artefacts, including microliths, have been found (see Chapter 3).

Pollen cores taken by Walker confirm the presence of human activity along the coast during the Late Mesolithic and Early Neolithic. The earliest human activity is dated to *c*.4780-4470 cal BC at Williamson's Moss where woodland clearance activity is recorded (Tipping 1994; Hodgkinson *et al* 2000), and at Barfield Tarn similar clearance activity was recorded at 4457-3825 cal BC (Hodgkinson *et al* 2000). This was followed at both sites by evidence for cereal cultivation dated to 3893-3381 cal BC at Williamson's Moss (Tipping 1994; Hodgkinson *et al* 2000).

Lancashire North of the Sands

This area of Cumbria is formed by the districts of Furness, lying between the Duddon estuary and Windermere, and Cartmel, the adjoining area to the east bounded by Windermere and the Winster valley. The landscape is largely dominated by undulating low limestone fells and ridges, from which a pastoral landscape with substantial woodlands has developed, penetrated by the valleys and estuaries of the rivers Duddon, Leven and Kent, all of which support wetland environments in their lower reaches along the broad expanse of Morecambe Bay, which lies to the south. To the north the Scafell massif separates the mountainous areas of Coniston and Hawkshead in High Furness from central Lakeland, whilst to the west the area is cut off from West Cumbria by Black Combe. As a consequence, this area has historically had closer ties to Lancashire than it has to the rest of Cumbria. This sense of cultural isolation from the north is embodied in the old Furness saying 'Nowt good ever came round Black Combe'. To an extent this sense of independence is reflected in the prehistoric archaeology of the area which often has closer affinities to that of sites to the south than it does to those in the north (see discussion in Chapter 9), reflected in what I have previously described as a prehistoric Morecambe Bay community (Barrowclough 2008).

The earliest pollen evidence for human exploitation of the natural environment in the area dates to the Neolithic. At Roudsea Wood, reductions in elm, oak and ivy pollen occurred between 3850 and 3150 cal BC suggesting small-scale clearance activity (Birks 1982), with the earliest, occasional, cereal pollen appearing from *c.*3150 BC. At Foulshaw and Helsington Mosses (Wimble *et al* 2000) the first indications of human interference occur slightly later at between 3000 and 2000 cal BC, when the pollen record contains small peaks of plantains and grasses, together with drops in elm, ash and lime. More substantial larger-scale clearances occurred here at between 2000 and 1300 cal BC and are characterised by steep falls in elm, ash, lime and hazel, with plantains, nettles and bracken increasingly evident, but cereal pollen was not recorded in the area until between 1300 and 900 cal BC. The delay in introducing cereal cultivation to certain parts of this coastal area has been put down to the rocky and marshy nature of the terrain close to the Morecambe Bay estuaries, which has traditionally limited arable agriculture, with many areas used for rough grazing (Evans 2008). Evans has argued persuasively that the available evidence illustrates that different *sorts* of landscapes, in different sorts of topographic zones, were used in different ways during the prehistoric period (Evans 2008). At a broad level, around Morecambe Bay, in common with the western lowlands and the eastern and central uplands, the evidence suggests a progressive intensity of clearance and cultivation over increasingly widespread areas into the Late Neolithic and Bronze Age.

The Eden Valley

The River Eden flows almost due north, from its source in the Mallerstang Common, through gently undulating country, created by the northward passage of the Eden valley glacier. The greater part of this valley is composed of Triassic shales and sandstones, cut in places by deep gorges. To the east the valley is flanked by the Pennine escarpment and to the west the ground rises more gradually to form the Lazenby Fell ridge. The Eden valley was the major prehistoric route through Cumbria, which to the south, crossed the Pennines via Stainmore to the Vale of York, and to the north, reached through the Irthing valley, the Tyne Gap, the principal route for those entering Cumbria from the east.

A palynological study of the southern Eden valley has revealed a rich and diverse history of prehistoric landscape exploitation (Skinner 2000). The study was based on four localised pollen catchment sites in different landscape zones, and included radiocarbon-dated sequences for each. The lowest lying site was Temple Sowerby Moss, a small basin mire on a terrace above the Eden floodplain. The earliest indication of human activity, in the form of charcoal associated with small-scale disturbance of the forest floor, perhaps associated with camp fires, is dated to soon after 5632 cal BC placing it in the Mesolithic. More substantial clearance can be detected in the Early Neolithic, dated to *c*.3899 cal BC, as a reduction in the number of birch, pine and oak trees, perhaps associated with agricultural activity, following which hazel and heather spread, and the herb component expanded.

The second site investigated by Skinner was Howgill Castle, a valley mire set below Burney Fell, where mixed deciduous forest conditions existed until the arrival of the first people in the Late Mesolithic, *c*.4009 cal BC. Their arrival is marked by the appearance of cereal pollen in the archaeological record. The evidence points to an agricultural economy involving an increasing reliance upon arable agriculture because from the Neolithic, *c*.3577 cal BC, the amount of land taken over for cultivation increases, evidenced by a marked decline in levels of woodland pollen, and a massive rise in plantains, bracken, sedges and other herbaceous plants.

Pollen samples taken from Bank Moor, an upland swallow hole located on the limestone above the 300m contour, suggests that during the Mesolithic and Neolithic, *c*.4300 to 3200 BC, the area was covered by open grassland with stands of birch, hazel and willow. In the Late Neolithic, *c*.2941 cal BC, high levels of charcoal are associated with a marked decline in the amount of birch and grass pollen, which suggests clearance by means of managed fire. Further evidence for clearance at this time comes from a contemporary increase in the amount of water induced erosion, interpreted by Skinner as clearance related erosion, exacerbated by worsening environmental conditions. Later in the Bronze Age, *c*.1950 cal BC, high levels of charcoal coincide with the first appearance of cereal pollen, whilst at *c*.1442 cal BC there is a significant increase in hazel pollen, mirrored by a dramatic drop in that of birch until *c*.1174 cal BC. For much of this 800-year period of the Bronze Age cereal pollen and charcoal were present intermittently, which may be interpreted as cyclical crop rotation within small-scale garden plots perhaps farmed by a series of extended households.

The highest of Skinner's sample sites was at Great Rundale on the Appleby Fells, an area of limestone uplands. The pollen sequence ran from *c*.3350 BC, but no clear indicators of human activity were present until the Bronze Age. Between *c*.1827 and *c*.1649 cal BC there is evidence for small-scale woodland management shown by a marked drop in hazel, and an increase in grasses, bracken and plantains, which were accompanied by charcoal. After this time the land reverted to woodland. Oak and alder increased along with grasses and heather, although high levels of charcoal suggest continued localised clearances. At *c*.1473 cal BC we see evidence for arable agriculture. Heather, grasses and alder were cleared, and together with charcoal and cereal pollen, indicate the presence of arable agriculture.

Skinner's (2000) study clearly illustrates the presence of naturally open landscapes with a variety of species of ground plants. Managed burning was taking place on the terraces of the Eden floodplain as early as *c.*5632 cal BC and continued into the Late Neolithic and Early Bronze Age on the limestone plateau. Cereal cultivation was taking place in the glacial valley at Howgill Castle at *c.*4009 cal BC, but did not take place on the limestone uplands until the Late Neolithic and Early Bronze Age. What is clear at the upland sites of Bank Moor and Great Rundale is that although the evidence suggests small-scale occupation from the Late Mesolithic and Early Neolithic onwards, this became more intensive only during the Late Neolithic and Early Bronze Age. This is consistent with other evidence of widespread settlement within the shelter of the Eden valley dating to the Neolithic and Early Bronze Age (Chapter 5), which takes the form of large stone circles, burial monuments, as well as stone implements of various types used to work the light sandstone soils.

The Central Lakeland Limestone Escarpment

The Carboniferous limestone rocks of central Lakeland form an extensive crescent-shaped outcrop which encircles the northern and eastern areas of the lake mountains in the form of an elevated ridge of subdued relief, from Ireby in the north, eastwards to Caldbeck and then southwards to Greystoke and Crosby Ravensworth. The continuous sweep of this elevated ridge, one of the most clearly defined natural regions in Cumbria, rises fairly abruptly to a height of about 1000ft above the Carlisle Plain, but is itself overlooked by the taller lake mountains lying to the south. The soil cover is thin, with the bedrock exposed in places such as Greystoke Park and the vegetation consequently light but in the form of rich sweet grassland which provides excellent sheep pasture, in contrast to the heavy clay lands of the Carlisle Plain and the sour, peaty soil cover of the ancient rock formations of the mountainous zone to the south, usually clearly defined by a marked change in the pattern of vegetation. The central Lakeland limestone escarpment was an important route for people travelling from the west and Ireland, and the most densely settled area of Cumbria with evidence of prehistoric activity all round the limestone ridge, from Aughertree Fell in the north-west, to Crosby Ravensworth and Crosby Garret in the south-east. The Iron Age and Romano-British 'native' sites in the vicinity of Carrock Fell are part of this pattern, although the contemporary hillfort was, for greater security, constructed on the neighbouring gabbro/granophyre intrusive complex that forms Carrock Fell (Chapter 8).

The evidence from pollen cores is that in the central fells, birch and elm populated the highland valleys, whilst alder grew in the valley bottoms, around tarns and in acidic hollows (Walker 1965). At the higher extents of the tree line, birch woodland predominated with some pine on more marginal soils (Pennington, 1975, 1997). At Langdale Combe the opening of zone VIIa was defined by an increase in alder, together with oak and elm, and low amounts of hazel, indicating relatively stable conditions (Walker 1965). Between zones V and VIIa, no herb pollen was recorded at Blea Tarn and Devoke Water (below 250m OD), and there was less than 10 per cent at Seathwaite, Blind Tarn and Goatswater (between 400 and 600m OD). High amounts of hazel pollen were recorded at the majority of these sites (Pennington 1997) which suggests an open canopy. Pennington (1970) suggested the upper extent of the tree line was at about 760m OD, however others believe it was lower, around 600m (Simmons *et al* 1981; Bradley and Edmonds 1993).

The Lazonby Fells

The Lazonby Fells form a ridge of high ground composed of red Lazonby Sandstone which is aligned parallel to, and lies on the western side of, the Eden valley. A property of the Lazonby Sandstones that distinguishes them from the Eden valley rocks is their excessive hardness, which explains why they now persist as a prominent ridge rising above the softer sandstones of the Eden valley. The soil cover of large areas of the Lazonby Fells is light and impoverished, and even with modern methods of agriculture much of the land is barren. There is, therefore, understandably little or no evidence of prehistoric settlement along this ridge.

South-West Cumbrian Fells

South of St Bees Head in south-west Cumbria, the Carboniferous limestone formations are completely faulted out and red sandstone rocks form a platform which is relatively wide in the Egremont/Gosforth area but narrows considerably towards the south where it abuts the Eskdale Granite rocks, terminating by the Duddon Sands. The passage inland at the Duddon estuary is restricted by the Skiddaw Slates that make up Black Combe mountain, which rises sharply a short distance inshore to a height of 600m (*c.* 2000ft). The restricted region with its neighbouring mountains and deep cut valleys, has been an area of relatively heavy settlement demonstrated by the Neolithic site of Ehenside Tarn (Chapter 4), and concentrations of field monuments and stray finds. The density of prehistoric activity is accounted for by the combination of lowland marine and lacustrine wetland resources associated with a relatively broad dry settlement site in close proximity to upland grazing.

Two distinct clearance episodes have been identified in the pollen record at Ehenside Tarn, spanning the period between *c.*3900 and 1500 cal BC, with increased charcoal between *c.*3000 and 2600 cal BC (Walker 2001). The first clearance episode took the form of reduced amounts of elm and oak, and the subsequent spread of hazel, ash and birch (Walker 1966a; 2001). The second phase involved clearance of the smaller trees, leaving the open herbaceous vegetation of ribwort plantain, grasses and cereal pollen.

The Central Mountainous Zone

Sitting at the heart of the Lake District, this area is composed of the oldest and hardest rocks in Cumbria, which form the highest mountains in England, Skiddaw and Blencathra (Saddleback) to the north and Helvellyn and Scafell Pike, at 978m (3210ft) the highest mountain in England, to the south. In fact all the mountains in England that are over 900m (3000ft)

OD are in Cumbria. Although the craggy profiles of the mountains dominate the scene, the district is best known for its lake-filled valleys. Silt deposits, which are thickly spread over the valley floors, provide areas of rich loam which supplement the grazing provided by the more impoverished upland areas. The presence of Castlerigg Stone Circle near Keswick demonstrates that settlement was established deep within the region as early as the Late Neolithic and Early Bronze Age.

Pollen evidence for woodland disturbance on the central and western fells is relatively well known, used both in the interpretation of axe production and the identification of processes leading up to peat formation (e.g. Pennington 1975; Bradley and Edmonds 1993). The earliest episode of clearance is derived from excavations at Thorn Crag. Sealed by peat, axe-working debris associated with a mineral soil and charcoal were dated to the Neolithic, 4209-3709 cal BC, with pollen data illustrating an elm decline at 4100-4030 cal BC (Quartermaine in Evans 2008). Downslope, the sequence from Blea Tarn is extrapolated from a single radiocarbon date of *c.*3700 cal BC for the first clearance episode (Pennington 1975). Here a rise in herbaceous pollen took place in pine-birch woodland and was maintained for around 200 years. This preceded more intense clearance extrapolated from about 3050 BC to at least *c.*2400 BC. At both Blea Tarn and Red Tarn, a fine band of mineral silt occurred at the second phase, illustrating increased soil erosion (Pennington 1964).

After the elm decline at Angle Tarn, the profile illustrated an inwash of acid mor soil. Pennington interpreted the accumulation and increasing acidity of soils as a response both to deteriorating soil conditions and the clearance of high forest trees (1964; 1975). At Angle Fell and Red Tarn Moss, charcoal layers were present alongside evidence for clearance of birch and pine around the Mesolithic VIIa/b boundary (Pennington 1964). Cores from Devoke Water, Seathwaite Tarn and Blind Tarn contained a band of mineral silt with organic debris containing mountain grassland species immediately above (Pennington 1975). Disturbance of this type can change the relationship between soils and vegetation: the replacement of deep rooted by shallow rooted plants initiates soil acidification, especially in upland areas with high rainfall (Dimbleby 1962).

The link between heathland burning and upland peat initiation is relatively well established (e.g. Casedine and Hatton 1993; Simmons 1993, 1996; Moore 1988, 1993). In many areas, whilst post elm decline episodes associated with burning do occur in such contexts, most are Mesolithic in date or occur around the zone VIIa/b boundary (Moore 1993). Other than at Angle Fell and Red Tarn Moss, there is no recorded evidence of such activity in the west and central fells (Pennington 1975). In eastern Cumbria however, managed burning was occurring as early as *c.*5632 cal BC and carried on into the third millennium BC (Skinner 2000).

The chronology of peat formation across the Cumbrian uplands is poorly understood, but it appears processes set in motion around the elm decline culminated in peat formation. Evidence from Blea Tarn suggests this began during the Late Neolithic (Pennington 1975) and at Thunacar Knott (Clough 1973; Pennington 1975) charcoal associated with an area of axe working sealed by peat dated to between 2850 and 3250 BC (Bradley and Edmonds 1993). At Great Rundale peat formation began at *c.*3300 cal BC (Skinner 2000). The spread of peat is, however, affected by very localised conditions, so cannot be assumed to have formed at the same time in different places.

The Pennines

East of the Eden valley running north-south is the Pennine escarpment, rising to a height of *c*.900m (3000ft) on Cross Fell, the highest point along the whole length of the Pennines forming the eastern boundary of Cumbria. The Pennine area is typical limestone country with the high ground cut by broad dry valleys. The pattern of human settlement has probably changed little since prehistoric times. From the northern end of the Pennines a fell-foot road skirts the base of the limestone escarpment and strings together a line of small villages from Castle Carrock in the north through Cumrew, Croglin, Renwick, Gamblesby and Melmerby to Skirwith and Kirkland beneath Cross Fell. The villages are small hill-farming communities exploiting the excellent sheep grazing on the lower slopes of the limestone fells and supplementing these resources with limited tillage on the Triassic rocks to the west. These same inducements attracted relatively strong settlement in pre-Roman times, and evidence of prehistoric activity is fairly common and evenly scattered over the entire area.

The Bewcastle Fells

The distribution of Lower Carboniferous rocks extends north of the Pennines to form the Bewcastle Fells. In this area the limestones are almost wholly replaced by sandstones so that the soil cover is light and impoverished, producing coarse grassland of indifferent quality. Even today settlement in the form of widely scattered farmsteads is sparse. A scatter of pre-historic sites has been recorded from the fringe areas, which in a region of limited potential is probably accounted for as an overspill from the more densely populated Eden valley.

From this overview the influence of topography on the main areas of prehistoric activity can clearly be seen, with settlement following the principal routes of communication: the low-lying coastal strip, the Eden valley and the central limestone escarpment. Most of the remaining areas, the central mountainous zone and the forested Carlisle Plain in particular, provided few opportunities for early settlement. The general settlement pattern was modified in places by the effects of local factors. Thus the successful exploitation of the Langdale fine-grained volcanic tuffs by the Neolithic axe manufacturers must have brought about a local increase of settlement in the vicinity of the factory sites. This supposition is to some extent confirmed by the scatter of polished stone axes which shows a relatively heavy concentration in south-west Cumberland and Low Furness.

Landscape Change and Site Preservation

The processes that have just been considered have to a large extent determined which parts of the prehistoric material record were preserved and then discovered. In order to assess whether the known sample of sites may be considered as representative of the original population it is useful to consider it against the background of the dynamics of the landscape.

Our present knowledge of the material record of the later prehistoric period of the region is rather uneven, both in terms of chronological distribution and in terms of classes of data. Many burial monuments dating to the Early Bronze Age have survived, only compromised in part by the efforts of early antiquarians. Domestic contexts for the same period, on the other hand, have proved elusive, primarily because domestic huts were built using much lighter methods of construction than those employed in funerary structures. In contrast, for the Late Bronze Age and Early Iron Age our knowledge of funerary practices is scant, perhaps as a consequence of shifting funerary practices in this period, whilst we have increasing evidence for settlement in both defended 'hilltop' enclosures and open farmsteads associated with their more durable construction. More significantly for the later period is the wealth of metalwork found either singly or in hoards, often interpreted as the product of ritual deposition.

The effect of these shifts in cultural practices in the later prehistoric period has resulted in a heavily biased repertoire of evidence, making direct comparison between one class of data across the whole period extremely difficult, with the possible exception of copper-alloy metalwork. This problem should not be allowed to obscure the fact that the remarkable survival of a considerable number of prehistoric artefacts, monuments and sites of different classes is also one of the greatest strengths of the evidence, which may present valuable opportunities for the researcher. The changing interrelationship between different classes of data remain our best evidence for gaining insights into the changing socio-spatial organisation of the prehistoric period, and this is the subject of the following chapters.

Before pursuing this line of investigation, it is useful to try to establish whether the known sample of archaeological data is representative of the overall picture, and to what extent it may have been distorted by selective destruction and discovery. Clarke's fundamental categories of pre-depositional, depositional, post-depositional and retrieval processes (Clarke 1973) provide useful pegs for a discussion of the known sample. Some of the characteristics and processes that may have influenced the deposition, preservation and retrieval of the archaeological record will be considered in turn.

Deposition

Monumental earthworks are by their very nature durable structures. The choice of raw material, location and size ensured their presence in the landscape was permanent. Cultural biographies of these monuments reveal that they were often multi-phased. For example, excavation of a stone cairn at Oddendale revealed a sequence of four phases beginning with a timber circle, followed by the removal of the posts and capping of the post-holes to create two concentric stone circles. In the third phase a ring cairn was constructed overlying the inner circle, to which was added in the final phase a platform of stone boulders (Turnbull and Walsh 1997; see Chapter 5). The effect of such re-use is that throughout the period of their use, they tended to grow in extent and mass, and consequently to become more conspicuous. Domestic sites, with the exception of Late Bronze Age defended enclosures – 'hillforts' – present a sharp contrast. The limited research that has been undertaken, such as the survey of settlement sites in Matterdale by Hoaen and Loney (above), has focused on stone-built structures and turf walls, as these are the most archaeologically visible features in a landscape given over to pasture. As a consequence 'archaeological features such as wooden built structures ... are unlikely to be visible ... and so we are likely to have missed any such finds' (Hoaen and Loney 2003, 53). Both stone and copper-alloy tools are durable and both have been preserved in large numbers, in part because of their intentional deposition, which ensured they were protected for posterity.

Preservation and Destruction

A variety of different processes, both natural and anthropogenic, have the potential to destroy or hide sites and monuments (see Kristiansen 1985). Natural processes actively at work in the region include sedimentation and erosion. Anthropogenic processes that have had a significant impact are urbanisation and mechanised agriculture. These will be considered in turn.

Erosion, Sedimentation and the Effects of Changing Sea-Levels

In the upper reaches of the county's major river systems river channels are constantly being re-cut and deepened. Potentially this could destroy much upland archaeology; in practice this does not seem to have been a great problem in Cumbria. The situation along the coastline is much more serious, with the evidence pointing to fluctuating sea-levels along the coast throughout the Holocene (Tooley and Shennan 1987) accompanied by periods of sedimentation and erosion (Zong 1997; 1998). For our purposes the process began in the Late Upper Palaeolithic, *c*.11,000 to 8000 BC, which nationally marked the final retreat of the ice belonging to the Devensian glaciation. At this time sea-level was below where it currently lies, so that Britain was connected by a land bridge to the European continent (*3*). As the climate warmed, and the ice cap melted, there was a rise in sea-level, which continued in the Early Mesolithic, *c*.8000-6500 BC, causing sea-levels to rise, so that by *c*.8000 BC the coastline lay only *c*.20m below OD (Tooley 1974, 33). At this time the area that is now Morecambe Bay was forested, the evidence for which can still be seen on occasion at low tide when oak stocks appear from beneath the sand. By *c*.5200 BC the sea-level had risen to 2m below OD, at which point Britain had lost its land bridge to the Continent and become an island, which it has remained to this day (Tooley 1974; 1978; 1985). Locally, from *c*.7000-6000 cal BC we see the first possible evidence for human and/or perhaps animal interference with the natural vegetation of the county that continued throughout the Late Mesolithic, *c*.6500-4000 cal BC (Chambers and Elliot 1989).

Focusing on the evidence for the Cumbrian coast, the pattern of sea-level change in relation to archaeological sites was considered by Tom Clare (2000). Drawing on research by Tooley (1974; 1978) and Zong (1993; 1998; Zong and Tooley 1996) he demonstrated that since the last ice age sea-levels have risen by more than 15m. Matters are further complicated by the effect of isostatic lift, a response to the removal of the weight of ice from the land surface as it thawed following the end of the ice age. This adjustment is seen in northern Britain where

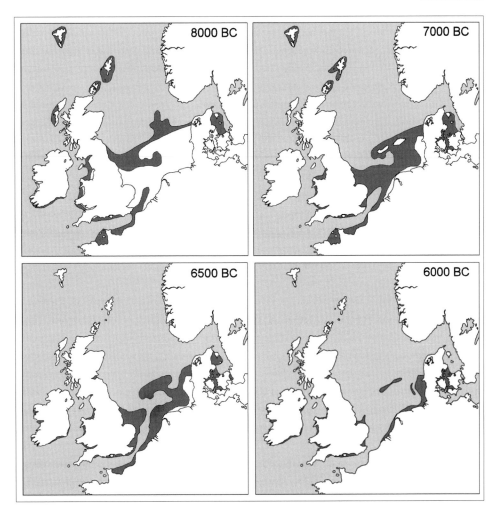

3 Changing sea levels following the retreat of the last ice sheets, showing the process of separation of Britain from the continent. *After Bradley 2007, fig. 1.4 based on Coles 1998; Shennan and Andrews (eds) 2000*

the land has risen more than sea-level, so that the overall effect is that the prehistoric shore-line has risen above modern day sea-level, creating raised beaches, which are also common along the Scottish coast. Further south this rise in the level of the land has been less than the rise in sea-level, drowning the prehistoric coastline. In Cumbria sea-level rises have led to the drowning of areas of limestone pavement in the south of the county, whilst in the north of the county sea-level change has led to the accumulation of deposits leading to the growth of land along the Solway Coast north of Dubmill Point. The effect of these changes has been to bury some sites whilst eroding others, leading to differential preservation of archaeological sites of different periods. In order to understand the preserved archaeological record it is therefore first necessary to consider the pattern of sea-level change through time.

The known distribution of archaeological sites may reflect the changes in sea-level. For example, the only known Upper Palaeolithic bone points from the county were found on the southern side of the Solway on top of peat derived from 'an ancient estuary' (Hodgson 1895 in Clare 2000), consistent with an uplift of the land surface. That none are found in southern Cumbria may be due more to the drowning of coastal sites than to an absence of human activity. Further credence is given to this explanation by the excavation of similar bone points at the inland wetland site of Highfurlong on the Fylde Coast of Lancashire, south of Morecambe Bay, suggesting that Late Palaeolithic hunting activity was taking place elsewhere in north-west England (Chapter 3). The problem of drowned sites along the coast of southern Cumbria may extend to the Mesolithic–Neolithic transition. Clare cites the example of Silverdale Moss where Oldfield encountered charcoal interpreted as being from a settlement below a marine layer (Clare 2000, 1-3).

Sea-level rise has been recorded starting before *c.*8980-7943 cal BC (9270±200 BP, Birm-141) along the northern coast of Morecambe Bay, so that by 7060-6707 cal BC (7995±80 BP, Hv-3362) the lowest reaches of the Kent and Levens Estuaries had been inundated (Kidson and Tooley 1977, 138-9). At the same time the sea was probably reaching its maximum landward penetration north of the Levens estuary in the valley of the Rusland Pool. Here, grey-blue clays containing the foraminifers *Globigerina sp* and fragments of *Radiolara* and sponge spicules have been found inland as far north as Crooks Bridge (Kidson and Tooley 1977, 138; Dickinson 1975).

A second rise in sea-level, dating to between *c.*5000 cal BC and 4000 cal BC (5865±115 BP, Q-261; 5734±129 BP, Q-256; 5435±105 BP, Hv-3844), has been recorded at Silverdale, Helsington, and Ellerside Mosses, and was probably short-lived, although its influence seems to have been intense, with sea-level rising to *c.*+3.72m to +3.85m OD at its maximum (Oldfield 1960; Huddart *et al* 1977, 138). A third period of rising sea-levels, reaching nearly +5.0m OD in places, seems likely to have affected Helsington Moss and the Duddon estuary in the north of Morecambe Bay, and Arnside Moss to the east, around 4400-3600 cal BC (5277±120 BP, Q-85; 5015±100 BP, Hv-3460; Smith 1958; Kidson and Tooley 1977, 139, 142).

Rising sea-level brought with it marine sediments drowning the original land surface, above which are subsequent deposits of peat and colluvium, reflecting the sequence of inundation by the sea followed by a more gradual retreat. Within these sediments, at Pennington, a stone axe was found 'twelve feet [3.6m] down' (Barber 1869, 30). Coring on the floor of Morecambe Bay suggests submerged forests lie on fossil interfluves between the palaeochannels of the rivers Kent, Leven and Keer (Tooley 1978) and further submerged landscapes are believed to occur around Walney and the Duddon estuary (Clare 2000). Pollen cores from southern and western mosses illustrate that coastal mires began as fens and reedswamps with some open water, and later became converted to raised bogs, often with saltmarsh represented by fossil tidal creeks (Oldfield and Statham 1963; Oldfield 1963; Tipping 1994). Similar environments have been identified on the Solway (Walker 1966a; Bewley 1994).

On the west coast the process of coastal formation differs from that on the low energy shores of Morecambe Bay. At Eskmeals coastal influx between *c.*5970-5480 cal BC and 5613-5240 cal BC meant a sea-level rise of *c.*2m OD, producing a series of shingle ridges between 1 and 1.5km inland (Tipping 1994). At Williamson's Moss, these formed a barrier isolating an inland basin from marine influence culminating in the development of a lagoon (Bonsall *et al* 1994; Hodgkinson *et al* 2000). This research provides a context for the buried Mesolithic

Number	Artefact	Context
1	2 axes	Ancient tarn
2	Stone axe	Unknown
3	Stone 'celt'	Shore
4	Axe hammer	Surface
5	Axe hammer	Surface
6	Axe hammer	In a wall
7	Axe hammer	Unknown
8	Axe hammer with tar coat	5ft down
9	Macehead	4ft down in clay
10	Perforated axe	Unknown
11	Polished axe	3ft down in boulder clay
12	Polished axe	Shingle
13	Polished axe	Scar above channel
14	Polished axe	Shore
15	Polished axe	Surface
16	Polished axe	Garden
17	Polished axe	Unknown
18	Fragment polished axe	Digging a grave
19	Fragment polished axe	Less than 4ft down
20	roughout	In 2ft of clay
21	Unfinished	Unknown

4 Records of stone axes found in the Barrow and Walney areas. *After Clare 2000, table 1*

sites identified by the Cherrys at St Bees (Cherry and Cherry 1983). One might imagine that these sites were originally located close to a valley floor covered by areas of peat moss interspersed with pools of water, whilst adjacent to the valley was a ridge of drier ground attractive to settlement.

The formation of peat mosses throughout the later prehistoric period similarly preserves copper-alloy metalwork and also some organic remains by means of sedimentation. As peat is strongly acidic wooden artefacts, human skin and also copper-alloy metalwork preserve well, but human bone does not. This has resulted in the preservation of a number of 'bog bodies' together with clothes and a wooden 'walking stick' at Seascale Moss, and of a wooden hafted axe at Ehrenside Tarn, but has also destroyed bone in inhumed burials on acidic moorland soils. Cremated bone is not destroyed to the same extent. The burial record is therefore biased toward bog bodies and cremations rather than crouched inhumation burials under cairns.

In addition to isostatic uplift and sea-level changes, a further factor affecting the preservation and recovery of archaeological sites is the movement of sand dune systems, which may have advanced over the original ground surface covering, and perhaps also in particular cases disturbing, the original stratigraphy (Clare 2000, 9). From an archaeological perspective the most significant dune system in Cumbria is the one on Walney Island where significant flint scatters have been recorded over the last 200 years. It has been suggested that, although the flint scatters were found amongst the dune slacks, these dunes have developed over the original land surface. Studies have shown that below the dunes lie both lacustrine and lagoonal peats, suggesting that the dune system advanced from the west over a series of different environments (Oldfield 1965, 250-1; 1971). Evidence from the peats suggested to Clare (2000, 10) 'that the flint scatters either side of the Barrow Channel may have related to the exploitation of a lagoon or estuary rather than the coast as previously assumed'. Radiocarbon dates are required to understand the chronology of these events, but in their absence an impression of the dates can be determined from the stratigraphy of Neolithic stone axes found in the Barrow and Walney areas (4). Further evidence comes from the discovery of a broken antler of an 'Irish Elk' found 17ft (5m) below the surface (Kendall 1900, 60) and of 'the horns and perfect skeleton of a red deer' found near Rooseholme (Kendall 1880, 58, 60). The deer was said to have been found on a 'curious bank of gravel and sand' that Clare thought may have been a fossil creek (2000, 10).

On the west coast, closely associated with the later shingle ridges in some areas, are similar windblown dune systems. These formed as sea-levels fell during the later third and early second millennia BC, a chronology borne out by the presence of Late Neolithic and Early Bronze Age lithic scatters in such contexts (Tooley 1990).

The evidence points to successive cycles of erosion and accretion that seem to have been the norm since the last ice age along the Cumbrian coast, and which make life difficult for the archaeologist attempting to map the prehistoric landscape. It is safe to say is that the fixed coastline as we know it is a product of modern sea defences and bears little resemblance to the fluid coastline that was the experience of previous generations of its inhabitants.

Industrial and Agricultural Intensification

During the nineteenth century the north-west of England experienced a sustained period of industrial and agricultural intensification. South of Cumbria the metropolitan centres of Liverpool and Manchester, and to a lesser extent Bolton, Preston and Blackburn, grew rapidly, whilst over the national border Glasgow saw similar growth. This growth impacted on Cumbria in a number of ways. First was the creation of new markets for Cumbrian raw materials, in particular coal, slate, limestone and iron ore. To meet this new demand new mines were opened and old ones upgraded along with the transportation infrastructure. Cumbria also developed its own industrial base, notably around the coast at Barrow-in-Furness and Workington. With the development of an efficient railway network mass tourism became possible for the first time, creating a new service industry focused on Lake Windermere. Finally, along with the growth of the North West's urban centres went a growth in population which led to an increased demand for agricultural produce and fresh water, both of which Cumbria provided.

The rapid building boom took place outside contemporary planning regulation and no provision was made for the protection of archaeological sites. Records of barrow disturbance and total destruction are numerous, revealing both an interest in, and recognition of, these ancient remains whilst acknowledging the need to destroy them in the name of progress, a desire which sits uneasily with modern attitudes. Fortunately the industrialisation of the region was accompanied by a plethora of literary and scientific societies who saw it as their duty to record the destruction of these monuments. Although the monuments are long lost, records and, in many cases, artefacts survive.

The destruction of an Early Bronze Age burial cairn at Low Field, Old Parks, Kirkoswald is a good example of this. Records show that the tumulus was sold to the County Council in 1892 for road metal, and that 30 cartloads of stone were removed from the cairn for this purpose before a number of prehistoric pots were found together with cremated human remains. At that juncture the tenant farmer, William Potter, who also happened to be a local county councillor, called a halt to the work so that a proper archaeological investigation of the site could be undertaken. Although the destruction of the cairn could not be prevented a photographic record of the site was made, the cremation urns were taken into safe custody, and a report was published by R.S. Ferguson (1894, 389-399).

A growth in population accompanied the growth of urban areas, and this led to increased agricultural activity in Cumbria. Much of the region, as we have seen, is given over to grassland, ideal for dairying and sheep rearing. The heavy clay soils of the Carlisle Plain are poorly drained and slow to heat in the spring, making cereal yields low. The effect of this is twofold: first, archaeological remains are preserved under grassland where otherwise they may be destroyed by plough action, but on the other hand, because the land is not being ploughed, stray finds, which often lead to the discovery of sites, are few and far between. Where arable agriculture is practised, notably in the Furness region, stone and metal objects have been regularly found. The bias is further compounded by modern metal detecting practices, which favour ploughed soil over pasture, reinforcing the biased pre-existing distributions, impacting on the question of retrieval.

Retrieval

Retrieval is the third important filter between past activity and the known material record (Renfrew 1979, 152; Fraser 1983, 235-261). We have already seen how the intensification of industrial and agricultural activity in the nineteenth century led to the discovery of new archaeological sites and artefacts. In many cases we are able to reconstruct the discoveries from published accounts, but it must be borne in mind that this is not always possible. In the mid-nineteenth century it was common for pedlars to travel around Cumbria going from farm to farm offering to buy any bronze weapons or tools that had been found. The going rate was two pence apiece, an attractive price to a farm labourer or servant. The pedlar would then sell the metal for scrap to the foundry making sixpence (Wilson 1901). Sadly, this practice seems to have been widespread, only hinting at the number of prehistoric metal objects that must have been found to make this business worthwhile. Only occasionally do we find mention of some of the objects melted down in this way, and then because they were made of precious metal. In Hutchinson's *Cumberland* (vol. I, 151) there is a reference to the destruction of a cairn made of sand and gravel at Hayton in 1790. Inside the cairn were found three gold open bracelets, 3-4in in diameter, all undecorated but each with a knob at each end. From the description we can guess that they were similar to others found in Bronze Age contexts, but we will never be sure as they were sold to a silversmith in Carlisle for £7 and £20 respectively, and then probably melted down.

If the recognition of metal artefacts, stone tools and pottery over time is plotted as a graph, the importance of the amateur archaeologist and lay public becomes readily apparent (5). The recognition of ancient objects when plotted produces a curve, which follows the three-stage model proposed by Fraser (1983, 240-246). In the case of stone tools, during the first phase, from 1750 to 1850, the number of sites and artefacts recorded increases only slowly. During the second phase the number of recorded sites increases rapidly, from 1850 until 1980. The leap in recognition is a consequence of a number of factors. The most important factor was the industrialisation of urban centres, such as Barrow-in-Furness. The construction work associated with development disturbed archaeological material. A second factor was the increased awareness of the antiquity of society and associated interest in archaeological sites and artefacts, evidenced by the formation of local archaeological societies, but not confined to them. A third factor was the formation of a network of local museums, and later legal protection for archaeological sites, which encouraged the identification, recording and preservation of sites and artefacts.

The third stage, from the 1990s onwards, is characterised by a sharp levelling off in the number of newly recognised stonetools. In Fraser's model, it is suggested this stage is reached when the number of recognised sites is nearing the limit of potentially recognisable sites (Fraser 1983, 243). The tendency towards levelling off, illustrated most dramatically in the case of stonetools, can also be observed in the case of pottery. In the latter case, stage two, when the number of discoveries increased most sharply, was much more intense, beginning in the late 1850s and ending before the turn of the century. During this period there was a flurry of archaeological activity with many of the known burial monuments, with which pottery is associated, being opened. Since then the number of pottery finds has been low, in line with the relatively infrequent discovery of new burial monuments. This suggests that the sample of pottery and associated burial monuments closely reflects the total number of potentially recognisable sites.

One of the stated premises of the model is that fieldwork techniques remain unchanged. In the case of metalwork a significant change has taken place with the advent of metal detecting. This change is clearly visible in the plot. The number of new finds had been slow-

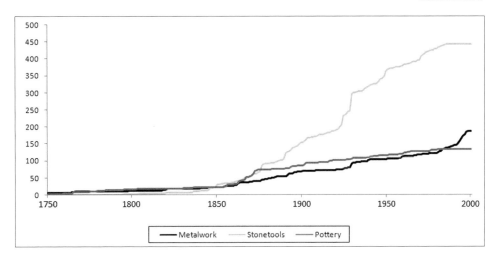

5 Cumulative totals for the number of artefacts recorded since 1750 in Cumbria. Metalwork = 187, Stonetools = 443, Pottery = 134

ing in line with Fraser's model. But since the 1990s there has been a rapid rise in the number of new finds. This reflects both the popularity of metal detecting as a hobby and also the steps taken to ensure that such finds are recorded, particularly the activity of the Portable Antiquities Scheme.

Assessing the Sample

The archaeological record for Cumbria and the surrounding area consists of 443 stone tools, 187 metal objects and 134 pots (mostly from burial sites). The artefacts, sites and monuments known at present are the ones that have filtered through the processes of deposition, preservation and retrieval that have been considered above. These considerations are useful to help create a better informed judgement of the extent to which the known sample may be considered representative of the original population. The number of known artefacts and monuments was large enough to permit statistical analysis of their distributions.

Primary Find Context

The samples of known funerary monuments, and of stone and metal tools and weapons, are most promising as representative samples of human activity that went on across the region during the prehistoric period. Analysis of the primary find context of funerary monuments revealed that antiquarian/amateur activity and field survey were most important in discovering monuments; surface finds, ploughing and gardening were the most common way to find stone tools; and metal detecting, construction, farming and quarrying were the main source of metal finds.

A practical way to assess whether the sample was representative is to consider collection strategies adopted in historical periods that may have introduced bias into the record. In order to do this the distribution of all known finds was plotted against modern land use. In each case fewer artefacts and monuments were found on grassland and moorland than would have been expected from a random distribution, and many more were found in urban, arable and woodland contexts. This suggests that finds are associated with human activity, of one sort or another, for example ploughing, coppicing and settlement. Object discovery is therefore biased toward populous locations and in those types of agricultural activity that involve disturbance of the soil.

Site Destruction and Preservation: Conclusions

It is certain that some monuments and artefacts have been destroyed and lost, but the total sample size is sufficiently large to enable one to use it to make some sort of interpretation of past human activity. It is clear that there exists a bias in the primary find context of the archaeological record. Certain locations, arable land and urban areas, are over-represented whilst pasture and moorland tend to be under-represented. This bias will have to be taken into account when interpreting the analysis in the following chapters.

CHAPTER 2

THE FIRST ARCHAEOLOGISTS
IN CUMBRIA

The proper business of an Antiquary is to collect what is dispersed, more fully to unfold what is already discovered, to examine controverted points, to settle what is doubtful, and by the authrority of Monuments and Histories, to throw light upon the manners, Arts, Languages, Policy and Religion of past Ages.

Borlase 1769, A short history of prehistory in Cumbria

Antiquarian Interest

Antiquarian research was a valued pursuit for gentlemen from the eighteenth century onwards, with the time and income required to cultivate and indulge their passion for antiquities. That passion was a reflection of taste and an instrument of competition amongst both aristocrats and gentry. It mattered to be able to converse about the contents of a cabinet of curiosities. To be knowledgeable on such matters bestowed a certain standing within polite society. In his *Itinerary* (Hearne 1710) Leland records travelling through Cumbria in the sixteenth century as part of his national tour, recording as he went points of geographical, historical and antiquarian interest. Subsequently, others, for example William Camden (1971 [1586]), found an interest in the prehistory of the region. The former's notes are relatively few and the publications of both were concerned more with Roman than with prehistoric archaeology. This general interest in the Roman period rather than prehistory reflects general antiquarian attitudes in both the north-west of England (Harrison 1910) and at a national level. For some antiquaries, such as Sir Robert Atkyns, there was little interest in pre-Roman Britain, when they believed the country was under the rule of a 'multitude of barbarous kings' (Atkyns 1712). For them British history was the history of religious and legal institutions, it was to be found in delineating the descent of property, questions which could not be addressed prior to Roman rule. Those concerned with emphasising the benefits of Roman rule were reluctant to concern themselves with barbarian inhabitants who represented mankind in its most polished form. But it could not be forgotten that the Romans were invaders who had conquered the native inhabitants from whom the British nation could be traced. Patriotic sentiment required that antiquarians study these earliest inhabitants.

Rosemary Sweet (2004) has persuasively argued that attempts to understand the history of Britain before the arrival of the Romans were closely linked to a sense of British nationhood forged during the eighteenth century (Sweet 2004, 119-20). This was forged out of a common Protestant faith, the experience of war, imperial expansion, commercial and manufacturing strength and the largely peaceful union of England, Scotland and Wales. For the earliest anti-quarian of the history of pre-Roman Britain, the study of what was then understood as the Celtic past, the term 'prehistory' had not yet been coined, we need to look to William Camden (1551-1623) whose influence over antiquarianism and history in the seventeenth and eighteenth centuries cannot be overestimated. He set the pattern for others to follow. A teacher at Westminster School, he spent his holidays travelling around Britain undertaking antiquarian research for his *Britannia* (1586), the first published topographical survey of the British Isles.

In *Britannia* he traced out the distribution of the British tribes, thus the counties of the north-west of England are considered under the tribe of the Brigantes; he identified monu-ments and barrows; and he collated sources of Roman history which yielded information on the ancient British inhabitants. Camden acquired a network of correspondents whose infor-mation was supplemented by journeys such as that made with Sir Robert Cotton in 1599 to Cumberland. The most notable of Camden's correspondents within the region was Reginald Bainbrigg, Headmaster of Appleby Grammar School.

When writing about the counties that make up modern-day Cumbria, Camden devotes most time to the Roman antiquities and subsequent history of the region, tracing the gene-alogies of the landed families of Cumberland, Westmorland and Lancashire. This pattern was followed later by both Todd and Hutchinson in their county histories of Cumberland. As one antiquary commented to Roger Gale:

> As for Dr Todd's *History of Cumberland* there are several good remarks and observations in it upon the Roman remains in Cumberland and Westmorland, but he has intermixt the affairs of the country familys and antiquities of churches with the Scottish incursions with a design to engage the gentry and clergy here to come into subscriptions.
>
> Lukis 1883, 73

Importantly for us Camden also considers the prehistory of the region as he encounters it. At Penrith he directs his attention to King Arthur's Round Table: 'not farre from the confluence of Eimot and Loder, where is seene that round trench of earth which the country people tearme Arthurs Table' (Camden 1971 [1586] paragraph 18). Camden was clearly struck at his first sight of Long Meg and her Daughters, for he unusually devoted all of paragraph 19 to a description of the monument and is for that reason worth recounting in full:

> After that Eden hath now given Eimont entertainment, hee turneth his course Northward by both the Salkelds, watering as hee goes obscure small villages and fortresses. Amongst which at the lesse Salkeld there be erected in manner of a circle seventie seaven stones, every one tenne foote high, and a speciall one by it selfe before them at the very entrance, rising fifteen foote in height. This stone the common people thereby dwelling name Long Megge, like as the reste her

daughters. And within that ring or circle are heapes of stones, under which, they say, lie covered the bodies of men slaine. And verily, there is reason to thinke that this was a monument of some victory there atchieved, for no man would deem that they were erected in vaine.

Camden, 1971 [1586]

Camden was not the last to be struck by their first sight of Long Meg. The seventeenth century generally saw little antiquarian activity, possibly because of the Civil War, but there were exceptions. William Dugdale and Hugh Tod[d] made observations of Cumbrian sites, later to be used by John Aubrey in his *Monumenta Britannica*, and the antiquary Thomas Machell toured Westmorland and Cumberland during the last decade of the seventeenth century keeping a detailed journal. Most notable of this generation of antiquaries was Celia Fiennes (1662-1741), who famously travelled England on horseback. When travelling from Lancaster to Carlisle in 1698, wrote:

A mile from Peroth [Penrith] in a Low bottom and Moorish place stands Mag and her sisters; the story is that these soliciting her to an unlawful Love by an Enchantment are turned wth her into stone; the stone in the middle wch is Call'd Mag is much bigger and have some fforme Like a statue of figure of a body, but the rest are but soe many Craggy stones, but they affirme they Cannot be Counted twice alike as is the story of Stonidge, but the number of these are not above 30.

Fiennes, 1888

Camden's contribution was more than to detail the prehistoric antiquities of Cumbria and the rest of Britain. He also provided a model whereby his reader could understand how it was that these islands came to be first settled. He argued that Britain had been settled from Gaul. The earliest inhabitants were Gomerians or Cimbri, descendants of Noah through his son Japhet, who spread out over Europe from the east after the deluge and the fall of the tower of Babel. Due to the success of *Britannia* this view of the early peopling of the British Isles acquired widespread acceptance as the authoritative version. There was an alternative theory, proposed by Aylett Sammes, that argued that the British were descended from Phoenicians settlers who had travelled to the south-west in search of trade. Both place their emphasis on Britain's connections with the ancient East.

The only constituency of the ancient British, which the classical sources discussed in any detail, were the Druids. The subject of both admiration and speculation, they featured in the verse of John Milton and Michael Drayton (Sweet 2004, 124). John Aubrey was the most famous of the seventeenth-century antiquarians to take an interest in 'druidic monuments', stone circles, devoting a chapter entitled 'Templa Druidum' in his book *Monumenta Britannica* (6). Previously there had been debate as to who had built the stone circles, and when. Aubrey's argument was, correctly, that stone circles must have been built by the ancient Britons as many were to be found in regions where neither the Romans nor the Saxons had been, such as Wales and Scotland. One of those influenced by Aubrey was William Stukeley, for whom the study of ancient religion was central. As he explained to William Borlase, the Cornish antiquarian, in 1749: 'All my studys in antiquity have ever had a regard to religion. Nor do I think any other studys are worth cultivating, but what have some aspect that way'.

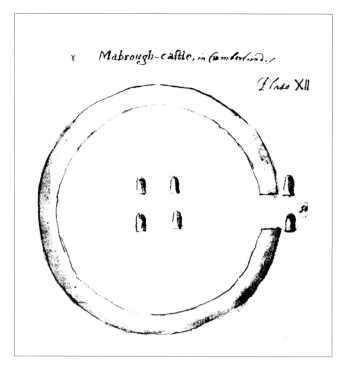

X Mabrough-caftle, in (umberland./

Plate XII

6 John Aubrey's plan of
Mayburgh that he deduced
from Sir William Dugdale's
description

Stukeley's theory that Druids were the heirs of a learned culture derived from the Egyptians, and that they had practised a monotheistic faith, had long-standing credence, going back to the authority of the classical world (7). They had built the stone circles which strengthened his conviction that the Druids had been highly learned and cultivated in the arts (Sweet 2004).

Stukeley's account of Stonehenge was published in 1740 and his *Abury: A Temple of the British Druids* followed in 1743. Although his books were very popular Stukeley had his critics. Samuel Pegge wrote: 'I am sensible that the Doctor has his admirers; but I confess I am not one of the number, as not being fond of wildness and enthusiasm upon any subject'. Richard Gough was more critical:

> had the author been less infected with Hutchinsonianism his book would be a useful compendium … Determined to fathom the utmost depth of Druidical science, he almost lost himself in an abyss which nothing but his strong imagination could have carried him through.

With mention of 'Hutchinsonianism' we return to Cumbria and to the work of the antiquarian William Hutchinson (1732-1814) (8). Beginning in the late eighteenth and throughout the nineteenth century the modern foundations of British archaeology were laid. It was at this time that county histories became popular. Thomas Pennant journeyed through Cumbria in the late eighteenth century, publishing his account in 1769 (9), closely followed in 1814 by the Lysons brothers who included Cumberland in their *Magna Britannia*. But it is Hutchinson's work on Cumberland that attracted most attention (1794-7).

Hutchinson, a Durham attorney, wrote a two-volume history of Cumberland, as well as an earlier history of County Durham. Hutchinson joined forces with Francis Jollie, a Carlisle printer, to prepare the *History of the County of Cumberland* (1797), which Jollie, writing in 1795, said took 'five years of incessant labour' (Jollie 1797, ix). Hutchinson was not highly regarded by his contemporaries, and the History is not free from fault. His History approaches the prehistory of Cumberland from the perspective of the Romans, using Classical sources to inform his discussion of the Celts. One effect of this is to obscure the great time depth of the prehistoric period, by conflating the great span of prehistory he reduces all prehistory to a snapshot of life at the time of the Roman invasion. As one might expect from this approach, he relies heavily upon Roman textual sources rather than studying the archaeological evidence. In turn the Roman sources, some of which are second-hand accounts, are known to have been selective in their presentation of life in Britain. This comes through most clearly in Hutchinson's over emphasis on the role of the Druids which left him open to ridicule, particularly by members of the Society of Antiquaries.

For example he devotes 28 pages to discussion of Long Meg and her Daughters (*10*, Hutchinson's illustration of Long Meg which follows the section on Wordsworth), of which only one page is spent describing the site. That page is, however, significant for its unwitting acknowledgement of the significance of the different colours and properties of the stones of Long Meg and her Daughters, which:

> forms nearly an exact circle of three hundred and fifty paces in circumference, of maffy ftones, moft of which remain ftanding upright. Thefe are fixty-feven in number, of various qualities and fpecies, not hewn nor touched with a tool; and their form fhews they were gathered from the furface of the earth: fome are of blue and grey limeftone: fome flint, but moft of them are granites-many of thofe that are ftanding meafure from twelve to fifteen feet in girt, and ten feet in height:-others much lefs in fize.-at the fourthern fide of this circle, about the diftance of 17 paces from its neareft part, is an upright column, naturally of a fquare form, of red freeftone,

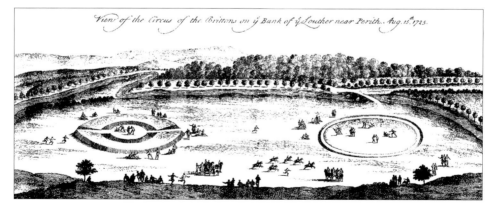

7 William Stukeley's sketch of King Arthur's Round Table and the Little Round Table. The sketch reveals Stukeley's belief that the Druids were influenced by the Classical world, leading him to interpret the Penrith Henges as a Druidical 'Circus'

8 Portrait of William Hutchinson from the title page of the third edition of *The Spirit of Masonry*, 1802

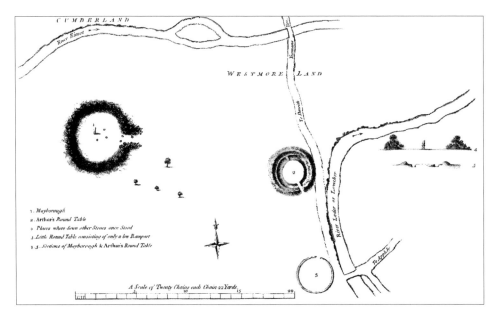

9 Thomas Pennant's plan of the three Penrith Henges, 1801. The plan shows Mayburgh (on the left) with the single central standing stone that is still to be seen today, together with three other socket holes suggesting that there were originally four standing stones in the centre. Another four holes are shown in the entrance indicating that there were another four standing stones there

with which the country abounds, and of which there is a fine quarry known to the Romans at Crawdundale, not many miles diftant from this monument. ... What creates great aftonifhment to the fpectator is, that the whole face of the adjacent country doen not fhew any ftones of the like magnitude or quality; and how fuch immenfe bodies could be moved, in an age when little of the mechanical powers (except the force of the lever) were known in this country, is not to be concived.

Hutchinson 1797 vol 1, 226

The remainder of Hutchinson's account is devoted to speculation, dressed-up as a detailed explanation, of the use to which the Druids would have put the site as part of their religious observance (Hutchinson 1797 vol. 1, 225-253). Similar explanations are given for Arthur's Round Table and Maybrough (Hutchinson 1797 vol. 1, 308-312):

We perfumed to declare our opinion of the Salkeld monument, that it was the place of druidical judicature; that there the affembled delegates met in congrefs, and that the criminals fuffered execution there. We conceive that Maybrough was appropriated folely to religious rites, and that here the pupils received their documents in the myfteries of that religion.

Hutchinson 1797 vol. 1, 311

Not surprisingly Castlerigg Stone Circle (*11*) is referred to as the 'Druids' Circle' (Hutchinson 1797 vol. 2, 191). The antiquaries' interest in Druids and ancient Celtic (British) antiquities became part of a wider fashion for primitivism and a rising tide of nationalist sentiment. This cultural trend has been described as a 'Celtic Revival' which exercised a powerful influence over both art and literature. The Druid was elevated as a symbol of patriotic valour, following Jean-Jacques Rousseau, the literary world lauded the 'primitive' qualities of a society uncorrupted by the commerce of a more advanced civilisation (Sweet 2004, 134). No wonder then that William Wordsworth, perhaps the Lake District's most famous resident, should draw upon and be drawn to these primitive qualities. In his *Guide to the Lakes* (1810) Wordsworth begins the second chapter with 'a description of the ancient and present inhabitants, their occupations, their condition of life' (1810, 63). Although no antiquarian himself, Wordsworth was clearly aware of the major prehistoric sites and of contemporary interpretations: 'a few circles of rude stones attributed to the Druids, are the only vestiges that remain upon the surface of the country, of these ancient occupants' (1810, 64).

In a footnote to this sentence Wordsworth expands somewhat upon his understanding, 'it is not improbable that these circles were once numerous, and that many of them may yet endure in a perfect state, under no deep covering of soil' (1810, 64). We also learn from the same footnote of how one of Wordsworth's friends had excavated a circle, taken to be 'a place of Druidical worship'. Although not named as one of the subscribers it must be likely that Wordsworth was aware of, or had indeed read, Hutchinson's *History* from which he would have learnt of the supposed association of stone circles and Druidical religion. Such was his feeling upon encountering 'the Daughters of Long Meg ... [and] Long Meg herself' that he wrote the following verse:

10 Long Meg and Her Daughters illustrated by Hutchinson, 1797

A weight of awe not easy to be borne
Fell suddenly upon my spirit, cast
From the dread bosom of the unknown past,
When first I saw that sisterhood forlorn;—
And Her, whose strength and stature seem to scorn
The power of years—pre-eminent, and placed
Apart, to overlook the circle vast.
Speak, Giant-mother! tell it to the Morn
While she dispels the cumbrous shades of night
Let the Moon hear, emerging from a cloud,
When, how, and wherefore, rose on British ground
That wondrous Monument, whose mystic round
Forth shadows, some have deemed, to mortal sight
The inviolable God that tames the proud.

In the nineteenth century archaeology was still firmly in the domain of the antiquarians and had yet to be institutionalised and embraced by the academic world. This was largely a male-based club culture, attracting middle class gentlemen for whom the pursuit of antiquities was either a hobby, if otherwise employed, or a full-time crusade, if privately financed. The Rev. Dr William Greenwell was one such gentleman who was able to devote considerable time to the exploration of barrows all across northern England. His annual campaigns took him to Northumberland, Cumberland, Durham, Westmorland and Yorkshire; he even found time to venture down to Gloucestershire, Wiltshire and Berkshire. His life's work *British Barrows* (Greenwell 1877) documents the opening of 234 barrows. A complete lack of plans and sections marks the book, leading to it being called 'the dullest book ever written' (Marsden

11 Castlerigg Stone Circle, described by Hutchinson as the 'Druids' Monument at Keswick', 1797

1999). Sir John Evans (1823-1908), perhaps the most influential archaeologist of the time (1872, 1881), described Canon Greenwell as a member of 'the bearded clerical order' who is, however, 'eminently un-clerical in his manners and manner of thinking, and a very sensible man' (Marsden 1999). Perhaps inspired by Greenwell, the study of antiquities was indeed a favoured pastime of the Anglican clergy. In Cumbria from 1883 until 1915 there were eight clergymen active in research and publishing their thoughts on prehistory in the *Transactions of the Cumberland and Westmorland Archaeological and Antiquarian Society* (the *Transactions*) (*12*). In addition to the contributions by these clergy very important contributions were made by the Rev. S. Pinhorne and Rev. J.W. Kenworthy who first identified the Neolithic site of Ehrenside Tarn, ensuring that its existence was brought to the attention of the Society of Antiquaries and that it was professionally excavated. Perhaps most influencial of all was Rev. Canon James Wilson who brought the two-volume *Victoria County History of Cumberland* to completion (Wilson 1901; see below).

   Increasing local interest in antiquarian activity prompted the foundation of the Cumberland and Westmorland Archaeological and Antiquarian Society in 1866. Like the many other local Societies that sprang up around the country at this time it was more like a debating club than a professional organisation. We learn from the accounts published at this time of the large number of barrows and cairns that were being opened by wealthy landowners such as the Lord's Muncaster (Dymond 1892) and Lonsdale (Mawson 1876). Many of these investigations went unpublished, whilst for others we have only sketchy accounts. Perhaps an exception to this general rule were the activities of Charles William Dymond (1833-1915). By profession Dymond had been a civil engineer, but after his retirement he devoted much of his time to antiquarian work in Cumbria. As the list of his contributions to these *Transactions* shows, he was prolific: *Gunnerkeld Stone Circle* (1880, 537), *A Group of Cumberland Megaliths* (1881, 39), *Mayburgh and King Arthur's Round Table* (1891, 187), *An Ancient Village near Yanwath* (1893, i),

Contributor	Year	Number
Rev. Bulkeley	1886	1
Rev. Gelderd	1912, 1914	2
Rev. Golland	1915	1
Rev. Rome Hall	1883	1
Rev. Heelis	1912	1
Rev. Canon Rawnsley	1904	1
Rev. Canon Simpson	1883	1
Rev. Canon Thornley	1902, 1904	2

12 Anglican clergymen contributing papers on prehistoric archaeology to the *Transactions of the Cumberland and Westmorland Antiquarian and Archaeological Society*. Contributors N = 8, Publications N = 10

An Ancient Village in Hugill (1893, 6), *Barnscar* (1893, 179), *Notes on an Ancient Village in Hugill* (with H.S. Cowper 1897, 460), *The Ancient Village near Threlkeld* (1897, 309), *An Exploration of Sunken Kirk, Swinside, Cumberland* (with W.G. Collingwood 1876, 53), *Note on Sunkenkirk* (1876, 354). What marks out Dymond's work is not just that he was at pains to publish, but that the plans accompanying his papers were carefully surveyed and elaborately drawn, which added greatly to their value even today (*13*).

A close contemporary of Dymond, and also one of the antiquaries who adopted a systematic approach to their researches was T. McKenny Hughes, (1832-1917) Woodwardian Professor of Geology at Cambridge. His love of antiquities was perhaps borne out of his close links to the Anglican Church, his father was Bishop of St Asaph and his brother Bishop of Llandaff. His connection to Cumbria was by marriage to the daughter of Canon Weston of Crosby Ravensworth, and it was with her that he undertook his archaeological research published in the *Transactions: Some Notes on Mound Opening, with a description of one recently explored on Sizergh Fell, Westmorland* (1904, 71); *On another Tumulus on Sizergh Fell* (1904, 201); *Note on the supposed 'burn' near Sizergh* (1904, 338); *On an Ancient Enclosure and Interment on Heaves Fell* (1912, 397); *On some Interments near Hyning, Westmorland* (1912, 403) *On the occurrence of a portion of the Skull and Antlers of Red-deer of exceptionally large size in the Estuary of the Gilpin* (1913, 59). Hughes' contribution to archaeology in Cumbria goes further than his own excavations, as his position at the University of Cambridge forged new links between the county and that University that were to prove significant for the direction of future research.

Finally in this period mention should be made of Robert Durkin Darbishire (1826-1908) for his excavation of the Neolithic settlement site at Ehrenside Tarn (Chapter 4), still to this day one of the most important sites in Cumbria. That this site still ranks in national importance is due largely to the professional approach to the excavation, and its timely

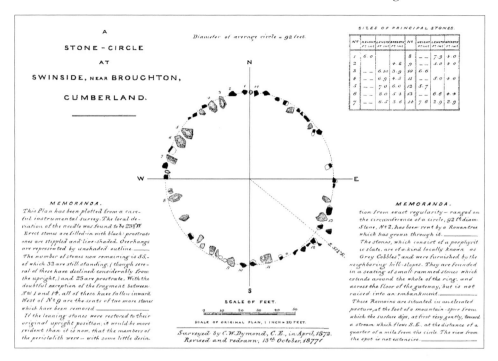

13 Plan of Swinside stone circle surveyed by C.W. Dymond 1872 & 1877

publication ensuring that the site has been available for successive generations of scholars to reinterpret. Darbishire was by profession a solicitor, in practice in Manchester, but his wide-ranging interests also included geology and conchology, and marked him out as an outstanding participant in the scientific and cultural life of Manchester. These interests were brought to bear as a powerful proponent of the future development of the University of Manchester and its museum.

The transition from Victorian antiquarianism toward the beginning of professional archaeology is marked by the father and son contributions of W.G. Collingwood and R.G. Collingwood. William Gershom Collingwood (1854-1932) was an eminent historian, as well as novelist, and secretary to John Ruskin (*14*). He undertook excavations of prehistoric monuments (1901; 1912; Cross and Collingwood 1929), but is best remembered for his inventories of the prehistoric and historic monuments first of Cumberland (1923) and then of Westmorland and Lancashire North of the Sands (1926). This research culminated in his guide *The Lake Counties* (1932). After his death in 1932 his equally influential son, Robin George Collingwood (1889-1943) (*15*) Professor of Metaphysical Philosophy and the author of *The Idea of History* (1946), took over his father's mantle as president of the Cumberland and Westmorland Archaeological and Antiquarian Society. R.G. Collingwood's most influential contribution was his paper *An Introduction to the Prehistory of Cumberland, Westmorland and Lancashire-north-of-the-sands* (1933), which outlined understandings of the region's prehistoric record, discussed below, and aimed to set a research agenda for the society's newly established Committee for Prehistoric Studies. Concerned with the lack of interest in pre-

14 *Left:* Self portrait of W.G. Collingwood, 1886

15 *Above:* Portrait of R.G. Collingwood

historic archaeology in the years following the First World War, Collingwood urged that if properly studied, the region's prehistoric remains could 'contribute their quota towards solving the general problems of prehistory' (1933, 165).

The Late Nineteenth and Early Twentieth Centuries and the Role of Women

In contrast to the male-dominated antiquarian interest in Cumbria's prehistory the late nineteenth and twentieth centuries saw the emergence, and even dominance, of a newly confident female archaeological community in Cumbria. The role of women can be traced back to the inception of the Cumberland and Westmorland Archaeological and Antiquarian Society in 1866 (Curwen 1933). Kate Sharpe (2007) notes that as early as 1876, 26 out of a total membership of 201 were female (13 per cent). Although this does not sound dramatic, it compares favourably with other regional archaeological societies, for example only two per cent in the case of the Bristol and Gloucester Archaeological Society in the same year (Hudson 1981, 18 quoted in Sharpe 2007). The role of women within the society is more important than can be revealed from the raw membership figures. An analysis of the prehistoric publications in the *Transactions* shows they seem to have been particularly active members, especially in the post-war period (*16*). Since the *Transactions* were first published women have contributed 43 papers on prehistoric topics compared to 150 by men. This is a significant number, approaching a quarter of all papers published on the topic of prehistory, and considerably more than

Contributor	Year	Number
Marjorie Cross	1929, 1939, 1942, 1947, 1948, 1950	6
Miss Cummings	1937	1
Mary Fair	1932, 1943, 1945, 1946	4
Clare Fell	1940, 1949, 1950, 1951, 1954, 1958, 1962, 1963x3, 1965, 1967, 1970, 1971, 1972, 1974, 1975	17
Ann Hallam	1993	1
Mrs Hodgson	1928	1
Miss Hodgson	1951, 1952, 1953, 1957	4
Elizabeth Huckerby	2002	1
Winifred Inglesfield	1972	1
Melanie Johnson	2005	1
Helen Loney	2003, 2004	2
Miss Noble	1907	1
Miss Simpson	1952	1
Deborah Walsh	1997	1
Ellen Ware	1891	1

16 Number of prehistoric contributions published by the *Transactions of the Cumberland and Westmorland Antiquarian and Archaeological Society* written by women between 1874 and 2008 (including six papers co-authored with men). Publications N = 43

might be expected from looking at the raw membership figures alone, which show that in 1881 women accounted for 15.5 per cent of the membership (Sharpe 2007).

Ellen Ware (née Goodwin) was the first woman to make a substantial contribution to prehistoric studies in 1890 with her paper on a Bronze Age *Gold armlet found in Westmorland* (Ware 1890, OS XI, 98), following other women who had contributed on other subjects, for example Miss Powley who had been a regular contributor since 1876 (Sharpe 2007). Nonetheless, in the early years of the society publications on prehistory were the domain of men, it was not until the late 1920s that women began to contribute in number, with papers by Mrs Hodgson, Marjorie Cross and Mary Fair (*17*). From the late 1930s until the late 1950s we enter a period in which publications by women on prehistory outnumber those by men, for the first, and so far only, time. Between 1939 and 1958 out of 27 papers, 19 were written by five different women. This may be seen as something of a golden age in terms of women's contribution to Cumbrian prehistory. Only Clare Fell continued to publish, and she was active until 1975. Since then, although there have been occasional contributions by women, only Ann Hallam's 1993 paper, *Irish food bowl vessel from the netherby Hall collection* (Hallam 1993, 43-50), stands in her name alone, the remainder are joint publications with male colleagues, notably the work of Helen Loney in Matterdale published with Hoaen (2003; 2004). It is perhaps worth noting in passing that, for whatever reason, of the six jointly authored publications the man's name always precedes that of his female colleague.

The first half of the twentieth century was a time of rapid change for both archaeology and the role of women in society. Archaeology was developing from a gentleman's pastime toward an institutionalised profession, whilst women began to enjoy a newly found independence that enabled them to begin to explore lifestyles and careers not previously open to them. In 1916 the first female council member of the society was elected. Mrs Hesketh Hodgson (1854 -1935) and her husband Thomas were keen members of the society, and were dubbed 'the firm' by the society president, Chancellor Fergusson (1936, 237). They contributed a great deal to the Excavation Committee, although their focus was on excavations on the Roman Wall rather than prehistoric archaeology, for example Hodgson, 1897. Another prominent female contributor at this time was Mary Cicely Fair (1875-1955). Fair joined the society in 1911, and served on the council from 1927 to 1932, becoming an honorary member in 1948 (Birley 1955, 307). She had a particular interest in prehistoric archaeology (Fair 1932; 1935; 1945) and was a founder member of the Committee for Prehistoric Studies (*18*). She published many articles and notes in the society *Transactions* including: *A reconsideration of the lakeside site at Ehenside Tarn* (1932, 57-62); *A note on some West Cumberland stone axes* (1935, 259-261); *A sandhill site at Eskmeals* (1936, 20-23); *The Gosforth area in Prehistory* (1943, 50-54); and early surveys of Bronze Age swords and daggers, and of types of bronze spearheads and axes, from Cumberland, Westmorland and Lancashire North of the Sands (1946, 34-38 and 172-178). Fell wrote of her: 'by stimulating local interest she came to hear of finds which would otherwise have gone unrecorded, and she visited all the known sites in her area, making notes and taking photographs' (1945, 309). Fellow antiquary Rev. M.K. Hodges observed that '… in her were combined a woman's sympathy to her neighbours and friends, a first-class intellect and a scholarly diligence and honesty …' (1945, 209).

Lady Henley became the first woman vice-president in 1930, the year that the Honourable Marjorie Cross joined the society. Her six articles on the prehistoric settlement of Walney Island (1938; 1939; 1942; 1946; 1947; 1949) received much acclaim. She also later served on the council, becoming vice-president in 1951, the year she was elected a Fellow of the Society of Arts, and an honorary member of the Cumberland and Westmorland Society in 1956. Prehistory seems to have been of particular interest to women as by 1936, just a year after its inception, the Committee for Prehistoric Studies included no fewer than five women. Alongside Fair and Cross, was Katherine Hodgson; her first paper was written at the age of 20 in collaboration with her mother (Hodgson and Hodgson, 1910). She studied at the Institute of Archaeology in London (Birley, 1974) but never moved permanently away, applying her knowledge and skills to the excavation of a variety of sites around Cumberland and Westmorland. In 1936 she became a member of the society council and 12 years later her services were recognised when she was elected president – the first woman to hold the position – for the triennium 1948-51 (Birley, 1974). She chaired the council from 1955 until 1965 and was elected an honorary member in 1962 (Birley, 1974), having made a big impression on

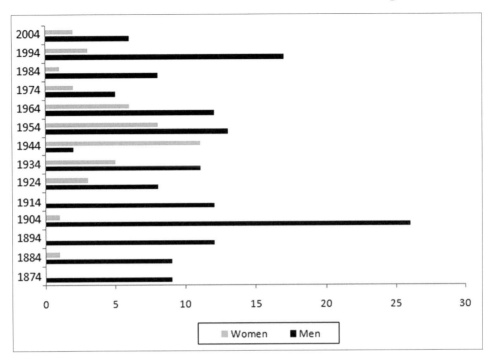

17 Graph to show the number of publications on prehistory published by the *Transactions of the Cumberland and Westmorland Antiquarian and Archaeological Society* according to sex, at 10-year intervals. Women N = 43, Men N = 150, Total N = 193

Cumbrian archaeology, her contributions ranging far beyond her own research and fieldwork.

Of all the women, and indeed men, working in Cumbria the dominant figure of the twentieth century was Clare Isobell Fell (1912-2002). Fell was one of the first students, male or female, to read archaeology at Cambridge University, taking a first in 1933 (although as a woman she was unable to graduate). Her contemporaries included Grahame Clark, Stuart Piggott and Christopher Hawkes, each of whom went on to become professors at Cambridge, Edinburgh and Oxford, and were influential in her approach to the archaeology of Cumbria. Fell's early career as an archaeologist was in Cambridge, where she was assistant curator in the Museum of Archaeology and Anthropology (*19*). Although interrupted by the Second World War, her career looked promising. In 1949 she joined the first season of excavation of the Mesolithic site of Star Carr in Yorkshire, excavated by Grahame Clark. Later that year she began her own research of the axe 'factories' in the Langdales. Her career in Cambridge was curtailed when family responsibilities drew her back to Ulverston in 1953. Thus began Fell's active research in the county which was to continue for the rest of her life. She joined the Committee for Prehistoric Studies (WDX 1408/2/7), which then included Hodgson, Cross and Fair, and in 1940 began a long tradition of publication in the *Transactions* with an article considering Bronze Age connections between the Lake District and Ireland (Fell 1940).

Fell used her Cambridge connections to good effect. In 1947 she published a short note on Bronze Age finds near her family home in Ulverston, having first sent the objects to Professor

18 Mary Fair in her later years

Hawkes for a second opinion (Fell 1947). She also acted as a consultant for Marjorie Cross, identifying the stone implements found at the Walney Island site, and reporting the opinion of her old friend Grahame Clark (Cross 1949, 9). When the Prehistoric Society visited Cumbria in 1949 for a joint meeting with the Cumberland and Westmorland Antiquarian and Archaeological Society (CWAAS), the speakers included a number of distinguished archaeologists, amongst them Stuart Piggott, Abercromby Professor of Archaeology at Edinburgh University, and Professor Gerhard Bersu, then Professor of the Royal Irish Academy in Dublin. Fell represented the CWAAS and delivered a paper entitled *Trans-Pennine communications in the Bronze Age*, later transcribed for the *Transactions* (1949, 191-193).

In 1949 she was invited by Grahame Clark, then a lecturer at Cambridge and editor of the *Proceedings of the Prehistoric Society*, to join his first season of excavations at the Mesolithic site of Star Carr over the Pennines in Yorkshire. There she was exposed to Clark's pioneering approach, working alongside respected botanists like Harry Godwin and Donald Walker to understand the environmental aspects of the site (Fagan 2001, 146-148). This excavation, with its momentous discoveries and huge variety of artefacts, must have been an exciting place to work, yet by September of the same year Fell had turned her attention to the Langdale Pikes back in Lakeland. Working with Brian Bunch, Fell was the first to recognise the importance of and draw attention to the Neolithic axe factory sites (Fell 1948; Bunch and Fell 1949; Fell 1951, 1955), a subject which would continue to fascinate her for many years, and with which she became closely identified. In 1950 Fell joined with ex-students of her old Cambridge master Hector Chadwick, to publish a volume of studies in his memory. She chose to write about her home counties and in her paper on the Beaker period in the North West (Fell 1950) she applied the knowledge and experience acquired at Cambridge to the pottery of Cumbria.

Drawing on the experience gained whilst working with Clark at Star Carr, Fell could see the value of scientific techniques to archaeology, which led her to develop an important research partnership, and friendship, with the botanist Winifred Pennington (Mrs Tutin) in the 1960s. Pennington (1915-2007) was born in Barrow-in-Furness, and educated at the town's grammar school. She was a pioneer in the study of pollen in sediments collected from open waters, which as we saw in the previous chapter, has been instrumental in our ability to reconstruct changes in the prehistoric landscape. She had a keen interest in archaeology which inspired her studies of human impact on the environment from the first tree clearances through changes in agriculture, and population expansion, all of which contributed to the enrichment of lowland lakes and the acidification of upland ones. She wrote *The History of the British Vegetation* (1969) and *The Lake District: a landscape history* (1973).

Fell was always keen to raise the profile of archaeology in the North West, believing that the area had been largely overlooked by prehistorians. Situated far from them both the capital city and the universities, for many years Cumbria, and the north-west of England in general, lagged well behind other parts of the country in attracting research programmes, particularly for the less glamorous field of prehistory in which she specialised. In a paper given to the British Association in Lancaster in 1976, Fell lamented:

> A variety of factors have combined to delay modern research into the prehistory of North West England. The absence, until recently, of universities near at hand which include archaeology in their curricula; the abundance of Roman military sites, including Hadrian's Wall, which have absorbed the bulk of informed research; acid soil, the high rainfall and mountainous nature of much of the area and the somewhat superior way in which southerners tend to look on the north as a backward area, have all acted adversely on this field of research.

Sadly, Lancaster University no longer offers archaeology in the curriculum, the closest academic departments now being in Preston to the south and Durham to the east. This lack of research attention has been considered elsewhere in relation to Lancashire (Barrowclough 2008).

Fell's greatest success in raising the profile of archaeology in Cumbria, and also the work with which she is most closely associated, is her pioneering research into the Langdale axe factories discussed in further detail in Chapter 4. Since her first report of the site, one of her regular notes in the *Transactions* of 1948, the Langdale valley has attracted the attention of leading archaeologists from across Britain, achieving Fell's wish to move the Lake District higher up the agenda of British archaeology. Her suggestion that other outcrops of volcanic tuff may also have been quarried has been confirmed, and when new modern studies of the Langdale axe factories were undertaken in the 1980s and 1990s (Claris and Quartermaine 1989; Bradley and Edmonds 1993), Fell was closely involved, corresponding regularly with the researchers including Mark Edmonds and Jamie Quartermaine (WDX 1408/1/1). One of the resulting books, published in 1993, was dedicated to Fell, as a tribute to her kindness and encouragement (Bradley *et al,* 1993). Fell was also interested in the stone tools themselves (Fell 1955; 1964; 1967; 1980; 1987) and her work with Vin Davis on the petrological identification of stone implements from Cumbria set a high standard for subsequent analysis. She was also very supportive of the County Archaeological Service, and the card index files on which she had recorded finds reported to the CWAAS went to help form the basis of the Sites and Monuments Record (later known as the Historic Environment) (WDX 1408/4/5).

Although Fell is known for her support of amateur and young archaeologists, what many accounts gloss over is that she was also a force to be reckoned with. Professional colleagues report how she could be 'bitingly critical on occasion' and had 'no tolerance for pretension of any sort' (Cramp pers. comm. 2004), and within the CW society she gained a reputation as 'she who must be obeyed' (Cramp pers. comm. 2004). When anyone comes to dominate a field of research, as Fell undoubtedly did with regard to the prehistoric archaeology of Cumbria, alternative interpretations and debate has a tendency to be subdued or even closed completely. This was an unfortunate side effect of Fell's domination, and is reflected in the narrow approach toward the archaeological interpretation of prehistoric sites in Cumbria,

19 Clare Fell (back row, second from right) outside the Museum of Archaeology and Anthropology, Cambridge, *c.* 1950. Also shown, from left to right: Geoffrey Bushnell (curator from 1948 to 1970), unknown, Joan Leversedge, Mary Cra'ster senior, Mary Thatcher (front row), Clare Fell (back row) and Meyer Fortes. Photograph possibly taken by Mary Cra'ster. *Courtesy of Pamela Jane Smith*

which became increasingly out of step with post-processual developments elsewhere in Britain during the 1980s and 1990s – a position that did not change significantly until after her death in 2002.

Always extremely generous with both her time and finances, Fell was herself a regular benefactor to many other trusts and charities, including the Armitt Trust, which funds and manages the Armitt library, collection and museum in Ambleside (the repository of many Langdale axes), and more recently the Fenland Archaeological Trust (set up in 1986 by Francis Pryor to help fund and look after Flag Fen), perhaps following on from her earlier association with the Fens whilst at Cambridge.

In many respects Cumbria can be seen as an enlightened place in the late nineteenth and twentieth centuries. The progressive approach of the CWAAS, seen in its attitude towards women, was undoubtedly unusual and provided an environment which nurtured female interest in prehistory, a network through which women could discuss and develop ideas, a framework through which they were able to pursue research and ultimately influence the shape of archaeology in Cumbria through publications. By the time Fell was elected a member in 1937 there was a strong tradition of female involvement in the society, with Hodgson, Fair and Cross (amongst others) setting a high standard for research as well as serving on important, strategic committees. None of these four women ever married or had children. The reasons for this may be complex, but research does suggest that in the first half of the twentieth century a high proportion of women in archaeology remained single (Nixon 1994). Analysis by Philips shows that single women accounted for 45-60 per cent of the female membership of four societies studied from 1900 to 1950 (1998, 137). Philips, quoted in Sharpe (2007), suggests that 'societies may have provided a venue in which single women could socialize with people of the same class and interest' (Sharpe 2007, 136). The reasons that Hodgson, Fair, Cross and Fell remained single may never be known, but they each found a 'family' of sorts in the many friends and colleagues who belonged to the CWAAS.

This enlightened approach only seems to have extended to the daughters and close friends of those middle class gentlemen that had dominated the antiquarian era. For example, Mary Fair was prompted to join the society in 1911 by the Rev. W.S. Sykes, who was her father's predecessor as parish priest, and a keen archaeologist (Birley 1955, 309). Clare Fell's father, Lieutenant-General Sir Matthew Henry Gregson Fell, was not only a member of the CWAAS, but its vice-president from 1936-1939, whilst Katherine Hodgson's parents had both played a significant role in the society, her mother having published in the *Transactions* in 1928, enabling her to take her mother's place on the Cumberland Excavation Committee. Although female, these pioneering women were at home in the company of their male contemporaries, typical of whom were Henry Swainson Cowper and Lieutenant Colonel Oliver Henry North. Henry Swainson Cowper (1865-1941) was a true antiquarian. Educated at Harrow, his financial independence enabled him to travel extensively in Mesopotamia, Egypt, Tripoli and Asia Minor, places for which he had a great affection. Closer to home he applied his archaeological interest to the study of Cumbrian prehistory. He made many contributions to *Archaeologia* and other national journals as well as to the *Transactions*. He also wrote a number of books, notably *Archaeological Survey of Cumberland, Westmorland and Lancashire North-of-the-Sands*, compiled in association with Chancellor Ferguson (Cowper and Ferguson 1893), and his monumental *Hawkshead, its History, Archaeology, Industries, Folklore, Dialect etc.* (Cowper 1899).

Oliver North's (1875-1955) upper middle class background, as the fifth son of a local landowner, first set him on course as a tea-planter in Ceylon until the Boar War broke out, setting him on course for a military career. North, a member of the Society since 1908, became a vice-president in 1935, and served as president from 1945 to 1947 (*20*). He was also an active member of the society's Committee for Prehistoric Studies, contributing a number of papers to the *Transactions* on the subject of prehistoric archaeology: *Some recent finds of stone implements* (1934, 113-115); *Stone circle, Summerhouse Hill, Yealand Conyers* (with J.E. Spence 1936, 69-70); *Local stone implements* (1936, 129-131); *Two recently discovered bronze Celts* (1936, 14.2-143); *Local stone and bronze implements* (1938, 155-156); *A bronze axe and other local finds* (1942, 232-233); *A Bronze Age Spearhead* (1943a, 70); *A stone axe-hammer from Threlkeld* (1943b, 161 and 200); and *A polished stone axe from Holme, Westmorland* (1943, 217). As we might expect of a man said to be equally at home 'as a rider and as a sportsman ... and ... there were occasions when digging had to be suspended so that he could go out with his gun' (Anon 1955, 305-307) he was no

20 Oliver North, shown here holding two Roman vessels from Burrow which he had restored

academic and his papers focus on description rather than explanation.

What both men and women had in common was financial independence which gave them the freedom necessary to devote their lives to archaeological research. In many respects the society was as much a means of socialising with members of the same, upper middle, class as it was with research. Marked by their absence are members of the working class, and even members of the lower middle classes are few and far between. In stark contrast to the county of Lancashire, to the immediate south, where skilled manual workers, school teachers mixed with local GPs and solicitors joined in common cause by an interest in prehistory (Barrowclough 2008) in Cumbria such people are the exception. Harper Gaythorpe, an engraver and illuminator, is one such person. He lived in Barrow and became interested in archaeology following his employment to work on Richardson's *Furness: Past and Present*. He became a great collector of archaeological artefacts joining both the Barrow Naturalists' Field Club, of which he was president 1902-14 and editor of their *Transactions* in 1895, and the Cumberland and Westmorland Society for which he was elected a member of that council in 1905. He published a number of papers, mainly on the archaeology of Furness: *Prehistoric Implements in Furness* (1897, 442-447; 1899, 161-171; 1900, 152-156); *Notes on the Bronze Celts from Urswick* and *Bronze Spearhead from Piel Castle* (1903, 373); *Prehistoric Implements from Furness* (1904, 325); *Notes on Stone Implements at Stain ton-in-Furness* (1904, 352); *Prehistoric Implements in Furness* (1906, 128); *Note on a Stone Celt from Urswick* (1907, 269); was a co-opted member of the Municipal Library and Museum Committee, and chairman of the sub-committee for the museum.

The contrast in participation between Cumbria and Lancashire may reflect the effect of urbanisation in Lancashire and the development of working class movements, such as trade unions, that encouraged education amongst their largely male membership. In Cumbria these movements were less developed with the traditional division between landed gentry and agricultural workers being more resilient. The pressure for change here was from educated women, encouraged by the North of England Council for Promoting the Higher Education of Women. It is worthy of note that, building on the intellectual links forged by McKenny Hughes, the first principal of Newnham College, a Cambridge college for women, was Anne Jemima Clough (1820-1892). Born in Liverpool between 1852 and 1862, she ran her own small school at Ambleside in Westmorland (Robinson 2009, 46). Clough was one of the founders of the council and acted as its secretary from 1867 to 1870 and as its president from 1873 to 1874. Clough's Cumbrian connections may have inspired women including Fell, who studied at Newnham, to take advantage of the new educational opportunities promoted by the council. Dorothy Garrod, one of Fell's tutors, completed her degree in history at Cambridge in 1916 and went on to be the first woman Disney Professor (Davies 1999; Smith 2000). By the early 1930s when Fell went up to Cambridge, Archaeology and Anthropology was a recognised field of study and the discipline had become more professional. A number of female graduates, for example Ann Hallam, went on to forge careers in archaeology, although excavation remained for many years a male dominated activity. The majority of women found positions in museums, or supported work done by male colleagues by recording, illustrating and cataloguing artefacts (Champion 1998).

The Later Twentieth Century

The later part of the twentieth century saw an expansion of professional archaeology in Britain. A number of archaeological units were established in the north-west of England: in Carlisle the city council founded one, with others growing out of the university archaeology departments at Lancaster, Manchester and Liverpool. Their business models have not always proved to be sustainable. Sadly the Carlisle unit was disbanded, whilst at Lancaster the Unit survived, ultimately becoming Oxford Archaeology North, now the major commercial unit operating in the county, only for the university archaeology department to close. Oxford North, under its different guises, has excavated a number of important sites, including the Bronze Age burial sites at Allithwaite (Wild 2003) and Borwick (Olivier 1987). The advantage of the commercial archaeological units is that they bring professional expertise to the excavations as a consequence the standard of excavation of these sites was much higher than that of previous excavations. In the south of the region, the archaeology department at the University of Liverpool became interested in Cumbrian prehistory for a brief period under the leadership of Professor Terrence Powell and undertook excavations at Skelmore Heads, Ulverston and Storrs Moss in North Lancashire (*colour plate 1*). Also out of Liverpool, at the end of this period, came Ann Hallam's study of the region's prehistoric pottery (1990), written later in life but recalling her undergraduate days at Cambridge and drawing on her practical experience in archaeology. University-funded work, this time Glasgow, was also responsible for new insights into upland settlement patterns with important new sites found at Matterdale (Hoaen and Loney 2003; 2004).

Important as excavation has been, most research since the 1980s has taken the form of archaeological survey. There is a long history of upland survey in Cumbria dating as far back as the work of Dymond in 1893, Spence in 1939 and the Royal Commission for Historical Monuments of England survey of Westmorland in 1936 (RCHME 1936). From 1982 onwards what is now the Oxford North Archaeological Unit undertook a major programme of survey work across the Lake District on behalf of the Lake District National Park Authority (LDNPA) and English Heritage, which mapped over 14,000 monuments (Quartermaine and Leech forthcoming). In addition there have been smaller surveys undertaken by the RCHME, English Heritage and other organisations and amateur groups. The extent of these collective surveys was monitored by a programme of surveys (LUAU 1995e). In the lowlands of Cumbria between 1990 and 1997 the North West Wetlands Survey, an English Heritage funded project, surveyed and assessed the archaeological potential for the county's wetlands. Further large-scale survey work of Cumbrian landscapes has been ongoing since 1987 and has been completed for some of the most famous valleys and landscapes including Great Langdale, Wasdale Head, Hartsop, Coniston, Wastendlath and Ashness, Borrowdale and Hawkshead, and Claife. This work is complemented by aerial survey where possible. Aerial photography in Cumbria and much of north-west England is hindered by the presence of extensive subsoils which are relatively insensitive to cropmark development, notably those over boulder clays and in areas dominated by permanent pasture and woodland. Despite this, concerted programmes of flying have had a revolutionary impact on the density, distribution and nature of past settlement in the county, producing a significant body of data. The work of J.K. St Joseph and the Cambridge University Committee for Aerial Photography from the 1940s to 1990s greatly increased the aerial photographic legacy for Cumbria, and increased the number of known sites for all periods. This work was significantly expanded during the 1970s by Tom Clare, then of Cumbria County Council, with the support of the RCHME and Nick Higham and Barri Jones of Manchester University (Higham and Jones 1975; Higham 1979). During the 1980s there were two significant advances. On the Solway Plain Bob Bewley (*21*) combined a study of aerial photographs with fieldwalking and targeted excavation to address the bias toward the Roman period, revealing much about the prehistoric occupation of the plain (Bewley 1994). Clive Bonsall did much to develop our understanding of the Late Mesolithic with his excavations at Eskmeals (Bonsall 1981; Bonsall *et al* 1989), discussed in more detail in the following chapter (*colour plate 2*).

The amateur still has a role to play in Cumbrian archaeology despite its increasing professionalisation. The most prolific amateur archaeologists in the county in the latter half of the twentieth century were John and Peter Cherry (*colour plate 3*) who have undertaken a long-term and wide-scale field walking survey in Cumbria which has begun to broaden the distribution and nature of prehistoric occupation in both coastal and upland areas. Their publications have focused, in the main, on the Mesolithic and Neolithic occupation of West Cumbria (1983; 1984; 1985; 1987) following their fieldwork amongst the sand dune occupation sites at Eskmeals (1963; 1966; 1969), Seascale (1967), Drigg (1965; 1982) and St Bees (1973), although they have also undertaken fieldwork on the limestone uplands of eastern Cumbria (1987). Another archaeologist worthy of mention is Christopher Salisbury who has led the excavation of a number of significant cave sites in the county. Of particular interest are his publications of finds from Kirkhead and Lindale Low Caves which have added considerably to our understanding of the Upper Palaeolithic (Salisbury 1986; 1988), as well as studies of the Mesolithic occupation of Mill Dam Meadow, Gleaston (1995).

Metal detecting has provided an alternative outlet for those amateurs with an interest in field archaeology. Beginning in the 1970s, but particularly since the 1990s, metal detecting has given rise to a huge increase in the amount of metalwork, and particularly Bronze Age material, from Cumbria, which is discussed further in Chapter 7. Professional archaeologists have often been mistrustful of a technique which they often believed to be no more than treasure hunting, whilst detectorists have been suspicious of formal archaeology's dismissal of

21 Bob Bewley excavating an Early Bronze Age Collared Urn at Ewanrigg. *Courtesy of Bob Bewley*

their work. To some great extent these barriers have been broken down in the last decade by the formation of the Portable Antiquities Scheme which, through the scheme's local staff, has provided a link between amateur enthusiast and professional practitioner. The advent of the Portable Antiquities Database, an online catalogue of metal detected finds, ensures that both academic researches and interested members of the public are able to gain access to new finds, whilst ensuring that they remain in the possession of the lawful owner.

Interpretations

A number of accounts have attempted to formulate an interpretation for the post-glacial settlement of Cumbria. We have already noted that the earliest interpretations were based on ideas derived from Aubrey and Stukeley that focused on the population of the British Isles by people from the East, possibly Phoenicians, from whom the Druid religion was ultimately derived. In the late nineteenth century an appreciation of the great antiquity of the human population became apparent and, following the work of the Danish archaeologist Thomson, the prehistoric period which had been synonymous with 'Celts' was divided into the Stone, Bronze and Iron Ages, with the Stone Age being further divided into the Old and New Stone Ages, the Palaeolithic and Neolithic. With these national and international developments archaeologists began to reframe their enquiries, the prevalent concern throughout the first half of the twentieth century being the cultural and racial origin of the region's prehistoric inhabitants. European prehistory during this period was dominated by culture-historical models, which often sought racial explanations for differences in material culture. The models invoked to explain the Cumbrian evidence were no exception.

Work on the *Victoria County History of Cumberland* began under R.S. Ferguson, who planned a four-volume history. Unfortunately Ferguson died in 1900 before any of the volumes were printed. His place was taken by the medievalist Rev. Canon James Wilson, vicar of Dalston, who published a two-volume history in 1901 and 1905. Volume one provides the first attempt at a comprehensive model for the prehistory of Cumberland, and also Westmorland, combining the evidence from the local archaeology with the then current interpretative framework for British prehistory. Although archaeologists would disagree with much that Wilson proposed, as they would with Hutchinson's earlier interpretation, the work was a landmark in advancing the public's understanding of Cumbria's earliest history.

Beginning with the Neolithic, he describes the people living in Cumbria as being of 'short-stature, with a long head [and] … probably had a mild countenance' (Wilson 1901, 226). This may seem an odd remark to us, but the *Victoria County History* bases its theory on measurements of crania, separating those with long heads, termed dolicho-cephalic, from those with round heads, brachy-cephalic, associated with the Bronze Age. According to the science of the time it was possible to identify two different groups of people according to the size and shape of their skulls, from which other information, such as their intelligence and temperament could be deduced. Needless to say modern science does not substantiate this idea and archaeologists no longer measure skulls in an attempt to deduce racial or temperamental characteristics. Wilson continues to argue that the Neolithic people lived a pastoral, semi-agricultural existence having begun to domesticate farm animals, something which modern archaeologists would not disagree with. Turning to the archaeological monuments, he correctly links the burial of the Neolithic dead in long barrows, distinguishing them from the Early Bronze Age burials which are associated with round barrows, which the author summarises as 'Long heads and long barrows go together; round heads and round barrows' (Wilson 1901, 227). Turning to discussion of stone implements, he also links polished stone axes with the Neolithic, although some of the other implements, such as perforated stone hammers which he also considers Neolithic are now thought to belong to the Early Bronze Age, although even today dating of stone tools is difficult and much work still needs to be done to understand many of the tools as previous research has largely focused on polished stone axes.

As a medievalist Wilson's knowledge of prehistory was a little weak; he was, for example, unsure when Neolithic people first settled Cumbria, indeed he offered no explanation for the arrival of people in the area, although it is implied that they must have moved into the county from elsewhere following the end of the last ice age. What is clearer was his view that they were 'intruded upon by another race … possibly somewhere about the year 1000 BC' (Wilson 1901, 229) this is a reference to the start of the Bronze Age which he believed was brought about by the movement of a new group of people into Cumbria, the round headed brachy-cephalic people. The presence of this group of people in Cumbria is marked by their burial monuments, the round barrows and cairns. Wilson believed that these people were a stronger and sterner race than the Neolithic people, and that judging by the skeletons were taller and more muscular, with 'broad jaws, turned up nose, high cheek bones, wide mouth and eyes deep sunk under beetling brows' (Wilson 1901, 229). Again, to the modern reader there appears scant evidence to support this vivid description. The skeletal record for the period is thin, as most bodies were cremated, and within this, as with any population, is a degree of natural variation which can make distinguishing between male and female adult skeletons difficult, and that of children virtually impossible. The best that can be said for the author's interpretation is that it is coloured by wishful thinking, and no archaeologist would support his interpretation today. What is more accurate is the association of the Bronze Age with the arrival of bronze (copper-alloy) metalworking, and the comment that the arrival of bronze did not mean the end of stone tools. It is the case that stone tools continued to be used in the Bronze Age and, what is more, the 'quality' of these stone tools appears to our eyes to be 'worse' than those of the Neolithic, something which the *Victoria County History* seems to be aware of as they describe the Bronze Age tools as 'cheaper articles' (Wilson 1901, 229). Wilson is also correct in pointing out that many of the Bronze Age burials are cremated and placed into a particular type of urn, what we now call Collared Urns, sometimes with a small range of grave goods, such as beads. The *Victoria County History* is prepared to offer an early attempt at interpreting why this might be so. For Wilson the reason is that they 'had a belief in a future state of which the conditions would be similar to the conditions of life upon this earth: conditions in which the man would still want his implements of war and of the chase, and the woman her ornaments' (Wilson 1901, 234). This interpretation differs little in substance to modern ideas, albeit that today we know that it is misleading to associate any particular grave goods with a particular sex, thus bead necklaces are in fact found with men as well as women in Bronze Age burials, as indeed they are amongst today's population.

The *Victoria County History* argues that the Bronze Age was caused by the invasion of Cumbria by a new people with particular physical characteristics which distinguished them from the Neolithic population, whom they conquered and 'enslaved' thanks to their superior physical attributes and their more sophisticated, bronze metal, technology. This is a contentious view and today archaeologists tend to favour a less bloody explanation which explains change in terms of the indigenous population acquiring the new technology, rather in the way that modern populations acquire technologies such as the computer which cause them to adapt their lifestyles. Put simply, we do not need to infer the movement of people in order to explain changes in either technology or behaviour. This is not to say that people never move, nor that warfare and violence are modern phenomena, clearly they do and they are not, but that in the absence of other evidence these should not be our immediate or first choice explanations for change in the past.

R.G. Collingwood (1933) expanded upon Wilson's (1901) model invoking settlement of Cumbria from outside, drawing on the ideas of Childe (1925; 1930) and Fox (1932). The strength of Collingwood's work was that his interpretation was based on the integration of different aspects of the prehistoric record. He combined the geographical patterning of monuments in different landscape zones and within and between the different regions of Cumbria with discussion of burial traditions and the distribution of stone axes and bronze metalwork in relation to settlement evidence. Helen Evans has pointed out that Collingwood's work illustrates the two key themes that have come to characterise studies of Cumbrian prehistory. The first has been the identification of links to the Irish Seaboard and eastern Yorkshire and the routes through which these were maintained. The second, a debt to Fox (1932), is that through its very physical location, the region has been understood as culturally backward and of little significance compared to its neighbours (Evans 2008, 8).

He envisioned the arrival by sea of 'Neolithic' people on the west coast, whilst the Early Bronze Age was heralded by the arrival of 'Beaker Folk' who migrated from the north-east of England travelling up the Eden valley (1933, 191). Beginning his interpretative scheme with the distribution of stone axes and stone circles which are at their densest in south and west Cumbria, Collingwood argues that Neolithic communities arrived on the Irish Sea coast, then worked northwards from Black Coombe and inland towards the Derwent and Eden valleys (Collingwood 1933, 177). The Beaker Folk entered the region from Yorkshire and worked their way down the Eden valley: 'We may regard the Beaker Folk from the east and the circle builders from the west as meeting there and combining to found a hybrid civilisation' (Collingwood 1933, 181). This argument has proved to be a persistent one. The Iron Age was similarly interpreted in terms of 'Celtic invasions', from the Rhine into the Marne valley and then to eastern England and finally Lancashire and Cumbria (Sayce 1956, 3).

The most developed model explaining culture change in the region was proposed by Bu'Lock (1961). Although he was working within the paradigm of culture-history, which fits uneasily with contemporary approaches, he was the first to recognise that Cumbria's archaeological record has to be explained in the context of the region, and that models imported from elsewhere in Britain cannot be applied uncritically. His interpretation is worth considering in detail as it identifies some of the main characteristics of the region's archaeological record and offers an interpretation that forms the basis of our current understanding. He argued that the north-west of England was a native enclave with its own distinctive 'north-western' styles of pottery surrounded by areas in which the single-grave Food Vessel tradition was either wholly predominant, as in the Peak District and east of the Pennines, or far more influential in amalgamation, as in North Wales, south-west Scotland and Ireland. This defined 'a geographic integrity sufficient to warrant the designation of a North Western Culture in Early Bronze Age England' (Bu'Lock 1961, 38).

According to his model the Neolithic population of pastoralists and hunters shared a common cultural heritage with their contemporaries around the northern shores of the Irish Sea, an idea that has recently received new currency in discussion of the Irish Sea Province (Fowler and Cummings 2003; see also Raftery 1972). He accounted for this in part by the trading of stone axes from the Cumbrian 'factories', and partly on common antecedents, expressed materially through burial rites and monuments, and the associated ceramics. Whilst 'Beaker Folk' colonised adjacent areas of Yorkshire and Derbyshire, establishing distinct cultural communities, the north-west of England retained its native traditions, which give it a distinct character. In the east of England he saw a fusion of immigrant and native elements out of which emerged the 'Food Vessel Folk', groups of whom penetrated into the North West in small numbers, following routes favoured by the trade in Irish bronzes. These immigrants are marked by single-grave burials under round barrows.

By the time that the Wessex Culture had established itself in the south the native tradition in the North West had reached the stage referred to as the 'Pennine Urn Period', that is the North Western Style of Collared Urns. This period was marked by an expansion of the population of the North West which, fuelled by its part in the bronze trade, was able to expand eastwards into the 'Food Vessel area' of the Peak District. He saw the 'native tradition' as experiencing a resurgence associated with either the absorption or the displacement of the food vessel single-grave groups.

The timing of his publication was unfortunate, coming just as culture-history interpretations were going out of fashion. In the 1970s and '80s, palaeoenvironmental research and models based on environmental determinism came to the fore (for example Hibbert *et al* 1971; Barnes 1975; Jacobi *et al* 1976; Cundhill 1981). According to them Cumbria was an environmentally marginal environment of lowland wetlands and upland mountains making subsistence difficult. Within the region ground-breaking work was undertaken by Pennington, synthesising archaeology and palaeoenvironmental evidence (Pennington 1975). Typology and chronology were similarly interpreted within a framework of geographical determinism for the Bronze Age of western Yorkshire, which includes parts of the region under investigation, by Manby and Turnbulll (1986). These interpretations were strongly influenced by geographical determinism originating in the work of Fox (1932) in his book *The Personality of Britain*. This placed Cumbria firmly in the highland zone. As such it was to be expected that influences were likely to be received from Yorkshire and Scotland channelled through the upland valleys of, for example, the Tyne and Aire Gaps.

More recent accounts have moved away from such deterministic interpretations. In a discussion of the later prehistoric archaeology of Cumbria, in the context of recent fieldwork, Hoaen and Loney (2004) argue that explanations of the region's data do not fit well with models developed for sites in southern Britain. They identify the need to devise interpretative models specific to the region. They have attempted this for the Bronze Age period in Matterdale (2003; 2004). Matthews (2001) explicitly rejects models based on south-eastern England and questions the core-periphery model that dominated interpretations of the Iron Age since the late 1970s in his study looking at consumption of material culture and how it worked to create distinct identities for people in the North West. Bewley (1994) offered a contextual study of settlement in the Solway Plain in the Romano-British period. A similar contextual approach to interpretations of the Late Neolithic and Early Bronze Age of the Furness Peninsula has been suggested by Helen Evans (2008), and will now be applied to the period from the end of the last ice age until the arrival of the Romans in what follows.

Discussion

The above review has traced some of the encounters with Cumbria's prehistory over the past four centuries. It did not set out to give an exhaustive account, but selected some key contributions that are representative of the history of ideas about Cumbria's prehistoric evidence. Present day attitudes to Cumbria's prehistory are the result of this stratification of ideas. In this sense, the history of Cumbria's archaeology reflects the history of prehistoric archaeology nationally. One of the reasons that this review is useful is that an understanding of how archaeological knowledge has been constructed allows one to identify the strengths and weaknesses in our interpretations more readily. One of the outstanding concerns that has emerged is a disjuncture between popular and scientific knowledge. Regional and national journals have become increasingly specialised; aimed at professional archaeologists they are written in increasingly technical language and are often inaccessible to a general reader. A second is the dislocation of archaeology from the regional context, as national narratives drawing upon evidence from other parts of Britain largely replaced understanding of the past based upon a reading of the regional archaeological record. Prehistoric archaeology became an activity for outsiders from which the communities living closest to these remains were often excluded. Another dislocation is the decontextualisation of Cumbria's archaeological record from the surrounding landscape. Beginning with the earliest collectors the emphasis has been on removing artefacts from the landscape and placing them first in private and then in public museum collections. These collections form the basis of the various artefact corpora which group objects according to the categories that archaeologists create, placing, for example, urns from different locations together, or separating objects that were found together in different corpora. The tendency to treat different classes of data in isolation from each other and from the landscape is not a trait that is particular to Cumbria, it is a tendency that has characterised approaches to prehistoric archaeology in Europe until fairly recently (Watson 2001, 296).

The series of disjuncture and dislocations outlined above are all interrelated. The creation of archaeological understanding is inseparable from the social context in which it occurs. The practices of archaeological investigation and site management that have been outlined were recognisably modelled on the mainstream paradigms of their period. They often became inseparable from the values that were driving research in the wider context of British archaeology. This array of global and local processes went far to create a sound foundation for the understanding of Cumbria's prehistory. Inevitably, it also had its limitations, some of which have been the focus of the present chapter. Such limitations are, of course, easier to recognise from the vantage point of the present. From our position we are better placed to begin to address some of these gaps in our knowledge.

CHAPTER 3

LIVING OFF THE LAND:

THE LATE UPPER PALAEOLITHIC AND MESOLITHIC, HUNTER-GATHERER OCCUPATION

Of the Eolithic and Palaeolithic periods we have nothing; these periods therefore may be ignored.

R.G. Collingwood 1933, 167

Introduction

The last ice age came to an end *c.*10,000 years ago. Tundra landscapes that supported reindeer herds were colonised by birch and soon became thick deciduous woodland with dispersed fauna including elk, red deer, auroch and wild pig. Sea-levels rose so that Britain, formerly a peninsula of Europe, had become an island by 8500 years ago. In this rapidly changing environment people continued to live by hunting and gathering for several thousand years until agriculture became established.

Stray finds indicate little other than the presence of Mesolithic people. Scatters of stone tools and the debris from their manufacture are the most abundant features of the record of the Mesolithic. The type artefacts from the period are microliths: small blades usually of flint that have been retouched occur in a range of shapes and sizes. Microliths are often found in hundreds if not thousands and were probably components of a wide range of tools including hunting equipment. The Early Mesolithic, the period before 8500 years ago was dominated by 'broad blade assemblages'. These are collections of relatively large microliths either shaped like isosceles triangles or described as 'obliquely blunted points'. Late Mesolithic assemblages, after *c.*8500 BP, are usually dominated by much smaller microliths in a wider variety of forms which are termed 'narrow blade assemblages' and include needle points and scalene triangles.

Late Glacial

The earliest evidence for human, hunter-gatherer, occupation of Cumbria dates to the Late Upper Palaeolithic *c.*16,000-8000 BC. The evidence is sparse as the ice sheet did much to obliterate and cover earlier landscapes and the sites that must have once existed. As a consequence it is impossible to reconstruct any meaningful pattern of occupation. Although limited, the Late Upper Palaeolithic material from Cumbria is the earliest evidence for settlement in Britain this far north-west and as such is of national importance (Wymer 1981, 77). Elsewhere in northern England it is rare to find artefacts of this period, with only two cave sites in the Yorkshire Pennines providing similarly limited evidence (Cowell 1996, 30). The main sites are found in the southern part of Britain with the exception of an important number of cave sites in Derbyshire (Jacobi 1980).

The occupation of Cumbria during the Late Upper Palaeolithic was focused around the northern, limestone, coast of Morecambe Bay where a series of caves have preserved occupation debris. No other evidence for human occupation during this period has been found in Cumbria. Although this is in part due to poor preservation elsewhere, it is also likely that it reflects the general pattern of human activity in the Palaeolithic. This general absence of activity was a response to the harsh climate that existed in Cumbria. The prehistoric

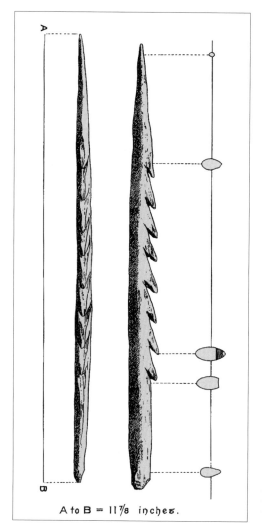

A to B = 11⅞ inches.

22 Bone point found at Crosby-on-Eden. This point is very similar to one found embedded in an elk at Poulton-Le-Fylde, Lancashire, dated to 13500-11500 cal BC. *Hodgson 1895*

environment of Late Palaeolithic Cumbria has been reconstructed from deposits dated to the Late Devensian period at St Bees (Coope and Joachim 1980; Coope 1994) and from the many tarns (Pennington 1970). From these data we are able to reconstruct the following sequence. As the ice retreated and the climate became warmer, the vegetation on the drier land developed into an open birch, juniper and willow scrub in the Early Mesolithic which was in turn ultimately replaced by more open grassland.

The evidence for the first post-glacial occupation of Cumbria comes from sites around the shores of Morecambe Bay. Lithic material from Kirkhead Cave, near Grange (Ashmead and Wood 1974; Gale and Hunt 1985, 1990; Salisbury 1986) has been dated to the Late Devensian zone III period of the Upper Palaeolithic (*c.*11,000-9500 BC; Young 2002). Radiocarbon dating of elk antlers, considered by Gale and Hunt (1985) to be associated with the artefacts in Kirkhead Cave, produced a date of 11,027-10,077 cal BC (10,650 ±200 BP, HAR 1059).

To the north-east, at the mouth of the River Kent, excavations at Lindale Low Cave recovered potentially the earliest evidence for occupation in Cumbria in the form of three possible Upper Palaeolithic blades (Salisbury 1988; Hodgkinson *et al* 2000). One of these, a large angle-backed blade of Creswellian type, was found sealed beneath a stalagmite floor (Salisbury 1988; 1992). A single flint bladelet similar to those from Kirkhead Cave and Badgers Hole, Warton was recovered from a separate location within the cave, and is unlikely to be contemporary. Excavations in caves at Blenkett Wood, Allithwaite (Salisbury 1997) may also have produced Late Upper Palaeolithic tools, alongside later lithic artefacts, faunal remains and human bone from highly disturbed contexts (Young 2002). More certain evidence comes from the site of Bart's Shelter, Furness, where 80 lithic implements of Late Upper Palaeolithic date were excavated, including a shouldered point (Jacobi in Hodgson and Brennand 2006, 25). The faunal assemblage at Bart's Shelter included reindeer and elk, the presence of which in the Morecambe Bay area was confirmed by the excavation of an elk on the southern side at Poulton-Le-Fylde near Blackpool (Barnes *et al* 1971; Hallam *et al* 1973; Barrowclough 2008, 47-48 figs 12-16). The bone points found embedded in the Poulton-Le-Fylde elk were similar to ones found at Crosby-on-Eden (*22*; Hodgson 1895), suggesting that hunting activity in the north of Cumbria, around the Solway Plain, was similar to that seen around the plain of Morecambe Bay and the Fylde in Lancashire.

Mesolithic

The potential of Mesolithic evidence from north-west England is amongst the best in the country because of the combination of upland and lowland sites, both in significantly large numbers, with detailed pollen studies which provide a range of associated evidence. Following the end of the last ice age the North Cumbrian Plain was colonised by a 'park tundra' vegetation, which at first consisted of juniper (*Juniperus* sp.) and willow (*Salix* sp.), and was then followed by birch (*Betula* sp.) and in turn hazel (*Corylus* sp.) to produce an open landscape with isolated small copses set amidst grassland. At the same time waterlogged basins populated by sedge created swamps, which as they became more acidic began to be colonised by *Sphagnum* sp. moss.

The pollen record from Scaleby Moss (Walker 1966, 42) shows that hazel, which had been present in small amounts for the previous thousand years or so, had by 8425-7576 cal BC (9009±194 BP, Q-161) expanded to become a major woodland-forming species in the area. In turn, elm (*Ulmus* sp.) and oak (*Quercus* sp.) became predominant, the elm establishing itself slightly ahead of oak. Finally, in common with most of lowland England, alder (*Alnus* sp.) expanded its cover rapidly between *c*.6500 cal BC and *c*.6000 cal BC (7700-7150 BP), the beginning of the alder rise being dated at Scaleby to between 6457 cal BC and 5888 cal BC (7361±146 BP, Q-167; Godwin and Willis 1959). By *c*.6000 cal BC (*c*.7150 BP) the vegetation of the North Cumbrian Plain is best compared with that of Northern Ireland (Walker 1966), having developed into what Walker described as 'an attenuated form' of the forest covering much of lowland England (Walker 1966, 179). That is, with less pine than is found further south and east, and with an absence of lime, because north Cumbria was not warm enough for it to survive.

Indications of human occupation can be detected in pollen cores from the Scottish side of the Solway estuary. At Burnfoothill Moss, in a core dated to *c*.5850-5750 cal BC (*c*.7000-6900 BP; based on interpolated radiocarbon dates), Tipping (1995b) records a small peak in microscopic charcoal which coincides with the appearance of pollen from plants such as *Pteridium* and *Plantago* which indicate woodland clearance, and the fire indicator *Melampyrum* (Simmons 1996, 119). He considered that this association suggested forest clearance, because it resembles similar activity at Thwaite House Moss in south Cumbria, also dated to the Mesolithic (Middleton *et al* 1995, 187). The presence of *Melampyrum* was also common in Mesolithic forest clearance recorded from the North Yorkshire Moors (Simmons 1996, 89-102). Hodgson and Brennand (2006) argued persuasively that given the evidence for Mesolithic disturbance at Burnfoothill Moss, it is likely that similar activity was also taking place in north Cumbria, only 15km away. Simmons and Innes (1987, fig. 1) considered that the presence of microscopic charcoal at Oulton Moss strongly suggested human activity around *c*.5000 cal BC (*c*.6100 BP). Similarly, at Bowness Common, peaks in grass pollen and a reduction in oak maybe an indicator of human activity in the surrounding landscape (J. Innes pers. comm. in Hodgson and Brennand 2006).

In addition to evidence of woodland clearance found in pollen cores the widespread presence of macroscopic charcoal, dated to the Mesolithic, in the north Cumbrian mosses may also be evidence of human activity (Hughes 1997, figs 5.4-8, 6.8-11). The North West Wetlands Survey of Cumbria (Hodgkinson *et al* 2000) found that charred and burnt plant remains are found regularly at the bottom of the peat mosses. Their survey of cleaned dyke sides on the southern and western edges of Solway Moss in 1991 revealed a continuous spread of charcoal at the interface between the mineral soil and the peat (Pl 32), which they thought likely to occur around the whole moss. This means that fire disturbance was common from at least 6080-5790 cal BC (7080±50 BP, GU-5277), when peat accumulation began, and reached a peak at 5240-4940 cal BC (6180±60 BP, GU-5315) coinciding with a sudden drop in the frequency of fragments of wood and the first appearance of *Eriophorum*, indicating a switch from fen to acid bog. This change corresponds to a sharp decline in alder and birch pollen. Taken together, the evidence suggests that carr woodland may have been destroyed by fire during the Mesolithic. Whether the fires were started deliberately or were a result of natural processes is unclear; however, burnt plant remnants remain an almost constant feature of the peat mosses into the upper layers dated to 3350-2890 cal BC (4400±80 BP, GU-5313; Huckerby and Wells 1993). It is possible that the fires were caused naturally by lightning, especially as the climate at the time was warmer and more 'continental' (Huntley 1993, 211), however human action remains a strong contender for at least some of the major fires (Simmons 1996, 129). The reason for burning back the vegetation in this way would be to create a grassy clearing where game would gather making hunting easier (Mellars 1976; Simmons 1996, 180). Similar strategies were employed by Native American hunters (Lewis 1977; Lewis and Ferguson 1988). It is therefore not inconceivable that some of the charcoal from Solway Moss could represent early attempts to manage the wetland landscape.

The evidence from the pollen cores points towards a Mesolithic population moving into the area and using fire to manage the landscape; however very few archaeological artefacts have been found to support this. The best evidence was provided by the North West Wetlands Survey (Hodgkinson *et al* 2000), which identified four separate findspots of Mesolithic/Early Neolithic material (CU1, CU6, CU7 and CU20). Most of the flint was waste from tool making, but they did recover a backed blade (CU1). Beyond this a single Late Mesolithic triangular microlith was found at Carlisle (Caruana and Cherry 1994), and a possible Early Mesolithic convex-edged blade was found at Crofton, north-east of Wigton (Fell 1985). Taken together, the north Cumbrian finds demonstrate the definite presence of groups with which to associate the tentative palaeoecological evidence, and suggest that further Mesolithic finds are likely in the future, particularly in view of the potential attraction of the coast and wetlands for hunter-gatherers and early farmers, which has been demonstrated on the West Cumbrian Coastal Plain (Bonsall 1981).

The west of Cumbria, south-west of St Bees, is known for its cliffs. Within these is a layer of organically rich sediment containing pollen (Walker 1956; 1966). Studies of this layer have revealed vegetation changes associated with the end of the last ice age, which can be dated to between 11,806-11,196 cal BC (11,500 ±120 BP, Birm-647) and 11,419-10,888 cal BC (11,180±120 BP, Birm-649). Coope (1994, 88) has even been able to estimate that the mean July temperatures at the time were *c*.15-16 °C during most of the Windermere Interstadial, falling to *c*.10 °C during the Loch Lomond Stadial phase. Evidence for the Early Mesolithic is in contrast lacking, however the Late Mesolithic/Early Neolithic transition is better understood, largely as a result of research in the Esk estuary. The Eskmeals area contains one of the richest concentrations of Late Mesolithic sites in north-west England and has been the focus for fieldwalking, excavation and palaeoenvironmental research since it was first discovered by Jim and Peter Cherry in the 1960s (Cherry and Cherry 1986).

All Mesolithic activity on the West Cumbrian Coastal Plain was played out against the backdrop of rising sea-levels which changed the outline of the coast. Between *c*.5970-5480 cal BC (6810±130 BP, Hv-6209) and 5613-5240 cal BC (6495±95 BP, Hv-5210) sea-level rose by 2m OD. The effect was dramatic; at Eskmeals it produced a perimarine fringe *c*.11.5km further inland than at present depositing a series of shingle ridges. These ridges began to isolate inland basins from marine influence, which encouraged the development of lagoon and estuarine environments (Huddart *et al* 1977, 142; Bonsall *et al* 1986, 178).

The Eskmeals sites are all found on seaward facing slopes overlooking the former coast-line. During the Mesolithic this would have been an esturine environment fitting with a

Europe-wide pattern of settlement location: during the Late Mesolithic settlements are typi-
cally found in sheltered locations around estuaries, lagoons or marine inlets (*23*; Bonsall 1981,
29). Other instances of this choice of location in north-west England have been described
on Merseyside (Cowell 2000, 169-174) and in west Lancashire (Barrowclough 2008, 3). The
reason is probably due to the variety and abundance of food resources combined with fresh
water and shelter that make estuaries more favoured locations than purely coastal sites (Jacobi
1973; Clake 1976; Bonsall 1981). In the case of Eskmeals, Bonsall has also pointed to other
specific factors, in particular that, in an area otherwise devoid of flint, supplies were available within the shingle deposits of the coastal foreland (Bonsall 1981, 29). Bonsall, who was
responsible for the excavations of the lithic scatters identified by the Cherrys, notes that many
of the scatters are associated with former stream channels. One explanation for this might be
that these streams were used as spawning grounds for sea trout and salmon, which would be a
protein rich food resource for the Mesolithic population (Bonsall 1981, 29).

Bonsall undertook excavation at two sites, Monk Moors and Williamson's Moss. At Monk
Moors two lithic scatters, on opposite sides of a small channel, were excavated (Bonsall 1981).
Within the excavated area of the lithic scatters over 30,000 artefacts were recovered including
hazelnut shells and wood charcoal, although the main component was flaked stone artefacts.
The tools were, in the main, scrapers and 'narrow blade' microlith types (*24*), which are typical
of Mesolithic sites throughout the north of Britain (see Barrowclough 2008 for consideration
of the tools found in the Pennines) and date to the period after *c.*10,350 cal BP. Also present
were numerous pieces of red ochre, stakeholes and hearths, which together point to human
activity that may suggest habitation, or as Bonsall prefers (1981, 31), indicate food processing
and storage. Radiocarbon dates establish that the site was occupied several times. One phase
of activity included stakeholes and a line of hearths; charcoal from one of the hearths was
dated to 6750±155 BP (BM-1216), placing it in the Mesolithic. Charcoal from an isolated
hearth elsewhere, and from a third associated with a pit, produced later dates (3650±120 BP,
BM-1395 and 4050±55 BP, BM-1385) suggesting that people had repeatedly returned to the
same location, presumably because of its rich food supply (Bonsall 1981, 33).

At Williamson's Moss Mesolithic occupation extends over at least 7500 square metres with
the greatest concentration in an area 50m x 30m. Excavation of the site by Bonsall (Bonsall
et al 1986; 1989) recovered 34,000 pieces of worked flint, chert and tuff, including over 600
microliths and other tools (Bonsall 1981, 34). Evidence for settlement in the form of hearths,
small pits and stakeholes were also found (Bonsall *et al* 1989), but more noteworthy were a
number of structures. A number of large stones had been laid in one area to create a floor
or 'stone pavement' (Bonsall *et al* 1986; 1989); in another oak branches were arranged in a
lattice and overlain by a layer of birch brushwood; and in a further area a revetment consisting of oak trunks and overlain with birch bark to make a floor was found (*25* and *26*). These
features were interpreted as 'platforms' by the excavator who, based on analogy with sites in
Scandinavia, thought that they were 'platforms' upon which houses had stood (Bonsall 1981,
35). Radiocarbon dates of the birch bark, for example 5555±40 BP (UB-2545), place them in
the Late Mesolithic.

Studies of pollen cores at Eskmeals have focused on the Williamson's Moss site (Tipping
1994). Not long after *c.*4780-4470 cal BC (5760±60 BP, SRR2658), the first possibly human

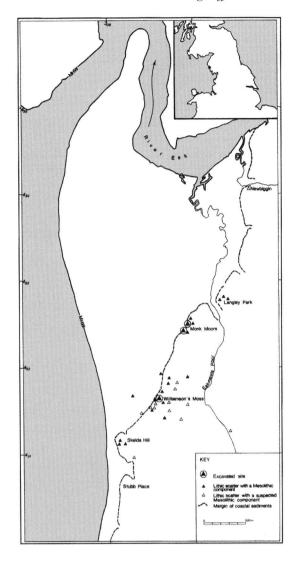

23 Distribution of Mesolithic sites in the Eskmeals area. *Courtesy of Clive Bonsall, Bonsall et al 1989*

indications of disturbance to the carr vegetation are discernible in the form of a slight opening up of woodland. Following this, Williamson's Moss produced evidence for a double Elm Decline, something seen elsewhere in Cumbria (Oldfield 1963; Walker 1966; Pennington 1975). Pollen cores taken from the channel to the east of Williamson's Moss, which contained the wooden platform, also records the primary Elm Decline. The radiocarbon dates for the elm decline match closely those of the timber platform, which hints that the activity at the site of the platform is connected with clearance in the wider landscape. At Barfield Tarn, 4.5km away, Pennington (1970; 1975) recorded traces of small forest clearings dating to *c.*4457-3825 cal BC (5340±120 BP, K-1057), whilst at Ehenside Tarn, 12km away, Walker (1966) registered the presence of similar reductions in tree pollen prior to the main Elm Decline. The wide distribution of this phenomenon seems to support the suggestion that the West Cumbrian Coastal Plain was a focus of Mesolithic settlement and it has even been speculated

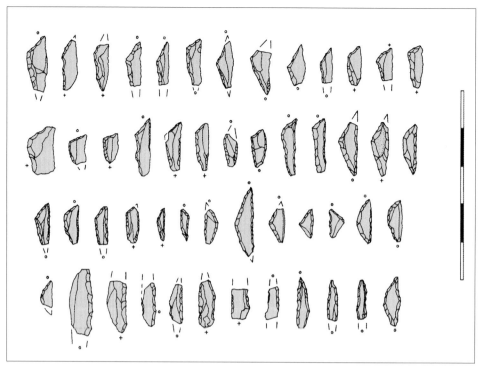

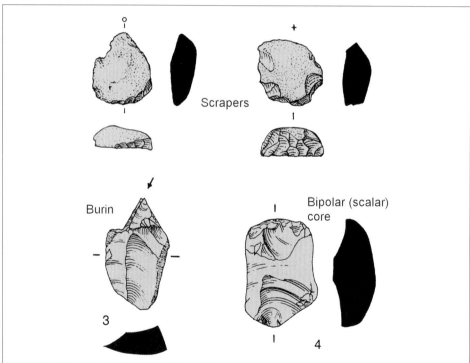

24a & b Lithic artefacts from Monks Moor site 1. Microliths and stone tools. *Courtesy of Clive Bonsall, Bonsall 1981*

that these initial falls in tree pollen represent the effects of small-scale forest clearance for agriculture (Tipping 1994, 126).

Such clearings were small-scale and temporary, and by *c.*3990-3650 cal BC (5010±70 BP, SRR-3067) woodland was reclaiming the open areas around Williamson's Moss. The 'main' Elm Decline followed, dated to *c.*3893-3381 cal BC (4850±80 BP, SRR-3068), from which the tree species failed to recover fully. At Barfield Tarn the main (secondary) Elm decline was accompanied by reductions in other tree pollen, especially oak, and an increase in cereal pollen. These changes in the composition of the pollen occur at the point when the sediment lithology changes from an organic mud to a pink clay. According to Winifred Pennington, this strongly suggested that at the same time as the Elm Decline large-scale woodland clearance took place, creating pasture and fields for cereal cultivation – an unforseen side effect of which was an increase in soil erosion around the tarn (Pennington 1975). Similar activity is also represented at Ehenside Tarn where the chronology of the sequence relies on proxy dating of palynological features by comparison with radiocarbon-dated analogues elsewhere (Walker 1966). Based on this, the indications are that major clearance may have begun here slightly later than at Barfield, the earliest cereal pollen occurring at the same time as the beginning of extensive and permanent clearance around Ehenside, possibly between *c.*2900 cal BC and 2600 cal BC (*c.*4300-4100 BP; Pennington 1970, 69). Taken together, the evidence from these three sites indicates that the West Cumbrian Coastal Plain began to be permanently cleared of forest during the Early Neolithic, making it one of the earliest recorded regions in the country to suffer this fate (Bell and Walker 1992, 165).

Evidence for Mesolithic settlement on the West Cumbrian Coastal Plain is generally confined to the raised beaches of former coastlines. The exceptions to this pattern, such as Fleswick, Tarnflat and Rottington, are located on the cliffs north of St Bees (Cherry and Cherry 1983, 8). On the coasts there is a widespread distribution of sites, from lithic assemblages in dunes at Pow Beck, St Bees, to more subtle signs of activity at Walkhole Bank near Silecroft (fig. 24; Cherry and Cherry 1987a). The location of sites on the coasts, and estuaries in particular, may suggest that they were taking advantage of the greater diversity of food

25 Williamson's Moss, Structure 1. Wooden raft-type foundation. *Courtesy of Clive Bonsall, Bonsall et al 1989*

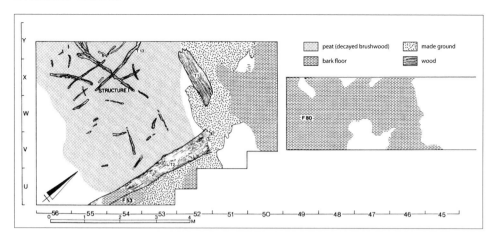

26 Plan of Williamson's Moss, Structure 1. *Courtesy of Clive Bonsall, Bonsall et al 1989*

resources that estuarine environments provide compared to other coastal habitats (Bonsall *et al* 1994, 93). In addition, the major sites of Williamson's Moss and Monk Moors were ideally positioned close to pebble flint sources on the coastal shingle bars. At Monk Moors two large microlithic scatters incorporating a variety of largely geometric microlith forms have been investigated (Cherry and Cherry 1986). Site 1 revealed an arrangement of hearths and stakeholes covering an area 7m x 2.4m, corresponding with highest densities of artefacts recovered from the ploughsoil (Bonsall 1989). Radiocarbon determinations from a hearth indicate occupation of the site at 5970-5630 cal BC (Bonsall *et al* 1986; Hodgkinson *et al* 2000).

At Williamson's Moss, extensive activity was centred around the banks of an inland lake formed after 5473-5074 cal BC (Bonsall *et al* 1994). Excavations revealed a lithic assemblage of more than 32,000 pieces and a variety of occupation remains that have not seen full publication. The wooden platforms dated to the fifth millennium BC, if accepted as true structures rather than natural features (Hodgkinson *et al* 2000; Croft *et al* 2002), may be taken to be indicative of year-round occupation of the site (Bonsall 1981). The lithic assemblages and the range of dates from both Williamson's Moss and Monk Moors span from *c.*5790-5360 cal BC to 1252-910 cal BC and are indicative of multiple activity phases, not solely Late Mesolithic as has commonly been implied.

Nearby basin fens may have provided other resources to supplement those of the coast. Eskmeals (*23*) might have been positioned to exploit both the adjacent marine environment and that of the inland wetland of Eskmeals Pool, while those at St Bees are similarly situated between the coast and the ancient alder carrs of the Pow Beck (*25*). It is conceivable that dune-slacks and fens to the rear of the dunes offered a similar suite of conditions at Drigg (*colour plate 1*). It is also possible to view the poorly defined Walkhole Bank coastal site in this light, positioned as it is in close proximity to both the coast and the mires of the Silecroft Beck.

The lithic assemblages of the Mesolithic sites share a number of physical and typological similarities, notably the predominance of beach pebble flint which has resulted in small artefacts of variable quality. The most common implements are geometric microliths and scrapers, with core axes and bevelled tools lacking (Bonsall *et al* 1994, 96). Cherry and Cherry (1984,

14) have suggested that the similarities in the assemblages from St Bees and Nethertown are so marked that in each case it may be the work of a single knapper, and that the scatters may represent a single family/hunting unit.

Within this widespread Mesolithic activity there is a concentration of settlement in the Esk estuary and it is this area which has received the most archaeological attention. Detailed field-work has identified *foci* of activity on Skelda Hill, Williamson's Moss, Monk Moors, Eskmeals Pool III, Eskmeals IV and V, situated near Langley Park, and a further site at Eskmeals near Newbiggin. All of these were initially identified as surface lithic scatters, some of which were subsequently excavated. Judging from the range of radiocarbon dates from Williamson's Moss and Monk Moors, obtained from hearth charcoal, *c.*5970-5360 cal BC (6752±156 BP, BM-1216) to *c.*1252-910 cal BC (2859±49 BP, BM-1386), which are statistically consistent (Ward and Wilson 1978) some of the sites have multiple phases of activity stretching into the Bronze Age (Burleigh and Matthews 1982; Bonsall *et al* 1994).

On the basis of the available evidence it is difficult to assess whether such a high density of artefacts reflects an actual preference by Mesolithic groups for the Esk estuary, or whether it may be simply a reflection of the fact that excavation has tended to be concentrated on the most promising flint scatters. The limited excavation of a superficially-similar surface scatter at St Bees golf course (St Bees Site VIII), however, yielded significantly fewer artefacts (Bonsall 1983, 13), and certainly seems to go some way towards bearing out Bonsall's theory that Williamson's Moss and Monk Moors were the *foci* of the Mesolithic groups, with the hinterland being exploited to a lesser extent. It has further been suggested that the scale of the activity in the vicinity of Eskmeals may indicate that the area was permanently occupied during the Late Mesolithic (Bonsall 1981, 469), perhaps as a result of the year-round abundance of food sources in the area (for example fish, gulls, gamebirds). It seems likely, however, that any change to a more sedentary way of life would have had a marked effect upon the surrounding landscape and that it should be possible to detect this signal in the palaeoenvironmental record. Such a signature may be represented by the extensive clearance activity recorded around the Elm decline.

In southern Cumbria shrubby mixed woodland, composed of birch and hazel developed at the end of the ice age. Hazel became the dominant woodland species after *c.*9000-8000 cal BC (*c.*9500-9000 BP). Whether this was wholly natural, or partly aided by the effects of human activity, in particular fire, remains unclear (Huntley 1993). Evidence suggesting human involvement comes from Little Hawes Water to the south of our study area in north Lancashire, where Taylor recorded the presence of charcoal in layers of peat which coincided with the expansion of hazel (Taylor *et al* 1994). This in turn was replaced by pine, oak, elm and, subsequently, alder.

There is only one published pollen study relevant to the Mesolithic period from southern Cumbria, this focused on the Carboniferous limestone belt fringing the south Cumbrian mosses at Roudsea (Birks 1982). Birks' pollen profile, which spanned the period between *c.*6000 cal BC, and 4000 cal BC (*c.*7200-5200 BP), confirmed that forests of Late Mesolithic date displayed a high biodiversity, qualitatively similar to the present-day wooded area. The findings tend to support the notion that many of the woodlands presently occupying the limestone headlands round the northern edge of Morecambe Bay are derived from original woodland cover, albeit heavily modified by millennia of subsequent human disturbance. The Late Mesolithic woodland assemblage represented in this particular study, however, displayed no evidence of local forest disturbance until the uppermost sediments, in which an Elm Decline is clearly discernible. However, given the very localised nature of the pollen catchment of the sample site (a small hollow set within dense woodland), and the very subtle and scattered nature of the Mesolithic clearance, the lack of evidence for disturbance is not surprising. It is possible, however, that more extensive investigation of suitable deposits in the area will reveal similar episodes of small-scale clearance to those recorded a few kilometres to the east around the rim of Morecambe Bay, such as at Little Hawes Water. There pollen evidence of possible Mesolithic activity *c.*7531-6646 cal BC (*c.*9200-8200 BP) occurs, marked by an increase of indicators of open ground, such as the plantains (*Plantago* sp.) and bracken (*Pteridium* sp.), together with a band of charcoal (Taylor *et al* 1994). These signals are amplified by the findings of work from Thwaite House Moss, a small basin mire located 8km to the south-east in the southern part of the Lonsdale limestone country. Here, what appears to be a small-scale clearance, associated with evidence of fires in the vicinity, occurred towards the close of Flandrian I, sometime between *c.*6500 cal BC and 5500 cal BC (*c.*7700-6500 BP; Middleton *et al* 1995, 183-9, 193). At this time a dense hazel-dominated woodland occupied the fertile limestone upland bordering the coast of Morecambe Bay. The landscape would have provided a variety of resources attractive to Mesolithic communities and it is possible that the disturbance from the moss may be recording a local example of this.

In support of this, fieldwork at Malham Tarn Moss (Pigott and Pigott 1963; Simmons 1996, 53-8), in the limestone uplands 40km to the east, has demonstrated that, during much the same period, a series of declines in tree pollen, similar to those described above from Lonsdale and again associated with charcoal, has been ascribed to Mesolithic disturbance. The presence of several substantial Mesolithic flint scatters around the tarn lend credence to this interpretation (Williams *et al* 1987).

In the light of all this evidence it seems probable that a similar level of Mesolithic activity, encompassing small-scale clearings and the use of fire, extended across the broad band of limestone country stretching across north-west England from the Pennines through south Cumbria. Furthermore, it is not inconceivable that this particular landscape was especially attractive, the fertility of its calcareous soils and its attendant biodiversity perhaps holding particular advantages for hunter-gatherer groups, especially when allied to the coastal resources available around Morecambe Bay.

There is limited evidence that the caves around Morecambe Bay continued to be occupied during the Mesolithic period. Continuing work at Bart's Shelter (D. Stables pers. comm. in Hodgkinson *et al* 2000) and Bonfire Scar Cave at Scales has revealed evidence for Mesolithic activity including bone and stone artefacts, and worked faunal material. A fragment of bone harpoon point has been dated to 6110-5883 cal BC (7160±60 BP, OxA-8069), which may also date the Late Mesolithic lithic material from a similar location on the platform outside Bonfire Scar Cave, although the harpoon point may have been re-deposited from within the cave (D. Stables pers. comm. in Hodgkinson *et al* 2000). It is too early to say what the material from Bart's Shelter represents in terms of settlement and subsistence activity in general. The presence of a harpoon point, however, may suggest links with the coast either in terms of the transport of the catch or people bringing back fishing equipment, although it could equally have been used for freshwater fishing.

Numerous excavations within other caves in the area have revealed faunal remains of the period, in some cases human, at Capeshead, Whitbarrow Bone Cave and Baycliff Haggs, although some are likely to be later in date. The limited amounts of Mesolithic material currently known from such cave deposits may suggest their use on an occasional basis, or the disturbance of occupation levels during subsequent use of the caves.

Hodgkinson *et al* (2000) have argued that it is also likely that smaller and finer Mesolithic lithic and faunal material was overlooked during antiquarian excavations. At Kirkhead, J.P. Morris and M.R. Bolton were keen to 'develop and explore the hidden mysteries of this primitive abode' and removed some four feet of cave earth in their investigations (Baines 1893, 628). The new work by the Morecambe Bay Archaeological Research Society in Furness is working to increase our knowledge of both Mesolithic occupation and, along with similar work at other sites with surviving stratigraphy, may expand considerably our knowledge of Mesolithic cave use in other parts of south Cumbria.

It is already apparent that not all Mesolithic activity was confined to the caves of the limestone crags. Scattered Late Mesolithic material has been recovered from fieldwalking in Furness (D. Stables pers comm. in Hodgkinson *et al* 2000) and evidence for a lakeside settlement has been claimed from excavations at Gleaston Mill (Salisbury and Coupe 1995). Excavations on a Bronze Age ring cairn at Levens revealed abundant lithic material with Mesolithic affinities from the buried soil; initial assessment of the assemblage of *c.*2000 pieces has suggested Late Mesolithic affinities (Turnbull and Walsh 1996, 17). Extensive concentrations of ash and charcoal were also within the buried soil horizon, perhaps suggesting some degree of settlement and subsistence activity. Further to the west, significant concentrations of Mesolithic material have been found, particularly on Walney Island, mainly chance finds from eroding dunes and coast (Wymer 1977, 162), at Trough Head, North End, and at the site of the Sandy Gap School (Barnes 1970a). Although the material has not been properly characterised, the sites are of sufficient density to indicate that the island was well frequented, with a preference for the western, seaward coast.

The overall pattern of Mesolithic activity in south Cumbria is clearly more dependent on the survival and recognition of material, rather than a real variability in the level of activity. The Levens Park material had survived owing to the protection afforded from erosion by the overlying cairn and the creation of Levens Park in 1393 (Farrer 1923-24, II, 126). Similarly, artefactual material from caves may be indicative not only of the use of convenient shelters but also of the good conditions for the survival of archaeological material in such locations. The results of recent fieldwalking in Furness, which has produced a less intensive distribution pattern (D. Stables pers comm. in Hodgkinson *et al* 2000) compared to that on Walney Island and in Levens Park, may suggest that there was concentrated activity in favourable parts of the landscape. This same pattern was noted in Lancashire (Middleton 1993b; Middleton *et al* 1995; Middleton *et al* forthcoming) and it was suggested there that reliable coastal locations, associated with favourable land, including wetlands, would have provided attractive areas for repeated visits. A similar case has been made for the Late Mesolithic of west Cumbria where work at Eskmeals has indicated the long-term and consistent use of favoured estuarine areas (Bonsall *et al* 1991). Hodgson and Brennand (2006, 25) have suggested that in south Cumbria such conditions are likely to have existed throughout the Mesolithic in variable configurations as relative sea-levels fluctuated, and that on Walney Island and in Levens Park we may be seeing the upper altitudinal limits of coastal Mesolithic sites similar to those identified on the eastern and southern sides of Morecambe Bay, at Heysham Head (Salisbury and Sheppard 1994) and in Pilling Moss (Middleton *et al* 1995, ch. 2). In south Cumbria assemblages occur at Bart's Shelter, where Early Mesolithic microliths, some composed of volcanic tuff, were excavated along with a bone or antler point dated to 6210-6190 cal BC (Jacobi in Brennand 2006, 26). Immediately to the south of Cumbria at both Borwick (Olivier 1987) and Levens Park (Cherry and Cherry 2000) assemblages of Late Mesolithic and Early Neolithic date were found sealed beneath burial mounds, suggesting repeated use of some locations through the Mesolithic and into the Neolithic (Hodgson and Brennand 2006, 26). The source of the lithics manufactured from volcanic tuff in the region is believed to be glacial drift originating from the central Cumbrian Massif (Bradley and Edmonds 1993).

The only current artefactual evidence for Mesolithic activity from the central Lake District is the find of a small number of microliths from the environs of the Roman fort at Waterhead, at the north end of Windermere (Fell 1971; CFA 1993; Manning and Dunwell 1995).

Discussion

The people of the Mesolithic, although basically continuing an Upper Palaeolithic hunting and gathering way of life, had to adapt to changes in the environment which included the disappearance of large herds of elk to be replaced by widespread forest cover. The most visible of these changes was the development of new types of tool. By the Late Mesolithic much of lowland Cumbria was covered in mixed deciduous forest. In the uplands the continuous tree canopy gave way to scrub at around 335-360m, where it included hazel, grassland and occasional patches of peat. This habitat was attractive to red deer who could browse on the shrubs, and also to auroch, a type of wild cattle, bones from which have been found in some of the cave deposits. Wild pig would also have been present in the woodland. Fish may have been another important element in the diet, as we have seen from the estuarine sites of Eskmeals where salmon and trout would have provided a seasonal variation to the diet. Wetlands around the Cumbrian coast would also have been a source of wild fowl, small mammals and fish. These would have been important sources of protein during the winter and early spring when plant food was at its most scarce. Grazing animals visiting sources of fresh water to drink would have provided the best hunting opportunities and may explain the clearance of woodland at the sites of Monk Moors and Williamson's Moss and elsewhere.

The Eskmeal sites may well have served as residential base camps occupied on a permanent or semi-permanent basis. A model for the Late Mesolithic subsistence economy of Eskmeals was proposed by Bonsall (1981). His model emphasised potential for permanent settlement and the role of fishing and coastal resources, the most persuasive evidence for which is the discovery of wooden house platforms (if we accept that this is what they are).

The construction of house platforms may indicate permanent settlement over a sustained period of years with food and raw materials generally coming from the immediate area around the site. The fact that the stone tools were fashioned from local pebbles is consistent with this model, but does not of itself confirm it. A permanent camp does not of itself rule out groups of hunters venturing further afield perhaps over a single or several nights in order to hunt game not available in the immediate area, or perhaps to meet with people from other social groups living elsewhere in order to exchange goods or stories.

A hunting group planning to be away for any period of time would probably choose a readily available natural feature, such as Bart's Shelter, if available. A natural cave would serve as a base from which to exploit the resources of the surrounding area over a period of several days to several weeks. Even for single night stays certain locations were more attractive than others and may have been occupied on more than one occasion. Several locations in the Lakeland uplands and others on the coast may well fall into this category. People dependent on hunting and gathering normally range over a considerable area during the course of a year, exploiting the natural resources from season to season in different parts of their annual territory. During the winter they would have sheltered longest at one base, such as Williamson's Moss, especially given that during the Mesolithic the climate was more extreme than now. Even in today's more moderate climate, red deer observe a seasonal rhythm in northern Britain, sheltering on low ground during the winter and moving to higher ground in the summer (Chaplin 1975, 41). The movements of individual herds would have followed the topography of the landscape, and this may account for the scatter of Mesolithic flints found in the Lakeland upland valleys.

Understanding of the Late Mesolithic occupation, based on the study of pollen and flint sites, shows that there were a variety of different sites. The presence of charcoal layers shows that the closed tree cover was suppressed by regular burning. Studies have described how burning improves both the quantity and quality of browsing for ungulates, presenting opportunities for easier hunting of herds and also imposing a degree of predictability on their movements (Mellars 1976a; Jacobi *et al* 1976, 315). People may have manipulated the woodland-edge habitat in this way, possibly reburning relatively small tracts of forest at 5-15 year intervals on a rotational basis (Jacobi *et al* 1976, 317). One effect of this burning would have been the encouragement of hazel (amongst other species), thus providing nuts for direct consumption. Besides those in the Furness Plain, others have been found on the west coast plain (Cherry and Cherry 1983; 1984; 1985; 1987). Thus it can be demonstrated that alterations of the ecosystem started before the Neolithic period.

In conclusion, the central Lakeland assemblages differ markedly from assemblages from the lowlands having a higher percentage of microliths. This indicates that many of the Cumbrian lowland sites at least appear to differ in function from the upland sites. The lithic evidence suggests that the lowlands might include both base camps and smaller specialised sites. The base camps were probably mainly in coastal areas, where larger groups may have congregated for longer periods of time, possibly in the winter. The specialised smaller sites may have included kill sites, butchery sites, hunting stands and bivouac sites. Small-scale manipulation of the woodlands was also taking place in the lowlands, sometimes associated with evidence of burning, suggesting fire-induced woodland clearance.

Natural flint is almost entirely absent from Cumbria. Pebble flint does occur in localised pockets of coastal shingle, and is likely to be a result of a disintegrating chalk formation lying beneath the Irish Sea (Cross 1939). Flint also occurs in small quantities in boulder clay. The presence of black and grey chalk flint within assemblages suggests sources in east Yorkshire (Jacobi 1978; Cherry and Cherry 1987a; 2000, 25-7; 2002) and the Flamborough Head area (Cherry and Cherry 1987a; Durden 1996) whilst an Irish origin is suggested for the rich reddish brown to pale honey coloured flint (Edmonds 2004). Antrim flint is known to have been exported from Antrim to Scotland and a similar trade seems to have existed with Cumbria. The occurrence of flint and chert tools, many miles from the stone sources, suggests the movement of people and goods and provides the possibility of identifying the economic patterns behind this mobility. The ubiquity of chalk flint in eastern areas has been taken to suggest the exploitation of sources to the east rather than the west (Cherry and Cherry 2000; 2002), which might in turn suggest the presence of long-distance trade networks and exchange, possibly integrated within seasonal movement of peoples. However, the evidence and sourcing of material remain equivocal.

In the Late Mesolithic such patterns are harder to identify. It may be that raw material exploitation and subsequent use was carried out on a much smaller, more local scale during the Late Mesolithic in the region. In the eastern Cumbrian uplands Late Mesolithic scatters primarily consist of local cherts, *c*.60 per cent, while pebble flint was also used, probably sourced from local and Pennine river gravels. The source for lithic forms manufactured from volcanic tuff in the north of the region is still believed to be glacial drift originating from the central Cumbrian Massif (Bradley and Edmonds 1993). There is as yet no evidence that the high-quality material in the central Lakes was exploited at source until the Early Neolithic (Bradley and Edmonds 1993).

The transition from the Late Mesolithic to the Neolithic began during the fifth millennium BC when disturbed ground and associated small gaps in the woodland cover became more common across Cumbria. They occur both around the coastal areas and around the central mosslands, and even continued into the fourth millennium BC (Hodgkinson *et al* 2000). At the coastal sites these phenomena are accompanied by cereal-type pollen at *c*.4900-4500 cal BC, mirrored at a number of other sites in north-west England and Northern Ireland (Edwards and Hirons 1984). If cereal-type pollen, rather than positively identified cereal pollen, is taken as representing the introduction of domesticated plants into Cumbria, the implications are that Mesolithic communities were adopting aspects of an agricultural economy (Simmons and Innes 1987). The sites where this phenomenon is found lie along the western seaboard of Britain, suggesting widespread contacts along the western coast (Edwards and Hirons 1984). The evidence suggests that small-scale agriculture may have gradually become part of the Mesolithic repertoire, in addition to the established lifestyle of gathering, hunting and fishing. It is notable that the occurrences of agriculture are found along the coast, where stronger evidence for the repeated use of the same locations is found (Bonsall 1981). The apparent lack of technological change between the flint assemblages of the Late Mesolithic and Early Neolithic suggest that a microlithic technology persisted in Cumbria into the Neolithic (Cherry and Cherry 2002; Evans 2004). The consistency in material between the two periods suggests that many aspects of Neolithic lifestyle and economy were already in place by the fifth millennium BC.

CHAPTER 4

SHAPING THE WORLD WITH STONE:
THE NEOLITHIC FARMERS

Let the reader now picture to himself a tarn … Let him imagine on the water rafts of oak, bound and covered with trees, to form the foundations of cottages or huts. Let him conceive this, and he will realise the idea of a lake dwelling of the earliest Britons … a dwelling which served at once for a home and a fortress … with a hollow tree and a paddle they went to and fro from the shore, which was surrounded by a thick forest. They gathered acorns and nuts, and captured animals, raised a little wild corn, and ground it in their stone hand-mills, specimens of which have been found on the spot.

Rev. J. W. Kenworthy 1870

Introduction

Traditionally narratives about the Neolithic, beginning around 4000 BC, have concentrated on the change from a transitory hunting and gathering lifestyle typical of Late Mesolithic groups to an increasingly settled agriculture. This change is marked by the appearance of a new artefact assemblage containing leaf-shaped arrowheads, scrapers and polished stone axes (*27*) together with pottery (*28*) and ceremonial and funerary monuments. The greatest change in the artefactual record of the period is the introduction of the polished stone axe, which was produced on an industrial scale in Langdale. It was only the presence of such axes that distinguished the Ehenside Tarn site as Neolithic to its excavator (Darbishire 1873). The only indicator for a Neolithic presence over much of lowland Cumbria is the evidence of individual axes which, on their own, are difficult to interpret as an indicator of settlement: there are few settlement traces represented either by physical structures or surface flintwork. Scattered finds of arrowheads, such as those from Walney Island, may potentially represent isolated hunting losses.

As was observed in the previous chapter, there is a suggestion that some degree of permanent settlement associated with the clearance of woodland has been seen during the Late Mesolithic, whilst it has been suggested that the Neolithic was less settled than had previously been proposed, and that people maintained a significant degree of seasonal or

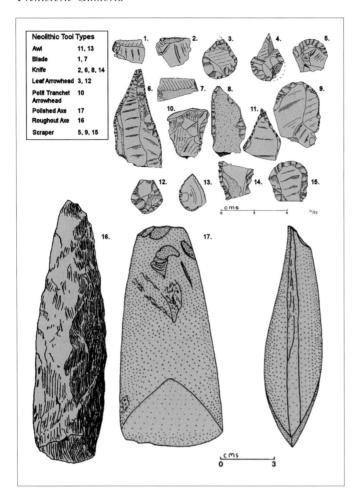

Neolithic Tool Types	
Awl	11, 13
Blade	1, 7
Knife	2, 6, 8, 14
Leaf Arrowhead	3, 12
Petit Tranchet Arrowhead	10
Polished Axe	17
Roughout Axe	16
Scraper	5, 9, 15

27 Neolithic tool types. Objects 1-15 from Little Ashby Scar, 16 from Braystones and 17 from Crosby Garrett. *Courtesy of Peter Cherry*

transitory movement, blurring the distinction between the two periods (e.g. Barrett 1989; 1994; Topping 1997; Whittle 1997). Contemporary interpretations also stress the regionality of this transition (Barrowclough 2007; 2008) with authors noting that whilst there are many shared elements of material culture and architecture across Britain, the manner and timing of the introduction of domesticated plants and animals, and the use of particular monumental forms may have varied considerably across different regions. Rather than a single model that explains 'the' British Neolithic we need to consider the variety of different ways in which a Neolithic package was adapted to local conditions. The Late Neolithic, 3000-2500 BC, is regarded as marking a phase of intensification of settlement, landuse and artefact production, and has been associated with the first indications for the existence of social hierarchies (Bradley and Edmonds 1993). There is evidence for long-distance communication and interaction, particularly in the realm of ritual and ceremony. In Cumbria, however, the period is also seen as one where distinctive regional characteristics become apparent (Piggott 1954; Bradley 1984; Harding *et al* 1996).

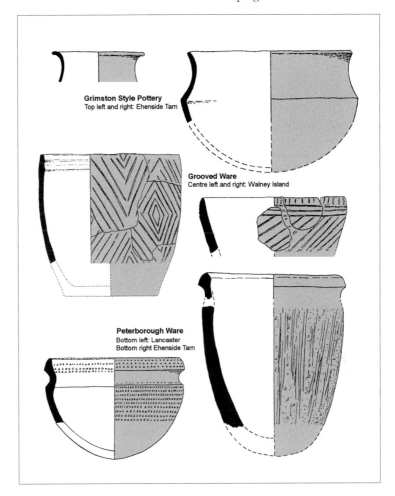

Grimston Style Pottery
Top left and right: Ehenside Tarn

Grooved Ware
Centre left and right: Walney Island

Peterborough Ware
Bottom left: Lancaster
Bottom right Ehenside Tarn

28 Neolithic
pottery types in
Cumbria

The Neolithic Package

The transition from the Mesolithic to Neolithic in Cumbria was a gradual process. Lithic scatters remain the most abundant source of evidence for human activity in the Early Neolithic as they are in the Late Mesolithic. The shift from one to the other may be identified in the archaeological record by the introduction of a characteristic new technology, the leaf-shaped arrowhead, which replaced Late Mesolithic microliths. These arrowheads are most often found in isolation, perhaps as casual losses from hunting and related activities. It has also been suggested that there are some indications that the range of raw materials became more restricted: black Pendleside chert disappears from assemblages at the end of the Mesolithic (Middleton 1996, 36), while better-quality flint material was sourced from areas outside Cumbria, arriving via networks of trade and exchange. Although many of the widely accepted typological or chronologically diagnostic forms for the Neolithic are represented, the most common of which is the scraper, assemblages are often characterised by informal or multi-use forms suggesting the expedient use of available raw materials. Mesolithic traits

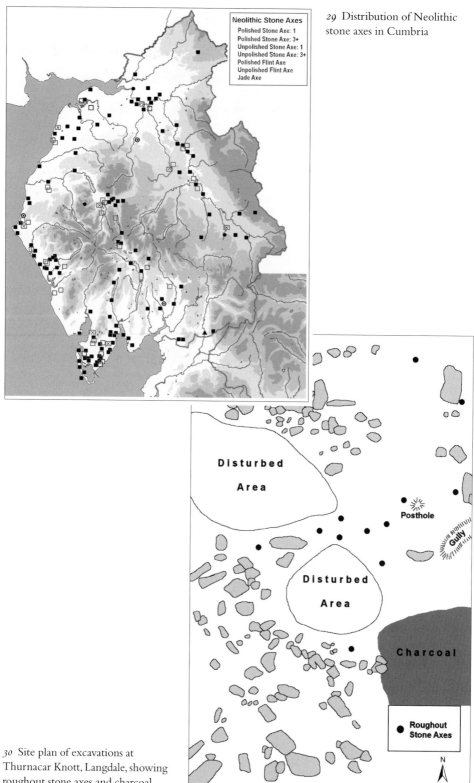

29 Distribution of Neolithic stone axes in Cumbria

Neolithic Stone Axes

Polished Stone Axe: 1
Polished Stone Axe: 3+
Unpolished Stone Axe: 1
Unpolished Stone Axe: 3+
Polished Flint Axe
Unpolished Flint Axe
Jade Axe

Disturbed Area

Disturbed Area

Posthole

Gully

Charcoal

● Roughout Stone Axes

N

30 Site plan of excavations at Thurnacar Knott, Langdale, showing roughout stone axes and charcoal

31 Distribution of Neolithic
pottery types in Cumbria

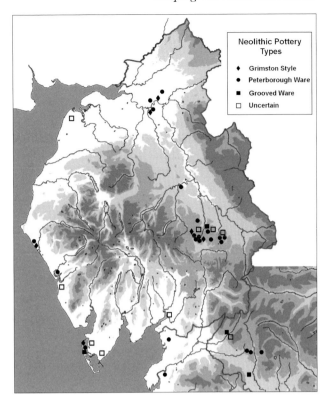

continue throughout a large part of the Neolithic, and in turn Neolithic types are found in
Early Bronze Age assemblages.

Another characteristic of the Early Neolithic are polished stone axes, part of the economic
changes associated with the adoption of agriculture and the domestication of animals (*29* and
colour plates 4 & 5). Most have been smoothed or 'polished' by rubbing or grinding on another
stone. The rounded end of the axeheads would have been set in a wooden haft, with the wider
end forming the cutting edge. In the Langdales, axe 'factories' have been identified, for example
at Thurnacar Knott (*30*), whilst complete, or near complete, 'roughout' axes have been found
throughout Cumbria in a range of different locations. A number have flattened sides, a typical feature of examples produced and found in the Lake District, and where thin-sectioning
has been undertaken, the results confirm that most originated at Great Langdale (Clough and
Cummins 1988, 219-221). Most of the axes date to the period *c.*2750 to *c.*2000 BC when agriculture was already established. From about this date the production of axes in upland areas such
as the Lake District, North Wales and Cornwall was highly organised and products from these
'factories' travelled hundreds of kilometres into areas that do not contain such rocks. The other
major new technological advance at the beginning of the Neolithic was the introduction of
pottery, augmenting the earlier use of organic containers by Mesolithic communities. Pottery
finds are, however, very poorly represented in Cumbria (*31 and colour plate 6*), perhaps as a consequence of the continued relative mobility of the population or perhaps because of the wet and
humid climate which has an adverse effect on pottery production (Barrowclough 2007).

Despite the apparently enormous implications of the change to farming, the gradual incorporation of Neolithic elements into existing society means that much of the economy may have remained relatively unaltered. The extensive evidence for burning episodes from both upland and lowland situations suggests that there was substantial management and control of wild resources by Mesolithic people (Zvelebil 1994). These may represent the clearance of scrub and light woodland to attract animals to specific locations at which they could be culled (Jacobi *et al* 1976). There is now substantial evidence from the mosses of Cumbria that such episodes were taking place from the earliest Mesolithic through to the Bronze Age. It is not clear how much of this was caused by people, although its ubiquity suggests it may represent deliberate management of the environment (Hall *et al* 1995, Ch. 6; Middleton *et al* 1995, Ch. 8).

Characteristics of the Neolithic Occupation

The character of earlier Neolithic occupation has much in common with that of the Late Mesolithic. The evidence suggests that some places were visited repeatedly over relatively long periods of time, whilst small, less dense occupation evidence in other areas indicates short-term or transitory occupation. Neolithic sites on the north Cumbrian Solway Plain have been studied by Bewley (*32*; Bewley 1986; 1993; 1994). During fieldwalking on the southern slopes of the Abbeytown Ridge, above Common Moss, a significant assemblage of Neolithic artefacts was found, marked 3 on the map. A leaf-shaped arrowhead was found together with waste pieces which included preparation and utilised flakes, as well as an end scraper and a point. Our best evidence for permanent settlement, however, comes from the site of Plasketlands, near Mawbray on the Solway Plain, marked 1 on the map, excavated by Robert Bewley (1993). Until this excavation, Neolithic domestic structures were unknown in Cumbria and most of the cropmarks identified in the area were provisionally dated to the Iron Age or Romano-British periods. The Plasketlands site (*33*) comprised a large sub-rectangular ditched enclosure, with an 'annexe' of large post-holes, each *c*.o.60m in diameter, on its north-eastern side; this suggested to Bewley a defensive function (Bewley 1993). Three radiocarbon dates, of 3970-3525 cal BC (4940±90 BP, GU-2573), 3775-3380 cal BC (4810±60 BP, GU-2571), and 4032-3720 cal BC (5090±60 BP, GU-2572) from charcoal within a post-hole established the Early Neolithic origins for the site. Bewley's (1993) work at Plasketlands may give some clues to the nature of Early Neolithic activity and our understanding of the archaeological record where it concerns early farmers. The site, possibly an enclosed settlement, may, from its location between wetlands, have been related to their exploitation. The work of the North West Wetlands Survey on Solway Moss complements the excavations and survey undertaken by Bewley and suggests that cereal cultivation was being undertaken during the Early Neolithic. The survey found two cereal-type pollen grains in peats dated to *c.* 4036-3780 cal BC (5110±60 BP, GU-5275) and *c.*3340-2707 cal BC (4370±90 BP, GU-5314) (Huckerby and Wells 1993). These observations represent the earliest cereal cultivation in north Cumbria.

The site of Plasketlands is the exception rather than the rule and, as with the remainder of the county, evidence for Neolithic settlement largely rests on the distribution of polished

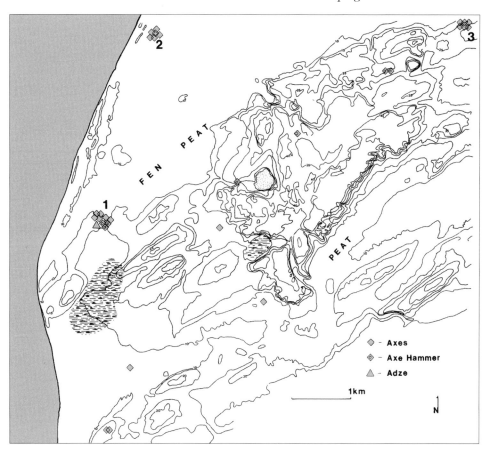

32 Neolithic sites in the Solway Plain: 1 = Mawbray, 2 = Beckfoot, 3 = The Hill on Abbeytown ridge.
Courtesy of Bob Bewley

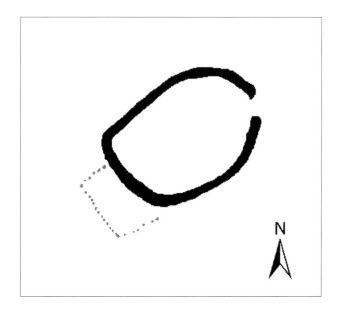

33 Site plan of Plasketlands.
Courtesy of Bob Bewley

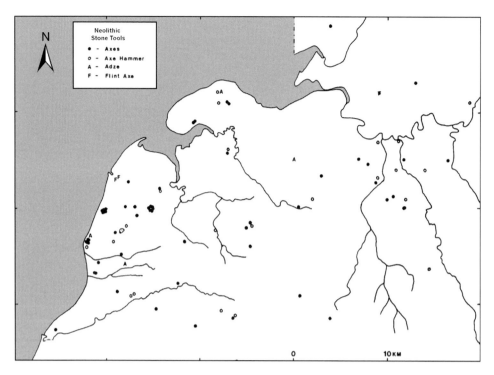

34 Distribution of Neolithic stone tools on the Solway Plain. *Courtesy of Bob Bewley*

stone axes. It has been estimated that approximately 100 axes have been found in the Solway Plain area (Bewley 1994, 56) of which a quarter were found in locations close to mosses (*34*). Bewley described three examples of axe clusters which might help us to understand the nature of Neolithic settlement (Bewley 1994). The most westerly cluster was at Mawbray, and was situated on a small rise, up to 10m, of sandy ground, overlooking the sea to the west and fen peat in the other directions. No traces of actual settlement were found, perhaps because the ridge is now occupied by farmhouses. Further north at Beckfoot (marked 2 on the map) the finds are similarly situated on an even smaller rise surrounded by marine alluvium to the east, and the sea, which is less than half a kilometre away, to the west. The third example, on the Abbeytown ridge (marked 3 on the plan) is perhaps the most similar to the setting of Ehenside Tarn, the well-known Neolithic settlement site on the west coast, discussed below. The site is on the north edge of the ridge, with fen peat a few metres below in the valley bottom. The ridge itself is surrounded by fen peat, with pockets of tarn, bog and moss on its top and sides.

In order to examine the possibilities for Neolithic exploitation of the plain, Bewley (1994, 72-3) undertook a Territorial Exploitation Analysis of Plasketlands together with the Hill Farm, Mawbray and Beckfoot Neolithic sites (*35*). The results indicate that the area around the sites contained a diverse range of land-types including potential arable land, pasture and sources of wild resources, such as the coast and wetlands. This suggests that in the Neolithic a mixed subsistence economy combining cropping, gathering and herding with hunting and fishing was relied upon (Bewley 1994, 73). For example at Hill Farm, which at 20m OD is comfortably above the floodplain, there is grazing potential in the 1km zone, beyond which is a large area within the 5km zone of arable potential. Further out, within the 10km zone, the sea and estuary provide both sea trout and salmon and also wildfowl and deer. On the basis of this evidence Bewley developed a model for settlement whereby small groups of people occupied sandy ridges around the coast, tarns and mosses. They supported themselves in part by growing cereals, but in the main depended upon natural resources taken from the local environment (Bewley 1994, 58). This is a pattern found elsewhere in the British Isles, for example by Alistair Whittle in Ireland:

> The pattern of small and dispersed but not necessarily isolated settlements could be compared with the Irish clachan system, varied and changing though this was … in which a mixed farming economy including some mobility particularly in the summer for grazing was combined with dispersed settlement. Communal exchanges are more than ever important for dispersed communities. They can be envisaged in the north and west of the country in the earlier Neolithic but without formal sites to mark them.
>
> Whittle 1977, 49

Most axes occur as single finds; most are situated on relatively high ground above either a peat moss or a river. For example, at Chapel Moss, Foulsyke, Dub Beck, 'The Hill' and Mireside, all skirting the valley bogs inland. Coastal finds are known from Anthorn and Allonby. Rough-out axes have been found at Mawbray, Kirkbride and Allonby. The wetland associations of some of these axes is notable: that from Pelutho is from peat to the north of the Abbeytown Ridge. Another is a polished stone axe from Solway Moss which was found during peat cutting '6ft deep' (*c.*2m) complete with haft (Evans 1897, 151-2); these, and other chance finds mentioned, may suggest a deliberate pattern of ritual axe deposition in wetlands which, as we shall see shortly, has been noted in other parts of the county.

The most famous Neolithic site on the West Cumbrian Plain is Ehenside Tarn. The site was discovered in 1869 when the eponymous tarn was drained revealing large numbers of artefacts including substantial amounts of pottery, and flint and stone tools, including polished axes. More unusual were two wooden paddles and axe-marked wood. The artefacts had been preserved because they had become waterlogged at the bottom of the tarn, this allowed aspects of day-to-day life that would not normally be preserved to survive such as the wooden paddles and also examples of their food, such as wild animal bones from cattle and deer, and also nuts. That we know about this discovery is due to the Rev. S. Pinhorne (Fair 1932, 57) and Rev. J.W. Kenworthy who recognised the significance of the site and used their local influence to protect and publicise it. The first published account appeared in the *Whitehaven Herald* in 1870:

> … Along the shore and continued round within a few yards of the watermark, was a line of white stones, burned white by the action of fire. Along with these, there was a very large quantity of charcoal, burnt wood, broken twigs, nuts and leaves, and some few, but not many, broken and charred bones of wild cattle and perhaps deer. Stone and flint implements, such as axes, knives and

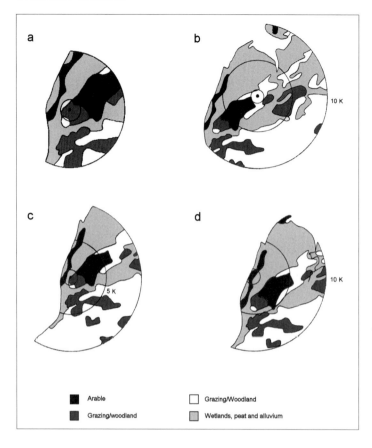

Arable

Grazing/woodland

Grazing/Woodland

Wetlands, peat and alluvium

35 Neolithic exploitation territories on the Solway Plain: a = Plasketlands, b = Hill Farm, c = Mawbray, d = Beckfoot.

chisels, were plentiful, still not one trace of iron, bronze or metal of any kind has come to light. The rude and primeval people whose existence these relics indicate were only in possession of implements of flint and stone ...

Rev. Kenworthy 1870

As a consequence, in 1871 the Society of Antiquaries of London sent R.D. Darbishire to excavate the site (*36*). Darbishire excavated a small part of the tarn edge using, what were for the time, the very best techniques. During the drainage works and subsequent excavations, a large number of finds were recovered (*37*) including: a fragment of wooden bowl, three wooden 'clubs', one of which was decorated, two possible wooden 'fish spears', a plain bowl and Peterborough Ware pottery, a stone saucer-quern, stone *polissoirs*, two stone axe-blade rough-outs, a polished stone axe blade in a wooden haft, a further wooden haft, a stone 'pot boiler', and the horn and metacarpal of *Bos longifrons*. Unfortunately, many of the wooden objects, having survived over 4000 years in the tarn, have not survived the last 130 or so years. We therefore have to rely on Darbishire's publication (1873), which is fortunately of a high standard, and which therefore allows for the reinterpretation and re-examination of the site (Fair 1932; Piggott 1954, 295-9; Walker 1966, 82-116; Coles and Coles 1989, 37-9; Bradley and Edmonds 1993, 136).

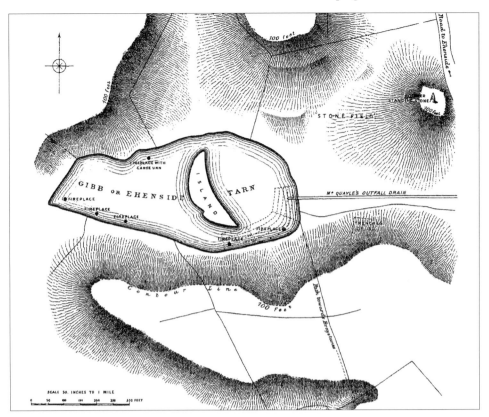

36 Plan of Ehenside Tarn with the locations of 'fireplaces' marked. *Darbishire 1873*

Using Darbishire's report the position of finds can be reconstructed. Some of the finds were directly associated with a series of 'hearths', others from what he terms the 'forest-bed' and which re-excavation in 1957 suggests was an artificial platform (Walker 1966, 91). The 1957 excavations, adjacent to the site of the earlier work, also produced two worked flints, an unidentified wooden object, and a possibly worked piece of wood (Walker 1966, 91-2). A further barbed-and-tanged arrowhead is also known from the site (Fell 1967, 230), whilst fieldwalking in the vicinity of Ehenside Tarn by the North West Wetlands Survey found iso-lated pieces of waste flint, two burnt blade fragments and two scrapers.

The diagnostic pieces amongst the assemblage of field-walked material clearly suggest a Neolithic date for the occupation of the area, as does the presence of the polished stone axes, although analysis (Fair 1932) and radiocarbon dating appear to suggest several phases of activity. The wide date range of the material assemblage, along with the manner in which the site was discovered and excavated, makes interpretation problematic and it is now impossible to associate finds directly with the stratigraphy and the dates. There may also have been a certain selectivity in the material retained and reported upon; flint implements, for exam-ple, are mentioned by Kenworthy (Coles and Coles 1989, 37) but not by Darbishire (1873). Nonetheless, the assemblage provides one of our best insights into the Neolithic of Britain and comparative examples for most of the types have yet to be discovered.

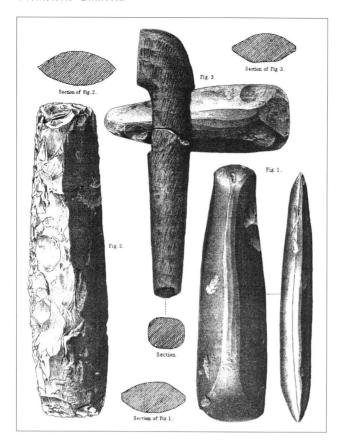

37 Polished and roughout axes excavated at Ehenside Tarn. *Darbishire 1873*

The presence of rough-out part-polished and finished axes in association with *polissoirs* (*38*) denotes the site's relevance to the production of axes in Langdale (Bradley and Edmonds 1993, 144). It should be noted, however, that polished axes with *polissoirs* are known from other wetland contexts, such as Roose Moss in Furness (see Chapter 2) and Pilling Moss, Lancashire (Middleton *et al* 1995, 57); in both cases it is assumed that the finds were deliberately deposited. The presence of plain bowl pottery would place the earliest demonstrable phase of activity within the Early Neolithic (Herne 1988), although closer dating is not possible. The site does show continuity between the Late Mesolithic and Early Neolithic in terms of the palaeoecological record (Walker 1966) and similarities exist between the wooden structures from Ehenside and those purported at the Late Mesolithic site at Eskmeals (Bradley and Edmonds 1993, 136). This supports the wider evidence for continuity between the last hunter-gatherers and first farmers, such as the use of volcanic tuff in Mesolithic assemblages (Cherry and Cherry 1984) from St Bees, Rottington, Nethertown and Ravenglass.

As elsewhere in the county, the most important indicator of Neolithic activity is taken to be the polished stone axe which has been used as the defining artefact of the period. The apparent occurrence of axes in wetland contexts, such as at Ehenside Tam, led to early theories that the west coast of Cumbria was settled by lake dwellers (Watson 1903). Subsequent chance finds and concerted archaeological survey has revealed a broader pattern

38 A grinding or polishing stone excavated at Ehenside Tarn. *Darbishire 1873*

of axe distribution, with an approximate total of *c.*35 rough-out and finished axes recovered from a wide variety of topographic locations throughout the West Cumbrian Coastal Plain, which changes our view.

A number of explanations have been put forward for the distribution of axes seen across the region, mostly concerned with trade routes (Barnes 1982, 45; Cummins 1980). Bradley and Edmonds (1993) outline a more persuasive case for the distribution of axes through a network of social contacts and obligations. The local axes can therefore be seen as a vital element for interpreting the distribution of Neolithic settlement, whereby the axes were used locally for various woodworking tasks. They may also have had a wider use, particularly as gifts and for other types of exchange, which is likely to have been a central feature of social relations between the small groups of farmers who lived in the area. The distribution of axes is therefore held to be important evidence for the distribution of the earliest farmers in Cumbria as there is an absence of other indicators of settlement such as pottery, flint scatters, and burial and ceremonial sites.

Flintwork from throughout the area continued to be characterised by industries based on beach pebble flint. Although surface material of Early Neolithic date is scarce, leaf-shaped arrowheads have been recovered from the sandhill sites at Drigg, fringing Williamson's Moss, and from St Bees (Annable 1987, table 8). These locations coincide with areas of Late Mesolithic activity, once again suggesting a degree of continuity between the two. The majority of those flint scatters identified are clustered around the eight metre contour (Cherry and Cherry 2002), probably in relation to the maximum marine transgression around *c.*3800 BC. A number of hearth sites have been identified on the west coast associated with limited amounts of lithic evidence (e.g. Cherry 1982), and although incompletely published, excavations at Eskmeals appear to have revealed dense evidence of prehistoric occupation ranging from the Late Mesolithic to the Early Bronze Age (Bonsall *et al* 1986; 1994).

As with the Mesolithic period, palaeoecological information directly relevant to South Cumbria during the Early Neolithic is limited. The lack of clear differences between assemblages of Late Mesolithic and Neolithic date has meant that there is a period in the late fifth and early fourth millennia for which sites are difficult to identify, particularly in the absence of well-dated ceramic and lithic assemblages and monuments. Our incomplete picture of human occupation at this time hints at small-scale activity around the coast at both High Furness (Smith 1958; 1959) and Low Furness (Oldfield and Statham 1963), suggested by the presence of plants associated with open ground such as plantain (*Plantago lanceolate*) immediately prior to, and continuing after, the primary Elm Decline dated regionally to *c.*4034-3700 cal BC (5060±80 BP, Q-913; Hibbert *et al* 1971). Evidence for the adoption of farming has proved elusive; from this we may infer that a small population, which does not appear to have been engaged in cultivation of crops, was living in the area.

We gain an insight into the nature of Neolithic life in south Cumbria from excavations at Bardsea (Middleton 1992b, 27). A very large red deer, with the teeth marks of a dog impressed into the bone, have been interpreted as representing scavenged remains dragged by a dog to a secluded area of stagnant water between *c.*3680-3350 cal BC (4725±65 BP, Hv-4348) and 3970-3340 cal BC (4830±140 BP, Hv-4347; Tooley 1978, 13). This suggests that the faunal remains were deposited sometime after the sea-level had declined sufficiently for a channel to be incised into the marine clays.

The remains of the red deer, although ephemeral, suggest several small-scale, local processes which would otherwise not be present in the archaeological record. The first is the possible presence of settlement in the vicinity of the site. If the bones were brought to the site by a dog, even a wild one, they may have been dragged from an area where the carcass had lain cooked. The second point is the fact that these were the remains of a wild animal hunted and possibly processed by Neolithic people. This may be a reflection of the continued use of wild resources in the Neolithic, and hunted game would surely have been an important part of the diet, even when crops were being cultivated. Red deer remains have been found widely in 'peat deposits all over Lakeland' and in 'the sands of Morecambe Bay' (MacPherson 1892, li), suggesting that the Bardsea finds may be a fragment of a much larger picture.

Excavations north of Castle Head Cottage at Meathop Moss, Lindale, in autumn 1982 unearthed a wooden trackway. Three vertical posts were found at a depth in excess of 2.3m aligned north to south and associated with worked wooden planks lain horizontally. The track linked Meathop or Castle Head with the 'mainland' across salt-marsh. In the absence of radiocarbon dates for the timbers it is difficult to be confident about their age, although based on the stratigraphy it is likely that the track is Neolithic or even pre-Neolithic in date (Hodgkinson *et al* 2000, 40). In terms of human activity, the find is significant as an indicator of the potential importance of the coastal areas in early prehistory, prior to the development of wetlands in the valley bottoms.

The possibility of a Neolithic round barrow tradition in Cumbria is suggested by the morphology of the excavated 'long' cairn at Skelmore Heads (*39*; Evans 2004; Clare 1979). The mound, which is more oval than long, was disturbed by an antiquarian group before being excavated by Powell (1963; 1972). Although the presence of some pottery and bones is recorded there is insufficient detail to comment on the details of the burial ritual. Excavations at Roose Quarry and Holbeck Park on the Furness Peninsula have produced assemblages including leaf-shaped arrowheads, flakes of polished volcanic tuff and Early Neolithic pottery (Jones 2001; Oxford Archaeology North 2002b). At Holbeck Park, deposits within a tree throw hollow contained 106 sherds of Early Neolithic pottery associated with rod microliths and two unpolished flakes of volcanic tuff (Oxford Archaeology North 2002b). Five radiocarbon dates, including one taken from a charred grain of wheat, have provided a date range of 4000-3700 cal BC for the assemblage (Huckerby in Hodgson and Brennand 2006, 32).

Excavations of a sand dune occupation site at Walney North End on the Furness Peninsula (*40*) revealed a substantial Late Neolithic and Early Bronze Age lithic assemblage together with hearths, middens and small amounts of Beaker pottery (Cross 1938; 1939; 1942; 1946; 1949; 1950; Barnes 1955; 1970b). At Sandscale, 3km to the north-east of Walney, a small post-hole structure and pits associated with a lithic assemblage of Late Neolithic and Early Bronze Age date were excavated (Evans and Coward 2004). The finds included characteristic Early Bronze Age barbed-and-tanged arrowheads and thumbnail scrapers, but the presence of a small polished axe of Langdale type suggests that the site was first occupied in the Neolithic.

With only limited evidence from excavations archaeologists have traditionally been dependent on the polished stone axe to identify activity across the Cumbrian landscape. It has long been recognised that south Cumbria, and Furness in particular, has produced a significant number of such artefacts (Clough and Cummins 1988, map 6). In part, this may be explained by the proximity of the area to the axe 'factories' in the Langdale hills. An analysis of the distribution of the polished stone axes can help to shed some light on human activity in the area during this period, although it should be borne in mind that axes were in active use for *c.*1500 years during which the role they had in society and manner in which they were used, circulated and discarded would have changed.

Polished stone axes generally have a coastal distribution and are particularly common in Furness and along the north coast of Morecambe Bay; the area accounts for approximately 67 examples, half of all the known axes in Cumbria. Of these 60 per cent were found within 5km of the sea, a figure that rises to 90 per cent when rivers are included (Collingwood 1932, 163-200). Of the 67 stone axes recovered from the coastal fringe of south Cumbria, only eight were found east of the River Leven and, of these, four were recovered from a valley bottom context. These include two from Winder Moor, near Cartmel, and another from Grange-over-Sands. The other eastern axes, such as one from Underbarrow and two flint axes from the Whitbarrow area, originated from the high, steep-sided limestone scarps, fringing the extensive valley mires of the Lyth valley and the Leven. A further reworked axe fragment has recently been recorded from this area at Little Strickland Hill, unusual in that it is a broken end which has been re-flaked to fit into a wood, or antler, sleeve leaving the original cutting edge intact (Fell 1991). An adze has also been recovered from Brigsteer. These axes, along with a single leaf arrowhead from Underbarrow (Annable 1987, 385), form the total Neolithic artefact assemblage from the eastern moss fringes.

To the west of the Leven there is a similar pattern with the stray finds restricted to the higher ground on the moss edge. These finds include an axe from the low-lying clay hills adjacent to Newland Moss, a rough-out axe from Leece on the fringes of Stank Moss (Robinson 1985, 36) and two polished examples also from Leece. A large sandstone polishing stone (*polissoir*), recovered from within the peat of Roose Moss, and associated with bog oak, has been interpreted as being Neolithic in date, after comparison with similar artefacts from Ehenside Tarn (Darbishire 1873; ch. 3). There is also a reputed 'celt' from Kirkby-in-Furness, close to Angerton Moss.

There are some hints that the pattern of intentional deposition of axes in mosses identified in south Cumbria is repeated in the central Lakelands and on the North Cumbrian Plain around the Solway Plain, and on the West Cumbrian Plain, for example at Ehenside Tarn,

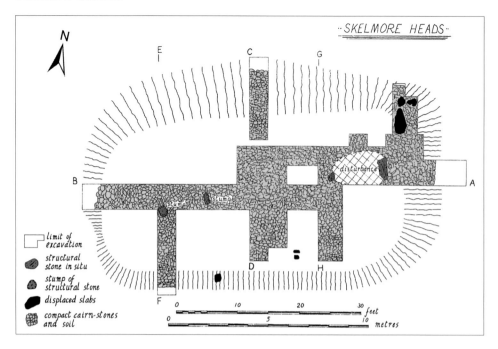

39 Site plan of Skelmore Heads long barrow. *After Powell et al 1963*

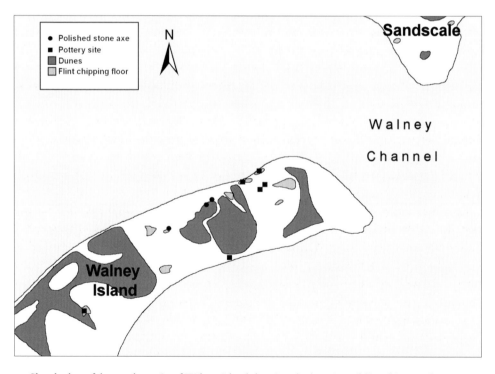

40 Sketch plan of the northern tip of Walney Island showing the location of flint chipping floors, polished stone axes and pottery finds. *After Barnes 1955*

at Portinscale (*41*) and also in North Lancashire (Middleton 1996, 38; Barrowclough 2008, 78). It has been noted that a number of axes come from the mossland edge, and it is possible that some derived from peat deposits. The axe and polisher from Roose Moss may be a more direct example of intentional deposition and mirrors the similar association of artefacts from Pilling Moss in North Lancashire, on the southern edge of Morecambe Bay (Middleton *et al* 1995, 57; Barrowclough 2008, 78). Recent work has established that the deposition of axes may have had a ritual significance, either related to the axe, or to the place of deposition (Bradley and Edmonds 1993). There is some evidence from elsewhere in Britain to suggest that rivers and wetlands were important places for deposition, and it is notable that some of the axes from Cumbria have a definite riverine and mossland distribution. The analysis of deposition suggests that they were not accidental losses and many of the axes must have been deposited deliberately. If that is the case then the wet places selected, whether river or bog, must have had a specific significance. It may be no coincidence that the same wetland locations were often selected for the deposition of metal axes in the Early Bronze Age. It is of particular significance that none of the five axe hoards from south Cumbria appear to have been associated with wetlands. Along the northern coast of Morecambe Bay polished stone axes have been discovered in small groups in fissures and gaps in out-cropping stone. At Skelmore Heads, near Ulverston, four flaked stone blades were found in 1959 in a limestone gryke (Barnes 1963). This pattern of deposition suggests a deliberate cache of axes, perhaps as part of a symbolic, possibly ritual activity, rather than an accidental loss (Bradley and Edmonds 1993). Ritual deposition was therefore not confined to wet locations, but rather may be seen to reflect the belief that a range of natural places and features had sacred meaning. As with bogs and mosses, we see a continuation of these beliefs into the Bronze Age, when bronze tools and weapons were placed in similar sorts of fissures (discussed in Chapter 7).

There has been much discussion of the Neolithic axe 'trade' and the role of the lowland settlements in the production and dissemination of completed axes from the quarry sites in the centre of the Lake District mountains. But, following Bradley and Edmonds (1993), it is no longer appropriate to talk of 'the' axe trade as if it were a homogenous process. Bradley and Edmonds distinguished between two phases of activity. There was an early phase during which axe production was characterised by ad hoc quarrying of material in the Langdales, which was then removed from the site for secondary working at settlements between 12 and 20km away (Bradley and Edmonds 1993, 144). The best evidence for this comes from Ehenside Tarn, where roughouts, polished axes and grinding slabs were all found together with structural evidence (Darbishire 1873). Later activity, on the other hand, focused all the principal stages of manufacture at the quarry site. What is more, later phases involved more systematic exploita-tion of the rock face with less waste. More attention seems to have been paid to preparing the stone and anticipating errors and higher efficiency. This change is exemplified by the site at Dungeon Ghyll (*42*), where earlier levels contained axes that were often irregular and worked in a 'summary' fashion; in contrast those from later levels were more symmetrical, even during the preliminary manufacturing stages (Bradley and Edmonds 1993, 132).

Focusing the manufacture of axes in one place has the potential for increasing efficiency, eliminating unsuitable stone before it had been transported. But as Bradley and Edmonds note, strictly speaking there was never any need to have created this problem as there were perfectly

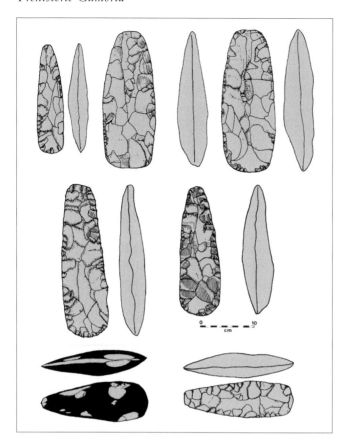

41 A possible hoard of polished and unpolished axes from Portinscale. *After Bradley and Edmonds 1993, 147, fig 7.6*

good sources of axe-making stone available in more accessible locations. That accessible sources were often overlooked in favour of more remote locations which were difficult and dangerous to reach, suggests that location must have had more to do with some social or possibly ritual qualities linked to their command of stunning views across the landscape (Bradley 1993, 2000; Bradley *et al* 1992; Bradley and Edmonds 1993). Bradley (2000, 86) observes that 'taken together, [axe] production sites are among the most remote archaeological monuments anywhere in England', and argues that such locations reflect an attempt to isolate axe production from the sphere of everyday activity during the Neolithic (Bradley 2000, 87). Bradley and Edmonds suggest that the locations of the quarries consciously established distinctions between places in which axes could be made by particular groups. If such groups undertook repeated trips to the area for the purpose of producing axes, this process may have been accompanied by specific notions of where it was appropriate for them to work. In addition, some of these locations would not have been easy to discover by chance, it was necessary to know exactly how to reach them (Bradley and Edmonds 1993, 134). Gabriel Cooney (2002, 93-107) argued that particular sources of rock used in the production of stone axes were distinguished by their colour, which the process of polishing served to highlight (see Whittle 1995). Colour was therefore a means of foregrounding the significance of both sources and those who had access to them; colour, place and identity were therefore intertwined.

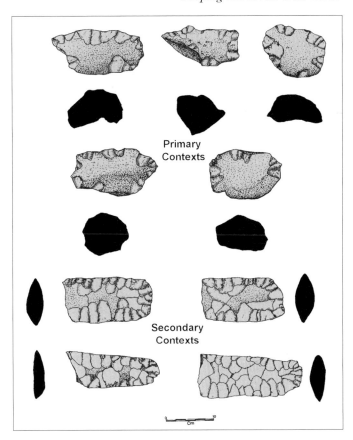

42 Roughout axes from Dungeon Ghyll illustrating the changing character of the axes. *After Bradley and Edmonds 1993, 133, fig 7*

Bradley and Edmonds (1993, 164) argued that the different phases of axe production could have been a response to changes in the social value placed on axes in the east and south of England. There, from 3300 BC onwards, a number of changes have been observed including the appearance of individual burials owing as much to northern practices seen in the Yorkshire Wolds as they did to local ones, the transformation of a small number of causewayed enclosures into defended settlements, and the replacement of local exchange networks based on flint mine products by the long-distance movement of axes originating in Cumbria. The changes that happened in southern England reflect the extension of exchange relations over a larger area than in earlier centuries. In forming links with more distant communities who conducted their lives in such different ways groups in southern England drew upon a powerful source of new ideas. The process of social differentiation observed at the end of the Early Neolithic may be understood as a result of these new relationships (Bradley and Edmonds 1993, 178).

It appears that axe production reached a peak toward the end of the fourth millennium BC. In the Late Neolithic there was a contraction in the areas in which Cumbrian axes are found with fewer examples found south of the Thames, and possibly south of Fenland (Bradley and Edmonds 1993, 179; Chappell 1987), although axes are still found in East Anglia and in Yorkshire, where they occur in large numbers (Manby 1979). At the same time changes are seen in the Langdales where quarrying seems to have come to an end, leaving manufacturing

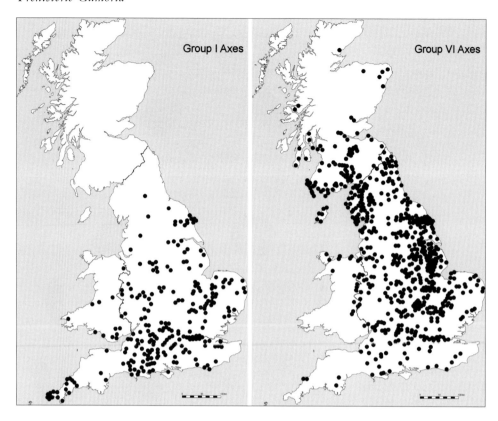

43 The distribution of Neolithic stone axes of Group I and Group VI. *After Clough and Cummins 1988*

with no option but to make use of stone obtained during earlier phases. Thus at Dungeon Ghyll the second phase of activity involved the systematic re-use of stone discarded during earlier periods of stone working (Bradley and Edmonds 1993, 180).

Contraction in Cumbria coincided with the expansion of production and distribution of Group I Cornish axes (Smith 1979). Significantly, the main distributions of Cornish and Cumbrian axes largely complement one another. Those made in south-west England seem to fill the void left as the distribution of Group VI axes contracted (Clough and Cummins 1988, map 2), whilst they are found less frequently in the North-East where Cumbrian axes retained a hold (*43*). Thus one exchange network extended along the south coast as far as the Thames estuary and East Anglia, whilst the other crossed the Pennines and the Solway Firth and reached down the North Sea coast to the Fens. In Burl's analysis the same broad areas are associated with different styles of henge monument (Burl 1976, fig. 13), and the geographical division can also be recognised in Barnatt's analysis of stone circles (*44*). It therefore seems that the movement of stone axes was caught up in larger political alignments (Bradley and Edmonds 1993, 194).

The shift toward greater use of the Eden valley and other areas close to the Pennine foothills beginning in the Early Neolithic may have taken place because people came into the area from north-east England, but this cannot be proved (Bradley and Edmonds 1993, 157).

This connection may help account for the unusually high proportion of Cumbrian axes found on the opposite side of the Pennines, and in particular on the Yorkshire Wolds (Manby 1979). This link would help explain the broad similarities of material culture that extend from Yorkshire into north-west England and south-west Scotland into Ulster, which provide evidence for interaction between these areas (see Discussion in Chapter 9). The most important link is with burials found on the Yorkshire Wolds. These belong to at least two series, which overlap in time. There are a considerable number of long barrows associated with collective burials in what have become known as 'mortuary houses' (Manby 1988). The Yorkshire Wolds also see the development of round barrows at a relatively early date (Manby 1988). These monuments can be associated with individual inhumations, accompanied by a distinctive suite of grave goods, particularly arrowheads, but collective burials are also found at these sites. One feature which characterises mounds belonging to both traditions is the use of cremation. This is mainly found with multiple burials and seems to have involved the firing of the charnel houses which are such a feature of this area.

Close to the Eden valley in Cumbria several features, which Canon Greenwell (Kinnes and Longworth 1985) who excavated in both areas would have recognised from his work in Yorkshire, also occur in a small group of monuments (Masters 1984). One of the more

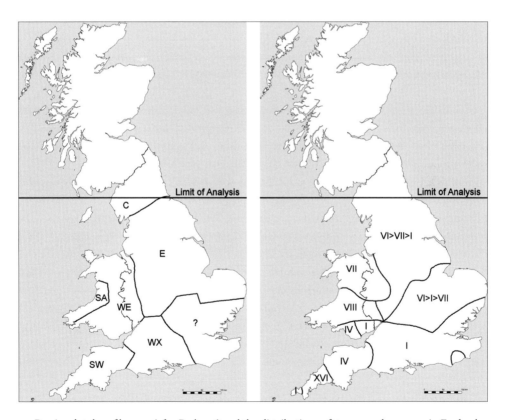

44 Regional styles of henges (*after Burl 1976*) and the distributions of stone axes by source, in England and Wales (*after Cummins 1980*)

informative sites was at Raiset Pike (*45* and *colour plate 7*), where two round cairns may have been incorporated into a later long cairn. Each of these early monuments contained a burial 'trench', which resembles mortuary structures found on the Yorkshire Wolds (Greenwell 1877, 510-13; Clare 1979). One of these had been set on fire. In common with earlier Neolithic practice elsewhere, the human remains from these deposits seem to have been disarticulated.

A third round cairn was recorded at Crosby Garrett nearby (Greenwell 1877, 387-9). In this case at least nine individuals were represented by disarticulated remains. Yet another round cairn, this time with a 'cremation trench', was found on Lamb Crag 30km south-west of the Eden valley (Masters 1984, 66-7). Although none of this evidence is of good quality, it may be no accident that all these sites are on the eastern side of the Cumbrian mountains. Similar evidence is absent from the coastal plain, but burnt 'mortuary houses' are also found on sites in Ireland at Doey's Cairn in County Antrim (Evans 1938) and Fourknocks Site II in County Meath (Hartnett 1971).

In Yorkshire, barrows of these types are a feature of the Wolds. Some of the round mounds had a complex structural history, extending into the Late Neolithic, and air photography has recently shown that in two cases these 'great barrows' are located at the centre of much larger circular enclosures, defined by a causewayed ditch. There is one site in Cumbria which closely resembles these enclosures. This is in the Eden valley, where a large earthwork monument lies alongside the stone circle of Long Meg and her Daughters (Chapter 5; Soffe and Clare 1988). Long Meg circle is thought to be among the earliest in Britain (Burl 1976, 89-92), but on one side it respects the position of an existing enclosure. The enclosure is about the same size as those in the Wolds, and its relationship to the stone circle recalls the juxtaposition of similar enclosures and henge monuments in the Vale of York (Bradley and Edmonds 1993, 161).

The concentration of activity at the edge of the Cumbrian Massif is paralleled by activity in Yorkshire. Between the Wolds and the eastern margin of the Pennines are a number of large enclosures and cursus monuments, where their distribution seems to focus on the major valleys extending into the higher ground. In effect these sites command the main routes across the Pennines into Cumbria (Bradley and Edmonds 1993, 162); a similar pattern was to develop around the edges of the Lake District during the Late Neolithic. The distribution of sites in Yorkshire is striking, with a group 75km to the north-west of the Wolds, where a second group of monuments is located, and the same distance from activity in the Eden valley. These monument complexes would have provided an opportunity for large numbers of people to gather together. Within the complexes there are often concentrations of elaborate artefacts from all over the country, it may have been during the ceremonies that took place there that Cumbrian axes were exchanged (Bradley and Edmonds 1993, 162). The data suggest that a significant percentage of the products of the Cumbrian sources were exchanged along networks that stretched across the Pennines and into Yorkshire. Axes may have been exchanged through gatherings taking place at specialised monuments, especially the large earthworks of the Vale of York. Some of the same objects are found on the Yorkshire Wolds, an area which had clear cultural links with the eastern fringe of the Lake District. Here a distinctive series of burial rites had developed which stressed the importance of the individual (Bradley and Edmonds 1993, 164).

In the Late Neolithic there is again a significant link between developments on the limestone above the Eden valley and those on the Yorkshire Wolds (Bradley and Edmonds

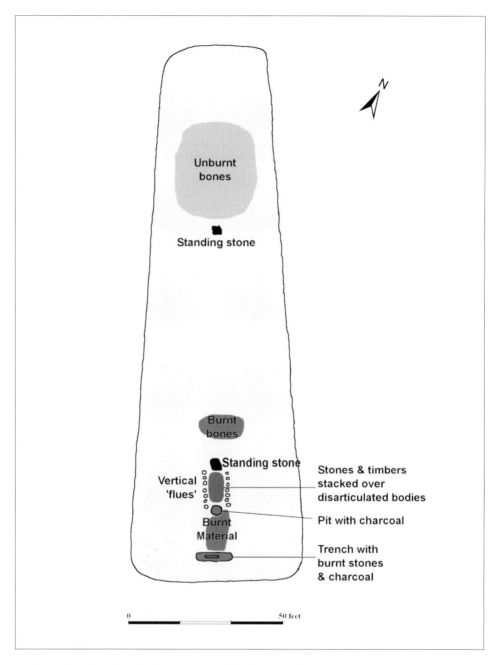

45 Excavation plan of Raiset Pike long cairn. *After Greenwell 1877*

197). Evidence for earlier Neolithic burial monuments in this area of Cumbria have features in common with examples in north-east England. That link remained in force during the Late Neolithic. The site of Crosby Garrett 174 was excavated by Canon Greenwell (1877, 389-91). It was an oval cairn with a number of burials two of which, both adult males, were accompanied by grave goods, including artefacts shared with Duggleby Howe, boar's tusks and an antler macehead. The remaining artefacts include a side-looped bone pin which would also be at home in Yorkshire (Kinnes and Longworth 1985, 98). Like Duggleby Howe, the body of the mound contained a series of human cremations. Other funerary monuments in the area may also date from the same period – for example Orton, associated with a polished stone chisel (Greenwell 1877, 395-6). These links are confirmed by the increased presence of Yorkshire flint in domestic contexts including the presence of knives, types that are common in Yorkshire. There seems to be a growing emphasis on the river valleys at this time, and it is here that a major group of henges is found in the vicinity of Penrith (see next chapter). The same applies to the large stone circles of Cumbria, such as Long Meg and her Daughters, which Burl considers to be of the same date (Burl 1976, ch. 4; Burl 1988) and which in the case of the latter overlies, as we have seen, an earthwork assigned to the earlier Neolithic (Soffe and Clare 1988).

Bradley and Edmonds considered the possibility that the exchange of Cumbrian axes was facilitated by the existence of large monuments in the Early Neolithic. Not only might these have provided focal points at which such transactions could take place, they also, like causewayed enclosures in the south of England, lay outside the orbit of everyday life. During the Early Neolithic two major groups of monuments, cursuses and possibly enclosures, were found to the east of the Pennines, one in the Vale of York and the other on the Yorkshire Wolds. These were well placed to command the major routes across the country. During the Late Neolithic henges developed in both of those areas, for example at Thornborough where a henge was superimposed on an existing cursus (Thomas 1955; Vatcher 1962). Only limited changes were made to the earlier pattern. The distribution of henges emphasised three crossing routes rather than two, and the main density of sites in the lowlands is found rather nearer the Pennines. In addition, henges were built in two of the major valleys leading into the high ground.

On the opposite side of the Pennines new developments took place. Where there had been only one large enclosure in Cumbria, a whole series of henges and early stone circles were built, with a distribution that picks out the main valleys leading to the Cumbrian Massif. The major concentration of these sites was in the Eden valley, towards the ends of the routes to north-east England: in one case the interval between sites on either side of the Pennines was as little as 40km. The same distribution of sites continues to the north, with a second group of henges and early stone circles around the Solway Firth. It has long been suggested that these monuments might have played some part in the movement of Group VI axes and poorly recorded finds of stone axes at three of the sites could lend a measure of support (Burl 1976; 1988, 83-4).

The Early and Late Neolithic systems have many features in common, but there is also a sense in which they differ radically. Although the basic pattern to the east of the Pennines remained essentially the same that was not the case in Cumbria, where only one ceremonial centre (the enclosure at Long Meg) was replaced by as many as 10. These seem to be concentrated in the lowland area where roughout axes were finished, and they most probably belong to a period in which the movement of specialised artefacts played an even more distinctive role. These sites were strategically located in relation to the easiest routes to the

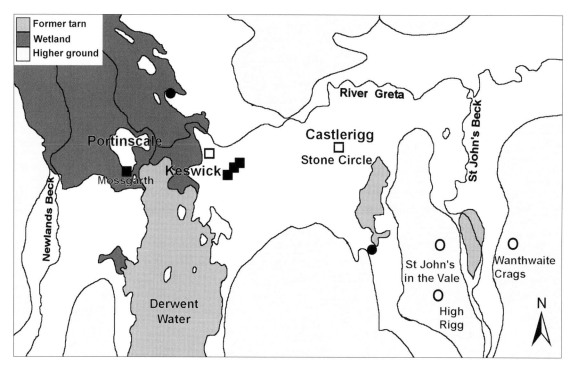

46 The distribution of stone axe finds in the Keswick area. After Clare et al 2002

stone source, but they also commanded the major crossing points of the Pennines (Bradley and Edmonds 1993, 198).

The presence of henge monuments in the Eden valley is important. Such sites lie at the heart of the axe distribution, and in the very areas where these artefacts seem to have been polished. Three sites, Grey Croft and Castlerigg stone circles, and the henge monument at Mayburgh, are actually associated with finds of Group VI axes (Burl 1976). We shall consider the possibility that it was through the aggregations that took place at such sites that the axes first changed hands. It may have been from there that they embarked on those journeys that were to take them to the opposite ends of the country.

In 1901 four unpolished axes, together with a number of 'chippings of similar stone' and a 'log … in an upright position, with the top rudely chipped as if by some clumsy instrument' were found when digging a pond, at Mossgarth adjacent to wetland at Ullock Moss (Rawnsley 1902). The following year a fifth, partly polished, axe was found in the same area within 'the blue clay'. The site of Mossgarth, at Portinscale, lies at the northern end of Derwent Water and is 4km west of Castlerigg Stone Circle (*46*), and has been important in discussions of the production of stone axes (Bradley and Edmonds 1993) as it was considered to be a settlement where axes quarried from the Langdales were 'finished' (Manby 1965, 3). An alternative interpretation was based on evidence from palaeoenvironmental studies and excavations undertaken in 1992 and 1994 (Clare *et al* 2002). These studies established that in the Neolithic Mossgarth was 'a body of slow-moving or stagnant water, surrounded by lush, emergent vegetation and shaded by deciduous trees which formed part of a woodland with a reasonable abundance of dead wood' (Davis *et al* 2007). The axes had therefore been placed into water, or at least deposited in a swampy waterside location. As such, Clare has argued that the axes should be interpreted as a cache, in which case the wooden timber could be interpreted as a post marking the place of deposition. A further two roughout axes were found in the same area when digging a drain, which may be a second cache as they are of similar size to each other and possibly the product of the same hand, a characteristic of caches (Pitts 1996, 341). The axes which constitute the main cache are of gradated size, suggesting deliberate selection for deposition. The stone chippings should also be seen in this context, as part of a votive deposit, placed with a cache and marked by a post.

Deposition of axes into the ground may be understood as a means of returning minerals to their natural state or place. Cooney (1998) has found clear evidence that material associated with the working of stone during the Neolithic period in Ireland was deliberately placed back into the earth during the course of activities that likely involved both placation of and dedication to the earth. A similar motivation may have acted upon the people of Cumbria, and if so then stone axes deposited in rock fissures may represent related types of activities (Bradley 2000).

Structured, ritual, deposition in wetlands is well attested in British prehistory; although most strongly associated with the Bronze and Iron Age, it is not unkown in the Neolithic. The site of Mossgarth represents a further early example of structured deposition of a practice seen elsewhere in the north-west of England at Pilling Moss, on the southern side of Morecambe Bay in Lancashire (Barrowclough 2008, 78). At Pilling Moss a number of Neolithic axes were recovered from locations that would have been pools of open water set amongst drier sand and gravel 'islands' covered in carr woodland at the time of deposition. Similarly, at Mossgarth there is evidence that the axes were placed in wetland on the edge of islands or otherwise near the junction of wet and dryer land. This suggests that roughouts were valued, and it was not just the polished versions of axes that had meaning. This is consistent with the view that the whole process of production was 'permeated with ritual' and that many 'were formally placed back in the earth in a range of contexts' (Cooney 1998).

A number of other axes from the Keswick area, although single finds, may also represent votive offerings rather than accidental losses (47). A polished axe was found 'hidden' in a crevice on Wanthwaite Crags, whilst another was said to have been found '5ft down [1.5m]' 'near St John's in the Vale parsonage' which would have been at Dale Bottom at the southwest corner of a former tarn which was open water in the Neolithic (Clare 1999; Clare *et al* forthcoming). It is possible that the axe had been placed in water, although, given the vagueness of the description, it may have been from dry land. It may also be that the partly polished axe found in the vicinity of Castlerigg Stone Circle was also a deliberate deposition. It is also possible that the axes found below Keswick town, all of which have a white patina similar to that on the axes from Mossgarth, may have been deposited in similar material to those at Portinscale, and therefore represent votive deposits of single axes.

The overall distribution of axes shows that both roughouts and partly polished axes were concentrated on the low-lying areas at the northern end of Derwent Water, this may represent a votive area, or be related to the proximity of settlement. This concentration also suggests that the movement of the axes would have been along the lake or lake shore, rather than along ridges as previously assumed (Clare 1999, 74). Indeed use of valley floors rather than ridges for communication is indicated by the location of cup-and-ring markings in Great Langdale (Brown and Brown 1999) (see Chapter 5).

In contrast to the pattern of roughout deposition at the head of Derwent Water in the adjacent valley of St John's in the Vale, all the recorded axes are polished. Clare has argued that the two contrasting patterns imply differences in the way that the landscape was perceived. In this context the location of Casterigg Stone Circle is significant (*colour plate 8*). A prominent feature of the valley floor is a former tarn, which would have been visible from Castlerigg circle (Clare 1999). At the time that the circle was built the vegetation of the valley consisted of: alder and birch carr along the fringes and on the surface of the former tarn and associated basins; birch and more open woodland on the high slopes; and oak-ash-elm woodland inbetween to a height of at least 200m OD. The circle lies on the ridge between the two areas; perhaps the circle is located on the periphery of the main areas of land use echoing arrangements in southern and eastern England where causewayed enclosures were probably at the edge and not centre of territories (Thomas 1999, 42-3). The stone circle was therefore one of several focal points in the landscape, along with places for votive deposits. Dates taken from Portinscale 2860-2464 cal BC (OxA-6215) are roughly contemporary with the axe production site at Thurnacar Knott, 2850-3250 cal BC (Bradley and Edmonds 1993, 81) and with Castlerigg Stone Circle (Burl 1976). The construction of the circle, contemporary with, or perhaps after practices of deposition had begun, suggests an ongoing relationship with the landscape, aspects of which were perceived as having ritual significance: the process of marking the landscape reflects ways of 'creating new kinds of relationships with place and with material substances' (Thomas 1999, 35). The spatial distribution of finds and monuments reflects changing perceptions of stone axes and monuments during the Neolithic similar to those recognised elsewhere, for example in Brittany (Bradley 1998, 48-75).

With the exception of the work on the axe quarries and that of Cherry and Cherry (1987b; 1996; 2002) little is known about the character of Neolithic upland occupation. The available evidence suggests that in the eastern uplands, Neolithic activity was clustered around the heads of major rivers, as well as in the vicinity of Neolithic monuments (Skinner 2000; Cherry and Cherry 2002). Much of the pollen data from upland contexts suggests a degree of continuity, with upland clearance in evidence from the Early Neolithic onwards. There are no secure dates for the onset of cairnfield construction in the region, though evidence from other areas of northern England is beginning to suggest that this may have begun during the Late Neolithic to Early Bronze Age (Evans and Edmonds forthcoming).

The sequence at Great Langdale shows that axe production changed through time, shifting from ad hoc production to a more systematic form, even though axes seem to have been polished in lowland Cumbria throughout the Neolithic (Manby 1965). From this we may infer the emergence of a class of specialised producers which reflects the increased emphasis on production for exchange (Bradley and Edmonds 1993, 201). Alongside the

SMR No.	Location/Context	Grid ref.	Number	Character
1100	In buried ditch	–	Single	End of polished axe
1112	Nr Castlerigg Stone Circle	–	Single	Unpolished
1114	Building extension to Blencathra Street	3271552349	Single	Unpolished
1115	Eskin Street	3269952324	Single	Partly polished
1116	Back of St Herbert Street	3270652333	Single	Partly polished
1118	Demolition of old Skiddaw Hotel	–	Single	Partly polished
1119	In garden	3264252371	Single	Grooved axe
1135	5ft below the surface, Naddle Valley (Dale Bottom)	–	Single	Polished
1137	On High Rigg	330521	Single	Polished
1138	At Reckow	331522	Single	Polished
4236	Crevice in Wanthwaite Crags	33245222	Single	Polished
–	In a sand pit near Keswick	–	Pair	–
–	Mossgarth garden, Ullock Moss	–	4	Unpolished
–	Ullock Moss	–	1	Partly polished
–	Mossgarth Garden, Ullock Moss	–	Pair	unpolished

47 Polished and unpolished stone axes found in the vicinity of Keswick. *Sources: Clare 2003, Clare et al 2002*

professionalisation of production limited ad hoc production continued, which implies that there were both local and export 'markets', the latter controlled by specific groups overseeing production and exchange with other communities, particularly those across the Pennines in the Vale of York and Yorkshire Wolds. The exchange of axes was mediated via monuments located around the limits of the region. For those acquiring axes different meanings and interpretations were attached to them in different areas. Variations in their treatment and deposition within particular regions suggest that the concepts associated with them may have been drawn upon in different ways. During the Early Neolithic some of them appear to have been deliberately smashed in the contexts of rites of passage; in other cases they were incorporated into formal pit deposits or thrown into rivers such as the Thames.

I would argue that the relative absence of Neolithic material from the uplands, with the exception of arrowhead finds, is notable. Only scattered Neolithic material within mixed assemblages has been recovered, for example from Shap (Cherry and Cherry 1987a). The blurring of the Mesolithic into the Neolithic hinted at by the combination of artefact types means that the 'end' of the Mesolithic may be impossible to trace. In common with the sites in the central Pennines, and others elsewhere in England, those in Cumbria have yielded Mesolithic flintwork associated with Neolithic artefacts (Cherry and Cherry 1987a). It is worth pointing out that it is no coincidence that the areas where Neolithic and Mesolithic equipment are found together are agriculturally marginal, areas which in all likelihood were used by farmers for hunting and not for agriculture (Bradley 1978, 101). The distribution of Neolithic arrowheads in the central Cumbrian uplands and elsewhere reflects this continuing use and disturbance of forest-edge habitats for hunting. The possibility that the Mesolithic mode of seasonal movement continued into Neolithic times must therefore be considered seriously. Neolithic clearings in the uplands may have been made in the course of hunting just as they were during the Mesolithic. Certainly it would appear that there was a different approach to the Neolithic in this part of the North compared with southern England. Early, and possibly even Late, Neolithic activities were not particularly different from Mesolithic practices, especially since pioneer agriculture may have been on too small a scale to register clearly in the pollen record. It is also likely that there were variations between different parts of the region in the frequency of cereal use as an adjunct to wild resources. Again, the type of forest clearance in the Cumbrian uplands differed from that of southern England, and probably also from that of the Peak District and central Pennines (Barrowclough 2008, ch. 4), in that small, temporary clearings were the rule compared with the widespread, longer-lived deforestation on the Downs. No evidence exists about the techniques used, but it does appear that pastoralism was almost universal in the scattered clearings on the fringes of the uplands, possibly nomadic, or more accurately transhumant, in character, with an emphasis on hunting on the higher ground. Many of these clearings were short lived, and there is widespread evidence of forest regeneration. In Cumbria, besides the strong suggestion of continuity from the Mesolithic into the Neolithic period, there is also the likelihood of a further continuity into the Bronze Age.

Late Neolithic/Beaker Period

Studies undertaken at Foulshaw and Helsington mosses (Wimble *et al* 2000) indicate a small clearance episode during the Late Neolithic, *c.*2570–2140 cal BC (3870 ±70 BP; Hodgkinson *et al* 2000). This was followed by regeneration of the woodland until 2300–1890 cal BC (3690 ±70 BP) when the first significant *landnam*-type clearance in this area of Morecambe Bay took place (Wimble *et al* 2000), creating a number of scattered clearings, each occupied for a few years, before the inhabitants moved to a new area, allowing the recolonisation of the clearing by secondary woodland. This activity is associated with Beaker style inhumation burials at Sizergh and Levens Park which mark the end of the Neolithic and the beginning of the Bronze Age (Turnbull and Walsh 1996).

On the Furness Peninsula excavations of a sand dune occupation site at Walney North End revealed hearths, middens, small amounts of Beaker pottery and a considerable assemblage of lithic forms of a probable Late Neolithic/Early Bronze Age date (Cross 1938, 1939, 1942, 1946, 1949, 1950; Barnes 1955, 1970b). Recent excavations at Sandscale, 3km to the north-east of Walney, have identified a small posthole structure and pits associated with an lithic assemblage of Late Neolithic/Early Bronze Age date including a small polished Langdale axe, a barbed-and-tanged arrowhead and thumbnail scrapers (Evans and Coward 2004).

Discussion

The region's broad topographical range and close juxtaposition of coastal, wetland and dry environments may have allowed gathering, hunting and fishing to remain of primary economic importance well into the Neolithic period after which domesticated crops and animals became common (Hodgkinson *et al* 2000, 151; Hodgson and Brennand 2006, 31).

The presence of Mesolithic coastal activity dated to the end of the fifth millennium cal BC in close association with Early Neolithic finds has given rise to a model which views the change from Mesolithic to Neolithic as essentially one of continuity, where new arte facts are integrated within existing patterns of subsistence and settlement. The scattered palaeoecological record for the Early Neolithic in the county suggests continued landscape management by burning, notably in the uplands (Bradley and Edmonds 1993, 138-9), and also of small-scale clearances.

We have noted the apparent continuity between the Late Mesolithic and Early Neolithic, and the importance of resource-rich wetlands for hunter-gatherers; the role of wetlands for early farmers is, however, less clear. The small amount of Early Neolithic flintwork from the coastal plain has been taken to suggest a move away from the coast inland where the monuments of the Neolithic tend to be located. An alternative view suggests that the same level of coastal settlement and exploitation that had been common in the Mesolithic continued into the Neolithic, but that in the later period there was also an expansion of activity into other parts of the landscape. Bradley and Edmonds' (1993) study of Neolithic Langdale has suggested an expansive use of the landscape with seasonal grazing. The continuous use of such high land, with its climatic restrictions, may suggest a more intensive use of valley bottoms and coasts, which had more clement weather and better soils. The widespread occurrence of charcoal, allied to small woodland clearances in the available pollen record, may be an indicator of this.

CHAPTER 5

CIRCLES IN STONE:
NEOLITHIC AND EARLY BRONZE AGE MONUMENTS AND ART

The stone circles of Cumbria are, however, sufficiently numerous to be of national importance as well as a major feature of local prehistory and, therefore, worthy of serious consideration.

T. Clare 1975, 1

Introduction

Cumbria has one of the largest number of preserved archaeological field monuments in England, far outstripping the number in the neighbouring counties to the south and east. The presence of prehistoric monuments in the landscape serves as a visible reminder of the past. Long Meg and her Daughters has been the subject of local folk lore for centuries whilst Castlerigg Stone Circle has been a popular tourist destination for over 100 years, 'During the Lake season huge chars-a-bancs daily discharge large numbers of tourists and trippers at the circle'(cw1, x, 272). Although they are the most enduring legacy of our Neolithic and Bronze Age predecessors they are also surprisingly obstinate research subjects. They vary in size, shape and method of construction and not surprisingly most attempts to understand them have begun by attempting to place them in categories based on these most visible features. The early antiquarians began the process applying terms such as henge, stone circle and barrow, which had been first coined for sites in Wiltshire where there is a concentration of prehistoric monuments, most famous of which is Stonehenge. In Cumbria, as elsewhere, this approach continues to be seductive and has led to the development of a local typology (Clare 2007, 132-4, fig. 72). This is at once both a necessary and obvious approach for archaeologists to adopt, and yet also misleading and potentially unhelpful. The problem is that although monuments are highly visible landscape features there is more to them than meets the eye. Excavation has demonstrated that many of the monuments have passed through several different phases, perhaps beginning life as a circle of timber posts which were later removed and replaced by stone settings, in turn incorporated into a cairn which at various times may have been used as a site for burial. Such sites defy simple classification, being both a burial cairn, and a timber circle. It also follows from this that the dating of monuments is complicated as in many cases the sites were utilised for about 1000 years, spanning the Neolithic and Early Bronze Ages.

As an alternative to discussing these monuments according to categories of different types the approach here will be to develop an understanding according to their landscape context, from which we may make some new suggestions about their meaning to the prehistoric people who first created and then recreated them. Using examples of excavated monuments it is possible to begin to identify the different phases of building activity from which we may reconstruct the life-history or biography of some of these monuments. At one time it was assumed that cairns were built out of whatever stone lay closest to hand, but this view is now changing and it is possible to detect an ongoing process of selection in the use of different materials used to build them. Beyond the mechanical properties of stone, texture and colour both seem to have been valued, to the extent that stone was sometimes carried considerable distances to be incorporated into the monument as at Stonehenge.

Studies elsewhere in Britain have done much to investigate this phenomena, for example Andrew Jones (1999) suggested that the use of coloured stones in the construction of chambered tombs on Arran, Scotland, related to the symbolism of the body. Research in Cumbria lags somewhat behind this, but from the limited evidence that we have it is possible to detect that the monument builders had similar preoccupations. The further embellishment of monuments with rock art motifs confirms the notion that monuments were appreciated for their aesthetic qualities, which may have been linked to their uses in a range of rituals. These links may have extended beyond the bounds of the stone circles, cairns and earth mounds to include standing stones and also natural rock outcrops and features, decorated examples of all of which have been found. An understanding of each will only be reached if they are studied together as ritual embellishments of a meaningful landscape.

Burial

The Neolithic has been categorised as a time of multiple, communal burials, often of disarticulated remains within tombs and long cairns. However, the paucity of both monuments and excavated evidence from the region does not provide a sufficient basis for an authoritative overview of funerary practice. A total of 25 possible long cairns have been identified in Cumbria (*48*; Collingwood 1933a; Manby 1970; Masters 1984; Quartermaine and Leech forthcoming). None of these have been excavated or recorded in detail and the majority have been identified solely through their external morphology. A number have been destroyed and the secure characterisation (and location) of others remain questionable. Some examples are present in cairnfield contexts, particularly on the south-western fells, but without excavation or dating evidence, it is difficult to distinguish between a funerary monument and clearance (Evans 2004). A tradition of long barrow construction utilising natural features is evidenced by Greenwell's excavation of Crosby Garrett in the Eden valley, which was partially formed from a distinctive limestone outcrop (1874).

The possibility of a Neolithic round barrow tradition in Cumbria is suggested by the morphology of the two excavated 'long' cairns at Raiset Pike (Masters 1984) and Skelmore Heads (Evans 2004; Clare 1979). The long cairn at Raiset Pike (Kinnes and Longworth 1985) was apparently formed from two separate round cairns conjoined to form a single monument

48 Distribution
of Neolithic
enclosures and
long cairns in
Cumbria

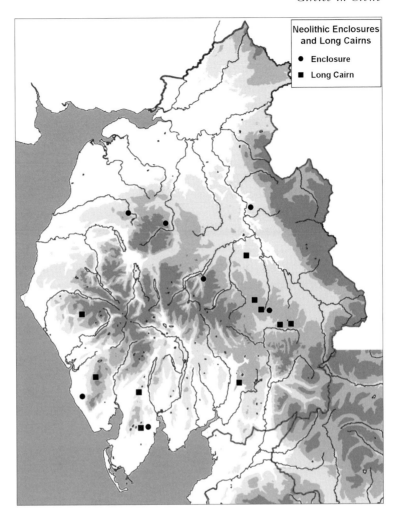

Neolithic Enclosures
and Long Cairns
● Enclosure
■ Long Cairn

(Clare 1979). Greenwell's (1877) description of the excavation of this feature left much to be desired, and it has been subject to a variety of interpretations (Manby 1970; Ashbee 1970; Kinnes 1979; Masters 1984; Annable 1987). What appears to have been a wooden and stone mortuary house, containing a number of disarticulated burials, had been burnt *in situ* before the construction of the cairns. Within the body of the mound were many un-burnt deposits of broken and scattered human bone, principally of children, and a variety of faunal remains including ox, horse, sheep or goat and pig. The burials at Raiset Pike may have been similar to examples in western Scotland where a number of early simple box graves in individual round cairns were later covered by a single long cairn (Lynch 1997). The mound at Skelmore Heads is more oval than it is long. The site was excavated by Powell (1963; 1972) but was found to have been subject to the attention of a local antiquarian group, who recorded the presence of some pottery and bones. The existence of a large transverse slab in the barrow adjacent to one end of the destroyed burial deposit has been taken to correspond to the mortuary structure at Raiset Pike (Manby 1970; Powell 1972; Masters 1984).

Landscape and Ritual

Prehistoric sites are known from much of Cumbria; their known distribution is illustrated in figure *49*. There is, however, considerable uncertainty even when it comes to stating the number of field monuments in Cumbria. At first glance it would seem a straightforward, if time consuming and labour intensive, matter of surveying the landscape to identify the number of extant monuments. In fact this has proved problematic. Although some monuments are easily identifiable, for example King Arthur's Round Table, the vast majority are more inconspicuous stone cairns (*colour plates 9, 10, 11, 12 & 13*). On the Cumbrian fells cairns, stones piled one upon another, come in a variety of sizes and range in date from the prehistoric to modern. Distinguishing between those built over burials from others constructed by farmers to clear scattered stones from their fields is often impossible without excavation. Of the thousands of cairns that are possible candidates for prehistoric activity only *c*.87 have been excavated (*50*). This is a sufficient sample for us to begin to understand their role in prehistoric society, although there is undoubtedly much still to be learnt.

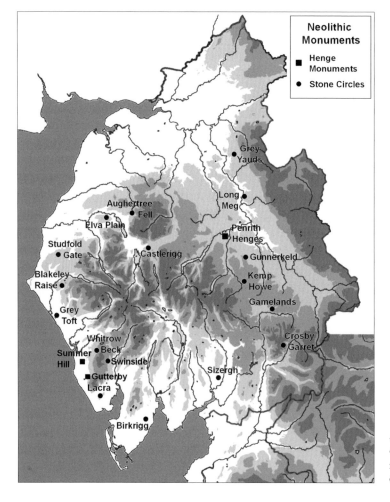

49 Distribution of Neolithic monuments in Cumbria

	Partially dug: research	Fully dug: research	Partially dug: rescue	Fully dug: rescue	Total	%
Pre-1900	46	5	2	0	53	61
1900-1935	4	8	0	0	12	14
1936-1970	12	3	0	1	16	18.5
1971-		1	1	4	6	7
Total	62	17	3	5	87	
%	71	19.5	3.5	5.5		

50 Analysis of excavated sites (excluding cairnfields). *After Clare 2007, table 2*

Previous studies of Cumbria's prehistoric monuments have often focused on the sites themselves (e.g. Clare 2007, Topping 1992). Such an approach downplays or even overlooks the landscape, which is often relegated to that of a backdrop to the monuments. The approach adopted here is somewhat different: rather than take individual monuments as the unit for consideration we shall consider the valley landscape of the rivers Lowther, Eamont and Eden, dominated by the larger ceremonial monuments of the Shap Stone Avenue, the henge monuments of Eamont Bridge and the stone circle of Long Meg and her Daughters. Around each of the larger and better-known monuments are a cluster of less visible but nonetheless important sites combining to create a ritualised valleyscape topography (*51*).

In the Lowther valley the southernmost of the monument complexes is found around Shap an area rich in Neolithic and Early Bronze Age field monuments. Focused on the eastern side of the river and surrounded by the modern village of Shap is the complex of monuments collectively referred to as the 'Stone Avenue', whilst to the east of them are a cluster of circular monuments including Oddendale Stone Circle and Hardendale Cairn Circle (*52 & colour plate 14*). Traditional accounts of the standing stones at Shap have described them as an avenue of standing stones, composed of the local pink granite, extending about a mile. Camden stated 'there be huge stones in the form of Pyramides, some 9 foote [7.75m] high and 14ft [4.3m] thick that ranged directly as it were in a rowe for a mile in length, with equall distance almost between' (Camden 1971 [1586]). William Stukeley (1776) gives us the first detailed account of what was visible of the avenue at the time of his visit in 1725:

70ft [*c*.21m] broad, composed of very large stones, set at equal intervals: it seems to be closed at this [south] end which is on an eminence and near a long flatish barrow, with stone works upon it; hence it proceeds northward to the town, which intercepts the continuation of it ... Though its journey be northward, yet it makes a very large curve, or arc of a circle, as those at Abury, and passes over a brook too. A spring likewise arises in it, near the Greyhound Inn. By the brook is a

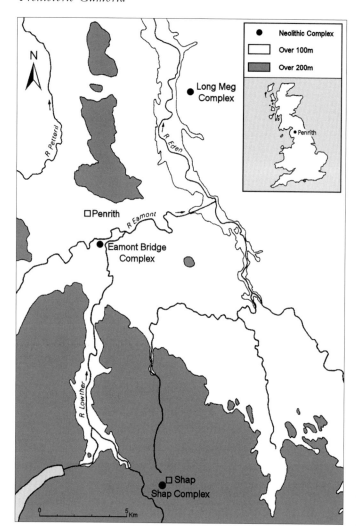

51 The valley landscape of the rivers Lowther, Eamont and Eden with the location of the major ceremonial monument complexes of Shap Avenue, the Eamont Bridge (Penrith) henges and Long Meg marked. *After Topping 1992, 250, fig 7. Courtesy, and copyright of, English Heritage*

little round Sacellum, composed of twelve stones, but lesser ones, set by one great belonging to the side of the avenue; the interval of the stones is 35ft [*c.*10.5m], half the breadth of the avenue; the stones no doubt did all stand upright, because 4 still do ... it ascends the hill, crosses the common road to Penrith, and so goes into corn-fields on the other side of the way westwards, where some stones are left standing; one particularly remarkable called Guggleby stone.

Such descriptions are over-simplistic ignoring the round burial mound of Skellaw Hill and glossing over the fact that in some places the stones form a single row, whilst beyond the area referred to as 'Carl Lofts' the stones form a double row (*53*). Acknowledgment of this feature led Tom Clare (Clare 1978) to argue that there were in fact two avenues: one made of single stones, widely spaced, to the west and north-west of Skellaw Hill (Shap Avenue North), and a second composed of a double row of more closely set stones consisting of the Carl Lofts arrangement and continuing beyond it to the south (Shap Avenue South).

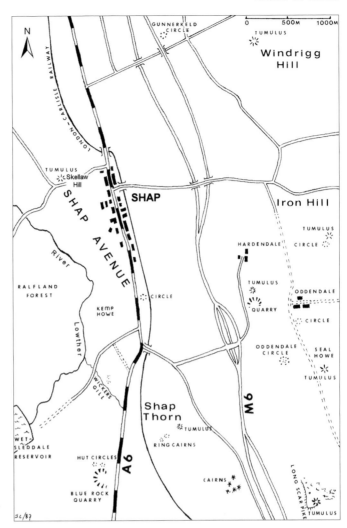

52 Location map showing
the Shap Complex
consisting of the Shap
Avenue, River Lowther, the
stone circles at Oddendale
and Gunnerkeld and
associated tumuli and cairns.
Courtesy of Peter Cherry

George Hall's account suggests that there was also one, and possibly two, large mounds at
the southern end of the South Avenue: a cairn of granite and cobble stone, 18m (20yds) south-
west of the southern end of the South Avenue, and a circle *c.*5.5m (18ft] in diameter and with a
central standing stone some *c.*91.5m (100yds) south of the avenue at Kemp Howe (Hall 1844).
The Kemp Howe circle was destroyed when the railway was carried through in 1844-6 and is
about 27.5m (30yds) across. A chain map of the railway itself dating from about two years after
the completion shows the circle to extend at both sides of the railway, so it would seem that
the railway embankment was simply thrown up across the circle leaving the stones in situ (*54
& colour plate 15*). These stones, variously named as Heppeshaw, Sapshaw and Shapsey, can be
seen on the western side of the railway only, and it seems that the eastern stones were removed
when the sidings for the quarry were built in the 1960s. From Kemp Howe circle the South
Avenue ran roughly north-north-west to Carl Lofts, north of the Greyhound Hotel, where
the road rises. The antiquarian, and vicar of Shap, Rev. Simpson (1859) described a tradition

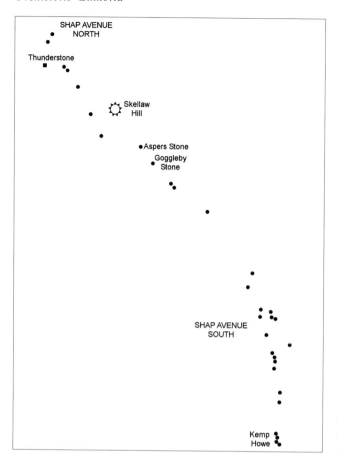

53 Shap Avenue showing the stones which probably formed part of the Avenue. *After Clare 1978*

that Carl Lofts was a stone circle 122m (400ft) in diameter with a large stone in the centre that was cut up into seven pairs of 'yat stoops' or gateposts.

Aubrey Burl agrees with Clare that Skellaw Hill was the focal point for the avenues (55) but argues that the South Avenue is better interpreted as two separate rows of single stones, rather than one row of paired stones. Whichever view is preferred the alignments probably date to the Late Neolithic, based upon excavation of one of the monoliths in the North Avenue known as the Goggleby Stone (Clare 1978, 5-15) (*colour plate 16*) and comparisons with other similar linear monuments such as the West Kennet Avenue, Wessex. The Rev. Simpson was also something of a pioneer in the field of prehistoric rock art and was the first person to describe and draw the cup and ring marking on the Goggleby Stone, a shallow wide cup mark with a smaller one beneath it on the vertical face of the stone, and in the next field north, Asper's field, a cup with a single ring on top on another huge stone, at a slight tilt (*colour plate 17*).

Whatever the precise arrangement of the stone avenues, rather than think of Shap as a single site consisting of a stone avenue, we need to think of it as a complex of sites including burial mounds, two rows of standing stones and stone circles. The choice of the distinctive pink granite for the standing stones, which was also favoured in the construction of circular monuments and the decoration of some stones with rock art, serve to connect the linear

54 The remains of the granite cairn referred to by Hall and depicted by Lady Lowther

55 Shap Avenue looking from the Goggleby Stone, past the Asper's field stone toward Skirwith Hill, in the background

monuments with the surrounding landscape (*colour plate 18*). The stone avenue's location seems to be tied closely to the valley topography. Clare identified three aspects of topography that may be significant: first that the high ground to the east restricted views, just as there are restricted views from some stone circles and megalithic tombs, although the mound on Hardendale Nab may just have been visible from the southern terminus; secondly, that there may have been a former tarn, south of Green Farm; and thirdly, the double row of stones at the southern end of the South Avenue appear to have ended at or deliberately crossed the stream. This arrangement can be compared with the ditched enclosure at Long Meg which embraces a valley that connected it to the River Eden and at Eamont Bridge where the entrances to King Arthur's Round Table are aligned with the River Eamont. Significantly, just as both Long Meg and the Eamont Bridge henges (below) appear to have been laid out with respect to a spring, so Stukeley (1776) noted at Shap 'a spring likewise arises in it'. Moving beyond the immediate setting of the avenues to consider the monument complex in the context of the valley allows us to note further significant similarities between it and the Eamont henges. In the hills surrounding Shap are the prehistoric stone circles and cairn circles of Castle Howe Hardendale and Oddendale, and near to it, Seal Howe, whilst in the vicinity of Eamont Bridge opposite King Arthur's Round Table was a cairn, to the north at Skirsgill a standing stone, whilst a second cairn is referred to as being at Ormstead Hill (below). In both cases we need to consider these monuments and their landscape setting in order to understand the context of ritual activity.

In the case of Oddendale we benefit from a modern excavation (Turnbull and Walsh 1997, 11-44), which has revealed something of the ritual complexity that is likely to have existed at the other sites that we are considering. In the case of most of the sites that are discussed in this chapter we lack a fixed chronology for their construction and development, having to rely on a broad approach which places them in the Neolithic/Early Bronze Age periods. In the case of Oddendale we are able to go further. With the benefit of radiocarbon dating the excavators were able to date four clearly identifiable phases of activity.

Phase one consisted of two concentric circles of timber posts set in pits. The inner circle, *c*.12m in diameter, consisted of 12 posts spaced closely but irregularly. The outer circle similarly had 12 irregularly spaced posts (56A top). The number 12 may be significant, perhaps linked to the number of months in a year, as the Clava stone circles in Scotland were also found to contain 12 stones in a circle. Charcoal samples show that the posts were made of oak (Jones in Turnbull and Walsh 1997, 23), radiocarbon dates from which dated the inner post circle to 4018 ±74 *c*.2872-2350 cal BC (UB-3421) and the outer circle to 4077±37 *c*.2869-2498 cal BC (UB-3400). The origins of the tradition of timber circles remain obscure although it is probable that they are directly related to stone circles. Horizontal lintels may be inferred to give the structure stability based on the example of Stonehenge where the lintels not only give integrity visually but appear to be tied to the uprights by skeuomorphic devices with their origin in carpentry techniques. The Stonehenge trilithons appear sufficiently unlike any other stone circle to allow the possibility that they are in fact a 'monumentalised' stone-built version of a timber circle.

Phase two is marked by the deliberate removal of the timber posts from the rock cut pits, the tops of which were sealed or capped with boulders, mostly of pink granite, to a depth of

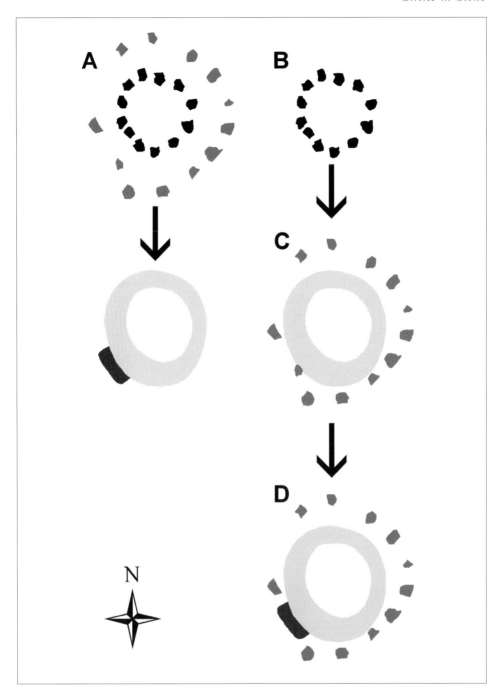

56 Alternative interpretations of the structural sequence at Oddendale, based on information from Turnbull (1997). 'A' summarises the excavator's sequence: two circles of posts (top) were replaced by a ring cairn (light grey) with an extended rubble platform (darker grey). Richard Bradley's re-interpretation began with a single circle of posts (B) which was replaced by a ring cairn with an extended timber setting (C). The rubble platform was added at a later date (D). *After Bradley 2005, 103, fig. 101*

25cm. The site would have appeared as two concentric circles of low round boulder settings, each group of pink stones with a diameter of a metre or a little more.

Phase three is dated to the Early Bronze Age when a ring cairn of *c.*12m diameter was constructed over what had been the inner circle. Given the presence of the phase two cap-stones, comparatively little additional stone would have been needed to create the ring cairn; in essence it was just a matter of filling in the gaps between the already close lying capping stones. Four types of stone were used, a grey gritstone and a hard blue igneous rock were used as the main body of the fill, alongside the pink granite that had already been selected for the capping in phase two and which was now selected to form the kerb around the edge of the cairn. There was also evidence that in places flat pieces of limestone had been added to the surface of the cairn. The excavators felt that this may have been a deliberate treatment of the face of the monument. When newly dug, the stone is a vivid yellow–white colour, which would have enhanced the cairn's visibility from a distance.

Associated with the ring cairn were a number of deposits of cremated bone distributed through the cairn. The deposits were quite small, insufficient to represent an entire burial, suggesting either 'token' burials or the removal of some of each burial to another site as part of the burial ritual. There were also 'token' grave goods, sherds of Food Vessel and Collared Urn pottery rather than entire vessels, suggesting a process of fragmentation. Other grave goods included two flint knives, perhaps symbolic of the severing of the ties between the living and the dead (see next chapter). Placed centrally within the ring cairn was a shallow grave-pit containing a crouched inhumation again with a sherd rather than a whole vessel, this time of Beaker pottery.

Phase four is marked by the addition of a rectangular platform to the ring cairn, which was itself modified. The platform measured 4m x 2m wide and was built out of large pink granite blocks, each a metre or more across. At the same time granite boulders were added to the southern, valley facing, side of the cairn to form a facade extending *c.*5m either side of the platform (56A bottom). On the surface of the platform several pieces of uncremated bone were found, suggesting to the excavators that it was used as an excarnation platform, perhaps prior to the bone being cremated. The presence of rectangular stone structures adjacent to the cairn on Hardendale Nab are similarly interpreted as being for exposure and excarnation, providing independent corroboration for the practice in the local area. A similar function is associated with the mortuary structures often found beneath long barrows. Much effort went into the construction of the platform, the boulders used being on average much larger than those of the sealing of the pits or buildings of the ring cairn and incapable of being carried by a single man.

An alternative interpretation of the site has been offered by Richard Bradley (56B, C and D) who suggests that phase one consisted of the inner timber circle, replaced in phase two by a ring cairn enclosed within a ring of upright posts. That outer timber setting was flattened on the south-west side as if, he argues, to anticipate the position of the platform added in phase three (Bradley 2005, 103-4) (*colour plate 19*). Bradley argues that Oddendale recalls the configuration of recumbent stone circles both in the distinctive form of the stone setting and in the possession of an outer ring of uprights. A parallel for the latter phase would be the site of Brenig 44 in North Wales (Lynch 1993). Whichever interpretation is preferred the excavation

	Earlier Monuments **Late Neolithic**	**Later Monuments** **Early Bronze Age**
	Passage graves, henges, timber circles, earlier stone circles	Later stone circles, recumbent stone circles, Clava Cairns, wedge tombs, stone rows
Raw materials	Wood, or stone replacing wood	Stone
Associations	Varied material culture; residues of feasting	Human remains, some quartz
Decoration	'Megalithic' art, some cups and rings	Mainly cup marks
Evidence of fires	Occasional	Locally abundant
Alignment	Solar, especially sunrise	Mainly lunar, occasionally sunset
Dominant association	Daylight	Darkness
Symbolism	The living	The dead

57 Earlier monuments of timber (or of stone which replaced timber) were generally associated with the movement of the sun, whereas later monuments of stone were generally associated with the moon. *After Bradley 2005*

and radiocarbon dating have revealed a long sequence of ceremonial activity at the site extending over at least several centuries and possibly a millennium.

Parker Pearson and Ramilisonina (1998) argue that timber circles are associated with the living and their activities, whereas stone circles are devoted to the dead, enclosing sites that had once been connected with the living, bringing their use to an end. In northern Britain, it is a sequence that applies to Oddendale circle, and also to sites at Balfarg, Moncreiffe and Machrie Moor in Scotland. Bradley adds that earlier monuments, like Newgrange, Knowth and some of those at Loughcrew in Ireland, and also to circular enclosures like Stonehenge and Woodhenge in Wiltshire, were generally associated with the movement of the sun at the summer and winter solstices, and most probably the equinoxes (Bradley 2005). In contrast, later monuments, such as recumbent stone circles and the Scottish Clava Cairns, which hardly ever had timber precursors, were more closely linked to the position of the moon (57). Individual monuments can be associated with deposits of quartz and cremated bones, and often they are embellished with cup marks (Burl 1980; 1981). This development extends from the late third millennium to the beginning of the first millennium BC, suggesting that it took place over approximately 1500 years.

Published accounts of sites suggest a basic division between monuments that had been associated with the sun and those related to the moon. On a broader level, the distinction between predominantly eastern and western alignments may correspond to the difference between day and night. This adds a further element to the contrast observed by Parker Pearson and Ramilisonina between those monuments constructed out of wood and those built from stone (Parker Pearson and Ramilisonina 1998). The earlier monuments are linked with the activities of the living, and associated with daylight and sometimes the rising sun. The later monuments are associated mainly with the dead, with darkness and the moon.

The predominantly Bronze Age cairn at Hardendale Nab may also have a Neolithic origin (Howard-Davis and Williams 2005), whilst excavations at Carlisle Airport in 1996 uncovered evidence for a complex of timber and possible stone settings, potentially contemporary with a single date of *c.*3500 cal BC (Flynn 1998), suggesting that the longevity of Oddendale was the norm rather than the exception. The deployment of different coloured stones, particularly red, blue/black, and white, within the Oddendale monument seems to have been of significance in ritual. The anthropologist Victor Turner (1967, 89) identified three basic colours: white, red and black, that have universal metaphorical significance relating to the basic fluids which the human body emits (*58*). Among archaeologists Christopher Tilley acknowledged this scheme as useful, applying it to archaeological examples in the Neolithic of southern Scandinavia (Tilley 1996, 321-2). Closer to Cumbria, Andrew Jones (1999) discussed the way in which red and white stones were used in the construction of Early Neolithic chambered tombs, linking them to the geography of the island of Arran, Scotland. As the deployment of red, black and white stones at Oddendale is reminiscent of the basic colour scale described by Turner and identified by him to be of ritual importance it seems a reasonable working hypothesis to assume that they too were associated with rituals linked to the corruption of the human body.

White	Red	Black
Semen – mating between men and women	Maternal blood – mother–child tie + process of group recruitment and social placement	Excreta or bodily dissolution – transition from one social status to another viewed as mystical death
Milk – mother–child tie	Bloodshed – war, feud, conflict, social discontinuities	Rain clouds or fertile earth – unity of widest recognised group sharing same life values
	Obtaining and preparing animal food – male productive role	
	Transmission of blood from generation to generation – an index of membership in a corporate group	

58 Turner's scheme for the universal physical experience of the colours white, red and black. *After Turner 1967, 89*

A second aspect of colour which is important at Oddendale is the effect of colour patterning. Gell pointed out that while the brilliance of certain bright colours such as red and white is significant, their effect is increased when contrasted alongside other colours, for example black or dark blue (Gell 1992). The red kerb is of importance in this context but perhaps more significant was the addition of pieces of limestone to the dark blue/black surface of the cairn. The limestone may have had a symbolic meaning, with the pieces representing a 'passport' to another world for the dead; for the living the white stone may represent the gateway to other dimensions through which they negotiate with the spirit world. All of these involve the selection of the stone, its movement through space and time by being carried to the site, and its structured deposition against the dark surface of the cairn bounded by the red kerb.

The longevity of the Oddendale monument in its various forms suggests that the site was the product of a society enjoying a considerable degree of social, cultural and economic stability.

Prehistoric settlement in the Oddendale area consists of worked flints in large numbers, and pottery, particularly Grooved Ware. These suggest intensive settlement of the area concentrated to the area between Seal Howe and the hamlet of Oddendale. No evidence of buildings is present today, suggesting they were timber built open settlements. Between the Seal Howe cairn group and the river is an extensive system of small rectilinear prehistoric fields defined by low banks of boulders. In places these underlie prehistoric cairns confirming their antiquity. This evidence suggests that the river valley was exploited for agriculture up to the zone of cairns and other monuments close to the watershed. Taken together the people living in the area must have had a complex multi-level and developing conception of the landscape. One set of local symbolic needs was filled by the siting of circular monuments in the immediate Oddendale landscape, overlooking the Lowther valley, but the community was simultaneously participating in larger-scale ceremonial activities associated with the linear stone alignments in the valley bottom which presumably brought together people from a number of local settlements. This nesting of monuments of different scales, bringing together people from wider geographic areas for economic, social and symbolic/ceremonial purposes, may be observed elsewhere within the valley landscapes of the Lowther, Eamont and Eden rivers.

Approximately 15km north of Shap lies the Eamont Bridge ritual landscape. Discussion usually focuses on the sites of Mayburgh, King Arthur's Round Table and the Little Round Table, collectively referred to as the 'Penrith Henges', but in order to understand these sites we need to consider the entire landscape. The henge sites need to be seen as components in a landscape dominated by steep sided valleys and fast flowing rivers. Sited on a narrow interfluve between the banks of the rivers Eamont and Lowther, but focused on a spring which lay between Mayburgh and King Arthur's Round Table, and which connected them to the River Eamont, are the henges, and on the other side of the Eamont are two less well known burial mounds (59). Considering the sites as part of a larger landscape helps makes sense of their location. The rugged terrain of the Lake District hills follows long-established routes of communication which follow the river systems through the valley bottoms. Significantly, the routes from the north-east, from Shap, from the Upper Eden, and down the Petteril valley to Carlisle and the Solway all converge at Eamont Bridge, which, as the name implies, is a natural and historic crossing point for the two rivers. The comparatively flat low-lying ground between the two rivers creates a place for travellers from the surrounding areas to break their journey, and it was here that in time they chose to construct their monuments.

Mayburgh lies on a knoll 110m south of the River Eamont, 155m to the west of King Arthur's Round Table which is visible from it (*60*), the Little Round Table lies 75m to the south of King Arthur's Round Table, to the south-east of Mayburgh, but is not visible. Mayburgh consists of a circular earthwork, *c.*90m across. Unlike other henge monuments, where earth from the digging of a ditch is piled up to form a bank, at Mayburgh the surrounding bank is composed of water-worn stones probably taken from the River Eamont (*61*) and is *c.*35-45m wide and *c.*4.5-7m high. As a consequence there is no ditch, but the position of the monument on a low knoll serves to further enhance the appearance of the site, especially from the south and east where it rises high above the low-lying ground (*62*), suggesting that it was deliberately constructed to be impressive when viewed from King Arthur's Round Table (*63*; Topping 1992, 250). The site is entered via a narrow causeway on the eastern side, oriented toward King Arthur's Round Table, leading to a level platform at the centre of which were originally four standing stones 'of a hard black kind of stone' (Stukeley 1776, 44), only one of which remains (*c.*2.8m tall) (*colour plate 20*):

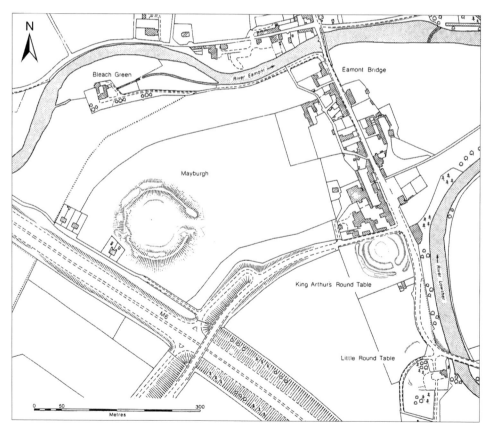

59 The Penrith Henge complex at Eamont Bridge. Locations of Mayburgh, King Arthur's Round Table and the Little Round Table. *Topping 1992, 251 fig. 2. Copyright English Heritage, reproduced with permission*

Near to the centre thereof are erected four stones of great magnitude, the biggest of them con-
teining eleven foot in highth above the earth, and six foot in breadth one way, and four foot in
thicknesse standing equally distant in a quadrangular forme about 50 foot [*c.*15m] asunder

Dugdale 1981 [*c.*1664]

Dugdale also mentions that stones stood on either side of the entrance, although no trace of
these stones remains. Neither is there any evidence of a ditch, a feature often associated with
henge monuments.

King Arthur's Round Table lies 170m south of the River Eamont, but only 75m from the
Lowther, on a relatively flat alluvial terrace. The monument has close affinities with the site
of Arbor Low in Derbyshire and consists of a bank *c.*10-13m wide and 0.5-1.8m high, and
an internal ditch *c.*12.5-16m wide and originally *c.*1.5m deep – a 'classic' henge arrangement
(65). There are two entrances, south and north, which cross the ditch by means of causeways,
the terminals of the southern entrance have been enhanced by the widening and heighten-
ing of the bank so as to focus attention on the entrance (64). As the northern entrance has
been damaged it is no longer possible to determine whether the entrance there had also
been elaborated.

The site was excavated first by R.G. Collingwood in 1937 (Collingwood 1938, 1-31) and
then by Gerhard Bersu in 1939 (Bersu 1940, 169-206). They demonstrated that the site had
been remodelled at least three times. The first phase of activity was associated with concentric rings of substantial timber posts, cutting across which was a timber-lined entrance-way
leading into the centre of the monument. The second phase is marked by the replacement
of some of the timber posts by standing stones, set in the timbers' sockets. At the centre of
the site a cremation trench was dug and beside it two standing stones were erected. The third
phase saw the deliberate destruction of some of these stones by means of a combination of
fire and water so as to fracture the stones.

Only vestiges of the Little Round Table now remain. The monument lies immediately to
the south of King Arthur's Round Table on the banks or the River Lowther. Projections of
the surviving earthworks suggest that it originally was *c.*90m in diameter and consisted of
a circular low earth bank, presumably a ditch based on the presence of upcast used for the
bank, and possibly with an entrance at the north-north-east, as recorded by Pennant in 1790,
although neither Stukeley's earlier 1725 plan nor Hutchinson's 1776 accounts refer to this
(Hutchinson 1794-1797). There are other important features that are only known from historic accounts of the area. Stukeley noted that between Mayburgh and King Arthur's Round
Table was a spring, which is no longer visible. Both Stukeley and Pennant reported a cairn on
the opposite side of the River Eamont. Pennant described it:

almost opposite Mayborough on the Cumberland side of the Eimot is a vast cairn or tumulus,
composed of round stones, and surrounded with large grit stones of different sizes, some a yard
square, which all together form a circle sixty feet in diameter.

The site is shown on Stukeley's sketch of Maybrough, placing it towards Eamont Bridge
and above a cliff north of the river. There is a further possibility of other lost monuments,

60 View of King Arthur's Round Table from Mayburgh

61 The stone pebble bank of Mayburgh

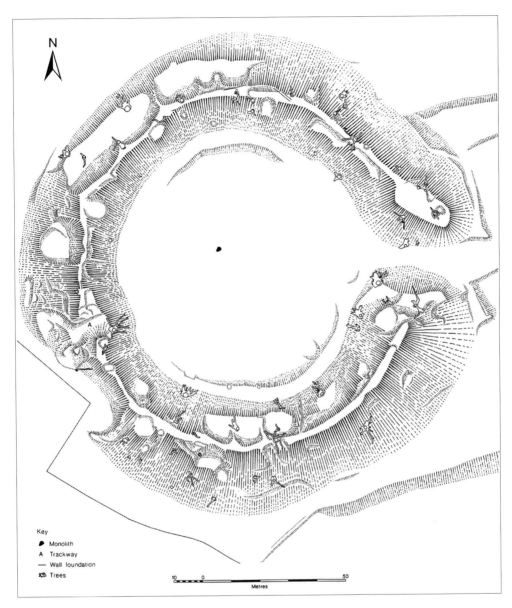

N

Key
- Monolith
- A Trackway
- — Wall foundation
- Trees

10   0   50
Metres

62 Topographical survey plan of Mayburgh. The eastern entrance to Mayburgh focuses on one of
the surviving four standing stones. *Topping 1992, 252 fig. 3. Copyright English Heritage, reproduced with
permission*

63 View of Mayburgh looking from King Arthur's Round Table

64 King Arthur's Round Table showing the causeway and entrance

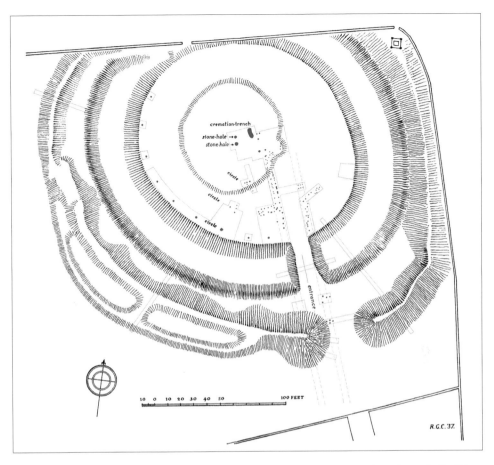

65 Topographical survey plan of King Arthur's Round Table. *Topping 1992, 256 fig. 6. Copyright English Heritage, reproduced with permission*

suggested by a standing stone at Skirsgill, whilst a second cairn is referred to as being at Ormstead Hill, although this is no longer to be seen (Hutchinson 1794-1797).

The setting of the monument complex at the confluence of two rivers seems to have been significant, as riverine settings were chosen for henges elsewhere – for example, Thornborough, North Yorkshire (Thomas 1955); the large group found in the Milfield Plain, Northumberland (Harding 1981); and the Dorchester complex (Atkinson *et al* 1951), all of which are found in riverine settings. The suggestion is that henges created localised or regionally based ritual *foci* (Harding and Lee 1987, 65). The nearest alternative focus to the henges at Eamont Bridge is that at the stone circle of Long Meg and her Daughters, 8km to the northeast of the henge complex on the river Eden.

The stone circle of Long Meg and her Daughters lies on a terrace above water and, as with the other monuments we have considered, should be seen as part of a complex of ritual monuments. Long Meg and her Daughters is a large ceremonial enclosure, 109m x 93m in diameter (*66*). Long Meg is the name given to a monolith that stands 25m outside the circle,

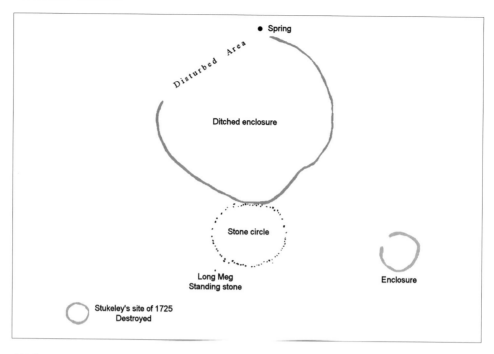

66 The Long Meg complex. The stone circle and standing stone of Long Meg, together with the associated ditched enclosure and spring. A further, smaller enclosure lies to the south-east, whilst Stukeley recorded an additional site in 1725 to the south-west. After Beckensall 2002, 63 fig. 68

the Daughters, and is the tallest of the 69 stones at *c*.3.8m high and weighing *c*.9 tonnes (67 & *colour plate 21*). It is made of local red sandstone in contrast to the daughters that are made of boulders of rhyolite, a form of granite, and the south-west face is encrusted with crystal, while the broad face that looks toward the circle is covered with rock art motifs (68). Unlike the glacial erratic that form the circle, Long Meg is sedimentary, and may have come from cliffs flanking the River Eden *c*.2.5km (1½ miles) away, or from the Lazonby fells. The site lies on a slight slope with Long Meg set on higher ground above the circle so that stone 1, the stone in the circle directly opposite Long Meg but furthest away, is 6m lower (69). Two of the largest blocks are placed singly to the east and west and weigh about 30 tonnes. The south-west entrance has two extra stones outside the circumference, and this forms a 'portal', a doorway into the circle. It is outside this portal that Long Meg is found, aligned from the centre of the circle on the point of the midwinter sunset. Instead of a bank and ditch like a true henge, large stones were used to construct a circle, flattened to the north. Originally there were about 69 stones but today there are 59, 27 of them still standing. Today the centre appears empty, but in the seventeenth century John Aubrey quotes from Sir William Dugdale that: 'In the middle are two Tumuli, or barrowes of cobble-stones, nine or ten feet high [*c*.3m]'. It is probable that later burials were placed inside the circle, covered with cobbles from the surrounding area.

Associated with the Long Meg circle was a huge enclosure formed by an interrupted ditch, that surrounds the present farm. The enclosure seems to predate the stone circle as the flattened part of the stone circle deliberately takes this ditched enclosure into account,

Right: 67 The standing
stone of Long Meg. The
monolith is made of
crystalline red sandstone

Left: 68 Carvings on the standing stone of
Long Meg

Above: 69 The Long Meg Stone Circle. The site on which the circle is built lies on a slope. From Long Meg,
at the top of the slope, to stone 1, directly opposite but at the bottom of the hill, is a difference of 6m in height

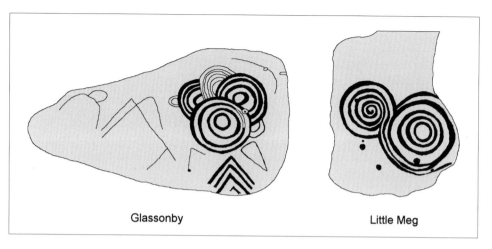

Glassonby   Little Meg

70 The stones of Glassonby and Little Meg are both decorated with concentric circles. In the case of Little Meg these flow into a spiral and are associated with cup marks. At Glassonby a series of concentric circles overlay each other and are associated with chevron marks

71 The Long Meg circle

Above 1 Terence Powell with John Corcoran examining a section at Drigg on the west coast of Cumbria. The section revealed a horizontal timber, 4m long, with a peg, interpreted as the 'ground framework of a rectangular, possibly square, structure' (Powell and Corcoran in Cherry 1982). *Courtesy and copyright of Peter Cherry*

Right 2 Clive Bonsall during excavations at Williamson's Moss, Eskmeals in 1982. *Courtesy and copyright of Peter Cherry*

3 John Cherry, holding a polished stone axe, and his wife, holding a copy of his book, at the cairn circle of Oddendale, Crosby Ravensworth. *Courtesy and copyright of Peter Cherry*

4 Rough-out stone axe from Williamson's Moss, Eskmeals. *Courtesy and copyright of Peter Cherry*

5 Polished stone axe from Levens. *Courtesy and copyright of Peter Cherry*

6 Neolithic Grooved Ware pottery from Raven Gill 3, Crosby Ravensworth. *Courtesy and copyright of Peter Cherry*

7 Long barrow at Raiset Pike. *Courtesy and copyright of Peter Cherry*

9 The stone circle at Gamelands, Orton. *Courtesy and copyright of Peter Cherry*

Below 8 Panoramic view of Castlerigg Stone Circle, near Keswick, showing the landscape setting of the circle. *Courtesy and copyright of Roger Broadie*

10 White Hag Stone Circle at Crosby Ravensworth. *Courtesy and copright of Peter Cherry*

11 An example of a round stone cairn. A Cumberland and Westmorland Society visit to the round cairn near Samson's Bratful, Miterdale. *Courtesy and copyright of Peter Cherry*

12 Small stone circle at Harberwain Rigg, Shap. *Courtesy and copyright of Peter Cherry*

13 Harberwain Rigg, Iron Hill Circle or kerbed cairn. *Courtesy and copyright of Peter Cherry*

14 Excavation of a stone cist at Hardendale Nab, Shap. *Courtesy and copyright of Peter Cherry*

15 The remains of the granite cairn that originally stood at the southern end of Shap Stone Avenue. The monument was destroyed when the railway was first constructed

16 The Goggleby Stone part of the Shap Avenue, with the Asper's Field Stone in the mid distance

17 The Asper's Field Stone with Skirwith Hill behind

18 Reconstruction of the stone avenue at Shap. *Courtesy of Nick Dooley*

19 Reconstruction of Oddendale Circle based on the interpretation suggested by Richard Bradley combining a timber circle with a stone circle and excarnation platform. *Courtesy of Nick Dooley*

20 The last remaining standing stone at the centre of Mayburgh Henge. Behind is the entrance to the henge with King Arthur's Round Table in the distance

21 The standing stone of Long Meg with the stone circle behind. Note the slope of the ground in which the monument is set

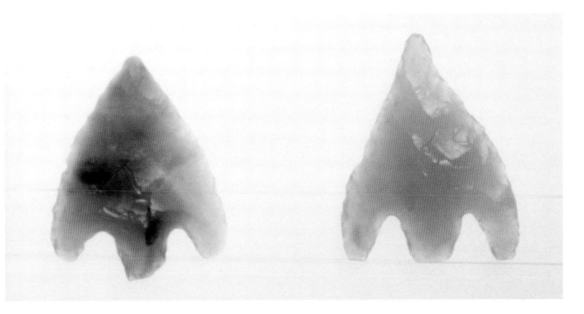

22 Early Bronze Age barbed and tanged flint arrowheads from Eskmeals. *Courtesy and copyright of Peter Cherry*

23 Jet ring from Hurlbarrow, Gosforth. *Courtesy and copyright of Peter Cherry*

24 Jet bead necklace from Mecklin Park, Santon Bridge. *Courtesy and copyright of Peter Cherry*

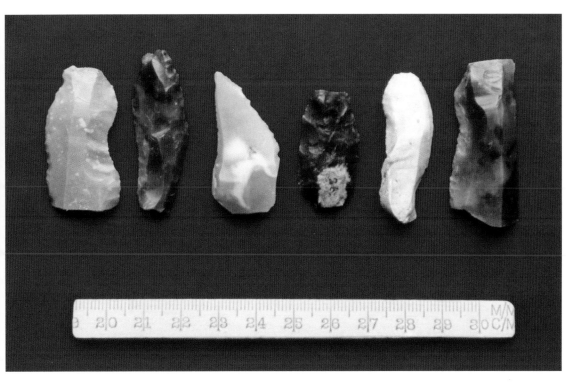

25 Flint knives found at Seascale. *Courtesy and copyright of Peter Cherry*

26 Flint blades found at Williamson's Moss. *Courtesy and copyright of Peter Cherry*

27 Standing stones at Kirksanton. *Courtesy and copyright of Peter Cherry*

suggesting that it was visible at the time the stone circle was constructed and in use at the same time (*66*). In addition to the large enclosure overlain by the stone circle of Long Meg (Soffe and Clare 1988) a number of enclosures in Cumbria have recently been recognised or reinterpreted as potentially Neolithic, including Carrock Fell (RCHME 1996a), Skelmore Heads (RCHME 1996b), Howe Robin (RCHME 1996c) and Green How (Horne 2000). Some of these had been previously identified as Iron Age hillforts (Powell 1963, 20; RCHME 1996a). We also know from Stukeley that in 1725 there was a smaller stone circle nearby, although there is no trace of it now, and further sites have been identified from aerial photographs which show an egg-shaped enclosure east of the large circle, and an enclosure south of what is now called Brustop Wood, all within *c*.200m of Long Meg and her Daughters. The whole terrace, however, extends along the river Eden toward Glassonby 2km away and includes the sites of Little Meg, a small stone circle 650m north-east of Long Meg, Glassonby Circle and Old Parks, all of which have been found, like Long Meg, to be decorated with rock art motifs (*70*).

Along with Long Meg of the 68 stones in the circle four are composed of non-local quartz crystal stone, numbers 2, 7, 10 and 53 (*71*; Hood 2004, 1-25). The closest source for this stone lies across the River Eden suggesting significant amounts of effort and labour to transport the stones to the site. Following Hood (2004) the quartz stones seem to have been deliberately selected for inclusion and placed at specific points in the circle that mark particularly significant calendrical events. Figure *72* illustrates the track of the sun and its approximate positions in relation to Long Meg as viewed from stone 9, as it sets at Samhain the sun can be seen

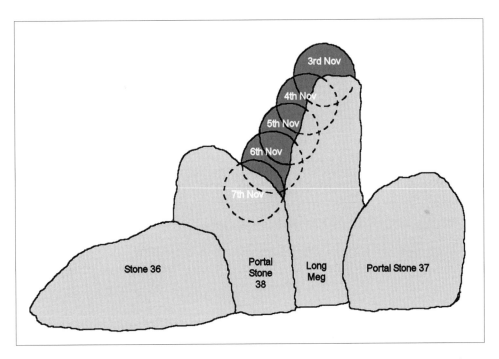

72 The position of the sunset in relation to Long Meg standing stone and the portal stones around Samhain. *After Hood 2004, 4 fig. 2*

Date	Stone Viewed From	Stone Observed	Iron Age Festival	Christian Festival
8 May	44	7	Beltane sunrise	Whitsun
8 May	13	52	Beltane sunset	Whitsun
21 June	42	2	Midsummer sunrise	Nativity of St John the Baptist
21 June	18	53	Midsummer sunset	Nativity of St John the Baptist
9 August	13	52	Lughnasadh sunset	Lammas Day
23 September	*48*	**10**	*Autumn Equinox sunrise*	Harvest
23 September	**10**	*48*	*Autumn Equinox sunset*	*Harvest*
6 November	51	17	Samhain sunrise	All Souls
6 November	9	38 & Long Meg	Samhain sunset	All Souls
21 December	52	20	Midwinter Solstice sunrise	Christmas
21 December	**2**	39-40	Midwinter Solstice sunset	Christmas
9 February	51	17	Imbolc sunrise	Candlemass
9 February			Imbolc sunset	Candlemass
23 March	*48*	**10**	*Vernal Equinox sunrise*	*Easter*
23 March	**10**	*48*	*Vernal Equinox sunset*	*Easter*

73 The relationship of quartz stones to solar events at Long Meg and her Daughters.
Bold = quartz stone

to slide down the top of portal stone 38 and into the quartz stone of Long Meg. Within the circle the stones seem to have been placed so as to mark out the positions of the sun throughout the lighter half of the year when observed standing outside the circle at the stone directly opposite. For example, the equinox sunrise is observed ascending over Melmerby Fell when standing at stone 48 looking toward quartz stone 10, and midsummer sunrise is observed standing at stone 42 looking at quartz stone 2 (*73*).

Quartz stone 2 is as involved in observations of the midwinter sunset at Long Meg. Standing at stone 2 the midwinter sun sets into Long Meg and portal stones 39 and 40.

Significantly this means that stone 2 is involved in the alignments of the two extreme solar points during the year. It is incorporated into the sunrise on the longest day when the sun is at its most northerly rising position and sunset of the longest night when the sun is at its most southerly setting position (Hood 2004).

Similar alignments have been noted elsewhere at Swinside and Castlerigg stone circles, suggesting that they are not merely coincidental. At Swinside Stone Circle the Beltane/ Lughnasadh sunrise is viewed from a position at stone 40 looking to stone 9. The Beltane/ Lughnasadh sunset occurs looking from the V-like join of stones 13 and 14 over to stone 44. The equinox sunrise alignment is to be seen from a position at stone 43 watching the sun rise out from the horizon above stone 12. The equinox sunset was seen from stone 12 across to stone 40.

In the case of Castlerigg the situation is somewhat different as it appears that it was the moon that was important. Some alignments involve the large northern portal stones. Figure 74 shows the circle as viewed from the north and has a diagrammatical representation of the track of the moon at its most southerly extreme along with the stones involved in these alignments. Standing at portal stone 50 and looking across to stone 24 we see an alignment with the extreme southerly rising position of the moon and when looking from portal stone 1 over to stone 31 we find alignment with the extreme southerly setting position, which occurs on that same day. The use of the large portal stones and small stones 24 and 31, which themselves are framed within the circle by larger stones on either side, exhibits an elegant symmetry within the structure and emphasises the various lunar alignments possible at these circles. Castlerigg is not just a stone circle; there is a rectangular stone box-like arrangement that projects into the circle (75). On the inward facing stone at the centre of the box, on the circle itself is a spiral motif. The stone is normally grey but at as the sun sets at the autumn equinox the stone has been observed to 'glow orange', illuminating the spiral. The spiral is clockwise, the outer curve running up against the natural strike lines of the rock. The configuration is the opposite of spirals at Long Meg and Little Meg. The stone to the left of the spiral (3) as you stand in the enclosure looking outwards, has a lozenge motif incised or pecked on it. Next to that, into the rectangle, a long stone (2) has what may be the beginnings of a circular or spiral motif. Opposite the rectangular setting of standing stones is the recumbent stone (5) which also has a lozenge-shaped motif, similar to the one on stone 3. Finally stone 4, near the entrance, has a small cup and incomplete ring. The discovery of the motifs emphasises the unique character of the rectangular enclosure attached to the inside of the circle.

The possible use of quartz stones is only seen using the suggested mode of viewing. The method of standing outside the circle and looking transversely from one stone to another may be relatively simple, but it would appear to work at the three great Cumbrian circles and, on another level, it could be said to maintain the sanctity of the circle, for whilst viewing an event, one stands at the edge looking across a sacred space.

At Long Meg, Swinside and Castlerigg there appears to be what might be termed an 'equinox stone' on the east side of each circle, that is a stone which is involved in both the sunrise and sunset alignments on this specific day. At Long Meg it is a red quartz stone, at Castlerigg it is a spiral-marked stone that glows red when the sun shines on it, surrounded by the unique 'box' feature, and at Swinside, the stone stands somewhat alone in the unusually

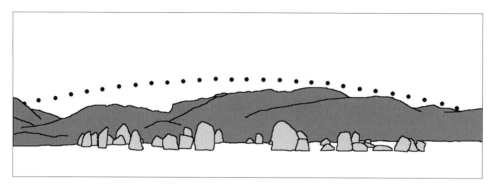

74 Castlerigg Stone Circle showing the most southerly moon positions. *After Hood 2004, 16 fig. 4*

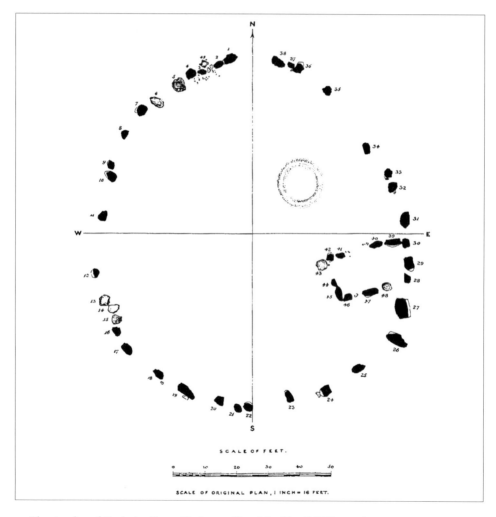

75 The site plan of Castlerigg Stone Circle near Keswick. *After C. W. Dymond 1877*

76 The standing stone of Long Meg
showing the different motifs carved
into the stone. These include concentric
circles, spirals and cup marks sometimes
linked by linear marks

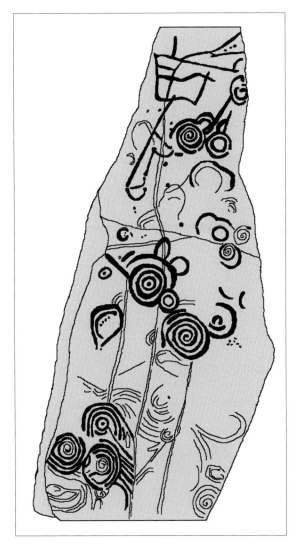

large gap on the eastern side of the circle. The use of stones of different colour and lithology
has been noted elsewhere, for example in the Irish Passage Graves (Bergh 1995; Cooney 2000,
135-8; Eogan 1986) and the Scottish Clava Cairns (Bradley 2000). In the case of the Clava
Cairns at different times of the year, particularly midwinter sunset and midsummer sunrise,
different zones of the monuments, constructed of different coloured stones, are highlighted.
This suggests a close relationship between stone colour and events of wider cosmological
significance (Bradley 2000, 126-8). The regular occurrence of these solar alignments could
suggest the possibility of a calendar with eight divisions of the year which would have been
in use throughout the Neolithic and Early Bronze Ages. The evidence from the circles suggests that Neolithic and Early Bronze Age people in Cumbria had observed specific solar
dates similar to Late Iron Age and Christian festivals, associated with, for example, the annual
harvest. The moon with its more extensive cycles may also have been important as research
at Castlerigg suggests.

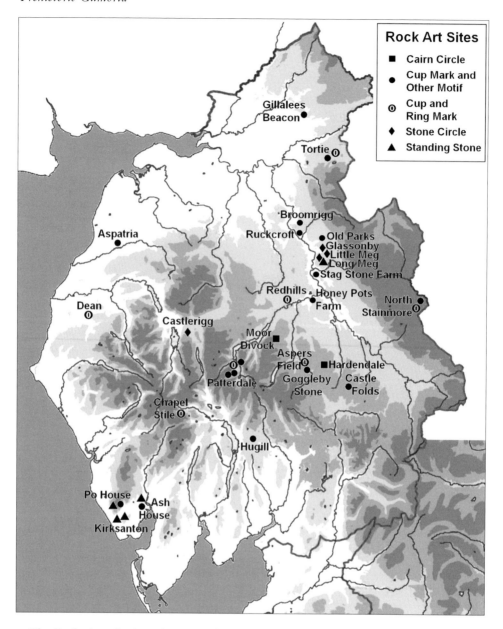

77 The distribution of rock art sites in Cumbria. *After Beckensall 2002, 15 fig. 8*

We have already noted how a large red sandstone block faced with quartz crystal was selected for the Long Meg stone, marking it out from the circle stones. This process was developed further by its elaborate embellishment with rock art motifs. The most obvious motif is the cup at the centre of three rings; however this is just one of many making its decoration highly elaborate (*76*). Amongst the Daughters of the stone circle there are other decorated stones: an anticlockwise spiral on stone 7, a spiral and a rectangular groove (possible shod foot sole) on stone 6, whilst stone 5 has some grooves marked on it.

78 The rock art motifs found at Chapel Stile, Langdale, include concentric circles, spirals, a chevron and linear grooves which are similar to those found at other sites in Cumbria. *After Beckensall 2002, 41 fig. 39*

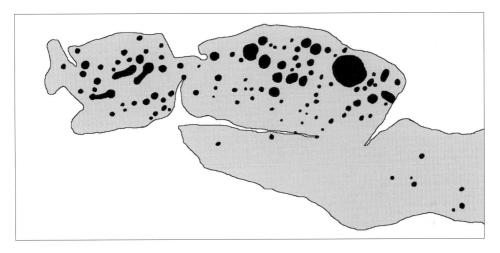

79 Rock art motifs at Patterdale Site 1. The motifs at this site are less diverse than those described elsewhere. They consist of a large number of cup marks, most of which occur singly, although three appear to have been connected or joined together. *After Beckensall 2002, 22 fig. 12*

Moving beyond the decoration of stone monuments into the surrounding landscape there is a suggestion of a similarly marked routeways through the Langdale and Patterdale valleys (*77*). At Chapel Stile is a marked rock located at a significant viewpoint in the valley above the floodplain (*78*). The motifs include a number of concentric rings, generally close together, with an unworked centre like the concentric rings on Little Meg, Maryport and Glassonby. There is also a chevron, like that on the Glassonby kerbstone, and a number of linear grooves, which sometimes utilise natural cracks in the rock. Not all the designs are complete, and the motifs may have been made at different times and over a period of time.

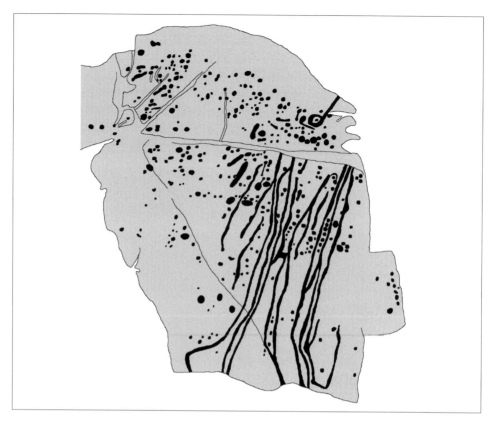

80 Rock art motifs at Patterdale Site 2. Most of the motifs are cup marks, as at Patterdale Site 1, one of which is associated with a ring mark. Site 2, however, also includes a number of linear grooves running down the face of the stone. *After Beckensall 2002, 25 fig. 17*

From Chapel Stile one looks north to the Langdale Pikes and prehistoric axe quarries, south the view is to the beginnings of Lake Windermere. The valley may have been a vital route for the export of stone axes and an access to the quarries themselves. The largest mass of decorated rock in the valley marks one of the natural routeways from Lake Windermere to the flaking floors high in the mountains, where the choice of such a difficult and precious mining area suggests that the rock being mined was not just attractive for use, but had a ritual significance.

The narrow, steep-sided Patterdale valley lies south of Lake Ullswater. North of Rooking in the eastern end of the valley, are three rock art sites. Each lies on a natural outcrop of rock located above the floodplain and at viewpoints commanding communication routes to the north and south. At site 1 the motifs are cups of varying sizes and depths, some joined, some ovals and some thin rectangles with rounded ends, repeating motifs found at Long Meg on the Daughter stones (*79*). Site 2 is a continuation of the rock outcrop of Site 1, but at a lower height. Some of the outcrop has been quarried away, and some is overgrown. What is left is 'almost unprecedented in Britain' (Beckensall 2002, 23). The motifs are simple cups, grooves and one angular ring around a cup. What is outstanding is the way the cracks in the fairly

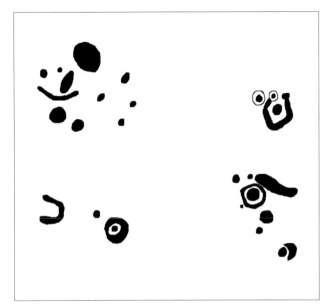

81 Rock art motifs at Patterdale Site 3(a). In common with the other Patterdale sites, 3a contains cup marks, but here they appear to cluster in a number of distinct groups. A number have been elaborated with the addition of rings, some of which are left open-ended. *After Beckensall 2002, 30 fig. 24*

smooth surface divide the rock from east to west into natural zones. The lesser cracks have been enlarged and new grooves pecked out. The main markings look as though they may have been influenced by the topography: the trails leading through the valley may have been echoed in the lines pecked out of the rock (*80*). Site 3 is a little different. It rests on the bend of a stream, where the land first falls away from a public path to the west, then rises gently again to form an outcrop where the art is found. The decorated outcrop lies at the edges of the mound and on top of it, and there is a suggestion that people made use of the natural shape to raise it into a mound that looks like an upturned boat or a long barrow. The motifs include cups, ovals, lines and thin rectangles with rounded corners, but there are also single rings around cups on a panel at the top of the mound. The outcrop stands just above the flood plain to the east, and may have been surrounded by marsh in the prehistoric period, creating in effect a small island (*81*).

Further along the Patterdale valley rock art was found at Beckstones also located at a site provided with good views up and down the valley confirming the theory that marked rocks indicate communication routes through the landscape. The prominent outcrop on the valley floor has been partly quarried away; it incorporates linear grooves and also cup marks, some of which reach the quarried edge indicating that there were more (*82*). There is a strong link between the locations chosen for panels of rock art and the most obvious path from the Kirkstone Pass through the narrow valley north to the lake, creating a link with the rich fishing and hunting grounds. The position of the marked rocks in this landscape differs from others in Britain in that they are almost on the floor of the valley, shut in by mountains.

The Langdale and Patterdale valley sites are similar, but different: both mark the easiest and most important routeways from the mountains through valley floors. Both are also associated with natural resources; in the case of Langdale the art makes a link to the stone quarries used for axe manufacture, and in the case of Patterdale the art is associated with sources of food

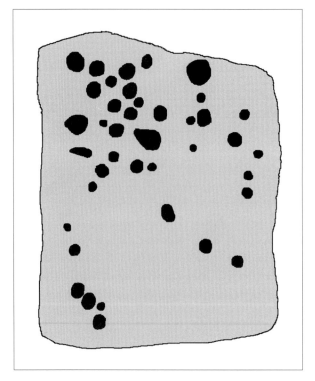

82 Rock art motifs at Beckstones
in the Patterdale valley. The motifs
here are cup marks, without
either rings or linear grooves. *After
Beckensall 2002, 32 fig. 26*

along the valley floors. The practice of decorating the landscape was therefore a means of
ordering the landscape and orientating the individual within it. By reading natural fissures
and cracks as ancestral lines of communication and responding to them with the production
of linear grooves people were situating themselves in a landscape they perceived as timeless.
In the context of the Kilmartin valley, Argyll, where similar panels of rock art are found,
Andrew Jones has argued persuasively that the production of images is a way of weaving a
sense of belonging and place, just as images are visually woven into the rock surface (Jones
2006). A similar process is at work in Cumbria where the motifs inscribed into the rock
surface are a way of visualising the relationship between people and place. The production of
images at locations commanding views of the landscape creates nodes which bind one place
to another.

Jones also suggests that by grounding images in the landscape a platform was created for
the use of images on standing stones and ceremonial monuments (Jones 2006). These monuments, as we saw in the case of Long Meg and her Daughters bring together carefully selected
stones, often brought considerable distances, and assembled in structured ways so as to give
the monument ritual meaning. The decoration of these sites offers a way of connecting the
natural landscape to the newly altered ritual landscape. The process of carving images on rock,
perhaps by successive generations of people, also created a way for people to comprehend
their own temporal existence and the capacity to alter the landscape through the production,
reconstruction and destruction of monuments as we saw at Oddendale. The production of
images at each stage of these events provided a way of tracing the history of events. Images

which perhaps began as panels of rock art, as a means of mapping the movement of the living in and around the landscape came, with the passing of time, to be a way of charting the movement of the sun and moon, and rituals associated with passing from life to death.

Discussion: Fire and Water, Life and Death

In order to interpret the valleyscape we need first to understand the significance of water to the monuments. The valleyscape is associated with the three interconnected rivers that run through it, the rivers Eden, Eamont and Lowther, and a series of monument complexes. Starting at the ruined stone circle and stone row of Grey Yauds, following the River Eden we encounter the now ruined complexes at Broomrigg, Old Parks, Glassonby, Long Meg and Little Meg. They take us first to the junction of the rivers Eden and Eamont, and then to the confluence of the Eamont and Lowther; 3.2km (2 miles) further downstream at Eamont Bridge are the triple henges of Mayburgh, King Arthur's Round Table and the Little Table. Following the Lowther south, it passes the standing stones of Clifton, the Long Barrow of Low Moor, the Moor Divock complex, the circles and enclosure of Knipe Moor and the nearby circles of Shapbeck Plantation, Wilson Scar and Gunnerkeld. Together these monuments constitute a significant ritual valleyscape that exists in a corridor between the western margins of the Pennines and the eastern margins of the Cumbrian fells. The connecting factor that links the monuments is water, which research elsewhere in Britain shows was closely tied to cosmological beliefs.

It is possible to speculate that the positioning of prehistoric monuments adjacent to springs and rivers had religious significance. An association between water and funerary monuments is seen elsewhere in Britain. On Salisbury Plain the River Avon connects Durrington Walls and Stonehenge with its avenue along which it has been postulated that the newly dead make their final journey to join their ancestors (Pitts 2000, 272-274). According to Parker Pearson and Ramillisonia (1998) Stonehenge was a ceremonial circle built for the exclusive use of the ancestors with ceremonies of the living focused around Durrington Walls. The Avon and the Stonehenge Avenue both physically and metaphorically link the domain of the living and that of the ancestors. One might speculate that the henge complex at Penrith comprising Mayburgh, King Arthur's Round Table and the Little Table all set in a riverine landscape may have functioned in a similar way. King Arthur's Round Table was excavated by Collingwood in 1937 and Bersu in 1939 (Collingwood 1939; Bersu 1940) when cremated bone was recovered from the interior of the monument.

An alternative interpretation of Stonehenge by Darvill (2007) focused on the mythical power of the stones to cure the ill and severely wounded, which links the henge on Salisbury Plain with the original source of the bluestones in the Preseli hills. Sites within the hills at Carn Meini are associated with 'enhanced spring heads', natural springs that have been elaborated with the construction of pools. For example at Ffynnon Beswch where rock art panels and round cairns are associated with the spring. Closer to Cumbria, in a study of Early Bronze Age barrows on the Lancashire moors of Extwistle and Worsthorne, it was found that of 12 barrows surveyed all were set on the west-facing Pennine slopes, half were grouped in pairs, invariably located adjacent to springs (Barrowclough 2005, 47 and fig. 2). I postulated that in Early Bronze Age ritual springs were metaphors for the birth of life. The human lifecycle is represented by the flowing water from springs into rivers and thence out to the Irish Sea. If this is indeed a metaphor for human life, then the horizon where the sky meets the sea, which can be seen from the Pennine peaks, below which the sun sets, represents death. In Cumbria a similar arrangement of monuments can be seen. For example, the Long Meg complex is similarly associated with a spring and lies close to a river which lies immediately below the complex to the west, whilst the alignments of Long Meg and the circle have a strong association with the setting sun. In his reinterpretation of Stonehenge Darvill (2007) interprets the central trilothon as a representation of the twin god and goddess of the sun and the moon. Known as Apollo and Artemis in the Greco-Roman pantheon, it was believed that each year Apollo left his home in Delphi, Greece, to spend three months of the year, around the winter solstice, in the land of the Hyperborians, what we now call the British Isles (Salt and Boutsikas 2005, 570). Apollo, who was god of healing and prophecy, may well be represented by the standing stone Long Meg, the association with the sun would explain the choice of red stone for the pillar and may give some insight into the activities that took place at the complex.

Cosmological considerations seem to have been central in deciding the location and orientation of monuments, which often combine solar and/or lunar alignments with a riverine setting. At Castlerigg Stone Circle the site is surrounded by mountains and valleys. At Long Meg all sunrises occur across the tops of the Pennine range, whilst the site is on a slope down toward the north-north-east, which can be seen to form an immediate skyline to the south-west as viewed across the circle. At Swinside Circle looking toward the south-east there are two distinct notches on the horizon from which the midwinter and the Imbolc/Samhain sunrises ascend. At Mayburgh Henge the position, between the rivers Lowther and the Eamont, gives a considerable view of the distant horizon, but once inside the structure the bank obscures the vast majority of the horizon from view with the rising and setting points of the equinox sun more or less framed. The connection between monuments and water is further strengthened in the case of Mayburgh Henge by the use of river cobbles to construct the large bank (*61*). The cobbles are a combination of the distinctive local pink and blue/grey stones and white quartz rock, and the visual impact of the colours would have been awe inspiring. Significantly, the same coloured stones were also selected for the construction of other monuments in Cumbria, for example the stone avenues at Shap, and the Long Meg and Oddendale circles. The use of this combination of coloured stones relates to the deliberate symbolic incorporation of the Neolithic worlds of the living and the dead through solar and lunar rituals that incorporate water. The use of different colours also provides an impression of contrast and depth (Jones and Bradley 1999, 114). This effect can be seen in the arrangement of structural stones in megalithic monuments (Jones 1999) or in the stone settings outside megalithic tombs, as at Newgrange and Knowth (Eogan 1986).

The combination of white, red and black coloured stone at Mayburgh and elsewhere is not limited to Cumbria. Both ethnographic and other archaeological studies have shown that white, red and black are used more frequently as basic ornamental colours than others. This has been interpreted as a reference to the significance of fire, whose colour spectrum encompasses these three colours, and to the production of meanings and metaphors that relate to fire cross-culturally. Previous studies of the British Neolithic (Darvill 2007) have focused on the preferential selection of white coloured stone, particularly quartz, which attracts attention not only because of its colour, but also because of its natural sparkle and luminescence. Quartz, and white stones generally, have been recognised in the construction of ceremonial and ritual monuments. The Thornborough henges in North Yorkshire, for example, were covered in gypsum, perhaps to imitate the great white southern henges such as Avebury or Knowlton (Thomas 1955, 436). Archaeologists have remarked on the impact that these white monuments would have had in the landscape when first built, but only recently have they begun to explore its wider symbolic implications (Lynch 1998).

The evidence is that white quartz became significant in the lives of people during the Early Neolithic when they selectively used it in the construction of monuments, and as part of the portable material culture associated with the actions and events enacted there. This tradition continued into the Late Neolithic when interest in quartz in all its manifestations, as outcrops, boulders and pebbles, intensified. The close physical association of quartz with water, and its place of origin in riverbeds and springs, suggests that there may be a symbolic link to the elemental force of water. Quartz is also widely found in the monuments of the Boyne valley in Ireland, such as Knowth and Newgrange, with their strong links to spiral decoration (Twohig 1981, 114), found in Cumbria at sites such as Long Meg. The moon is also regarded as significant in the operation of Late Neolithic and Early Bronze Age sites that used copious amounts of quartz. Burl speculates that the white pebbles within some stone circles, soulstones, symbolised the moon to which the spirits of the dead had gone (Burl 1981, 93).

This chapter has adopted a contextual approach focusing on landscape and association as a means to gain some insights into the meaning of Cumbria's prehistoric monuments. What has been revealed are patterns in things that can be observed at the sites in Cumbria that are repeated in sites elsewhere in Britain. From these, inferences may be drawn about the meanings and rules of the prehistoric complexes and their component sites, which suggest they were part of a scheme of ritual and belief.

CHAPTER 6

IN MEMORY OF THE ANCESTORS:
THE LATE NEOLITHIC AND EARLY BURIAL TRADITION

An area as small as Cumbria is liable to receive cultural influences from many directions. Because of the essential geographical unity of the Lake Counties, it might be thought that these influences would affect all parts of Cumbria equally. However, this unity somewhat contradictorily relies on the radial distribution of numerous valleys and hill-ranges whose characteristics are highly individual, so that impulses which are strongly felt in one quarter may hardly register in another. There is a tendency towards parochialism, as a result of which the distribution of datable archaeological material may vary strikingly. At no time are the variations more impressive than during the Bronze Age.

T.H. McK. Clough 1969, 28

Introduction

Nationally the Early Bronze Age was marked by technological and ritual innovation. Archaeologically this is seen in the adoption of copper-alloy (bronze) metalwork, the introduction of new pottery styles, first Beaker Ware and then Collared Urns (*83* and *84*) and the construction of new forms of earthworks. In Cumbria and the neighbouring areas, the innovations that are seen at a national level in the latter half of the third millennium BC are reflected in changes in both social and religious practices. Equally there is considerable evidence for a continuity of practice between the Late Neolithic and Bronze Ages. As was observed in the previous chapter, many sites occupied in the Bronze Age had also been occupied during the Neolithic. Stone utilised in the Late Neolithic continued to be exploited for the production of axe-hammers during the third millennium BC and there is a suggestion that the population retained a degree of mobility in their lifestyle.

The distinction between 'Late Neolithic' and 'Early Bronze' Ages is therefore somewhat artificial as others have pointed out (Burgess 1976a) and for this reason there will be an inevitable overlap between the two. During both the Neolithic and Eary Bronze Age locally available flint sources appear to have been exploited extensively, whilst better-

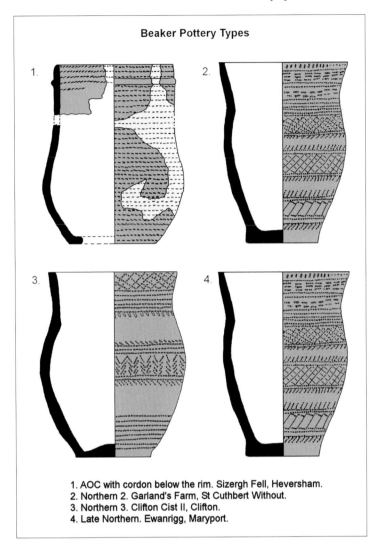

Beaker Pottery Types

1.

2.

3.

4.

1. AOC with cordon below the rim. Sizergh Fell, Heversham.
2. Northern 2. Garland's Farm, St Cuthbert Without.
3. Northern 3. Clifton Cist II, Clifton.
4. Late Northern. Ewanrigg, Maryport.

83 Different types of
Beaker pottery found
in Cumbria

quality flint material was sourced from areas outside Cumbria, in particular the areas around Flamborough and Bridlington in East Yorkshire (Cherry and Cherry 2007, 173-182), presumably arriving via east-west networks of trade and exchange. Although many of the widely accepted typological or chronologically diagnostic forms for the earlier Bronze Age are represented, such as the barbed-and-tanged arrowhead (*colour plate 22*), assemblages are often characterised by informal or multi-use forms which suggest the expedient use of available raw materials where these were easily available (*85*).

Many of the Late Neolithic and Early Bronze Age burial monuments were excavated in the nineteenth and early twentieth centuries, and an absence of recent analysis and radiocarbon dating means there is sometimes difficulty understanding the fine-grained chronology of these sites. To an extent this difficulty is offset by more recent excavations which provide a chronological framework for the whole region. The transition from Neolithic to Bronze

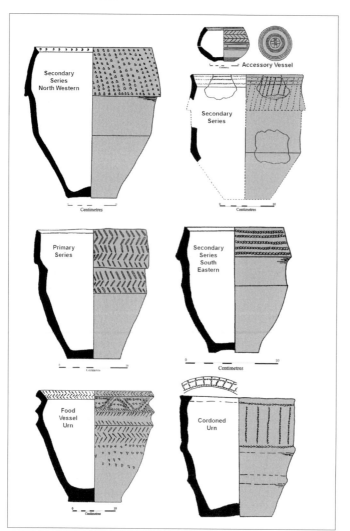

84 Different types
of Early Bronze Age
pottery. Collared Urns
are often associated with
Accessory Vessels, smaller
'miniature' vessels (top
right). Top and middle
rows: Collared Urns of
different types. Bottom
row: Food Vessel Urn and
Cordoned Urn

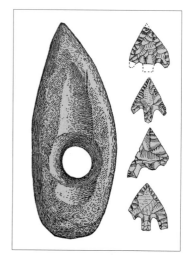

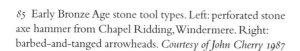

85 Early Bronze Age stone tool types. Left: perforated stone
axe hammer from Chapel Ridding, Windermere. Right:
barbed-and-tanged arrowheads. *Courtesy of John Cherry 1987*

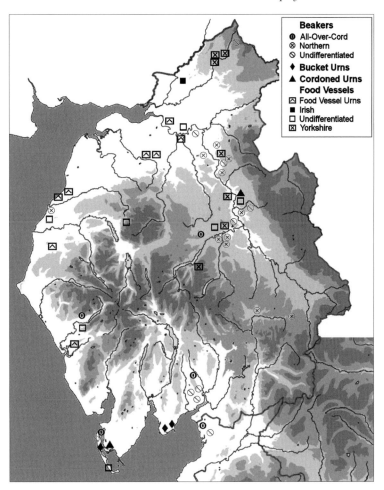

86 Distribution
of Beaker Ware in
Cumbria

Age is marked in southern England by the Beaker Period but in Cumbria, as elsewhere in
north-west England, Beaker burials are rare (*86*). North of Lancaster and in Cumbria the
pottery becomes slightly more common than in Cheshire and Merseyside, with a handful
of burials accompanied by Beakers recorded (Taylor 1881; Turnbull and Walsh 1996). Beaker
sherds have been found in a variety of different contexts, sometimes implying ritual cura-
tion of vessels, as in the case of deposits in 'natural' places. Examples include Beaker sherds
deposited in a limestone fissure with a polished stone axe placed in a gryke close by, both in
the vicinity of the Sizergh funerary cairn (McKenny Hughes 1904; Edmonds *et al* 2002; Evans
and Edmonds 2003). In place of the widespread adoption of Beaker style burials, in Cumbria
circular structures of wood and stone incorporating burials and later sealed by funerary or
ring cairns appear to have been the common monumental form during the Late Neolithic
and Early Bronze Age, as we saw in the previous chapter. Excavations have demonstrated the
variety, complexity and longevity of these sites, and perhaps a long-term commitment to particular sites, by the communities who built and maintained them (Turnbull and Walsh 1997).
Continuity rather than innovation is once again a characteristic of prehistoric Cumbria.

The Early Bronze Age Settlement

On the North Cumbrian Plain and Solway Firth the Early Bronze Age was marked by an increase in woodland clearance to make way for cereal cultivation. Evidence from several sites where pollen cores have been taken shows that inroads were made into woodland, for example at Bowness Common and at Abbot, Scaleby and Oulton Mosses where the activity was dated to *c*.2000 cal BC and 1500 cal BC (*c*.3700-3200 BP) with cereal cultivation becoming increasingly important. Despite the evidence for significant increase in clearance activity and for cereal cultivation in the pollen record, archaeological evidence for human occupation is scarce. For the most part the archaeological remains consist of scattered finds of stone axe-hammers; three have been recovered from near Mawbray and another three are known from Bowness-on-Solway, whilst single examples have been found south-west of Cockermouth (Jackson 1906) and near Silloth (anon 1917) (*87*). A stone axe-hammer from Solway Moss, which was found during peat-cutting, may suggest that stone implements were deposited in wetlands as part of ritual observance. Other finds hinting at contact with the world beyond Cumbria include a broken fragment of a jet bead found at Brownelson (Caruana 1989). The general absence of finds may be a reflection of the lack of systematic survey over most of the plain, however it cannot be the whole answer as intensive survey by the North West Wetlands Survey on the Abbeytown Ridge suggests that settlement sites are either not represented by large scatters of flint, or are located lower in the landscape. The survey discovered ten separate sites scattered

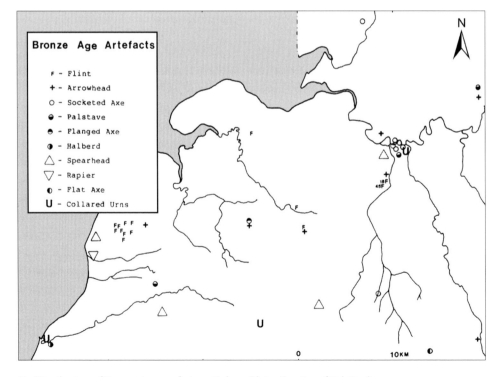

87 Distribution of Bronze Age artefacts on Solway Plain. *Courtesy of Bob Bewley, 1994*

along the ridge. Of particular note was a flake knife from south of Tarns Dub, and another approximately 1km to the north-east, in addition to a thumbnail scraper amongst the largely earlier assemblage from Lowsay Farm (Hodgkinson *et al* 2000, 113).

A 'palisade' found during peat cutting on Bowness Common in 1903 would potentially provide evidence for occupation during the Early Bronze Age, assuming that it was contemporary, but is difficult to interpret from the sketchy excavation report (Hodgson 1904). It comprised a single row of roundwood stakes of various spieces, including oak, birch, hazel, and possibly alder. Each was *c.*50mm in diameter and *c.*1m long with one third of the length driven into the sand beneath the peat, overlain by *c.*0.6m of peat at the level created by peat cutting. Most of the stakes had been sharpened to a point with 'a heavy tool having a clean cutting edge' (Hodgson 1904, 211), and then secured in place with stones. In the area seen by Hodgson only a single line of stakes was visible, although several such structures, most with double lines of posts, were known from other parts of the moss. The description favours interpretation as a fence or palisade similar to those known from the site of Fengate, near Peterborough (Pryor 1982). The fence would have acted to divide the moss edge into discrete parcels suggesting a formal organisation of the landscape. The closest parallel may lie at the site of Bonds Farm on Pilling Moss in Lancashire where a similar arrangement of light posts was discovered (Barrowclough 2008, 102 figs 49 and 50; Edwards 2007, 211–236).

A number of other potential settlement sites have been identified from aerial photographs, however without test excavations it is notoriously difficult to confirm, let alone date them. It is against this background that the work of Robert Bewley should be judged as having been particularly important. Bewley analysed the morphology of sites first identified from aerial photographs with a view to understanding the settlement pattern of the Solway Plain (Bewley 1994, 65). Bewley's analysis was based on a study of the soils on the plain, which he grouped according to their workability (Bewley 1994, 75, fig. 5.1). He identified a number of sites to serve as case studies, for each of which he looked at the soils within a 10km radius to understand how these would have serviced the settlement. One of these, Hill Farm, was a Neolithic site located at 20m OD above the floodplain (Chapter 4, 35). Within 1km of the settlement there is only grazing potential, but beyond this is arable potential within the 5km zone. Outside this, within the 10km zone, the sea and estuary probably played an important part in the economy. The Solway Firth provided salmon and sea trout whilst the mosses provided good hunting for wildfowl and deer.

Similar patterns were found for other Neolithic sites at Mawbray and Beckfoot (Bewley 1994, 73), although they are situated on the arable soils and nearer the coast (Chapter 4). He proposed that the proximity of the sea and the fens was an important factor in the early settlement of the plain as they provided for year-round subsistence needs. In the Neolithic he suggested there would have been a 'very mixed' economy which combined arable crops with gathering of wild foods, with fishing, hunting and increasingly herding. As the pollen record shows, lightly wooded areas around the mosses would have been the first to be cleared to create agricultural plots.

Based on his study of the Brownelson site Bewley proposed a continuity of settlement from the Neolithic into the Early Bronze Age (Bewley 1994, 73). The site of Brownelson lies south of Carlisle and is situated on a bend in the River Caldew on a thin strip of arable

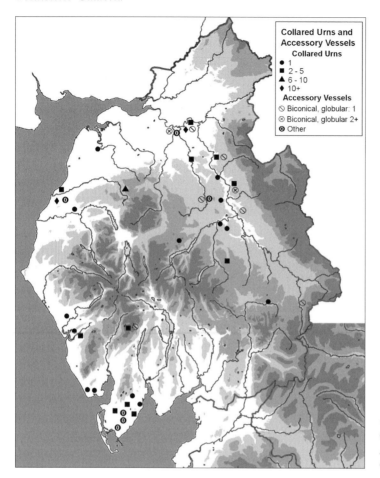

88 Distribution of
Collared Urns and
Accessory Vessels in
Cumbria

potential soil surrounded by grazing land. Bewley first identified it as a crop-mark on an aerial photograph, he then followed this up by fieldwalking the area, which led him to discover a number of flint artefacts spanning the Neolithic to Early Bronze Age periods. Turning our focus to the Early Bronze Age, Bewley inferred from the distribution of burial sites that occupation continued to favour the lighter soils with sites along the southern edge of the Abbeytown ridge. His analysis of the site of Plasketlands, identified from aerial photographs and fieldwalking, usefully illustrates the Early Bronze Age exploitation strategy of the area (Bewley 1993) (Chapter 4, *35*). Within a radius of 5km around Plasketlands there is a combination of arable, grazing, peat, alluvium and marine resources. This suggests a mixed economy compatible with the fieldwalking finds from the site which included a flint scraper and net sinker (Bewley 1994, 73). Overall the evidence points to a pattern of agriculture that had developed by the Bronze Age, from shifting agriculture to more permanent agricultural settlements (Bewley 1994, 72-3). This way of life, with an agricultural economy largely based on animal husbandry, but with small-scale cereal cultivation supplemented by marine and wildfowl resources, seems to have continued in much the same way at least until the arrival of the Romans (Bewley 1994, 77).

89 Engraving of Collared Urns found at
Garlands, Carlisle, 1861

For the Early Bronze Age the best
evidence of human occupation comes
not from settlement but from the burial
sites and their associated Collared
Urn assemblages (*88*). A number of
sites are known from early publications, including the sites of Garlands
Hospital in Carlisle, Aughertree Fell
and Aglionby. Unfortunately, accounts of the discovery and 'excavation' of these sites are poor.
At Garlands Hospital at least 15 urns were found, although there is no excavation report and
our best record comes from a near contemporary drawing of the urns (*89*). The records of
the Aughertree Fell finds are little better and the urns 'lost'. All that we can safely say is that
they were found by: 'Mr Robinson … arranged in a circle around the centre of the tumulus'
(Ferguson 1883, 191), that they 'proved that the Aughertree Fell circles … be prehistoric, for
in a tumulus near he has found no less than twelve urns of the usual British type, which as yet
are not dry enough to be fully examined' (Ferguson 1883, 190).

We know that at Aglionby there were five urns but there is also confusion about the nature
of the site. The description asserts that the urns were covered in sand and that 'there were no
vestiges of a tumulus', however it does not necessarily follow that this was a flat cemetery as
Hodgson suggested (Hodgson 1956, 15). Bewley suggests that there may have been a tumulus constructed from sand which was subsequently flattened as at Aldoth, discussed below
(Bewley 1994, 61). These examples point out the limitations of working with sites and artefacts studied before the advent of modern scientific archaeology.

What was needed in order to develop a deeper understanding of the Early Bronze Age of
the plain was a contemporary excavation undertaken under modern scientific conditions.
Bewley once again made an important contribution using the same approach as he had for
identifying settlements; starting with aerial photographs he suggested that 21 circular crop-
marks could be interpreted as barrows. They are mostly located on the Abbeytown ridge and
only one of them had been excavated under controlled conditions – by Prof. Barri Jones of
the University of Manchester. That site at Aldoth was shown to be a ring ditch with a cremation inside an inverted urn found in the centre of the ring, but unfortunately was neither
independently dated nor fully published, following the untimely death of the excavator. The
best evidence therefore comes from the site of Ewanrigg, located south-west of the Solway
Plain near Maryport, identified by Bewley whilst fieldwalking (Bewley 1992, 325-354; 1994,
61-2). In the adjacent field was a large double-ditched enclosure marking the location of settlement, which first prompted him to investigate the general area; both are sited on a sandy
promontory surrounded by marsh and only 1km from the sea (Bewley 1994, 62). Excavation
of the site identified it as a natural mound crowned by a primary cist burial surrounded by
a series of secondary cremation pits, many of which contained Collared Urns (*90*). Study
of the cremations enabled an analysis of the age/sex of the individuals, whilst radiocarbon

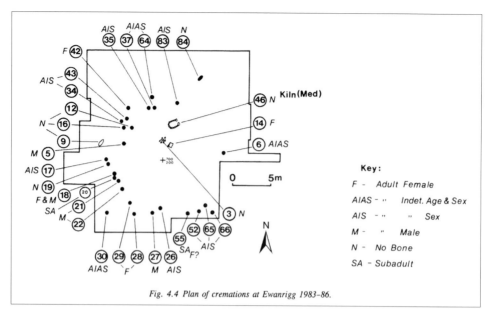

Fig. 4.4 Plan of cremations at Ewanrigg 1983–86.

90 Site plan showing the location of cremation burials at Ewanrigg. *Courtesy of Bob Bewley, 1994*

analysis gave a date range from 2470 cal BC to 1520 cal BC for the site (Bewley 1992; Bewley *et al* 1992) reinforcing the pattern of ritual continuity for areas in the landscape discussed in Chapter 5.

Continuity between the Neolithic and Bronze Ages is also observed on the West Cumbrian Coastal Plain. Although many of the monuments are now lost, using records it is possible to reconstruct the original distribution of occupation represented by stone circles and monuments, which often span the Neolithic to Bronze Age transition. Individual monuments are known from: Gretigate near Gosforth, from Greycroft west of Egremont, and near to Sellafield, whilst small groups of sites are clustered around Kirksanton and Lacra. The chronology of these monuments may be inferred from the excavated circle at Greycroft which, typologically, belongs to the period *c*.2670–1975 cal BC, although phases of activity are present, suggesting that the monument was in use for several centuries. Excavations revealed a fragment of polished axe within the packing of one of the stones, linking the monument with axe production and exchange during an early phase of use (Fletcher 1957). Later phases of activity were marked by the construction of a cairn containing a cremation burial associated with Bronze Age artefacts (Waterhouse 1985, 64). Similar longevity was also noted at Lacra, where Circle A surrounded an Early Bronze Age cremation burial, and at Circle D a Collared Urn also indicates Bronze Age use of a Neolithic monument.

Evidence of settlement on the coast is more ephemeral. Amongst the sand dunes at Drigg a horizontal timber, 4m in length, and associated vertical peg *c*.0.05m in diameter, was interpreted as the 'ground framework of a rectangular, possibly square, structure built on the peaty surface' (Powell and Corcoran in Cherry 1982). Within the organic deposit was a hearth, dated to 2456–2039 cal BC (3780±55 BP, UB-905; Cherry 1982, 5). Generally the evidence for occupation, in the form of lithic material recovered by fieldwalking, suggests that much of the lowland was settled. Significant sites have been identified south of Beckermet (Cherry and Cherry 1984, 7). At Eskmeals Bronze Age flint-knapping sites were discovered on raised gravel beaches (Fair 1936, 1937; Spence 1937) and similar material has been found at Walkhole Bank, where the dunes appeared to have been a focus of activity (Cherry 1963; 1965). These assemblages are all characterised by the poor quality of the raw materials which, with the exception of Beckermet, are derived from beach flint. In spite of the poor raw material more finely worked artefacts also occur, notably barbed-and-tanged arrowheads which are spread throughout the area, particularly on the coastal sites: examples have been found amongst the dunes at Drigg, at Ehenside Tarn (Fell 1967, 230) and two from Williamson's Moss (Cherry 1969). In the latter case, and at Monks Moors, hearths were also found dated to 2480-1890 cal BC (3755±105 BP, BM-1396) in the case of Willimason's Moss (Bonsall *et al* 1994, 99) and 2883 -2403 cal BC (4050±55 BP, BM-1385) in the case of Monk Moors. Remnants of a lowland burial tradition have been observed at Ravenglass and Herding Nab, Seascale, comprising a 'clay burial urn with small bones' (Fair 1943, 50). Isolated metal and stone finds are rare on the coastal plain, just a 'copper battle axe' from Rainors or Bolton Wood and a stop-flanged axe from Town End, Santon Bridge (Fair 1943, 52), and five stone axe-hammers, including examples from Ehenside, Winscales, and Silecroft (Cross 1950).

Occupation of the west Cumbrian coast was therefore continuous during the transition from the Neolithic to the Bronze Age. During the Neolithic the uplands were used extensively for seasonal grazing, however the evidence from pollen cores taken from Ehenside (Walker 1966), Barfield Tarn (Pennington 1970) and Drigg (Pennington 1965) is that in the Early to Middle Bronze Age *c.*2000-1500 cal BC (*c.*3700-3200 cal BP) the clearance of woodland increased dramatically, reflecting the increasing importance of arable farming in the agricultural economy of the coastal strip. This expansion forced people to build more permanent settlements further inland and up-slope. Beaker sherds from Mecklin Park, Santon Bridge (Clough 1968, 2; Annable 1987, 601), may suggest that the limit of settlement, denoted by burials, was already moving upward by the late third millennium cal BC.

Further south around the northern shore of Morecambe Bay the evidence from pollen cores at Foulshaw Moss represents a local clearance episode during the Late Neolithic, *c.*2570-2140 cal BC (3870±70 BP, CAR-544; Dresser 1985). This probably reflects a genuinely low level of human activity in the hinterland of Morecambe Bay, as other studies from around its fringes show (Oldfield and Statham 1963; Wells *et al* 1997), a situation which is in marked contrast to the West Cumbrian Coastal Plain which saw intense clearance during the Neolithic. The Early Bronze Age evidence from the Lyth valley (Wimble 1986; Wells 1991) also points towards a picture suggestive of low intensity, but widespread human activity around Morecambe Bay, in contrast to that seen in the West Cumbrian Coastal Plain, where activity in the Bronze Age was extensive.

The first significant clearance episodes in south Cumbria coincide with a marked increase in the frequency and variety of archaeological material from the north Morecambe Bay area. These include a pair of barbed-and-tanged arrowheads found in Underbarrow and a single barbed-and-tanged arrowhead from Gilpin Bridge (Anon 1903). Several others have been found on Walney Island (Annable 1987, 488). Generally there are few Early Bronze Age metal artefacts: a flat axe from Gleaston Castle (McK. Clough 1969, 29), an Early Bronze Age flanged axe of late Migdale tradition (*c.*1650-1350 BC; 3400-3100 BP) from Roose (Gaythorpe 1897, 446; Fell 1940, 121; McK. Clough 1969, 2), and an awl from a potential cremation burial at Appleby Hill, Birkrigg (Gelderd *et al* 1914, 468). One of the more unusual finds which, unfortunately, lacks context, is a Grooved Ware bowl of Late Neolithic date from Walney Island (Barnes 1956). This may have been associated with finds of Food Vessels and Beakers from the same area. Taken together there is significant evidence for settlement on Walney Island, as Walney North End I excavation of a sand hill midden revealed a flat rim ware vessel sitting on a cobble stone and containing periwinkles, mussels, cockles, limpets and oysters. Finds from North End VII consisted of a clay hearth surrounded by midden deposits which included the remains of a flat rim ware bucket-shaped vessel in which shellfish had been boiled, a flat perforated disc had acted as a lid for the cooking pot. Implements of bone and antler were also found, as was a sharpening stone streaked with red raddle on one side. Taken together the evidence points to domestic activity which gives insight into daily life during the Early Bronze Age (Barnes 1970a).

There are two concentrations of Beaker burials to the east of Morecambe Bay, at Sizergh and Levens Park (Turnbull and Walsh 1996). At Sizergh five inhumations were excavated from a cist and fragments of All Over Corded Beaker Ware were found nearby (McKenny Hughes 1904a, 1904b; Fell 1953, 1-5). The excavation of a funerary cairn at Levens Park (Sturdy 1976) revealed a large circle of boulders surrounding a central Beaker inhumation with Beaker pottery and a pair of flint knives (Turnbull and Walsh 1996). Two further inhumations and a covering barrow were added later. To the north at Allithwaite an Early Bronze Age crema-tion cemetery associated with the slightly later Collared Urn tradition was excavated west of Levens producing dates of *c.*2023-1747 cal BC (3545 ±50 BP; Wild 2003). The excavation, undertaken by Oxford Archaeology North, revealed that a minimum of 12 individuals had been buried there, some in urns and some not. An interesting feature of the site is that the burials had been inserted into small solution holes and in linear fissures, grykes, in the natural limestone bedrock.

In many areas of Cumbria, and extending into north Lancashire, there is strong evidence for the deposition of artefacts and burials in natural features over the course of the Late Neolithic and Bronze Ages. Deposits in 'natural' places include Beaker sherds deposited in a limestone fissure and a polished stone axe placed in a gryke close by, both in the vicinity of the Sizergh funerary cairn (McKenny Hughes 1904; Edmonds *et al* 2002; Evans and Edmonds 2003). This association suggests the articulation of a depositional practice whose origins lay in the Neolithic and which may have been further developed at the site of Allithwaite.

The distribution of perforated stone axe-hammers also resembles Early Neolithic distri-butions of polished stone axes. Comparatively little is known about axe-hammers, which seem too heavy and blunt to have been used as axes whilst the suggestion that they were agricultural implements used for ploughing remains unproven (*91*). Petrological studies show that the majority were made of stone of Group XV, which originates in the southern Lake District, possibly around Coniston and which was suitable for manufacture by pecking (Fell and Davis 1988, table 29). They appear to have a chronology that lasts throughout the Early Bronze Age, tailing off by *c.*1300 BC.

91 Perforated stone axe-hammer

Perforated axe-hammers are found in Furness, Cartmel and along the northern coast of Morecambe Bay but are rare elsewhere in Cumbria (Collingwood 1933, 181). The *c.*85 known examples are confined to low, often wet, ground and the valleys leading up from them, such as that from Egton with Newland, on land adjacent to Newland Moss; a further example has been found in peaty ground at Colton, at the head of Rusland Pool. At Stakes Moss a perforated whetstone was found below '5 feet' (1.5m) of peat and an axe-hammer is also recorded from Low Park Wood on the limestone of Sizergh (North 1934). Further north, in the Lyth valley, a perforated stone implement, possibly a mace head, was discovered near Whitebeck, whilst perforated stone implements have been recovered from the immediate moss fringes at Lindale. Concentrations of stone hammers have been recorded at Winder Moor, near Flookburgh, fragments of a stone adze from Grange (North 1934), and 'many hammers as well as Celts of brass, copper, and stone found in the Cartmel District particularly at Nab Green' (Stockdale 1872, 250). Whether such finds represent deliberate deposition or the first marginal wetland settlement is difficult to establish with certainty from the small number of isolated artefacts.

The distribution resembles that of polished stone axes; the difference is that axes tend to be more coastal than the hammers whose distribution includes the valleys that run up from the coast in to the interior. Collingwood interpreted this as evidence for the expansion of the population inland, extending the area of cultivation in response to population growth (Collingwood 1933, 181). The very number of these implements from Furness may suggest a real concentration of activity in the area, although the precise nature of this activity is difficult to determine. The distribution of perforated axe hammers continues around the coastal area from the Lancaster and the Lune, south to Pilling Moss in Lancashire.

The pattern of distribution points toward occupation around the shores of Morecambe Bay. Lithic finds suggest a large group of quite small sites, consisting often of only one or two pieces (Middleton *et al* 1995). This thin distribution of largely single finds is also found further south in the central Fylde and inland Merseyside, and may suggest that non-intensive or temporary occupation on a repeated or seasonal basis was the norm. The bay and its adjacent wetlands would have provided opportunities for the collection of shellfish, bird's eggs and the hunting of wildfowl, whilst the light soils of the coast would have been more easily ploughed than those further inland. Rather than a barrier the bay may have acted as a communication route connecting the people who lived around it. These people may have shared not only technology but also perhaps a common identity focused around the shared concerns and preoccupations of coastal communities.

Burial Traditions

Both inhumation and cremation were practised in Cumbria during the Bronze Age, though the latter was far more numerous: only 51 inhumations have been definitely recorded compared to 268 cremations. We have already encountered some of the different types of monuments and natural features that were deemed appropriate places for burials, including stone circles, cairns and barrows, and also natural features such as limestone grykes. The full extent of the variety of places chosen for burials is demonstrated by figure 92, which demonstrates that although circular monuments of various types were favoured there were also linear cemeteries and burials associated with standing stones. The image suggested by the term flat cemetery can be misleading as although these site were not covered by mounds in several cases they were constructed on natural knolls and eskers and thus had the appearance of barrows. At Urswick, for example, a flat grave containing a Secondary Series Collared Urn with cremation accompanied by a bronze razor-knife was constructed on a sand knoll, whilst at How Hill, Thursby a Food Vessel urn containing a cremation was found in a pit dug into the sand of an esker. A rarer form is the linear cemetery where burials are arranged in a line rather than in the more common circle. Two examples are known, both from southern Cumbria, at Ireleth Mill, Dalton and Aynsome Lane, Cartmel. To these should properly be added the linear cemetery at Lancaster, which although outside the county is in the same general area. The site at Ireleth Mill is typical: eight urns with cremations were buried in a straight line, arranged on a north-east to south-west axis about a metre apart.

Type	Number
Stone circle	9
Ring cairn	4
Kerbed cairn	3
Cairn	26
Round barrow	14
Tumulus	2
Flat cemetery	12
Linear cemetery	2
Standing stone	1
Limestone gryke	2
Natural mound	1
Sandpit	2

92 Monuments and natural features selected for burials. N = 78

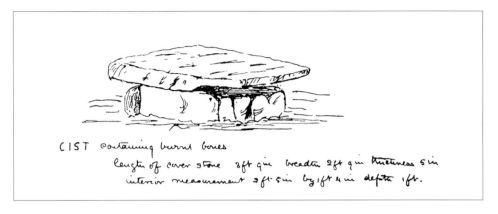

93 Sketch of the cairn at Bleaberry Haws, Torver, showing the cist. *Swainson Cowper 1888*

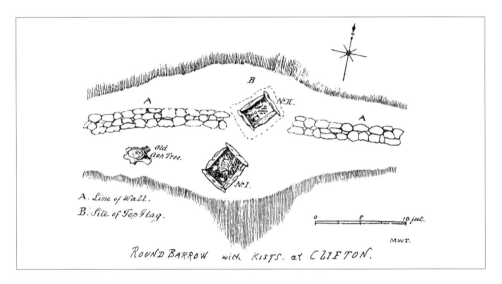

94 Sketch plan of the round barrow at Clifton showing two cists containing inhumations, 1881

Inhumation burials in barrows and cairns occur on the natural surface, as at Oddendale, or in a pit, and in the latter case they may be in a cist, roughly enclosed by stones, or laid on a pavement. Inhumations were found in cists at several sites (*93*). At Moor Divock, Askham, a crouched inhumation laying on an east-west axis was buried in a cist and covered with a capstone. At Brackenhill Tower, Arthuret, a short double cist contained two inhumations, whilst a second cist contained sherds of possible Collared Urn together with the jaw of a young woman and a younger skeleton.

The simplest form of grave pit is commonly associated with Beaker burials, illustrated by Beaker inhumations in the Peak District (Lewis 1970, 52). Beaker burials are generally poorly recorded in north-west England, but we are fortunate to have several examples in Cumbria, at Moorhouse Farm, Brougham, a cist contained the burial of a young man

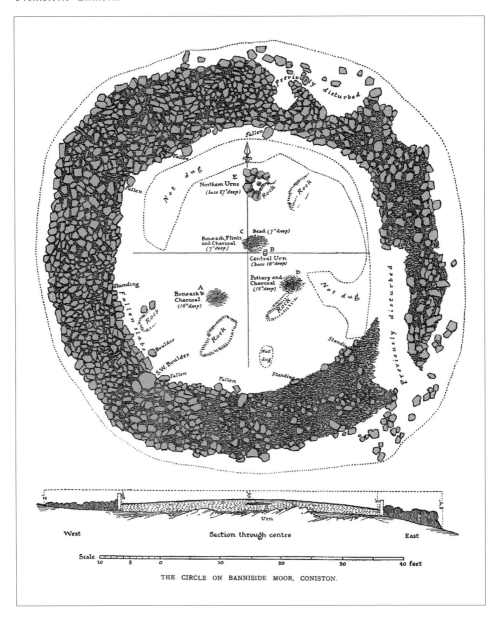

95 Site plan of the stone cairn on Banniside Moor, Coniston, showing the location of urns, cremated material and artefacts

accompanied with a Beaker of Northern Type 3 and a Food Vessel. At Leafy Hill I, Castle Carrock, a cist inserted into a natural rise contained an adult male of mid to old age, crouched on his left hand side on a north-east axis. One arm was extended, the other was placed over the chest and a Beaker of Northern Type 3 was placed behind the head. The barrow at Clifton contained two cists: buried in the first were two crouched inhumations, that of a woman aged 20-30 years, 5ft 2in (c.1.5m) tall, lying on her right side, with head to the south and a Beaker of Northern/North Rhine type by her knees and a bone pin (*94*). In the second cist was the crouched inhumation of a small man with two beakers, a Northern Type 3 and Northern Type 2/North Rhine, at each side of his legs. The barrow at Shield Knowe, Bewcastle contained a primary inhumation in a cist with two Food Vessels of Yorkshire Vase type, whilst a secondary cist contained an inhumation and a single, inverted, Food Vessel of Yorkshire vase type. Both cists were filled with sand. A more unusual arrangement was found at Levens Park, Heversham, where a wooden plank-lined grave was found within a ring cairn below a low mound. The grave contained three beakers and two flint knives.

Cremation burials, too, may be in a pit, cist, below a pavement, or roughly enclosed by a stone cist. A Secondary Series North-Western Style Collared Urn containing a female cremation was buried in a hole beside an outcrop of rock near the centre of the ring cairn at Banniside Moor, Coniston (*95*). Other urns and cremations were placed in cists (*96*). At Moorhouses, Penrith, a Collared Urn was found upright and full of cremated bone in a small cist covered with a capstone, a similar rite had been applied to burials at Yealand Conyers in the vicinity of Warton Crag, North Lancashire. At other sites the cremation was placed directly into the cist without an urn, as at Penhurrock Circle.

Thus a mixture of grave traditions obtains, and when these are considered together with the nature of the actual burial structures and the pottery, many survivals from the Neolithic can be discerned. It may be suggested that this is entirely in keeping with the other aspects of continuity seen in Cumbria and more widely in north-west England (Barrowclough 2008). A further example of which are multiple burials within a monument, which are common. At Ewanrigg, in the north of Cumbria, 28 burials were discovered. Two were inhumations, one of which was a Beaker burial and the other a cist burial with Food Vessel, and 26 were cremations buried together with a number of Collared Urns, mainly Secondary Series, and worked bone artefacts. Of the 26 cremations it was possible to identify six female and five male burials. Radiocarbon dates give a range for the Collared Urns of 2460-1520 BC (Bewley *et al* 1992). Also in the north of the county at what was Garlands Hospital, St Cuthbert Without, a flat cemetery was disturbed to reveal at least 21 urns and six accessory vessels; of those identified four were Primary Series Collared Urns and 13 Secondary Series. At Old Parks, Kirkoswald, a stone cist contained the remains of an inhumation while two further disturbed cists may each have contained a further inhumation. To the west of the cists were 32 cremations in pits; mostly unurned, they were placed around the circumference of the cairn. Pottery included a Cordoned Urn, a Collared Urn and two accessory vessels, one of which contained 12 jet beads. A round barrow at Aughertree Fell, Ireby, contained 12 Collared Urns, mostly Secondary Series, ranged in a circle round the centre of the barrow. Further south at Allithwaite a minimum of 12 individuals were excavated, the most striking feature of which was the unusually high occurrence of double burials, where two individuals are buried together. What is noteworthy is that seven of the eight double burials consist of an adult and immature individual, a pattern that is repeated elsewhere in both inhumation and cremation contexts (*97*). Inhumation burials at Arthuret II and Urswick consisted of a woman and child, and cremations at Homrook and Seal Howe consisted of adult and child. The case of Sunbrick II is particularly interesting as it

Type	Cremations in Cist
Collared Urn, upright	1
Urn, upright	2
Urn, inverted	0
Collared Urn	1
Urn	5
Unurned	7
TOTAL	16

96 Analysis of cremations in cists showing relationships between burials and urns

combines an adult female and male, with a child aged four years and a newborn infant. In contrast there are only three recorded instances where an adult was buried with another adult in the absence of a child.

The association between adult and child burials may be informative. Lucy (1994; 1997) cautions that children were buried by adults, so we never experience the world of children, only the experiences of adults coming to terms with, and ascribing meaning to, their brief lives and premature deaths. Although she was writing in the context of early medieval cemeteries the point is relevant to the prehistoric period. What we see in the archaeological record is to some extent an idealised version of adult–child relationships.

For the majority of children, burial on their own was inappropriate and in 20 cases they were buried with adults. A simple explanation, that the children had died in childbirth, can be ruled out as there are only four cases where the child was a foetus or neonate, and in one of those the foetus was buried with a male adult, and in two others the neonate was buried with an older child and a female adult. In 16 cases young children in the age range 3-12 years were buried with adults, both female and male. The most likely explanation is that the children died of childhood diseases, but it is more difficult to understand their relationship with the accompanying adult. If the child were being buried with a parent it would suggest that a considerable period of time might have elapsed between the death of the child and the death of a parent. During this time the child, who presumably had been already cremated, must have been stored above ground awaiting the death of the parent. An alternative explanation is that the adult with whom they are buried is not always a parent, but is another member of their social group who may, or may not, have been related in a more distant way. If the rite required that the child was buried with an adult who was not necessarily a family member, it would mean that it was less likely that the child's body would have to be stored above ground awaiting interment for an extended period of time. There is also a suggestion that only a small proportion of the adult population were placed in barrows following criteria unknown to us and that stricter additional criteria were applied to those children selected for burial. Given

Site	Inhumation	Cremation
Allithwaite I		Male & female adult
Allithwaite II		Adult male & child (5–8yrs)
Allithwaite III		Adult & infant
Allithwaite IV		Female & infant
Allithwaite V		Female & neonate
Allithwaite VI		Female, child & neonate
Allithwaite VII		Male & child
Allithwaite VIII		Female & child
Arthuret I	2 unsexed	
Arthuret II	Young female and child	
Banniside Moor		Female & child (2–3 yrs)
Clifton Cist I	Adult male & adult female	
Ewanrigg		2 adults and child
Gaythorn Plain	2 males	
Homrook		Young adult and infant
Holmrook Hall		Young adult and female
Leacet Hill II		2 adults and infant
Oddendale	Uncremated bone adult male &infant	
Seal Howe		Female & infant
Sunbrick I		Male and foetus
Sunbrick II		Adult female, adult male, child (4 yrs) & newborn
Urswick	Woman and child	

97 Analysis of inhumation and cremation burials according to site. Both inhumation and cremation burials frequently combine adults and children

the generally low numbers of children found it must have been thought inappropriate for young children to be buried in barrows as a rule, and that they were dealt with in some alternative way that is not archaeologically visible.

These cremation cemeteries of the Early Bronze Age can be seen to continue Neolithic ideas of multiple burial (Burgess 1970, 210). Single burials associated with standing stones hint at a different ritual practice to that employed in the cairns and linear cemeteries. At Kirby Thore a cup and ring marked standing stone was destroyed in 1860 revealing an unurned cremation below it, and it is tempting to interpret the stone as immortalising the individual buried below it.

Focusing on the practice of burying cremations in urns, it is possible to determine that a decision was made whether to invert the urn or place it upright (*98*). Analysis of urns where their position has been recorded reveals that significant numbers were buried inverted with the mouth facing downwards, as at Moor Divock I and Barnscar. The figures suggest that there is a slight tendency towards urns containing men to be buried upright and those containing women to be inverted, however given the small sample size this view must be treated with caution. What is more certain is that the dual practices of inversion became a firmly entrenched tradition which began with burials in Food Vessels and continued through the Primary Series to the Secondary Series of Collared Urn burials, spanning a period of 500 years. It is not uncommon for a monument to contain both upright and inverted burials; at Leacet Hill I, Brougham, of five urns four were buried upright and one inverted.

A feature of both urned and unurned cremations is that they were often capped by placing a flat stone over the mouth of the urn (*99*). Examples of capped urned cremations include that of an adult man, aged 30-60 years, buried in a Collared Urn with an accessory vessel and fragments of bronze at Broomrigg site C, Ainstable, and the site of Culgaith Moor, Kirkland, where four upright urns containing cremations were found in 1784, each covered with a flat stone. Unurned cremations found below capping stones include that of a child placed in a central hollow within a kerbed cairn at Mallerstang, Kirby Stephen. All together there are records of 10 urned cremations and 11 unurned cremations closed with capping stones. In urned burials the practice of capping is first seen in the Secondary Series Style Urns placed upright, as at Kirkoswald. Presumably for those urns inverted, the base of the pit, or cist, was often considered sufficient to seal the urn, removing the need for a cap, although examples do occur where the urn was inverted over a flag stone placed at the bottom of a pit. At Hadrigg, Ravenstonedale, a round barrow built mostly of earth with some stones contained a Secondary Series Collared Urn cremation of a young woman with a clay bead inverted over a flagstone. In other cases, for example Banniside Moor, Coniston, coarse cloth has been recovered which may have been tied round the urn neck, covering the mouth and sealing it off.

Whatever the method, containment was important. It may be understood that the corpse was considered unclean, and therefore polluting, and perhaps socially dangerous. A considerable body of literature exists around the binary concept of pollution and purity first developed by the anthropologist Mary Douglas (1966). The period following death, but before burial, when the corpse is 'betwixt and between' is a particularly unsettling time for society (Douglas 1966; also Leach 1976, 1977, 171-3). The living are confronted by the danger brought about by death of a torn social fabric, a time when long-standing social

Type	Female	Upright male	Unsexed	Female	Inverted male	Unsexed	Female	Sideways male	Unsexed	Not known
Beaker			2							1
Food Vessel			3			3			1	6
Collared Urn, Primary Series			2	1		2				3
Collared Urn, Secondary Series		1	2	1		4				9
Collared Urn, Secondary Series North Western	1		5	1	1	3				12
Collared Urn, Secondary Series South Eastern										
Collared Urn, unclassified		2	4			6				1
Urn, unclassified			10			1				20
TOTAL	1	3	28	3	1	19	0	0	1	52

98 Sex of burials in urns placed upright, inverted and on their sides. The figures suggest that male cremations tend to be placed upright and female burials are inverted. However, the dataset is very small, with a large number of 'not knowns' and unsexed burials, so the results should be treated with caution

relations have to be renegotiated. They also have to confront the physical contamination of a decaying body. It is this liminal stage of the final rite of passage in the human life cycle that is most dangerous and must be contained.

Containing the corpse is a preoccupation of many cultures and what we see in the cremated remains of the funerary urns may be the final stage in a process of containment that began when the deceased first passed away. The requirement to prepare the corpse, including some form of purification, is almost universal among contemporary cultures. There is evidence that the Early Bronze Age was no different. The final phase of construction at Oddendale included the addition of a boulder platform, interpreted as an area for exposing corpses for the purpose of excarnation prior to cremation (Turnbull and Walsh 1997, 22). A similar structure was found at the nearby Hardendale Nab cairn, also made of large boulders, but in this instance detached from the cairn (Williams 1986, quoted in Turnbull and Walsh 1997). Prior removal of flesh and soft tissue would make the process of cremation easier and would reduce the

	Adult Female	Adult Male	Adult	Child	Juvenile	Unknown
Beaker						
Food Vessel						
Collared Urn, Primary Series						
Collared Urn, Secondary Series		I				
Collared Urn, Secondary Series North Western						
Collared Urn, Secondary Series South Eastern						
Collared Urn		I	I			
Urn, unclassified						7
Unurned				I		10
TOTAL	0	2	I	I	0	17

99 Cremations with capping stones. Urns were all placed upright. N = 21

amount of fuel required. Edmund Leach (1977) argued that all humans are interested in what distinguishes the outside from the inside of their bodies, especially with orifices which connect the two: anus, urethra, penis, vagina, nipples, mouth, eyes, nose and ears. These orifices have major symbolic significance (Leach 1977, 171) and require careful control. In corpses these boundaries begin to break down: the bowels, for example, generally move once after death unless action is taken to prevent it. As transgressors of boundaries, corpses are sites of power and danger (Kristeva 1982). This idea echoes that of Mary Douglas that 'interest in [the body's] apertures depends on the preoccupation with social exits and entrances, escape routes and invasion' (Douglas 1973).

Further evidence of preparation of the body prior to cremation comes from the sites of Mallerstang, Allithwaite and Ewanrigg. Excavation of cremation burials at these sites provided evidence for clothes fastenings. A carefully worked bone button with two perforations measuring 210mm was found with the cremation of a child at Mallerstang. The button, which is now lost, showed evidence of having been burnt suggesting that it might have fastened a light shroud-like garment. At Allithwaite a similiar practice may have been employed. A worked bone toggle was excavated from one of the cremation deposits (*100*). It comprised a short cylinder of bone into which a single hole had been bored. It was also burnt and found mixed with the cremated human bone, suggesting that it too had fastened a light garment that the corpse had been wearing when cremated. A similar function may explain the presence of bone pins which were found with cremations at both Allithwaite and Ewanrigg, and elsewhere. This practice was not confined to Cumbria: the best parallel for the practice from elsewhere in the North West comes from Pendleton in Lancashire where a diamond-shaped bone button with two perforations was excavated from amongst cremated remains (Barrowclough 2008, 128 and fig. 80). Wrapping the corpse in textile is another common form of containment, which may be imbued with symbolic meaning (Schneider and Weiner 1989). For example, Feeley-Harnik's (1989) study of the *lamba mena*, the funerary shawl used for wrapping and enclosing corpses in Madagascar, explores the symbolism of how kin relations are represented through these fine cloths (Parker-Pearson 1999). At this distance, and with so little to go on, it is impossible to reconstruct the symbolism attached to the shrouds from Mallerstang and Allithwaite. However, it highlights the need to be aware that the act of containment involved several stages beginning with the moment of death.

The inversion of urns may also have a specific ritual significance as the performance of actions backwards, and of things being inverted or turned inside out, are common ritual elements in funerary practices. Ucko considers the case of Zulu ceremonies in which the coffin bearers walk backwards, a hole in the house wall is used instead of the door and 'yes' is used to mean 'no' and vice versa (Ucko 1969). The eschatology is that of a world of the dead inverted to that of the living. Turning inside out the clothing on the corpse is a common practice in many societies; among the Lo Dagaa the smock worn by the corpse was turned inside out. Reversal reinforces the normality and naturalness of everyday practices by defining their opposite in ritual time. It also serves to separate the dead and their realm from the living.

Evidence suggests an overlapping sequence of urn usage from Beakers and Food Vessels to Primary then Secondary Series Collared Urns (*101*). This evidence also suggests that even the latest examples were evidently deposited within the Early Bronze Age (Challis and Harding 1975, 31). The term 'Secondary Series North Western Urn' is somewhat misleading as these vessels are not contemporaneous with the Secondary Series, which are somewhat later. Analysis of the position of urns in funerary monuments confirms this (*88*). Beaker Vessels

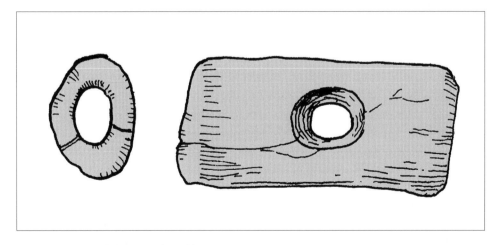

100 Bone toggle, Allithwaite. *After Wilde 2003, 23-50*

were almost always found in primary positions, invariably with inhumations (15 examples), but not exclusively. Food Vessels are also associated with primary positions in the monument, both cremations (6 primary examples) and inhumations (8 primary examples), although there were rare finds in secondary positions (4 and 2 examples). Collared Urns are always associated with cremations, never with inhumations, and largely in primary positions. Only Secondary Series North Western Style Urns follow the entire sequence being found in primary, secondary and also outside the main monument. Secondary Series South Eastern Style Urns are rare restricted to secondary positions. Unurned burials are numerous, with 47 examples, and are always found at the end of the sequence in secondary positions and most commonly outside the monument, 36 examples.

In 11 burials accessory vessels were present, in most instances, eight, they accompanied urns containing cremations: three accompanied Secondary Series North Western type Collared Urns. Among these was a Secondary Series North Western Collared Urn containing a female cremation and an Accessory Vessel inside which were the teeth and bones of a child aged two to three years. Three accompanied unclassified Collared Urns, including Broomrigg C where a Collared Urn and cremation of an adult male was found upright with an accessory vessel under a stone slab, and in two further cases 'urns' of unknown type were found with Accessory Vessels. There were also three cases where unurned cremations were found with accessory vessels including Skirwith Moor, Kirkland.

Sherds of Beaker Vessel, or less frequently Collared Urn, accompanied the cinerary urn in some instances. At Crosby Garrett Beaker sherds were found in the cairn with the body of an adult male; Beaker sherds were also found at Oddendale with a crouched inhumation, whilst Collared Urn sherds were found with a secondary cremation burial at the same site and also at Moor Divock, Askham. These sherds may be understood as part of a process of fragmentation whereby, during the burial ceremony, relatives or friends broke the original pot and placed a sherd with the burial while they retained the others as a memento. The original pot must have had meaning to the group, perhaps because it belonged to the deceased or to one of their ancestors. The focus here is on the reproduction rather than the production of objects. By exchanging and sharing sherds of the vessel a link is created between all the owners or users of the artefact who themselves become part of the pot's distinctive biography.

The Cumbrian burial assemblages contain other examples of fragmentation. Beads are found, but rarely as entire necklaces. Instead single or small numbers occur, as at Mecklin Park, Santon Bridge, where jet beads were found in a possible ring cairn; at Ewanrigg where a single bead was found with a cremation in a Secondary Series Collared Urn; and at Hadrigg, Ravenstonedale, where the cremation of a young woman was accompanied with a clay bead. There is a sense that sets were being broken and perhaps redistributed, as part of the symbolism of regeneration. Fragments of Beaker pottery from the time of the ancestors were incorporated into the burial of the deceased, while some of the possessions of the deceased were divided amongst their living descendents or friends. In exchanging objects people are also exchanging themselves. The exchange of ceramics and beads establishes a chain of personal relations, which Chapman terms 'enchainment' (Chapman 2000). Enchained relationships are established through fragmentation. To establish a social relationship, a specific

	Primary inhumation	Secondary inhumation	Primary cremation	Secondary cremation	Outside monument/ inserted above	TOTAL
Beaker	15	2	1			18
Food Vessel	8	1	6	4		19
Collared Urn: Primary Series			3	2		5
Collared Urn: Secondary Series			6	4		10
Collared Urn: Secondary Series North Western			5	2	1	8
Collared Urn: Secondary Series South Eastern				1		1
Collared Urn: unclassified			6	6		12
Urn	6		9	3	1	19
Unurned				11	36	47
Inhumation/cremation: no urn	18	7	6			31
TOTAL	47	10	42	33	38	170

101 The Early Bronze Age burial sequence in Cumbria according to type of urn. N = 170

artefact is broken in two or more pieces, each party keeping one or more parts as a token of the relationship. In turn each fragment can be broken further so that new relations with a third party can be entered into. These fragments are kept until the reconstitution of the relationship, which may occur at death, when parts brought together and deposited in a structured way. This may account for the incorporation of ancestral Beaker sherds into the burial in one way or another.

The process of enchainment operates at different levels – at one, between fragments and the complete vessel, that is between entire vessels and sherds placed in the burial; and at another, between complete objects and sets of objects, that is, single beads and necklaces. The interaction between parts, wholes and sets provides part of the dynamic of prehistoric communities.

Funerary urns should not be considered in isolation, but as part of the assemblage that accompanies the dead. This includes metal and stone implements, exotic materials, accessory vessels, animal parts and personal ornaments. The sacrifice of possessions, whether living or not, may be a means of communication with the other world. They may be viewed as gifts, tribute or even fines to be paid to the supernatural as expressions of a reciprocal relationship, rather than a material exchange. These gifts do not necessarily force a repayment from the supernatural but link the living to that realm. Grave goods should not be seen just as personal trappings, whether or not polluted by association with the corpse, but as items bound up in gift exchanges with the dead, as in the case of personal equipment which was definitely never used, but instead made specifically for the deceased. Heirlooms may be placed in the grave, possibly because there was no successor to inherit them. An example is the placing of jet necklaces in British Early Bronze Age burials (*colour plates 23 & 24*), a Cumbrian example of which was found at Broomrigg C where 13 jet beads were found in a pit accompanying the cremation of an adult man. From the wear on the beads and the evidence for multiple repairs and replacements of beads, many of these necklaces were clearly very old by the time they went into the grave (Sheridan and Davis 1998).

Artefacts found in burials include: bone pins and buttons; flint implements; jet, slate and clay ornaments; and ochre, red porphyry and quartz crystals. In one of the urns in the cremation cemetery at Birkrigg, Urswick, quartz, red porphyry and green stone were found. A third inhumation of a young woman with child included a double ended bronze awl. At Sunbrick one cremation was accompanied by a boar's tusk and part of a bronze dagger; elsewhere in the barrow one deposit of teeth was accompanied by ochre and another included a human bone which had been worked as a polisher. Besides the grave goods mentioned in the burials above flint knives are frequently found in burials. A plano-convex flint knife was found in a cremation burial at Allithwaite. The knife was badly burnt suggesting that it had been amongst the pyre goods. At Mazon Wath two bone awls and two boar tusks accompanied a flint knife, whilst other flint knives were found at Hawkeshead Moor, Oddendale, Leafy Hill II and Mecklin Park.

A useful way to study grave goods is to consider the types that are found with particular types of urns, as that way the ceramic typology can be used to help us study changes in preferences of grave goods through time. Generally the idea of placing some sort of object with the dead can be seen throughout the Early Bronze Age. However, the type and number of objects deposited varied through time, starting with the Beaker and Food Vessel burials and increasing during the Collared Urn phase, starting with the Primary Series, and reaching its maximum with the Secondary Series Collared Urns. This pattern reflects that already described in the case of the field monuments whose most active and varied forms occur during the same period.

Certain limited types of object recur throughout the period; this suggests that objects were being selected to fulfil specific cultural requirements. Consideration of the objects might usefully reveal something about society in the Early Bronze Age. One of the most frequent objects deposited in graves is the knife or dagger. This can be made of flint, 10 examples, or metal, one example. Interpretation of the significance of these items is difficult. They may have been possessions of the deceased, or they may have been mourners' gifts to the dead. They may have been placed with the burial to equip the dead for the world of the afterlife, or to prevent the dead from coming back to haunt the living. Parallels drawn from anthropology may assist us to explore the range of possibilities, without excluding others.

What is interesting about the selection of knives and daggers is that they are artefacts associated with the act of cutting, with separation of one thing from another. One possibility is that the placing of a knife or dagger on or in their grave by their survivors may represent the dead's severance from the living. The aim of placing the object with the burial may serve to prevent the deceased from remaining in the world of the living. For example, among the Iban of Borneo a knife may be included in burials to symbolise the cutting of those ties (Uchibori 1978).

Hunting equipment, such as leaf and barbed-and-tanged flint arrowheads, flint blades and scrapers, animal parts including unworked bones from fish, red deer, boar and birds, and 11 accessory vessels, often accompany the dead. These could be accoutrements to feed the dead in the afterlife, or complex symbols, which express the values, aims, and attitudes of mourners. For example, the presence of fish placed with a burial may have cosmological significance according to Kaul's reconstruction of prehistoric cosmology, as evidenced by the decorated metalwork of Bronze Age Denmark (Kaul 1997).

In his interpretation of the cosmology a ship draws the sun across the sky. At different stages in the cycle, a horse, a snake and perhaps significantly, a fish assist it. The passage of the sun during the night, its absence from the world, in a symbolic sense its death, is associated with a fish (Kaul 1997). If we accept that this interpretation has some validity for the prehistory of Scandinavia and by extension to the north-west of England (Barrowclough 2007, 123-4) then we can begin to understand some of the rationale behind the choice of objects placed in the grave.

The fish recalls the association between water, in general, and rivers and the sea, in particular, that is a characteristic of northern mythology and the Early Bronze Age funerary monuments. Immediately to the south of Cumbria, at Lancaster, a burial on Lancaster Moor contained the remains of a fish identified as that of the genus *Salmonidae*. This may be significant because the life cycle of the salmon involves cyclical movement from rivers down to the sea, and then back to the river to spawn before its death. We saw in the discussion of monuments at Penrith (Chapter 5) that funerary monuments are often separated from the world of the living by flowing water and it may be that this choice of location had further symbolic significance, linking the world of the living to that of the dead through flowing water.

Conclusion

A Neolithic to Early Bronze Age continuity is clearly demonstrated in Cumbria's archaeological record. Evidence for Early Bronze Age occupation consists mainly of burial monuments, their associated grave goods and lithic implements – the same classes of evidence as were used to construct an understanding of the Neolithic. The origins of the practices that have been identified in the Early Bronze Age may likewise be traced back to the Neolithic. In particular surviving Neolithic traits in monuments demonstrate a close relationship between the two periods. The Early Bronze Age was also a time of increasing diversity, seen in the variety of burial monuments, interments and grave assemblages, accelerating a pattern that began in the Late Neolithic.

In the lowlands, particularly around the coast, but increasingly moving on to heavier soils further inland, indications are of a largely pastoral economy supplemented by some cereal cultivation. Pollen evidence suggests widespread but irregular and spasmodic forest clearances during the period, although generally small-scale in character. From which it may be inferred that there was a larger population in the Early Bronze Age than in the Neolithic period. The presence of barbed-and-tanged arrowheads on the upland moors, including the highest ground, presumably means that hunting remained a means of food gathering, reflecting the continuing disturbance of the forest cover on the higher ground. This was possibly a seasonal activity carried on from settlements of more lasting status on the lower ground.

CHAPTER 7

LAND AND WATER:
THE DEPOSITION OF BRONZE AGE METALWORK

The implements and weapons of the later bronze period exhibit a variety of form, a frequent elegance of design, and an excellence of workmanship, which evince, on the part of the artificers, consummate skill, and a thorough knowledge of the metallurgical qualities of the alloy.

M.W. Taylor 1884, 279

Introduction

At a national scale the Bronze Age is associated with the introduction of copper-alloy (bronze) metalwork. In the previous chapters we have seen how aspects of the occupation of Cumbria exhibited considerable continuity across traditional period divisions. This continuity can likewise be traced in practices of metalwork deposition. Collingwood (1933, 184), for example, noted an association between the distribution of bronze implements and perforated stone axe hammers in Furness. The distribution follows an earlier pattern established in the Neolithic. Half the known examples of polished stone axes in Cumbria come from Furness and the area along the northern coast of Morecambe Bay similarly, of *c.*200 bronze implements known from Cumbria approximately half come from southern Cumbria with concentrations around Furness and Cartmel. We have also seen in the previous chapter how some aspects of culture fail to respect traditional period boundaries, the barrow building tradition for example begins in the Late Neolithic and continues to the end of the Early Bronze Age. What gives meaning to the 'Bronze Age' in Cumbria is metalwork, it is the one category of data that crosses boundaries between the Early, Middle and Late Bronze Age giving coherence to the period.

The metalwork of the British Bronze Age has been extensively researched, for example Lort (1779), Evans (1881) and Burgess (1979; 1980; 1988). Locally Bronze Age metalwork has been catalogued and its distribution considered (Fell 1940, 118-130; McK. Clough 1969, 1-39). As a result there exists a number of chronological sequences for the different types of metalwork. Needham (Needham 1996; Needham *et al* 1997) divides the metalwork of the British Bronze Age into eight time periods (Chapter 1, Figure 1) with different types associated with particular periods (*102*). The extent to which the types identified by contemporary archaeologists reflect prehistoric reality is open to question. The typological approach is, however, often the only available tool when dealing with unassociated and undated 'stray finds' and is applied here for that very reason.

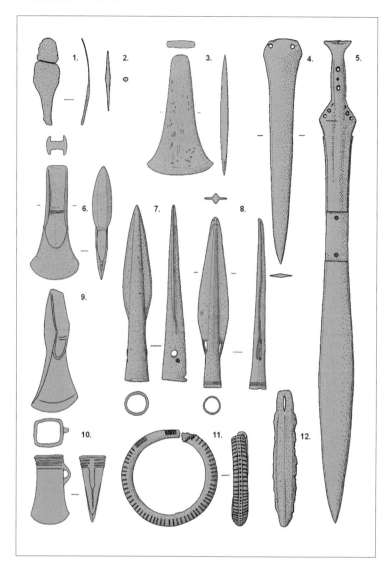

102 Metalwork types found in Cumbria

Interpreting Change Through Time

Overall, of *c*.200 bronze objects known for Cumbria and the surrounding areas the most numerous types represented are the flanged axe and spearhead – 21 of each are recorded – followed by palstaves, 20, and flat and socketed axes, 16 each, with other types making up the remainder. Chronologically 69 objects can be ascribed to Period 5, the Middle Bronze Age Acton/Taunton/Penard (Wallington) phase of activity dated *c*.1500–1150 cal BC. The preceding periods 1 and 2, 3 and 4 reflect a consistent level of activity. After a brief relapse in Period 6, Period 7 represents a further fluorescence of activity in the Late Bronze Age, Blackmoor/Ewart phase dated *c*.900–750 cal BC (*103*).

Period Year cal BC	Metalwork Types	Total
1 and 2 2500–2050	Flat Axe 10, Copper Dagger 1	11
3 2050–1700	Awl 3, Flat Axe 6, Knife Dagger 2, Knife 1, Pins 2	14
4 1700–1500	Chisel 1, Dagger 1, Flanged Axe 10, Razor 1	13
5 1500–1150	Armlet 1, Dirk 5, Flanged Axe 11, Knife Dagger 1, Palstave 20, Rapier 6, Socketed Axe 3, Spearhead 19, Spear Ferrule 1, Sword 2	69
6 1150–920	Spear 1	1
7 920–750	Brooch 1, Neckring 1, Socketed Hammer 1, Socketed Axe 8	11
8 750–510	Bucket 1, Cauldron 1, Socketed Axe 8	10
9 510 BC–AD 40	Flanged Axe (Iron) 1, Harness Fitting 7, Personal Ornament 4, Razor 1, Spoons 2, Tool 1, Torque 1	17
'Bronze Age'	'Axes'	12

103 Metalwork types found in Cumbria according to chronological period. N = 166

The earliest evidence for the use of metalwork in Cumbria comes from artefacts deposited with burials in the 'metal using' Neolithic, Periods 1 and 2, *c.*2500-2050 cal BC. There were hints that a bronze object had once formed part of the burial assemblage at Ewanrigg near Maryport. When excavated although no bronze artefacts were present there was a green residue suggestive of copper-alloy on the bones of one of the cremations (Bewley *et al* 1992). In Cumbria seven bronze artefacts have been found in definite association with burials. At the College, Kirkoswald, a bronze pin was found associated with an adult male cremation in a Secondary Series Collared Urn and at Birkrigg, Urswick, the inhumation burial of a young woman and child was accompanied by a double-ended bronze awl. The barrow at Sunbrick contained part of a bronze dagger placed with a boars tusk with a cremated burial, whilst at Urswick a bronze razor-knife was deposited with a cremation in a Secondary Series Collared Urn at Stainton Head I, and at Stainton Head II a second razor-knife accompanied an Accessory Vessel and Secondary Series North Western Style Collared Urn. Also worthy of note is the burial site at Little Mell Fell, Matterdale; although it was impossible to identify the original artefact, two pieces of copper-alloy metalwork were found with cremated bone, charcoal and sand within a Secondary Series North Western Style Collared Urn.

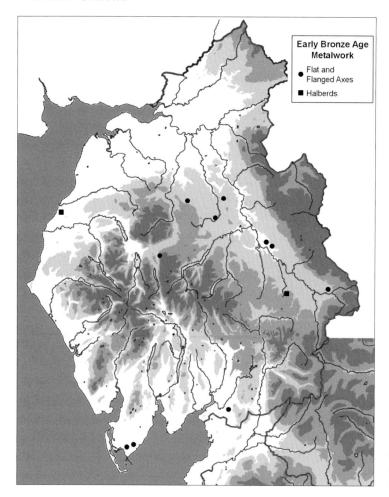

104 Distribution
of Early Bronze
Age metalwork in
Cumbria

The geographical distribution of Early Bronze Age metalwork in Cumbria is restricted
largely to the valleys and valley sides, and to the plains of Furness and West Cumbria (*104*).
It is particularly associated with the better drained areas, including examples of flat axes
of Migdale-Marnoch type from Gleaston Castle and Migdale type ones from Roose,
Barrow-in-Furness. Other examples are associated with possible routeways through the
hills following the Eden valley, including an Arreton type flat axe from Brough-under-
Stainmore high in the Eden valley. This axe is decorated with an engraving of hatched
and unhatched lozenges of a type usually associated with Irish objects suggesting that the
Cumbrian example was inspired by, if not an actual import from, Ireland (McK. Clough
1969, 4). Connections with Ireland are reflected in halberds found at Maryport on the west
coast and at Harbyrnrig, Crosby Ravensworth in the Eden valley (Chapter 9). The example
from Maryport is particularly interesting in this context because it has three rivets, an angular three-sided butt with ogival sides and bevelled edge, placing it in type 4 (O Ríodáin
1936). This type is thought to be an insular form strengthening the connections between
Cumbria and Ireland at this time (Fell 1940).

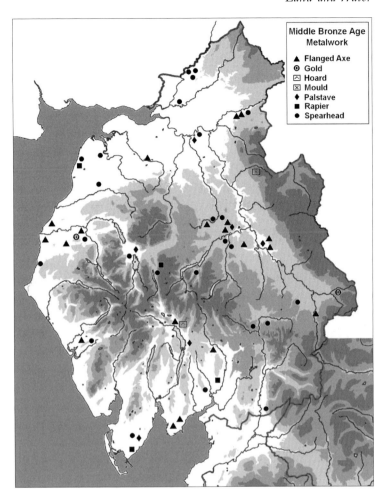

105 Distribution
of Middle Bronze
Age metalwork in
Cumbria

Metalwork forms the main evidence for the Late Bronze Age in Cumbria, as elsewhere.
The largest number of metal objects of Middle Bronze Age date, 1500-1000 cal BC, Periods
5 and 6, are palstaves and spearheads, of which 20 of each are known. Also present are 11 haft
flanged axes, nine rapiers and five dirks. During the Middle Bronze Age, deposition shifted
away from burials toward 'ritual' wet places. This is reflected in the distribution pattern of
bronze artefacts according to underlying superficial geology, elevation, aspect and proximity
to water, all of which indicate strong preferences for 'wet' lowland or river valley locations.
In particular Period 5, the Acton/Taunton/Penard (Wallington) phases, was a time of intense
activity associated with unprecedented amounts of metalwork (69 objects), significantly larger
than that which came before and was to come after, and of different types.

There is a concentration of material around Penrith reinforcing the pattern of occupation observed during the Neolithic, testament to the continued importance of the valley
networks as a means of communication and as prime areas for settlement. Known examples
of flanged axes come from Castletown near Penrith, Ravenstonedale and Penrith itself (*105*).
Other objects are known from the coast, for example from Wraysholme Tower, Allithwaite

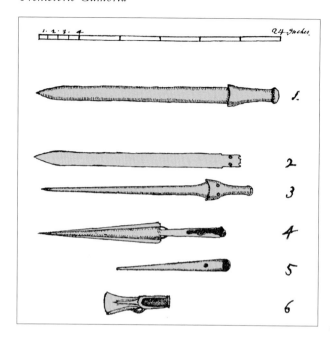

106 The Ambleside hoard of bronze weapons. The artefacts were found wrapped in a bundle and include two swords (1 & 2) one of which (1), along with a rapier (3), has a solid cast hilt. Also found were a spearhead (4), spear ferrule (5) and palstave (6). *Illustration taken from a letter written by the Hon Peregrine Bertie to Maurice Johnson, 17 December 1741*

and from a peat moss near Cartmel. McK. Clough made an interesting observation about the distribution of these axes, dividing them into angle- and convex-flanged axes, following Coles' typology (1963-4). Angle-flanged axes tend to be found in the eastern half of Cumbria, with none known to him west of a line drawn from the Crake/Leven estuary to the mouth of the Eden. In contrast half of the convex-flanged axes come from sites west of the line. This distribution may, in part, be explained by stronger contacts on the west coast with people from Ireland, who may have brought convex-flanged axes to this part of Cumbria. Possible Irish influence is also seen in some of the spears; examples of spears with kite-shaped blades and raised ribs from Blindbothel and Whinfell Tarn have close affinities with Irish examples where they occur in larger numbers, with a smaller number of other examples coming from just over the border in southern Scotland. One further piece of evidence pointing toward Middle Bronze Age Irish influence in Cumbria is provided by two finds of gold. A twisted gold armlet was found at Eaglesfield and another at Winton Common, between Kirkby Stephen and Brough-under-Stainmore (Fell 1940, 124). The closest parallels for these objects lie in the Bishopsland phase of the Irish Bronze Age (Eogan 1964, 277).

A common feature of the metalwork distribution in the British Late Bronze Age period is its bias towards wetland areas and rivers, particularly in the form of hoards (Bradley 1984). This is seen as occurring at, or shortly before, a time of climatic deterioration, which is a possible cause for the changes seen at the end of the Early Bronze Age (Burgess 1974). In Cumbria, as generally in the north-west of England, hoards are rare, the pattern being dominated by single finds (Barrowclough 2008, Ch. 6). Where they do occur, for example at Skelmore Heads, Urswick; Ambleside at the northern end of Lake Windermere; and at Netherby, they are considerably smaller than those in the south of England. At Skelmore Heads six socketed axes were discovered in a limestone fissure (below). Swords, although present, are comparatively

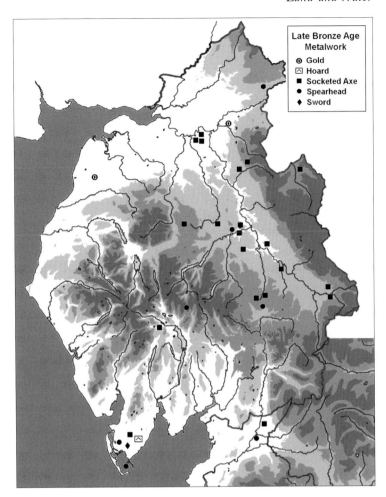

107 Distribution
of Late Bronze
Age metalwork in
Cumbria

rare, not only in Cumbria but throughout the north-west of England. The Ambleside hoard
is therefore important regionally and is also the largest yet found in Cumbria, and the only
one in which the objects were wrapped in a bundle (*106*). Found in 1741, the hoard contains
swords including an early type with solid cast hilt, which are rare in Britain, a spearhead, spear
ferrule and palstave (Barrowclough 2007; Needham 1982). The hoard found at Netherby is
less secure. Said to have been found in the vicinity of the Roman fort it has been argued that
the artefacts represent a hoard (Burgess 1968, 57), and although not conclusively proved that
argument is accepted here. The hoard consists of a protected loop spearhead, part of another
spearhead and two socket fragments, one with a single loop together with another spearhead
recorded as having come from 'Carlisle'. All five socketed spears share the same uniform pagi-
nation and general condition as well as the same find spot at the fort.

The Late Bronze Age and Early Iron Age Periods 7 and 8, 920-750 and 750-810 cal BC,
are dominated by socketed axes of which there are 62 (*107*). West Cumbria is not only dif-
ferentiated by the absence of angle-flanged axes, but also by the absence of Late Bronze Age
socketed axes. Elsewhere in Cumbria socketed axes are found in the Eden and other valleys,

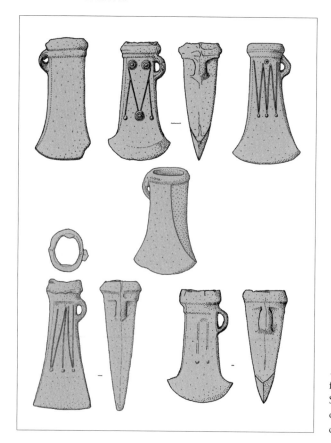

108 Hoard of six socketed axes found in a limestone crevice at Skelmore Heads, Urswick. Three of the axes were of the elaborately decorated Sompting type

but most interesting are a hoard of six socketed axes found in a rock crevice in the limestone at Skelmore Heads, Urswick, in the Furness District. Three of these axes are of Sompting type, the most elaborately decorated of all the socketed axes, in this case with distinctive rib, ring and pellet motifs (*108*). Other examples are less remarkable, two Yorkshire type axes were found on King's Meadow, Carlisle, another from Lowther and one from Brough. This period marks the end of metalwork deposition in watery places. Analyses of metalwork distributions reveal a resurgence in activity on the northern coast of Morecambe Bay, the location of a series of hillforts, extending from the Irish Sea coast through North Lancashire to Warton Crag, and into North Yorkshire at Ingleborough.

The changing relationship between metalwork deposition and wet-dry locations is unsurprising given the substantial body of literature that exists describing Bronze Age practices of deposition elsewhere in Britain and Northern Europe (Bradley 1990). In this sense Cumbria can be seen as part of the wider European Bronze Age. However, the detail of practices in the region are worthy of closer scrutiny as they show differences with practices elsewhere that give the region a unique identity. This may lead to a reconsideration of Bu'Lock's suggestion that a 'North Western Culture' existed (Bu'Lock 1961, 36-8).

Closer analysis of the particular contexts of deposition reveals the nature of the practice. 'Wet' locations have already been separated from 'dry' locations, but each can be further subdivided into particular types of wet or dry places (*109*). Three major types of wet location can be distinguished: rivers/streams, lakes/tarns and peat bogs. Four major types of dry locations may be distinguished: burials/monuments, dry hoards, limestone clefts and caves. Cave sites are somewhat ambiguous: although located in the dry limestone uplands they are also associated with drainage of water and therefore can be described as wet locations. This ambiguity may have been part of their attraction. For the present purposes they are placed in the dry category, and cognisance will be taken of their potential 'wet status' in the discussion that follows.

It was possible to determine the context for 112 artefacts, 71 for wet and 41 for dry (*109*). From this a number of patterns are discernable. First, in a number of instances particular types of object are only ever found in dry and some only ever in wet contexts. Thus, razors, awls and knives are confined to dry locations. Palstaves, flanged axes, rapiers and spear ferrules are always found in wet locations. These are the exceptions, however. In most cases objects can be found in either wet or dry locations, but what is significant is the relative proportions in each. Although dry land examples exist, by far the majority of each type are found in wet locations: flat axes, four dry and nine wet; socketed axes, six dry and eight wet; and spearheads, three dry and eight wet. The distribution mostly favours wet locations, but this is not universal – armlets, 12 dry and two wet, and socketed spears, two dry and one wet, are most often found in dry places.

In order to begin to understand these distributions it is helpful to look at the particular type of wet or dry context. For example, Late Bronze Age buckets and cauldrons are not only never found in dry locations, they are also only found in one type of wet context, bogs. Similarly, some other types are only found in dry locations, awls and razors in particular are associated with Early Bronze Age burials. What I want to focus on is the distribution of metalwork in different wet contexts. The analysis of depositional practices may offer insights into continuity and change in belief during the Middle and Late Bronze Ages, a period for which we lack burial data, the usual source of information on such questions.

Within wet conditions particular types favour particular contexts, thus as we have seen bogs are the focus of deposits of buckets and cauldrons (1 each), swords (2), palstaves (bogs 2, lake/tarn 1) and rapiers (2). Rivers and streams, the focus of socketed axes (3), axes (2) and spoons (2), the later being found in a spring at the head of a stream. The only object type to be found predominantly in lakes and tarns were spears (lake/tarn 2, bog 1) although that serves to mask their general significance as a 'second choice' location for objects more frequently placed in bogs: palstaves, flat and flanged axes.

This distribution suggests a diachronic pattern. Artefacts found in bogs tend to date to the metal-using Neolithic and Early Bronze Age, Periods 1, 2 and 3, with further deposition in Period 5, the Middle Bronze Age. Those found in stream valleys are restricted in type to dirks, and to Period 5, whilst major rivers were the focus of activity in Period 7, the Late Bronze Age. Spearheads represent an exception to this pattern of distribution; they are found in all three wet contexts: 16 in bogs, 14 in rivers and 5 in streams. This distribution is interesting, as the spearheads found in these contexts date, in the main, to Period 5. The Middle Bronze Age has already been identified as representing a peak in depositional activity, and it may be this intensity of deposition that first motivated the deposition of objects outside bog contexts, which, up until Period 5, had been the only site of wet deposition.

Object	WET				DRY				Total
	River/Stream	Lake/Tarn	Peat Bog	'Wet'	Limestone Cleft	Burial/Monument	'Dry'	Cave	
Axe	2			4	5				11
Armlet				2	3	6		3	14
Awl						3			3
Brooch								1	1
Bucket			1						1
Cauldron			1						1
Dagger				1					1
Dirk			1	3					4
Ferrule			1						1
Flanged Axe	1	1	1	7					10
Flat Axe		1	3	5	1		3		13
Harness Fitting				1					1
Knife						1			1
Neckring				1					1
Palstave		1	6						7
Pin				1				1	2
Rapier			2	2					4
Razor						1			1
Socketed Axe	3			5	6				14
Socketed Spear				1		2			3
Spear		2	1	5	1	1	1		11
Spoon	2								2
Sword			2			1			3

Object	WET				DRY				Total
	River/Stream	Lake/Tarn	Peat Bog	'Wet'	Limestone Cleft	Burial/Monument	'Dry'	Cave	
Tanged Chisel								1	1
Tanged Knife				1					1
Total	8	5	19	39	16	15	4	6	112

109 Analysis of the deposition of bronze artefacts throughout the whole of the Bronze Age in Cumbria according to whether they were found in 'wet' or 'dry' contexts. N = 112

The deposition of metalwork in wet places has been widely interpreted as one aspect of Bronze Age ritual practices, the majority of which are lost to us. Many key aspects of people's lives and social personas are embedded within, framed by and organised around forms of ritual practice that we may broadly term 'religion'. At one end of a continuum are the relatively intangible structuring principles of social life, the *habitus* embedded in, and reproducing, habitual forms of social existence (Comaroff and Comaroff 1989, 272). At the other, and more visible, we can see in the deposition of metalwork the end product of highly elaborated, structured and overt practices and displays. These practices may have been integral elements of a political project that maintained religious identities so as to construct and manipulate, either inclusively or exclusively, both community affiliation and social boundaries.

Identity, at the level of the regional group, is created in opposition to other group identities, as part of an ongoing historical relationship. This view of cultural identity as an aspect of relationships contains the idea that the group has to be constantly maintained. In its maintenance over time, it will be subject to small changes, which will lead to its gradual transformation. The interest lies in how that reproduction of feelings of solidarity happens in society through time.

One of the most powerful ways to reproduce feelings of cultural identity and belonging is to make use of symbolic resources, especially material culture and everyday practices. The role of dress and bodily adornment is a good example that has received attention in previous studies of the Bronze Age (Treherne 1995; Sørensen 1997). While rarely consciously articulated, the ways in which people dress are subject to a range of culturally informed ideas and expectations. Cultural differences in dress are one resource that can be seized upon in the articulation of difference, as can be seen with national or regional costumes, or differences in military dress. The same may be true of the articulation of ritual among, and between, different groups which, when expressed through practices of deposition, are rendered visible to archaeological analysis.

The symbolic resources drawn on in the construction of group identity are not arbitrary. The cultural practices and representations that become objectified as symbols of the group have to resonate with people's usual practices and experiences (Jones 1997, 90). It is pre-existing differences that are drawn upon in the creation of shared feelings; it is interaction with others, of a different cultural tradition, that makes people think about the observed differences in a conscious way (Eriksen 1993, 34; Jenkins 1997, 76-7; Jones 1997, 95). A study of metalwork deposition therefore has the potential to inform our understanding of regional identity.

To those familiar with the pattern of metalwork deposition in Britain throughout the Bronze Age what may be most striking about the preceding analysis of the Lancastrian metalwork is the relatively small quantity. The point is reinforced by examination of hoards (*110*). A defining practice of the British Middle Bronze Age is the deposition of large amounts of metalwork together in wet places as hoards, and yet this is a practice rarely encountered in Cumbria. Of 196 artefacts where data are available only 47 were deposited in hoards (defined as two or more objects placed together), and of those many were placed in pairs, 12 objects. Only occasionally were multiple objects deposited. I feel that the absence of hoards defines Cumbria in this period, substantially contributing to a sense of regional identity. Understanding why hoarding, apparently, played such a small part in ritual practice is central to the formation of a model for social organisation within the region, and yet, although widely recognised, it has received comparatively little attention.

The most common, and tacitly accepted, explanation is functional. Following Cyril Fox (1932) it has been argued that the north-west of England, along with other areas of the highland zone, was peripheral, both economically and socially to the south. A characteristic of the highland zone was that it was a 'difficult' area to live in. A cooler, wetter climate led to a shorter growing season and lower yields than lowland areas. As a consequence, the population was characterised as stressed, struggling to survive, with little time for either cultural or technological pursuits. People relied upon technological advances imported from 'core' areas. According to this model, the relatively small amount of metalwork, and the almost complete absence of large hoards, was easily explained. For a 'marginal' population, reliant on expensive imports, metal was simply too scarce and valuable a commodity to 'waste' by throwing it away.

This account does not bear close examination. First Cumbria, although firmly within the highland zone, contains, as we have seen in earlier chapters, significant amounts of lowland around the Solway Plain, West Cumbrian Coastal Plain and Furness areas. Environmental conditions alone cannot explain the different distribution. Second, the notion of marginality does not fit with aspects of the evidence that show that contacts between the region and the rest of Britain and Ireland were widespread. The Langdale axe 'trade', for example, flourished during the Neolithic. Widespread trading links established contact across Britain and these appear to have continued into the Bronze Age, evidenced by the presence of a wide range of different metalwork types, although in low numbers.

In order to understand the absence of hoarding as a widespread activity we need first investigate the nature of those hoards that do exist. It is possible to date each hoard using the known typo-chronological sequence, taking the date of the youngest artefact as the date for the deposit. The temporal sequence of 14 known hoards generally follows the pattern that has already been described for individual objects. There were low numbers during the Early Bronze Age, followed by an increase of activity in the Middle Bronze Age, Period 5, which peaks in Period 7 before it tails off toward the Early Iron Age, Periods 8 and 9.

	Ambleside	Back Hagg	Butts Beck	Fell Lane	Flookburgh	Grayber	Hayton	King's Meadow	Kirkhead Cave	Long Rigg	Netherby	Rogersceugh	Skelmore Heads	Sleagill
Armlet							⬜		⬜	□				□
Axe										▲				
Axe (copper)		□												
Chisel (tanged)									○					
Palstave	○				⬜									
Pin									○					
Rapier	○													
Sock'd Axe				○				□				□	◆	
Sock'd Speahead	○		○	○							▼			
Spear Ferrule	○													
Spoon					□									
Sword	□		○											

110 Composition of hoards: ○ single instance, □ two instances, ⬜ three instances, ▲ four instances, ▼ five instances, ◆ six instances

We have already seen that many of the hoards are small, comprising just a pair of objects. Although the number are two few to justify statistical analysis, some patterns do appear noteworthy. Objects were not deposited arbitrarily, only certain pairings were considered appropriate. In particular it was appropriate to place objects of the same sort together. As in the case of pairs of: copper axes at Back Hagg, armlets at Sleagill, socketed axes at King's Meadow and Rogersceugh and spoons at Grayber. Homogeneity continued to play an important role in some of the larger hoards, with three armlets at Hayton and three palstaves at Flookburgh, five spearheads at Netherby and six socketed axes at Skelmore Heads. Although more diverse in types the contents of the Ambleside hoard were all weapons: swords, plus a rapier, spearhead and ferrule and palstave axe. Likewise the Butts Beck and Fell Lane hoards had a martial theme, sword and spearhead, and spearhead and socketed axe respectively. Of the larger hoards only the material from Kirkhead Cave, three armlets, a pin and tanged chisel; and Long Rigg, two armlets and four axes have a more personal and domestic feel.

The composition of the larger hoards, three or more objects, also reveals repeated deposition of a restricted range of objects. Objects appropriate for placing in hoards were swords, rapiers, spearheads and, in particular, socketed axes. To understand why this might be is to understand that communal identity is an aspect of social practice. Identity has to be continually constructed and generated and this is most effectively done through shared ways of doing things. Studying group identity involves paying attention to the uses of material culture in social interactions. One approach has been to investigate material culture in respect of style, attempting to read this as if it were a text. The problem with that approach was that little consideration was given to the role of living human beings in the interactions made possible by those artefacts (Boast 1997, 181-2). As a consequence, interpretations 'overlooked the contexts within which the variation arose, how the artefacts in question were used, and that they were a part of the production of meaning to prehistoric peoples' (Conkey 1990, 10).

Social Identity: A Biographical Approach

There is more potential in biographical approaches (Kopytoff 1986) that take account of all the stages of production and use of artefacts, the *chaînes opératoires* (operational sequences), including deposition (see Mauss 1979 [1950]; Conkey 1990, 12-13; Lemonnier 1993, 2-3; Dietler and Herbich 1998). Within this perspective the knowledge drawn on in the creation and use of artefacts, and ways of doing things, such as deposition, is constituted in social and historical worlds. This knowledge is generally context specific and not necessarily explicitly discussed (Edmonds 1990).

This idea has implications for discussing group identity in Cumbria. Previously it was thought that group identity could be inferred from artefacts by looking at static features, for example, axe decoration, which defines the various types and sub-types, and then plotting distributions of the various sub-types to map material culture groups. Taking his lead from Childe this was the approach adopted by Bu'Lock, which led him to posit the existence of a 'North Western Culture'. The life-history perspective is somewhat different: 'not only decorative patterns or secondary aspects of shape are used to define one's status or ethnic identity but also the use of given artefacts or entire processes of production' (Lemonnier 1993, 20). Material culture is actively involved in social practice, and social practice cannot exist without material culture. Social practice involving material culture is how the idea of the group, whether social, familial, ethnic or other, becomes articulated: it is not something that can be 'read off' from the artefactual evidence without regard for its contexts of use and production.

An important distinction that should be made for the present study is that between 'specific' object biographies and 'generalised' biographies (Gosden and Marshall 1999, 170-1). Specific biographies are about the idiosyncratic histories of objects, whilst generalised biographies describe the characteristics of widely shared features of an object's life-path. In this study of object deposition I am referring to generalised biographies. Archaeologically, it is much more difficult to come to terms with specific biographies, since they are outside established patterns.

Every biography commences with production. In making an object the smith is both constrained by practical factors, such as availability of materials and skill, and cultural factors, such as which objects were considered appropriate to produce and what they should look like. Evidence that hints at copper ore extraction in Cumbria, from sources around Coniston, is based on the discovery of prehistoric stone hammers, but as yet there is no evidence for the production of copper from its ore in the county. The most certain evidence for early mining in the north-west of England is that from Alderley Edge, Cheshire, some considerable distance from Cumbria. More certain evidence for metalworking in the Early Bronze Age comes from excavations of the flat cemetery at Ewanrigg (discussed above; Bewley *et al* 1992). A clay tube, which would have connected a bellows to a nozzle feeding air into a furnace, was found in one of the Collared Urn burials (*111*). Such tubes are known by the technical term tuyère and are rarely found in Early Bronze Age contexts (Howard 1983). The Ewanrigg example is 1cm long with external diameter of 3.7cm and internal hole *c.*1cm. Examination of the tube by P. Craddock suggested that it had been made from a single flat piece of clay which had been wrapped around a wooden stick to form the tube, and then fired at high temperature under oxidising conditions, leaving it an orange colour (Craddock in Bewley *et al* 1992, 343-5). Of the few tuyères known from Britain most are of Late Bronze Age date, for example those from Mucking, Essex and Breidden, Wales. Closer to Cumbria in time and space is a possible nozzle from Woodhouse End, Cheshire (Rowley 1977). The Ewanrigg example was probably part of a composite tuyère; one end would have been tied to the bellows and the other would have fitted into a larger tapering nozzle that would have connected to the furnace (*112*). This design was successfully used by African smiths until recently and had the advantage of reducing the risk of hot gases being sucked back into the leather bag of the bellows. The presence of bellows points to metalworking rather than pottery production, as only metallurgy needed the higher temperature they generated. That is not to say that the furnace was being used to separate copper from its ore, more likely the furnace was used to raise the temperature sufficient for annealing of bronze scrap in a crucible (Craddock in Bewley *et al* 1992, 345).

Further evidence for metal production comes from moulds. The earliest metal artefacts were made using open stone moulds, none of which have been found in Cumbria. Later more sophisticated two-part stone moulds were used, examples of which were found at Croglin in Cumbria (anon 1884, 279). These would have made a twin-looped, leaf-shaped spearhead (Burgess 1968, 25) of Period 5 and spearshaft ferrule (*113*). No spearhead fitting the mould has yet been discovered, however the spear ferrule found in the Ambleside hoard is very similar to that of the mould.

Consumption of metalwork is one of the factors that emphasise communal similarity and difference. The ownership of metalwork and activities such as deposition which went along with it were social markers used in group affiliation. Deliberate deposition of particular objects suggests that they had specific meaning; this meaning came about during the life of the object (Munn 1986; Rowlands 1993, 147, 149). This implies that during its life an object

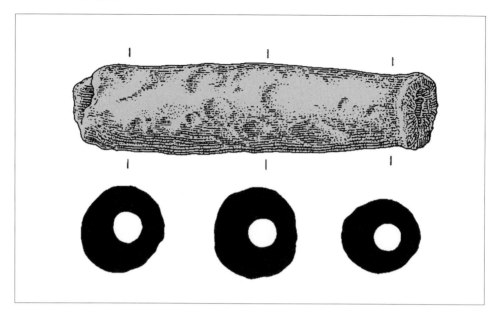

111 Clay connecting rod for a furnace, found at Ewanrigg, Cumbria. How this object was used is illustrated in figure *112*. *Courtesy of Bob Bewley 1992, 332 fig. 7*

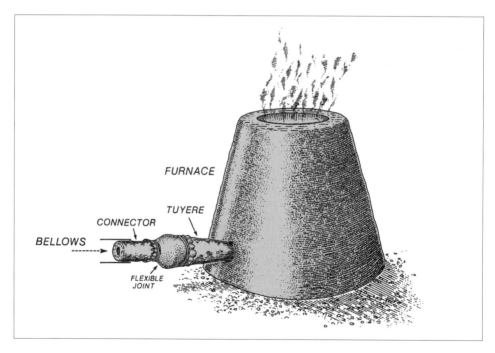

FURNACE

TUYERE

CONNECTOR

BELLOWS

FLEXIBLE
JOINT

112 A hypothetical reconstruction of a Bronze Age furnace. *Courtesy of Bob Bewley 1992, 344 fig. 13, illustrated by Philip Dean*

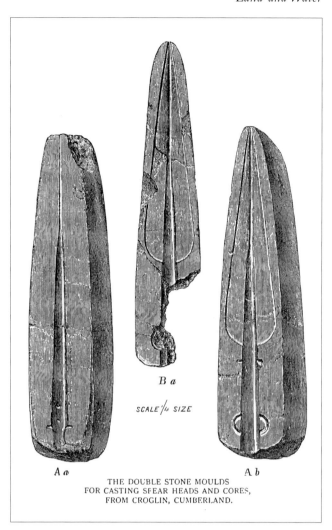

B *a*

SCALE ¼ SIZE

A *a*   A *b*

THE DOUBLE STONE MOULDS
FOR CASTING SPEAR HEADS AND CORES,
FROM CROGLIN, CUMBERLAND.

113 Two-part stone moulds
found at Croglin. The
moulds would have made
a twin-looped, leaf-shaped
spearhead and a spearshaft
ferrule. *Anon 1884, 279*

is likely to undergo transformations of meaning. In order to become valuable and earn the
right to be ritually deposited artefacts must fulfil specific expectations. If they do not fulfil the
expectations, and follow the life-path considered appropriate, they may lose their significance.
This is something which has been recorded for several ethnographic case studies on the use
of valuables (Weiner 1992). In the case of metalwork it is unclear whether objects began their
lives as commodities, later transforming their status to that of valuable, or whether they always
existed as valuables. It is likely that bronze objects may have been both gifts and commodities
(Bradley 1990, 144-8) with different spheres of exchange co-existing (Bloch and Parry 1989,
15; Kopytoff 1986, 71-2). As Mauss (1993 [1923/1924]) has shown, during gift exchange an
object is to some extent seen as imbued with the presence of the former owner, hence the
inalienability of the object. It becomes, to an extent, personified. Godelier (1999) has argued
that in the case of valuables perceived as very special, objects are not only seen as signalling
the presence of former owners, but of very special persons, and even ancestors or gods.

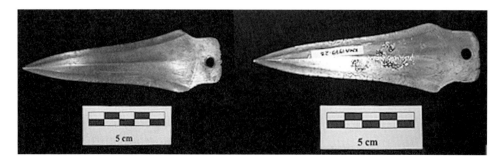

114 Dirk, modified for rehafting. Found at Foulshaw/Helsington Moss, Cumbria. *Museum reference number: Kendal Museum KMA 1979.28*

The transactions themselves are hard to recognise archaeologically. One way that we may identify the existence of spheres of exchange is through use-wear analysis. Valuables are likely to have passed through several hands in order to accumulate complex biographies (see Malinowski 1922 for discussion of the *kula*) before being deposited. They are therefore likely to have achieved considerable age and to bear the marks of circulation at the point of deposition. Repeated resharpening and reworking of objects has been noted elsewhere in the European Bronze Age (for example Vandkilde 1996, 32). In Cumbria a number of instances of resharpening can be identified in spears. Even more striking is a Group II dirk of Period 5, Acton phase, found at Foulshaw/Helsington Moss, Cumbria (*114*), which has had its butt reworked to form a broad tang with a secondary hole drilled through it for rehafting (Barrowclough 2007, fig. 6.29). With each event the artefact acquired additional meaning imbuing it with individual character.

Support for the hypothesis that objects, which circulated over long periods of time, acquired extensive biographies prior to deposition is provided by hoards. When objects of different types, and therefore different origins and ages, are found together in hoards it is possible to estimate the distance and time that some of the objects were in circulation. This is because the more distant objects would have taken time to travel to their point of deposition and because older objects could not have been deposited until at least the date that the younger objects were manufactured. Taking data from the Ambleside hoard for which the typology of the contents could be determined it was possible to determine that some of them had travelled considerable distances. Amongst the hoard were a sword and rapier with solid cast hilts, similar to one found at Salta Moss in Cumbria. These weapons are generally rare in Britain and are thought to be imports, probably from France, as they share many features with French weapons of the Rosnoën group (Briard 1965, 153). The objects in the Ambleside hoard are dated to the Middle Bronze Age, Penard Phase of Period 5, 1300-1150 cal BC and thus the oldest objects were *c.*150 years old at the time they were deposited. Although the dating is approximate it is possible that the objects, particularly the solid cast hilted weapons passed through several generations before they were deposited.

Exchange takes place between people and also between people and supernatural forces, ancestors, spirits and gods (Godelier 1999), and it is this that leads to consideration of the final stage in the life cycle of metalwork: deposition. For the purposes of the discussion that follows a distinction must be made between objects that were placed in the ground with the intention of leaving them there forever, and those that were only temporarily stored but never retrieved. The former marks the intentional end of an object's biography, from the point of view of those making the deposit, the latter the unintentional interruption of a biography. Objects that were lost are another example of an unintended interruption of an object's life.

When objects are deposited they are taken out of circulation. It is this economic aspect of hoarding that has often received greatest attention. In this study I wish to emphasise another aspect, that of the relationship between the people making the deposit and the location in which it is made. The act of deposition brings together histories of people, of objects and of places. This aspect of deposition is generally neglected in studies (Bradley 2000), perhaps because detailed palaeoecological reconstructions are rarely possible. In the case of lowland Cumbria it has been possible to reconstruct the Bronze Age landscape in some detail (see Chapter 1) making this approach possible.

The Furness district of Cumbria lies on the northern edge of Morecambe Bay. During the Late Neolithic the lowest lying ground was inundated with water, but as sea-levels fell, as they did throughout the Bronze Age, substantial areas of wetland 'moss' were created. Human activity in this area is evidenced by the presence of stone tools, pottery and in particular by a concentration of metal artefacts. In all, 32 bronze artefacts have been found in this area, more than anywhere else in the study region (*115*). They include the Skelmore Heads hoard already considered as part of this discussion. The density of deposited objects and the period of time that they represent, from Period 2-8, 2300-500 cal BC, suggests that this landscape was held to have particular meaning over a long span of time making it particularly appropriate to the deposition of metalwork. This case makes the point that significance may reside not in a single event but in the repetition of events, each of which contributes to the construction of a cultural landscape.

Within this long timespan, depositional activity concentrated on certain types of object, in particular axes and spears. Deposition was clearly selective as both flanged axes were of type Caverton, both palstaves were of Primary Shield Pattern type and all of the socketed axes deposited in Period 8, Llyn Fawr Phase, were of the same type, Sompting. This strongly suggests that selection was taking place, arguably as a means of maintaining group identity through material culture. The increase in Late Bronze Age material deposited in the Furness area may suggest that strong socio-political control was established across the landscape, an interpretation consistent with the rise of the defended hilltop settlements flanking the northern shore of Morecambe Bay from Urswick to Warton Crag. During the Late Bronze Age, hilltops begin to be developed as enclosed sites, usually seen as the precursors to hillforts. Rather than being primarily defensive, it is a strong possibility that these sites had specialist functions, perhaps associated with metalworking, gatherings of some sort or high-status individuals. Skelmore Heads in Furness (Powell 1963), has revealed at least two phases of occupation, since the prominent stone-banked enclosure was preceded by a timber palisade, but little artefactual material was recovered during the excavations and almost no occupational debris was encountered within the trenches. Parallels to the structural sequence at Skelmore Heads have been found in Scotland and at Huckhoe in Northumberland, which have a suggested Late Bronze Age origin (Annable 1987, 255; Higham 1986, 121). It has been

Period	Phase	Type	Sub-type
2	Mount Pleasant	Flat Axe	Migdale
2	Mount Pleasant	Flat Axe	Ballybeg/Roseisle
2	Mount Pleasant	Armlet	Unclassified
2	Mount Pleasant	Armlet	Unclassified
3	Overton	Awl	Tanged
3	Overton	Awl	Double ended
3	Overton	Flat Axe	Unclassified
3	Overton	Flat Axe	Bandon
3	Ewart Park	Hammer	Socketed
4	Arreton	Chisel	Tanged
4	Arreton	Flanged Axe	Caverton
4	Arreton	Flanged Axe	Caverton
4	Arreton	Razor	Unclassified
5	Acton	Rapier	Keelogue
5	Acton	Rapier	Unclassified
5	Acton/Taunton	Palstave	Primary Shield Pattern
5	Acton/Taunton	Palstave	Primary Shield Pattern
5	Taunton	Armlet	Unclassified
5	Taunton	Spearhead	Basal looped, leaf blade
5	Taunton	Spearhead	Basal looped, leaf blade
5	Penard	Socketed Axe	Gillespie
5	Penard	Spearhead	Pegged socketed, leaf blade
5	Penard	Spearhead	Pegged socketed, leaf blade
7	Ewart Park	Socketed Axe	Meldreth
7	Ewart Park	Sword	Ewart Park
8	Llyn Fawr	Socketed Axe	Sompting
8	Llyn Fawr	Socketed Axe	Sompting
8	Llyn Fawr	Socketed Axe	Sompting

Period	Phase	Type	Sub-type
8	Llyn Fawr	Socketed Axe	Sompting
8	Llyn Fawr	Socketed Axe	Sompting
8	Llyn Fawr	Socketed Axe	Sompting

115 Metal artefacts found in the Furness district, Cumbria, classified according to period and type.
N = 32

argued that the clustering of Late Bronze Age metalwork in the vicinity, allied to the Iron Age enclosure, indicates the presence of an *oppida*-like settlement – a focus of local power exerted over the surrounding area. Although the chronology of occupation is poorly defined, the finds suggest that this may have been established in the Late Bronze Age as a palisaded enclosure and continued through the Iron Age (Higham 1986, 121-35). Excavations at Urswick Stone Walls, also in the Furness Peninsula, have indicated similar continuity between the Late Bronze Age and Iron Age. The excavations on a hut circle revealed a mixed assemblage, including a Bronze Age flint scraper, large quern stones and a decorated bronze fragment, dated stylistically to 200-100 BC (*c.*2200-2100 BP; Smith 1907, 99).

The nature of the objects deposited in the Furness district may be a clue to the people involved in the act of deposition (Traherne 1995; Ehrenreich 1997; Sørensen 1998, 262; Bradley 2000, 56). In line with the general evidence on prehistoric weapon graves, it is assumed that activity around Furness was primarily a male one. I would not want to place too much emphasis on attempts to identify the people involved in the act of deposition, but I feel safer in asserting that the choice of depositional location appears to have been steered by cultural considerations. Given the combination of selected location and selective deposition, rules and perhaps taboos may well have existed which stated that a particular type of object should only be deposited in a particular place.

The act of deposition brings about change to the people, the object and the place involved. The object is removed from society, and with it the biography of its past owners; the people, who no longer possess the object, are perhaps transformed in status, especially if the object was associated with illustrious owners; and the place itself, which in the memory of the participants will be linked to the act of deposition. The setting in which the act took place, a wetland environment prone to seasonal flooding, may also be perceived as symbolically changed by the act. As a result the location, already redolent with communal memories of earlier acts of deposition, can have added resonance in the memories of the participants. Although knowledge of the ceremony may be transferred from generation to generation the exact details will fade, be reinvented and embellished. With no permanent marker, so far as we are aware, the narrative is open to 'rewriting' and manipulation by future generations.

We have seen that deposits were placed cumulatively around Furness over a period of several centuries. The mechanism that triggered these acts of sacrifice is unclear. One interpretation of metal deposited in natural places would be to see the deposits as funeral hoards.

This is an explanation offered by Warmenbol (1996) with regard to deposits in Belgium, but based on the earlier ideas of Wegner (1976) and Bradley (1990, 102). They observed that weapon sets first deposited in graves were, at later stages of the Bronze Age, placed in hoards. I favour this mechanism as it fits the pattern of activity found in Cumbria and elsewhere in north-west England.

In Early Bronze Age burials, for example Borwick, to the east of Furness, single or occasionally a pair of axes were deposited. Later, in the Middle Bronze Age, deposits of axes, again often singly or in pairs, formed the basis of deposits in natural places. Stronger evidence for the link between death and hoarding comes from a rare Late Bronze Age burial at Butts Beck Quarry, Dalton-in-Furness, where a pegged socketed leaf-blade spearhead was found with a Ewart Park, Northern Step 1, sword and human bones in a stone cist along with the bones of a horse (Gaythorpe 1899, 164-66).

Hoards in natural, 'wet' locations may be interpreted as hoards of personal equipment, deposited at the moment of death, but buried separate from the body. The implication is that weapon deposits are related to the conceptualisation of the deceased, but in a skewed manner. Blok (1994, 34 cited in Fontijn 2002, 231) argues that using violence against others is a polluting action, since it transgresses the boundary between the category of life and death. As such it may have repercussions for the way in which people deal with weapons, both in daily life and in ritual. For this reason, the use of violence is often related to rituals (Blok 1994, 34). In the case of the Butts Beck burial the sword had been deliberately bent, perhaps as an act of decommissioning, and similar acts of deformation have been observed in swords and rapier deposits in watery locations just outside our study area in Lancashire, for example a rapier found bent in the River Ribble at Ribchester.

The separation of certain classes of artefact: bronze spears, axes, and also swords, implies that they represent an ambiguous category in material culture. Weapons are often seen as ambiguous, even dangerous in ethnographic studies. Politically, weapons are dangerous because their presence in a social group implies 'haves' and 'have-nots', and thus potentially a group who can impose their will upon others (Claessen 1988, 7-8). In small-scale society where there was previously no authority with an effective monopoly of force (Roymans 1996, 14), the presence of weaponry may have threatened established social cohesion. Thus, ideologies are reflected and constructed in the practices and lifestyles of people. In the evidence from metal deposition we can see at least a glimpse of the connection between ideological values and real life.

Conclusions

The analysis of the landscape context of metalwork during the periods of the Bronze Age leads to the following conclusions. First, deposition was selective, both in terms of artefacts selected, and of places in the landscape chosen for deposition. Secondly, deposition was also cumulative, with repeated acts of deposition occurring in the same place, and other places therefore being repeatedly ignored. Thirdly, deposition was ideological, it was used to construct and maintain identities, elements of which were regional.

This discussion has demonstrated that when we start to examine the detailed local contexts of use and deposition of artefacts that previously would have been interpreted as evidence for 'migration' or 'invasion' (or centre and periphery) we will start to identify subtle local variations pointing to the appropriation of items of material culture for particular purposes. It is at the local scale that we may be able to identify certain patterns of use that point to the deliberate articulation of cultural differences. It is also in the historical depth that archaeology provides that we may be able to trace the formation of new types of identities through the use of material culture. Such patterning may be due to different types of communal identity such as familial lineages or territorial groupings, discussed further in Chapter 9.

CHAPTER 8

CELTIC CULT PRACTICES:
IRON AGE CUMBRIA

When Aulus Plautius founded the Fosse frontier in the years AD 44-7 he was simply emphasizing a geographical and political truth. Britain could be divided into two parts about a line drawn along the Jurassic ridge from Lincoln to Lyme Bay. To the south and east lay a densely settled region with authority centralised about oppida and with a subsistence economy depending to a large extent on the production of grain. To the north and west settlement was more scattered and in places sparse, there was little centralisation of power and, while cereals were widely grown, there appears to have been a greater reliance on stock rearing.

Cunliffe 1991, 213

Evidence for ritual and belief in Iron Age Cumbria includes a variety of different classes of data including direct evidence for the disposal of the dead in the form of regular burials and also the 'bog burials'. The deposition of bodies in bogs was part of a varied repertoire of artefacts that were deliberately deposited in selected parts of the landscape. Beliefs seemed to have focused on particular wet places: springs, tarns, lakes and rivers; and also on dry sites, in specially dug holes or in existing pits and ditches, and in natural features such as caves and limestone grykes. Overall these deposits may be interpreted as displays of belief, to which we may add the possibility that excarnation took place, but has left no visible trace; and a few literary references, from Roman sources, concerned largely with the Druids. Together these sources create the impression of a highly complex belief system pervading the everyday life of the people and governing their perception of the Cumbrian landscape.

Iron Age Background

Generally, the evidence for Iron Age activity in Cumbria, as in the rest of north-west England, is thin. In the lowlands of North Cumbria during the Early to Middle Iron Age there is a scarcity of archaeological material (Bewley 1994, 63). With the exception of hillforts found on the southern edge of the plain at Carrock Fell and Swarthy Hill, dated to c.500 BC (c.2450 BP; Bewley 1992), the only sites dated to this period are an Iron Age burial with pottery at Rise Hill (Bellhouse 1984) and a bog body from Scaleby Moss which may be of later prehistoric date (discussed below). It has been argued that this may in part be explained by the relative lack of archaeological excavation and difficulty in identifying Iron Age sites (Bewley 1986;

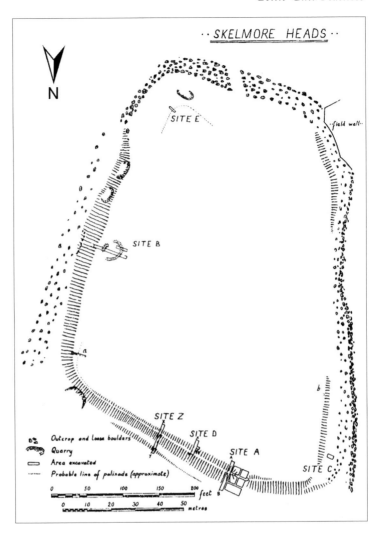

116 Site plan of
the Early Iron Age
defended hillfort
at Skelmore Heads,
Furness. *Powell et al
1963*

McCarthy 1995), certainly the evidence from pollen cores confirms that in the lowlands of
North Cumbria there was steady but low-level agricultural activity in the first millennium
BC. This includes indications of cereal cultivation in the vicinity of Bolton Fell Moss (Barber
1981, 112). On the basis of current knowledge the clear picture which seems to emerge from
both strands of evidence is of a sparsely populated landscape in the North Cumbrian lowlands for the first part of the Iron Age.

The appearance of a large number of enclosures on Solway Plain, detectable through
cropmarks, coincides with a major expansion of forest clearance and agricultural activity
in North Cumbria, identifiable in pollen cores dated to the final centuries of the first
millennium BC (Bewley 1994, 63). The clearance of forest has been observed at a number
of sites, for example at Walton Moss intensive clearance started before 111 cal BC–cal AD 83
(2000±45 BP, SRR-4531), before declining at 8 cal BC–cal AD 139 (1925±40 BP, SRR-4530;
Dumayne and Barber 1994). Across the Solway at Burnfoothill Moss, Tipping (1995b) records

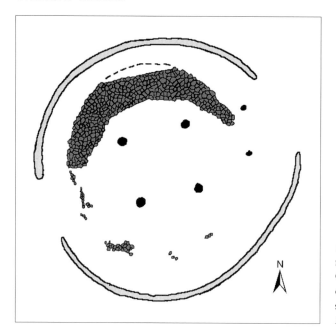

117 Plan of an Early Iron Age
roundhouse at Wolsty Hall,
Cumbria. The house has two
entrances and a central four-post
setting. *After Blake 1959 &
Harding 2004, fig. 2.6(5)*

a similar process beginning before 157 cal BC-cal AD 76 (2015±45 BP, SRR-3752), while the
pollen diagram from Midgeholme Moss, situated immediately to the north of Hadrian's Wall
at Birdoswald, also shows a Late Iron Age clearance initiated before 355 cal BC-cal AD 125
(2040±80 BP, OxA-2325; Innes 1988). On the Solway Plain, small-scale excavation suggested
the Roman re-use of a prehistoric circular enclosure at Boustead Hill, and a possibly similar
situation at Fingland (Bewley 1986), at the Ewanrigg settlement (Bewley 1992), and at
Edderside (Bewley 1998). If the circular enclosures are Iron Age in origin, in contrast to the
Roman rectangular and square examples (Bewley 1994; cf. Bewley 1998, 114), their ubiquity
would suggest a widely settled landscape in the Iron Age.

Despite the paucity of securely dated sites, the evidence suggests that individual enclosed
farmsteads were the normal settlement pattern which appears to have existed across (at least
parts) of the Solway Plain by the end of the first millennium cal BC. The economy of such
settlements is likely to have been mixed, with possibly a strong element of seasonal stock
movement; such a pattern of settlement and subsistence has been noted in other parts of
northern England where archaeological visibility and survival are better (Cunliffe 1991,
275-9; Haselgrove 1996).

Evidence for Iron Age activity on the West Cumbrian Coastal Plain is also scanty and con-
trasts with the Furness evidence (below). The only lowland sites to have produced artefacts of
Early Iron Age date are Eskmeals, consisting of a pair of blue beads found in association with
an earlier flint scatter (Cherry 1963, 50) and Seascale Moss, where a bog body may date to the
later prehistoric period (see discussion below). Such limited evidence is insufficient to prove
continuity of habitation of the sand-hill sites from the Bronze Age. To the south, at Whicham,
a double-ditched enclosure, interpreted as a bivallate hillfort, has been found by aerial photography (Higham 1986, 130). This site, which has not been excavated, may be similar to other

sites around the northern shore of Morecambe Bay, at Skelmore Heads, Castle Head and Warton Crag and the enclosed settlement at Urswick.

Skelmore Heads (*116*) follows a sequence from stockade enclosure to earthwork fort, which may have included a timber box-rampart (Powell *et al* 1963). A Late Bronze Age hoard from the site may be contemporary with one of the early phases but precise dating is unavailable for Skelmore Heads and also Castle Head and Warton Crag 'hillforts'. Approximately 1.5km (1 mile) south-west of Skelmore Heads lies Urswick Stone Walls (Dobson 1907) where excavations revealed a stone enclosure wall within which the principal roundhouse was also constructed of stone, including massive undressed boulders. The distribution around Morecambe Bay may suggest that local communities were controlling access to and from the Irish Sea routes to arable resources. The Cumbrian hillforts, together with those of Lancashire and Cheshire (Barrowclough 2008) and the rest of northern England, differ from those of southern England and in particular Wessex. In Cumbria there are no 'developed hillforts' (Cunliffe 1991, 352), indeed the evidence suggests that few if any hillforts were still occupied in the immediate pre-Roman Iron Age.

As in the Scottish Borders, the distinction between small hillfort and more substantial ditched homestead blurs, with the great majority of sites being under an acre (around half a hectare) in an enclosed area. Examples of excavated Iron Age roundhouses in Cumbria are few, but at Wolsty Hall a roundhouse with two entrances and a central four-post setting was found (*117*). Of the three adjacent enclosures: oval, circular and rectangular, the latter two both produced clear evidence of occupation in the Roman period. But in the case of the oval enclosure Hadrianic pottery occurred in the upper levels of the ditch filling, suggesting that it was long since out of use by the early second century, whilst the roundhouse occupation within the enclosure produced no Roman material.

A potential regional *oppidum* is the site of Carrock Fell (*118*). At over two hectares (five acres) R.G. Collingwood (1938) thought it could have formed a tribal centre, it is however unlikely that it was permanently occupied. There are no traces of habitation and at 650m it would have been inhospitable. Higham (1986, 129) argued that permanent settlement was confined to lower locations such as Dobcross Hall (Higham 1981), a univallate enclosure of three hectares in which the ditch was of defensive proportions. Among smaller enclosed sites, the triple-ditched cliff-edge enclosure at Swarthy Hall on the Solway Plain produced a single radiocarbon date from its ditch filling of 450±50 BC (Bewley 1992).

With the apparent abandonment of the hillforts, evidence for the Late Iron Age and Early Romano-British period is sparse in Cumbria. Pollen cores show that the episodes of extensive clearance, associated with cereal cultivation, date from *c.*2400 BP (*c.*700-400 cal BC) in the Duddon valley and *c.*2200 BP (*c.*350-200 cal BC) in the Lyth valley (Wells 1991). Evidence from Coniston Water, immediately to the north (Pennington 1997, 44), has also yielded additional evidence of this phenomenon with major deforestation beginning just before *c.*110 cal BC-cal AD 120 (1980±50 BP, SRR-1872), suggesting a resurgence of clearance activity across much of South Cumbria. These results are directly comparable those from the North and West Cumbrian Plains that we have already considered and also with those from the upland fringes, such as the episode of upland cereal cultivation from the south-western fells, which is dated to *c.*cal AD 210-680 (1560±130 BP, NPL-116) at Burnmoor Tarn and *c.*20 cal BC-cal AD 592

(1750±130 BP, NPL -117) at Devoke Water (Pennington 1970, 72). The pattern continues over the county boundary in Lancashire at the Forest of Bowland (MacKay and Tallis 1994) and at Fenton Cottage, in the Over Wyre district of Lancashire situated immediately across Morecambe Bay (Barrowclough 2008, ch. 7), where a major deforestation begins at the end of the first millennium BC (Middleton *et al* 1995, 151, 170; Wells *et al* 1997). A small rise in sea-level may explain the absence for low-lying settlement. A study of the Leven estuary at Roudsea, near to the Duddon valley, identified a previously undetected rise in sea-level of >0.5m OD sometime after 800-380 cal BC (2420±80 BP, Beta-88434; Zong 1997). Rising inland water tables resulting from this may have caused waterlogging or flooding in low-lying areas around the Duddon estuary resulting in abandonment of settlement.

The evidence from upland areas points to a relatively high density of settlements, such as the extensive habitations, enclosures and fields on Crosby Garrett and Crosby Ravensworth fells, and the crop-marks identified from aerial photographs in the Eden valley and Solway Plain make it unlikely that the county was sparsely settled. This confirms the account of Tacitus that the territory of the Brigantes was reputedly the most populous in the entire province (Agricola 17).

At Crosby Garrett fields radiate around the Severals settlement in a way that suggests an integral system (*119*). Many sites display a degree of complexity that suggests longevity of occupation from the mid-first millennium BC to the mid-first millennium AD. In his survey of the Crosby Ravensworth sites R.G. Collingwood (1933, 204) noted the frequent occurrence of barrows of presumed Bronze Age date in proximity to Iron Age and Romano-British 'native' settlements, but failed to understand that this was evidence for a continuity of occupation of the landscape. More recent work in the North Yorkshire Moors (Harding 2004, ch. 2) has demonstrated an older genesis for the landscape pattern of dykes and settlements there that applies equally to Cumbria (Harding 2004, 50). This is shown by the site of Wolsty Hall.

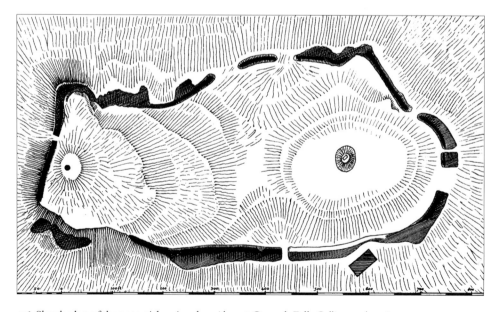

118 Sketch plan of the potential regional *oppidum* at Carrock Fell. *Collingwood 1938*

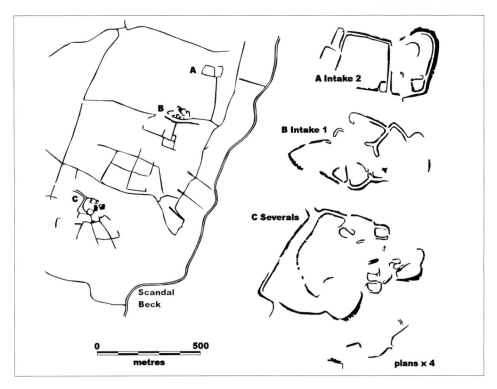

119 Plan of Late Iron Age/Romano-British settlements at Crosby Garrett, Westmorland. *After RCHME 1936*

The Wolsty Hall roundhouse was of a type that underlies the regional diversity of Iron Age roundhouse architecture. Its external wall, 13.5m in diameter, was based on a ring-groove, with two opposed entrances, each with a pair of post-holes marking the inner limit of a porch. Around the inner edge of the ring-groove the excavator detected traces of a turf wall or revetment, which in turn was defined on its inner edge by an arc of cobbled flooring. A setting of four posts in the centre of the house is unusual. Within the considerable diversity of roundhouse construction in the Early Iron Age in northern England there are recurrent elements including ring-groove construction and the use of double entrances. These features are also found in the roundhouses of the Borders and south-west Scotland (Harding 2004, 53).

Following the Roman invasion of Britain in AD 43 Roman control quickly spread across lowland England and South Wales up to an informal frontier running across the Midlands and marked by the Fosse Way. To protect this frontier the Romans reached an arrangement with the Brigantes, the main tribal grouping of northern England led by their queen Cartimandua. Within Cumbria the local tribes were the Carvetii and perhaps also the Setantii, who may have extended from Lancashire into southern Cumbria, encompassing Morecambe Bay (Chapter 9). Along with the other tribes of northern England they would have been under Brigantian control (*120*). This sense of semi-independence is captured by the Roman author Pomponius Mela (*de Chorographia* III, 6, 51) who, talking of Britons, states that '... all are uncivilised, and the farther away they are from the continent, the more they are unacquainted

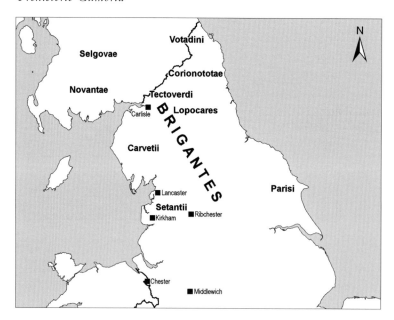

120 The tribes of northern England with the location of some of the major Roman forts indicated

with its other blessings'. In terms of ritual and belief it also suggests that at this point the local population would have continued to hold faith in the Celtic gods and ways of doing things. Certainly we know that Anglesey was a Druid stronghold, described by Tacitus as a 'source of strength to the rebels' (Agricola, xiv). Tacitus' description of the storming of the island in AD 59 is vivid: 'The enemy lined the shore in a dense mass. Among them were blackrobed women with dishevelled hair like Furies, brandishing torches. Nearby stood the Druids raising their hands to heaven and screaming dreadful curses'. Overcoming their fear, the Roman soldiers pushed on to victory and destroyed 'the groves devoted to Mona's [i.e. Anglesey's] barbarous superstitions' (Annals xiv, 30).

Unrest in North Wales led to the establishment of the fort at Chester in the AD 50s (Petch 1987) and was followed by the collapse of the relationship with the Brigantes, triggering the Roman army's move northwards to suppress Brigantine resistance. The process of conquest was begun by governor Petilius Cerialis (AD 71-74) and completed by Agricola (AD 77-84). Working from the south, northwards, after the fort at Chester auxillary forts were built at Northwich, Middlewich and Manchester. In Lancashire forts were built at Preston, Kirkham, Ribchester and Lancaster. Following the river Lune, in Cumbria the fort at Burrow-in-Lunesdale may be of early date as are those at Low Borrow Bridge, Kirkby Thore, Carlisle and Blennerhasset. Other sites with important Roman forts are Ravenglass, Maryport, Brougham and Brough. On the northern frontier the constant rebuilding of the military frontier of Hadrian's Wall implies that native rebellion was a constant threat.

The Roman invasion changed political organisation in Cumbria, but outside the civilian centre of Carlisle, known as Luguvallum, the basic pattern of economic and social life probably continued largely unchanged. Brigantian landowners did not, or were not allowed to, adopt Roman ways and amongst the existing pre-Roman native population the pattern of small dispersed settlements or farmsteads of the Iron Age continued. In Brigantian territory this pattern of settlement is well established in Cumbria and North Lancashire (Higham and Jones 1975; Higham 1980), where the population remained thin, though with concentrations of new settlements occurring around Roman forts. A site within Levens Park (Turnbull and Walsh 1996, 15), known as 'The Temple of Diana', has yielded first-century material with superimposed post-Roman structures. A similar enclosure (the Sizergh Fell Barrow), excavated by McKenny Hughes on Heaves Fell, revealed a skeleton within the corner of one of the walls, interred with a blue melon bead, a bronze fibula and ring, dated to the second to third century AD (McKenny Hughes 1912a).

Burial Rituals

Evidence for burial or funerary practice is extremely rare. An inhumation burial associated with sherds of pottery was cut by the construction trench of the Roman milecastle at Risehow and was most likely of Iron Age date (Bewley 1994, 85; Bellhouse 1984). More certain evidence comes from Butts Beck Quarry, Dalton-in-Furness, where a Late Bronze Age 'warrior' burial was found in 1873 (Gaythorpe 1899, 161, 164-166). A stone cist *c*.1.8m x 1.2m x 1.2m contained a single adult inhumation together with the bones of a horse and an assemblage of weapons. The latter included a sword which had been deliberately bent in the middle and a peg-socketed leaf-shaped spear.

Possible Iron Age burials include a group of three crouched inhumations at Crosby Garrett (Whimster 1981, 169, 403) whilst an Iron Age inhumation cemetery was excavated at Nelson Square, Levens (Parsons 2004; Rachel Newman pers. comm.). An area of 140 square metres was stripped of topsoil revealing five Late Iron Age graves containing five, or possibly six, inhumation burials, all cutting into the limestone bedrock (*121*). Grave 5 measured 1.35m x 0.85m, with the long axis aligned north-east to south-west (*122*). A skeleton was found within the grave in a crouched position lying on its left side. Grave 6 measured 1.35m x 0.76m, hourglass in shape and aligned north to south. An inhumation lay in a semi-crouched position on its left side. Grave 9 measured 0.85m x 0.55m aligned north to south. The skeleton was poorly preserved. Grave 12 measured 1.06m x 1.77m aligned north-east to south-west. The skeleton was again poorly preserved. Grave 15 measured 1.1m x 1.15m and irregular in shape, it contained the mandible from a second skeleton and there is a possibility given the 'unnatural' placing of the limb bones of the main interment that they had been disarticulated prior to burial (Parsons 2004, 17). No dateable finds were recovered from the graves but radiocarbon assay of Grave 5 skeletal material placed the burial in the Late Iron Age at 172-44 cal BC (2089 ±24 BP, KIA-24385).

Inhumation cemeteries of Iron Age date are very rare in Britain with only *c*.30 examples recorded in England, the majority of which are in Cornwall and Dorset (English Heritage 1990; Cunliffe 2005, 551 and fig. 20.6). They first appear in the fourth century BC, in the Middle Iron Age, and continued into the Roman conquest. Most articulated inhumations occur as isolated burials within pits and ditches, and often crouched as in the case of the Risehow burial. Both the Butts Beck and Nelson burials are exceptions to the general national pattern and worthy of more detailed consideration.

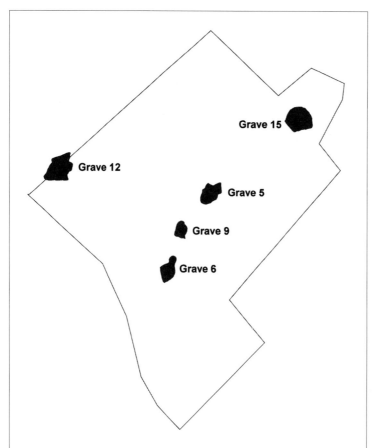

121 Site plan of
the Late Iron
Age inhumation
cemetery at Nelson
Square, Levens. *After
Parsons 2004*

Grave 15

Grave 12

Grave 5

Grave 9

Grave 6

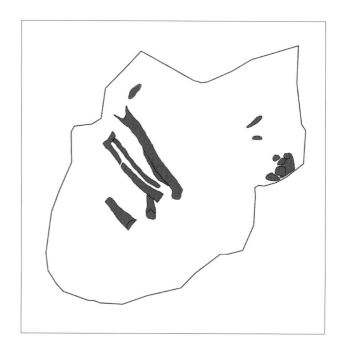

122 Excavation plan of Grave 5
at the Late Iron Age cemetery
at Nelson Square, Levens,
which contained a crouched
inhumation. *After Parsons 2004*

The burial at Butts Beck of an adult man together with weapons and a horse is usually described in the literature as a 'warrior burial'. Warrior burials form a distinct group characterised by the combination of weapons and male inhumation in burials without barrows (Cunliffe 2005, 555-557 and fig. 20.10). Such burials characteristically occur in Yorkshire at North Grimston, Bugthorpe, Kirkburn, Rudston and Garton Station; outside this they are less common but may still be found, for example at Shouldham in Norfolk, Deal in Kent and as far as Bryther in the Isles of Scilly. Given their wide distribution it would not be a total surprise to find a warrior burial in Cumbria, however I believe that there may be an alternative interpretation for this burial as none of the warrior burials were accompanied by horses, distinguishing the Butts Beck burial. Returning to the evidence for burials in Yorkshire we find a distinctive burial practice focused in east Yorkshire, associated with the Arras Culture (Stead 1979, 1991; Dent 1982, 1985). Within the Arras Culture are a number of cart burials, characterised by male inhumations associated with horses and carts and in some cases personal equipment and harness fittings, for example the Wetwang Slack burials (Cunliffe 2005, 548-9). Outside Yorkshire such burials are rare, but not unknown. At Mildenhall in Suffolk an extended inhumation was found, accompanied by a sword, axe and gold torc and flanked by the skeletons of two horses. Although there was no certain evidence of a barrow or of a cart this burial is considered to be a cart burial. Like the burial at Butts Beck, found in 1899, the discovery was made some years ago and is 'ill-recorded', and therefore it is highly likely that in both cases the organic remains of a wooden cart, had one been present, would have gone unnoticed. Prof. Barry Cunliffe of the University of Oxford lists several other similar burials, where a man was found with a horse but without evidence of a cart, for example at Newnham Croft in Cambridge and Fordington in Dorset, all of which he classes as cart burials (Cunliffe 2005, 550). On this basis we might also consider placing the Butts Beck burial in this category of cart burial rather than that of the warrior burial. Alternatively, it may be that we have identified an additional category of inhumation burial: that of the warrior and horse.

Nelson Square is an exception to the most common form of individual burials and has parallels with the larger cemetery at Worton Rectory Farm, Yarnton in Oxfordshire, where nine of the 35 crouched, north to south orientated, burials were radiocarbon dated to the Middle Iron Age (Hey *et al* 1999). Most prehistoric inhumation cemeteries have been located on relatively low-lying land, the majority under 120m OD, and many are near to rivers, with Iron Age examples showing a preference for burial in a crouched position with the head to the north. The Nelson Square site fits this trend as it lies at approximately 45m OD and overlooks the rivers Kent and Gilpin (Parsons 2004). Where bone preservation was sufficient to establish orientation and position, all the burials were crouched with the head to the north. Tightly crouched burials, often suggestive of the binding of the corpse after death, are a common feature in the treatment of the corpse in the prehistoric periods. Iron Age regional variations in funerary rituals, such as the Arras Culture and Durotrigan warrior burials, also predominantly involve positioning the corpse on its side in a crouched position (Taylor 2001, 73-5), as do most Iron Age pit burials (Cunliffe 1978, 312; Whimster 1981, 211; Wait 1985, 83). The rather unnatural positioning of the skeleton in grave 15 and the presence of the mandible of another individual within the same grave are suggestive of excarnation before burial (Parsons 2004, 28). These 'bag' or 'sack' burials, where largely disarticulated bones were interred, are known from other Iron Age sites, such as that at Fengate, Peterborough (Pryor 1982, 369).

Before we move to discussion of the bog bodies there is a further type of inhumation identified by Cunliffe as involving a separate ritual practice (2005, 557-8). At Burnmouth in Berwickshire and Mill Hill, Deal in Kent, extended inhumations have been found, each with a pair of bronze spoons. In each pair one spoon was marked with a cross, the other had a small hole punched to one side. Spoons of this kind have been found in various parts of Britain, some in contexts which suggest ritual deposits. At Grayber, Crosby Ravensworth, a pair were found by a spring in a bog. At Penbryn in Cardiganshire another pair had been buried under a pile of stones; the River Thames produced a single spoon and some of those from Ireland were probably from bogs. Cunliffe argues that 'it is difficult to resist the conclusion that these spoons were in some way connected with ritual procedures' (2005, 559).

Beyond Nelson Square possible evidence for burial in the Iron Age consists of two bog bodies from Scaleby and Seascale Moss, although precise dating of these bodies is difficult (Turner 1988, 1-7; 1989, 21-23). At Scaleby Moss, north of Carlisle, a bog body was found on the 25 May 1845 whilst digging peat on the moss. The find was reported in the *Carlisle Journal* of the 7 June 1845:

> ... he came to the remains of a human skeleton buried about eight or nine feet beneath the surface, and closely embedded in the lowest stratum of black peat. The skeleton was wrapped in what appears to have been the skin of a deer, and has evidently formed a garment, as the hair has worn off in some places. This garment has been composed of different pieces, united by seams, which had been executed with considerable neatness, and had even been repaired in some places, but in a manner inferior to the original workmanship. The whole was bound together by thongs of strong leather. From the discoverer apprehending at first that he had come to the remains of a beast of some kind, less care was taken to preserve the interesting relique. The writer of this, who visited the spot two days subsequent to the discovery, saw several ribs, a bone of the arm, (*Os humerus*) a scapula or shoulder blade and a part of the spine; the vertebrae still attached to each other by ligaments. There were also parts remaining of the bones of the pelvis, thigh, legs and forearm. It is curious, however, to observe that the skull was wanting. A part of the intestines remained, which seemed to have undergone something like the process of tanning, as they were tough and had parchment-like appearance. From the size of the bones, the writer infers that they must have been those of an adult, of slender form, a low stature, and if a conjecture were hazarded, he thinks that the skeleton was that of a female. The circumstances of the bones being buried so deep in the moss (a considerable portion of which might be the production of ages) and of their being wrapped in a skin, which, in all probability, was the clothing of the age in which the deceased lived – forcibly bring us to the conclusion that the remains were those of an Ancient Briton, and that the preservation through so many centuries was effected by the well-known preservative properties of peat moss. The Rev. John Hill, rector of Scaleby, who has taken great interest in investigating the circumstances of the discovery, has in his possession some of the best preserved bones and pieces of skin.

The recovery of the body continued throughout June as Hill records in a letter dated 28 June 1845:

> The Rev. J. Hill presents his most respectful compliments to the Rev. J. Isaacson and his pleasure in forwarding to that Gent, the enclosed portions of the human skeleton discovered in Scaleby Moss, on the 28th.
>
> The skeleton was found nearly 9 feet [2.75m] from the surface and almost 3 [1m] from the bottom of the moss, enclosed in the skin of some wild animal tied with thongs of white, strong, tanned leather. Had the body been carefully dug up, and not mangled and scattered in the manner it now is, the skeleton as well as the garment in which it had been enclosed would most probably have been complete.
>
> Other portions have this week been found especially the upper and lower jaw, parts of the skull with black hair preserved whole, many of the teeth, together with a large portion of the brain, quite firm and beautiful, much resembling *marl*.
>
> It appears from the remains of the deceased to have been a full grown person, of little stature, as the arm bones are quite short and that the person in question had been lost and bewildered in the wild forest, unfortunately sunk into a morass.
>
> A paper on the subject will be forwarded according to your direction.

There is one further important detail contained in the records of All Saints Church, Scaleby, and made by Hill: 'Within the grip of the bony fingers was a stick, three feet [1m] long and 12 inches [30cm] in circumference, from which it is conjectured that he must have perished accidentally on the spot'.

The current whereabouts of the body are uncertain. We know that it was passed on to the Derbyshire antiquarian, Thomas Bateman, in 1853, who wrote that the brain was 'in the state of adipocere' and 'from the body of an Ancient Briton' – adipocere being the condition where tissues are converted into a mixture of soaps, fatty acids and volatile substances; this occurs after death, particularly in submerged and boggy conditions. Subsequently in 1893 his collection of antiquities including the body and a piece of wood from the ship the *Mary Rose*, Lot No 428, were sold at auction in London by Sotheby, Wilkinson and Hodge where

---

428   A Glass Frame containing portions of a skull, brain, and hair, also skin garments of an ancient Briton found 9 ft. below the surface in a peat mass, in Cumberland; two old English packhorse Bells, *from Haddon Hall*; a Piece of Oak, *from the Mary Rose*, sunk at Spithead, in 1545, and recovered in 1840 ; a piece of polished Oak, *from*

Rathbone   £ 14

---

123 Extract from the Bateman auction catalogue, which describes lot 428 as the skull, brain, hair and clothing of 'an ancient Briton'. The handwritten notes in the margin refer to the purchaser and the price he paid

records show that it was bought for £4 14s by 'Mr Rathbone' (*123*) from where it found its way to the Natural History Museum, although they have unfortunately been unable to locate it more recently.

Historic sources suggest that other bodies may have been found in the lowlands of North Cumbria. Writing about Solway Moss, 10km to the north-west of Scaleby, Nicolson and Burn say that out of this bog 'have frequently been dug human bones, silver coins, of the later ages, earthen pots, iron and brass weapons' (Nicolson and Burn 1777), suggesting that the bog may have been a focus of ritual deposition during the later prehistoric period. The *Cumberland Pacquet* of 3 June 1834 records the finding of another bog body at Seascale Moss, identified by Turner as being located at Seascale Moor, east of the Seascale-Gosforth road, on the west coast of Cumbria (Turner 1989, 21-23):

> A very singular discovery, which has offered abundant scope for the recollections of the local anti-quarian, and for the enquiries of the curious, took place on Friday last, in the parish of Gosforth. Mr Aaron Howe was engaged in cutting peat at Seascale Moss, when about one foot from the surface, he discovered a substance which resembled in shape part of the human form, and on fur-ther inspection found the remaining parts of a body. From the length of time which it had laid in the earth, however, the bones were mouldered to dust, but the moss water had acted, it is evident, as a preservative to the skin, and gave the hands the appearance of a pair of fine leather gloves: the nails still continuing on the fingers. The left ear and the feet are quite perfect, part of the scalp had the hair upon it, and the chin still showed a vestige of the beard. Unfortunately Mr H had cut away part of this singular remnant of a former age before the discovery was made. A walking-stick of hazel was lying by its side. How long the body had laid there, or why its last home was made in such a place, must ever remain shrouded by the dark hand of oblivion: it may have laid there for centuries, for it is well known that peat-moss acts as one of the strongest preservatives of the skin, and it must evidently have been some time embedded to cause the decay of the bones. The oldest inhabitants of the district, say that the place where the body was found was formerly a tarn or pool of water, and that about 23 years ago the water was let off and the land drained: arguing upon the shadowy ground here created, some persons imagine that the man had been drowned; but if that were the case how do they account for the walking-stick which was found lying by his side? All, however, is mere conjecture, but the probability is that the English mummy had laid there for centuries; and now it 'revisits the glimpses of the moon' to awaken the curiosity of what would be to him a strange and unborn people. Looking upon this frail wreck of humanity, the moralist is forcibly reminded of the language of the poet …

Comparison between the Seascale and Scaleby Moss finds shows that different types of tissue were preserved at Seascale when compared with the body from Scaleby Moss. This suggests that the chemistry of the moss or the layer of peat in which the two bodies were found was different. At Scaleby, the bone was described as if it were in quite good condition, whilst only the most robust of the tissues, the hair, intestines, ligaments and brain were preserved. At Seascale, the bones had almost dissolved away whilst the skin, hair and nails were remark-ably well preserved. This implies that the body from Seascale probably came from the upper layers of a true raised bog which receives its water from precipitation alone. In contrast, the

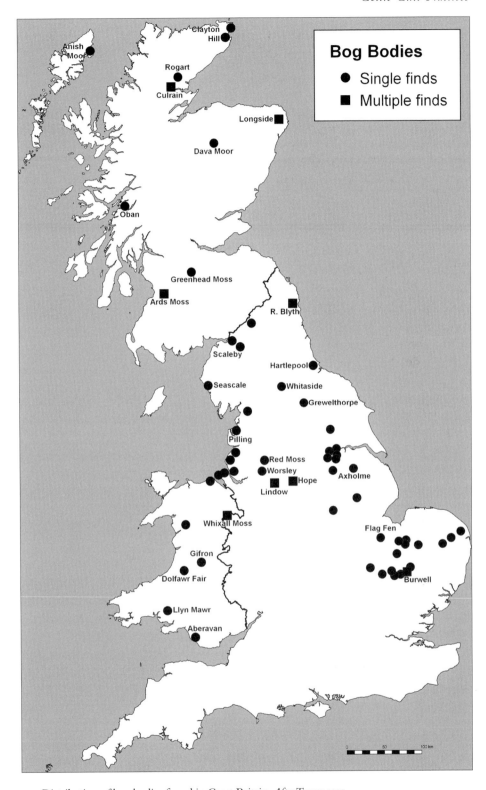

124 Distribution of bog bodies found in Great Britain. *After Turner 1993*

Site	Sex	Cape	Stick	Date	Mode of death
Bockhornerfeld	?	Skin cape	3 branches	Late Iron Age/ Roman	?
Borre Fen	Male	2, sheepskin	1m long, 4.5cm thick	650±80 BC	Blow to head and strangulation/ hanging
Castle Blakeney	Male, young man	deerskin	2 staffs	Iron Age 2040±90 BP	?
Derry Keighhan	?	Animal skin	None	?	?
Drobnitz	Female, girl	Skin cape	None	?	?
Elling woman	Female	2, sheepskin	None	Iron Age, 220±55 BC	Hung
Emmer-Erfscheidenveen	Male	calfskin	Several sticks	?	?
Gallagh	Male	Leather cape	2 pointed stakes	Late prehistoric	Strangulation by willow rope
Horby	?	Cape	None	?	?
Huldremose	Female	2, sheepskin	None	?	?
Ruchmoor	Female, girl	Deerskin	None	?	?
Scaleby	Female	Deerskin	1m long, 30cm circ.	Late Bronze Age/Early Iron Age	?
Seascale Moss	?	No	Hazel stick	Late Iron Age/ Roman	?
Søgårds 1	Male	3 skin capes	None	Late Iron Age	?
Søgårds 2	Male	1 calfskin	None	?	?
Tued	?	Cape	None	?	?

Site	Sex	Cape	Stick	Date	Mode of death
Underlev	Male	2 skins	3 hazel rods	?	?
Whixall Moss	?	Leather apron	None	?	?

125 Analysis of bog bodies found with skin capes and/or wooden sticks according to the sex of the body, mode of death and date

Scaleby body was described as being in the lowest stratum of the 'black' peat. In lowland bogs in north-west England, humified black peats are found below a major recurrence surface, a temporary cessation of peat growth, dated to about 600 BC. This suggests a minimum age for the body at the transition between Bronze and Iron Age, although depending whereabouts in the 'black peat' it was found it could conceivably be as old as the Neolithic or Early Bronze Age. We may perhaps be more confident in dating the Seascale body, whose position in the moss and mode of preservation are consistent with a date after 600 BC, sometime in the Late Iron Age or Romano-British period.

Outside Cumbria bog bodies have a wide distribution in the north-west of England, and beyond, consideration of which helps us to understand the significance of the local bodies (*124*). In Britain bog bodies are unevenly distributed, falling into two distinct groups. One is a westerly distribution running from South Wales into north-west England, and ending in the west of Scotland, following the distribution of lowland wetland bogs found in this part of the country; a second quite distinct group lie in the Fens of East Anglia, again utilising an area of lowland wetland. Of the British bodies the most well known is that of the Lindow Man, one of two or perhaps three bog bodies found in Lindow Moss, which lies south of Manchester in Cheshire (Stead *et al* 1986). Outside Britain large numbers of bog bodies are also known in Ireland, the Netherlands, Germany and most famously Denmark, where the discovery of a number of bodies in the 1950s brought the phenomenon of the bog body to the attention of the public through the publication by P.V. Glob of his popular book *Mosefolket* translated into English as 'The Bog People' (1969).

Taking the known examples of bog bodies from north-western Europe more specific comparisons can be made to the details of the Scaleby burial (*125*). The body was wrapped in a cape or cloak made from deer skin and sewn with thongs of strong leather. Burials in similar wrappings have been found in Britain, Ireland, Denmark, the Netherlands and Germany consideration of which is illuminating. One of the bodies found at Whixall Moss (Shropshire) is described as wearing a leather apron. In Ireland the circumstances surrounding the finding of a well-preserved body of an adult man at Castle Blakeney, County Galway, are very similar to those from Scaleby. The body was found 9ft (2.75m) down in a bog in 1821. It had much more tissue surviving, enabling it to be identified as a young man:

> The heads, legs and feet, were without covering, but the body was clothed in a tight dress, covering also the limbs as far as the knees and elbows. The dress was composed of the skin of some

animals, laced in front with thongs of the same material, and having the hairy side inwards; and it is not improbable that it might have been that of the Moose-deer. He had no weapon, but near him at each side of the body was found a long staff or pole, which it was supposed he had used to cross a rivulet.

The radiocarbon date of this burial shows that it is late prehistoric, 2040±90 BP (HAR-6908), placing it in the Iron Age. Also in Ireland the find of a male body at Gallagh, County Galway, at a depth of 9.5ft (2.9m), and clothed only in a leather cape has interesting parallels with the Scaleby body. The cloak was gathered at the neck with a band of sallow (willow) rods and a pointed wooden post or stake was placed at each side of the body. The 'band of sally rods' around the neck may have been a rope with which the victim was strangled. Radiocarbon dates suggest it is late prehistoric. A similar cape of animal skin, woven with sinew, was recovered from a bog at Derry Keighhan, County Antrim, in 1861 (McAdam 1861-62).

Several of the Danish bog burials, both male and female, were associated with skin capes. From the same bog which produced Tollund Man came the Elling Woman (Fischer 1979). The woman, with long plaited hair, was clad in a cape of sheepskin, with the fur inside. The front edges were doubled over to make a hem and it was sewn together with very fine thread. Remains were identified of a second cape or cloak of cowhide which had been wrapped around her legs. Elling Woman met with a violent death, having been hung by a leather halter which survived around her neck. She has also been dated to the Iron Age, 220±55 BC (Tauber 1979).

Other examples of women found with capes are a girl from Ruchmoor, near Damendorf in Schleswig, found in 1934. She had amongst other clothing an oval cape made from four tanned sheepskins which were sewn and repaired with coarse leather stitching (Jankuhn 1938, 89-137). Huldremose Woman was found in 1879 with two skin capes. Both capes were made of sheepskin and measured 0.8m long with a maximum width of 1.8m. Huldremose Woman was wearing both capes at the same time, the inner cape with the wool on the inside, the outer cape with the wool on the outside; an extra layer of skin, with the wool facing inwards, had been sewn to the inside of this cape at shoulder height. The outer cape was made of several differently coloured pieces of sheepskin and was a particularly decorative garment. Several patches had been sewn onto the cape made of four pieces of skin that was found with Dröbnitz Girl, Poland, in 1939 (van der Sanden 1996, 111).

Also in Central Jutland, at Borre Fen, three bog bodies were found in the late 1940s. The first was a man found in 1946. He had been dumped in an old peat working in a sitting position, having been killed by a combination of blows to the head and either hanging or strangulation using a hemp rope. The body was naked, but rolled up at his feet were two capes, sewn together from pieces of light and dark sheepskin. Lying alongside the body was a birch branch, 1m long and 4.5cm thick (Glob 1977). This find has been dated to 650±80 BC. In 1942 at Søgårds Mose, near Daubjerg in the northern half of Jutland, a male body dated to the Late Iron Age was found with a well-preserved skin cape lying to his right, and the remains of two more capes to the left of the body. In 1944, in the same moss a second male body was found near to which was a cape made of calfskin. Several more fragmentary discoveries have been made in Denmark associated with skin capes or coats. These include the finds from Søgårds Mose, Tued Bog and Horby Fen (Glob 1977, 98). An earlier discovery was made in 1797 in

126 A red sandstone carved head on a plinth. Found on the bank of the River Eden at Rickerby Park, Carlisle. Possibly Iron Age or Romano-British

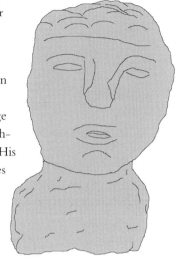

Underlev Fen, of a male bog body wrapped in two skin capes, where three hazel rods were found alongside.

In Holland a male bog body dating to the Bronze Age was found in 1938 at Emmer-Erfscheidenveen in the southern part of Bourtangermoor (van der Sanden 1996, 126). His body was wrapped in a skin cape, made of several pieces of calfskin, which also contained several sticks. Finally, a body found at Bockhornerfeld dates to the Late Iron Age/Roman period. The body was covered by a woollen fabric, a skin cape and three branches.

There are also cases of severed heads found wrapped in skin capes, at Roum in Denmark and Osterby in Germany (Glob 1977, 100, 116-7). Closer to home, at Pilling Moss on the southern side of Morecambe Bay in Lancashire, the head of a woman with long plaited auburn hair was found in Pilling Moss in the Over Wyre district in 1864 (Edwards 1969; Middleton *et al* 1995, 66). The head was reportedly wrapped in a piece of coarse woollen cloth and with it were two strings of cylindrical jet beads, with one string having a large amber bead at the centre. The association with jet beads suggested that it should be dated to the Early Bronze Age (Edwards 1969), although there is no independent evidence for this date. To the south of the find, *c.*10km away on the Fylde Coast, the head of a man aged 25-35 years was found at Briarfield, close to Poulton-Le-Fylde (Wells and Hodgkinson 2001). The skull was dated to the Late Bronze Age, 1260-840 cal BC (2845 ±65, AA-28733). Other finds of heads from the north-west of England come from Red Moss, Bolton, again with plaited hair, but undated (Hall *et al* 1995, 86), and from Worsley Moss, Greater Manchester, where the second cervical vertebra shows a deep cut caused by a sharp instrument used to decapitate the body of a man who had first been garrotted. Finally, from Lindow Moss is a severed head (Lindow I) found in 1983, thought originally to be that of a woman, it may in fact belong to a decapitated male bog body (Lindow III) dated to AD 25-230 (Turner and Scaife 1995) found subsequently in 1987. In addition to the cases of decapitation there are also a large number of carved stone heads, for example at Anthorn (Richardson 1998, 51 and 52) and Rickerby Park, Carlisle (*126*; Richardson 1990, 31 and 33). Their distribution, focusing on north-west England, follows that of Brigantine territory which may point to a particularly strong belief in the Celtic Cult of the Head, which I have previously discussed in greater detail (see Barrowclough 2008, ch. 7).

The Seascale Body was found naked but like the Scaleby body was accompanied by a wooden stick, described as a 'walking stick' at Seascale, whilst at Scaleby the stick was more robust. Wood has been found on top of, beneath or next to bog bodies at several findspots in a number of different combinations and orientations (*127*). We have already seen that 17 of the bodies found with capes, and in addition to the Scaleby Moss find, seven were also accompanied by wooden sticks. The original description of the Castle Blakeney body states that 'near

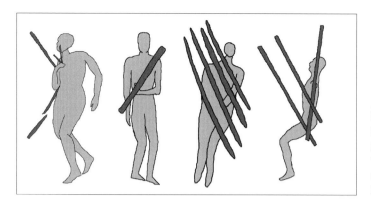

127 Examples of bog bodies accompanied by wooden sticks. From left to right: Windeby, Huldremose, Clongownagh, Bockhornerfeld

him, at each side of the body was found a long staff or pole, which it is supposed he had used near a rivulet'; a similar arrangement was described at another Irish burial at Gallagh, County Galway, where the posts may have served to anchor the bodies in the peat (van der Sanden 1996, 99-100). At Borre Fen in Denmark a substantial birch stick was found alongside the body of a man dated to 2600±80 BP, at Underlev Fen the body was found with three hazel rods alongside, whilst the body from Bockhornerfeld was covered by three posts said to have been pointed so as to secure the body in the peat (van der Sanden 1996, 99-100). One post had been placed parallel to the body, two others at right angles to the first. The latter two posts had been inserted into the walls of the wet depression, so as to clamp the body down. Finally that from Emmer-Erfscheidenveen was found wrapped with several sticks.

To these cloaked burials may be added a number of others found with sticks. A single pole came from alongside a skeleton in a bog in Drumcroon, County Derry in Ireland, and a headless male body found at Baronstown West in Ireland was held down by thick birch or hazel branches (van der Sanden 1996, 99-100). According to the report describing a body found at Landegge it lay beneath two thick branches, which were crossed over the man's back. A fully clothed woman was found in Huldremose, Denmark, in 1879 with a willow stake about 3ft 6in (*c.*1m) in length and 1.5-2.5in (38-63mm) in thickness, lying across her breast (van der Sanden 1996, 99-100). The body has been dated to 1920±10 BP. The posts that were found in association with Haraldskær Woman also served to hold the body down. Windeby Man was likewise anchored to the peat with wooden posts. Fortunately, a good drawing was made of the latter find in 1952 (van der Sanden 1996, 99-100). The man was held down by no fewer than eight thick stakes, which had been obliquely inserted into the peat (*128*).

In each of these discoveries, the stick or sticks must have had a purpose; this was probably symbolic but may also have been functional. In some cases a single thick branch was found lying obliquely across the body, for example at Bernuthsfeld, Vester, Torsted, Borremose (1946) and Huldremose. Other bodies lay beneath two or three parallel branches, for example at Hokkerup, or piles of twigs as at Aschbroeken. At some findspots one or more branches were lying next to the body. In other cases the branch was said to be in the body's hand, as at Scaleby and in the case of Windeby where a thick birch branch rested in her right arm. In many cases, but not all, the stick was made of hazel.

We cannot be certain how the two Cumbrian bog bodies met their end because the bodies are no longer available for study. Studies of bodies from elsewhere have shown that drowning, strangulation, stabbing and clubbing to death have all been utilised, sometimes in combination as in the case of Lindow Man, who was also associated with mistletoe as discussed below. No mention is made of any signs of mortal wounds in the Cumbrian examples, although their poor state of preservation may have destroyed such evidence; nor is there mention of a noose as is sometimes recorded – as with Lindow Man and some of the Danish bodies – and of course death by drowning would leave no visible marks upon the body. In the case of the Seascale body the original report states that only 'part of the scalp had the hair upon it'. This feature of the report appears to have passed without comment, however it is noteworthy because in the case of both the Danish Windeby and Yde Girls the reports show that one half of the head had been shaved before the person was killed. In the case of the Yde Girl it was the right half of the head, and in the case of Windeby Girl it was the left side. The lack of hair on part of the head of the Seascale body may be explained in a similar way, leading to the conclusion that he was also subject to a ritual death.

As we have seen, there is too much evidence, in the form of patterns of dress, accompanying wooden stakes and acts of violence, to believe that the majority of the bodies could be the remains of individuals who sank to the bottom of the bogs after accidentally losing their way. Instead the structured nature of the deposits points to the deliberate killing of the bodies as the final stage of a ritual act of sacrifice. It is difficult given the fragmentary nature of the archaeological record to fully understand what this ritual may have entailed, however a number of scholars have attempted to reconstruct something of the belief structure of those taking part, combining the evidence from the bogs with that from the surviving, mainly Roman, texts (Caesar VI, 16; Cassius Dio LXX, vi, 7; Diodorus Siculus V, 32; Strabo IV, 5). Although we have to approach the classical sources with caution they do provide an additional source of information that complements the material remains discovered by archaeologists.

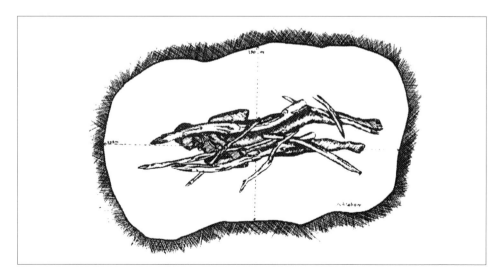

128 Windeby Man, buried in a dug grave and then pegged into the peat with wooden stakes

129 Roman altar to the god Teranis, the Thunderer or Sky God, found at Foregate Street, Chester. The inscription reads: I(oui) O(ptimo) M(aximo) Tanaro/L(ucius) [Bruttius?] Galer(ia tribu)/Praesens [Cl] unia/Pri(nceps) leg(ionis) XXV(aleriae) V(ictricis)/Commodo et/Laterano co(n)s (ulibus)/U(otum) s(oluit) l(ibens) m(erito) To Jupiter Tanarus, Best and Greatest, Lucius Bruttius(?) Praesens of the Galerian voting tribe, from Clunia, princeps of the Twentieth Legion Valeria Victrix, willingly and deservedly fulfilled his vow in the consulship of Connodus and Lateranus. *After Collingwood and Wright 1965, 149 No 452*

A combination of excellent preservation and modern scientific techniques have allowed a general model for the treatment of bog bodies to be developed based on the find of Lindow Man, from Lindow Moss in Cheshire, which is arguably the most certain British example of ritual death (Cunliffe 1997, 192). Reconstruction of the complex and violent acts leading to his death show that he died a three-fold death. That is to say that in rapid succession he was strangled with a garrotte, hit on the head and his throat cut (Stead *et al* 1986; Turner and Scaife 1995). Such a mode of death is referred to by both the Roman poet Lucan in the first century AD, and the later Irish vernacular literature. From Lucan's *De Bello Civili* (I, 444-6) we learn that the Celts worshipped three main gods: Teutates, the god of the tribe; Esus, the god of the underworld; and Teranis, the Thunderer or Sky God. All three seem to have been important in the north-west of England. Esus is frequently linked with Cernunnos, the Celtic horned god, a popular deity in northern Britain. Teranis also seems to have been popular as a Roman altar excavated at Chester (*129*) was dedicated jointly to Jupiter and Teranis, whilst a pottery mould of the god comes from Corbridge, and an inscription to the god Teutates was excavated from Cumberland Quarries (RIB 1017). The three gods were propitiated by sacrificial offerings involving a different kind of death: hanging and stabbing appeased Esus; fire appeased Teranis; whilst drowning satisfied Teutates. Interestingly, in some of the Irish myths death by burning is sometimes replaced by death by hanging (Ross 1986, 162-4). Lindow Man was killed by the noose, his throat was cut with a weapon, and he was deposited in a bog satisfying all three gods.

The Classical sources provide a number of references to human sacrifices and to religious belief in general; they are, however, to be approached with caution. The intention of the writers was usually to communicate some other message and references to Celtic beliefs are at best anecdotal. Caesar's account of Gallic custom *de Bello Gallico* makes it clear that there may have been little distinction between ritual and judicial deaths in Celtic society. According to Caesar, some tribes, as well as performing regular state sacrifices, actually chose to sacrifice those caught in the act of theft or some other offence on the grounds that the gods preferred such persons to innocent men, although, if there were a dearth of criminals, the innocent would be sacrificed without hesitation (*de Bello Gallico* VI, 16). This account is echoed by those of Strabo (IV, 5) and Diodorus Siculus (v, 32). Both Casaer and Diodorus' accounts name Druids as performing the sacrifices which, according to Caesar, were intended to ward off serious diseases as well as to protect those who were exposed to dangers in battle. Cassius Dio (LXX, VI, 7) states that 'the Britons have holy places and offer human sacrifices to Andraste in a sacred wood'. The *Rennes Dindshenchas* attests to sacrifice by drowning among the Irish and the first century AD Latin poet Lucan describes sacrifices to Teutates which involved drowning the victim in a cauldron. Sacrifice by throat slitting is attested by Strabo (VII, 2) among the Germanic Cimbri. White-cloaked priestesses who accompanied the wives of the warriors on expeditions would utter prophecies and cut the throats of prisoners of war while the latter were suspended over huge bronze cauldrons. Other priestesses would inspect the entrails of victims to see if victory would ensue in the forthcoming battle.

Mention of the word Druid conjures images of people wrapped in white sheets promenading around Stonehenge. This contemporary behaviour, derived from the seventeenth-century Romantics, serves to cloud our image of Druidical activity. The sentiments expressed through New Age festivals owe more to a modern recreation of Druid activity than to historical sources and are better referred to as neo-Druid. A more historical version of events tells us that Druids were the intermediaries acting between the people and the gods. Our main source was Caesar writing of his observations in Gaul, who states that Druidic religion originated in Britain whence it spread to the Continent. He even comments that 'even today anyone who wants to make a study of it goes to Britain to do so' (BG VI, 14). The Graeco-Roman historians often emphasise human sacrifices in their accounts, perhaps in a deliberate attempt to disgust their readers, with the aim of painting the Celts in general, and Druids in particular, as uncivilised barbarians. For example, when Tacitus describes the assault on the Druid stronghold of Anglesey in AD 59 he writes that 'their religion encouraged them to drench their altars with the blood of prisoners and to find out the will of the gods by consulting the entrails of human beings' (Tacitus *Annals*, xiv, 30).

Although sacrifice seems to have played a part in ritual life, Tacitus' focus on this element portrays his, and his readers', own bias. Archaeologically it is difficult to identify the presence of natural places such as groves, the closest we may get is to identify springs such as that at Grayber where the deposit of bronze spoons marks it out as a meaningful place. In reality the Druids were more than bloodthirsty tyrants, they served society in several ways: they were responsible for administering and guiding the religious life of the people, supervising ceremonies and sacrifices, and divining the future from such omens as the death struggles of a sacrificial victim. They also maintained the theory and practice of the law and were the teachers of the oral traditions of the people, holding schools where the novices learnt verses off by heart. Caesar reports:

> ... they seem to have established this custom for two reasons: because they do not want their knowledge to become widespread and because they do not want their pupils to rely on the written word instead of their memories; for once this happens, they tend to reduce the effort they put into their learning ...
>
> BG VI, 15

Pliny the Elder provides an insight into Druidical ritual and practices, which as well as conveying some of the richness of their beliefs, also helps to explain the presence of mistletoe found in the gut of Lindow Man by archaeologists:

> Here we must mention the awe felt for this plant by the Gauls. The Druids – for so their magicians are called – held nothing more sacred than the mistletoe and the tree that bears it, always supposing that tree to be the oak. But they choose groves of oaks for the sake of the tree alone, and they never perform any of their rites except in the presence of a branch of it; so that it seems probable that the priests themselves may derive their name from the Greek word for that tree. In fact, they think that everything that grows on it has been sent from heaven and is a proof that the tree was chosen by the god himself. The mistletoe, however, is found but rarely upon the oak; and when found, is gathered with due religious ceremony, if possible on the sixth day of the moon (for it is by the moon that they measure their months and years, and also their ages of thirty years). They choose this day because the moon, though not yet in the middle of her course, has already considerable influence. They call the mistletoe by a name meaning, in their language, the allhealing. Having made preparation for sacrifice and a banquet beneath the trees, they bring thither two white bulls, whose horns are bound for the first time. Clad in a white robe, the priest ascends the tree and cuts the mistletoe with a golden sickle, and it is received by others in a white cloak. Then they kill the victims, praying that the god will render this gift of his propitious to those to whom he has granted it. They believe that the mistletoe, taken in drink, imparts fecundity to barren animals, and that it is an antidote for all poisons.
>
> Pliny the Elder, *Nat Hist* XVI, 249

This account goes some way to explaining why Lindow Man might have taken mistletoe in his last drink: it would be a means of ensuring his potency, which his sacrifice would then confer on the community. The account also demonstrates that time was crucial to the proper

130 The fragmentary bronze calendar found at Coligny, Ain, France. It is divided into 16 columns each of four 29- or 30-day months, containing a total of 62 months. Propitious or unpropitious times are indicated and the dates of two festivals are recorded

enactment of ritual. The mistletoe had to be cut from the oak, sacred to Teranis, 'on the sixth day of the moon'. In order to understand the significance of this we need to consider the details of the Celtic calendar.

The Celts had a sophisticated understanding of time which we are able to reconstruct through a combination of literary and archaeological sources. Importantly, fragments of a bronze calendar were found at Coligny, Ain, France in 1897 (*130*). The calendar is divided into 16 columns each subdivided into four months, and the months are divided into 29 and 30 days, making a year of 354 days. Each month is also divided into a light- and dark-half, the divide signified by the word *Atenoux* ('returning night'), and the months are divided between those that are auspicious and those that are not, with the abbreviations MAT ('good') and ANM ('not good'). The division of the month between light and dark is a reference to the phases of the moon, which as it passes from new moon to full moon goes from dark to light. The sixth day is interesting as at this point in the cycle the moon resembles a sickle, which was used to cut down the mistletoe. The days are numbered and some are also marked by abbreviations which must have been significant for those who were informed: there are indicative signs for the festivals of Beltane (1 May) and Lugnasad (1 August).

Agrarian societies need to be able to chart the passage of time and to know when to initiate essential activities such as sowing seeds, moving animals to upland pasture and harvesting crops. This knowledge lay at the basis of human existence and, as we have seen in discussion of the Neolithic, the measurement of cycles of time has been well understood by people long before the Iron Age. From Irish literary sources we gain an understanding of the seasons.

The old year and the beginning of the new was marked by the greatest of the ceremonies, Samhain, which took place on 1 November. It was a liminal time between the two years and as such was dangerous: the spirits of the dead could roam free. Samhain was the time when all the important communal acts, meetings and sacrifices took place. The strength of tradition which lay behind the festival has ensured its survival as Hallowe'en.

The next festival, Imbolc, which took place on 1 February, is less well known. In all probability it was associated with the goddess Brigit, a goddess of fertility, learning and healing. In Christian mythology Brigit became a saint and her festival falls on 1 February and is still widely celebrated in Ireland. It probably signified the beginning of the period of lactation of ewes, when the sheep could be moved to upland pasture.

Next came Beltane, held on 1 May a ceremony associated with the Celtic god of fire, Belnus. The fires lit may have been used to fumigate cattle before they were turned out to graze on the summer pastures.

Finally, on 1 August the festival of Lugnasad was held, presided over by the god Lugh. The timing might suggest that it was when the propitiatory offerings had to be made to the chthonic deities in anticipation of a fruitful harvest. Lugh has particular meaning for Cumbria as demonstrated by his preservation in the place name Luguvallum, present-day Carlisle, and it is possible that offerings and sacrifices, potentially including the human sacrifices that are preserved in the Cumbrian bogs, were made to Lugh on that day. In this context it is noteworthy that Esus may have been synonymous with Lugh (Ross 1986).

Against this background we can understand why the monthly cycle with its dark and light halves and its propitious and unpropitious days had to be recorded and accessible to those whose task it was to attend upon supernatural matters.

Mention by Lucan (*De Bello Civili* I, 444-6) that victims were sacrificed to Teutates, the god protector of the tribe in times of war, by being drowned in a vat or cauldron is noteworthy. Many cauldrons and buckets have been recovered from bogs in north-western Europe, the most famous of these being the cauldron recovered from the bog at Gundestrup, Jutland, Denmark, which shows the deity pushing his victim into a vat or well. At Bewcastle

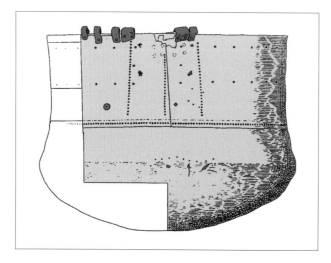

131 A bronze cauldron found at Bewcastle. *After Davenport 1996, 229*

in Cumbria a bronze cauldron of suggested second-century date was found during peat-cutting on Black Moss, High Grains, *c*.1907 (Davenport 1996). The cauldron was made from three pieces of bronze riveted together and measured 63cm in diameter, was 48cm deep and weighed 4kg. Two pairs of rivet holes near the rim, on opposite sides of the cauldron, indicate where handles could have been attached. There are also six loops of bronze attached to the rim (*131*). Interestingly the cauldron seems to have had an eventful life because before it was deposited in the bog it had been damaged several times and repaired with bronze patches. There are thirteen inner- and six outer-patches. Three similar cauldrons have been found with repairs, one from Carlingwark Loch, which lies to the north of Cumbria in Dumfries and Galloway and two from Ireland: one from Urlingford, County Kilkenny and one of unknown provenance. This suggested to Davenport (1996) that these large bronze cauldrons were highly valued possessions and were patched and repaired to make them last as long as possible. Stuart Piggott dated the Carlingwark Loch example to the second century AD because it contained a hoard which included dateable Roman pottery; this gives the latest date for its deposition, but it could have been made some considerable time before, as it had also been repaired several times. This example is so similar in form to the Bewcastle cauldron that Davenport thought that they could both have been made by the same metalworker, the only difference between the two being in the manufacture of the rivets. Both are of Santon type, so named after the cauldron found at Santon Downham, Suffolk.

The cauldron was in all likelihood filled water from a sacred pool within the bog, or per-haps from a sacred well or with some alcoholic beverage such as ale or mead, and may have been suspended over an open fire, in which case combining death by drowning and death by fire. After death the victim may have been disposed of in the sacred bog into which the cauldron was finally laid to rest as an offering to the deity. The discovery of a bronze bucket in a peat bog at Ravenstonedale is another rare example of a ritual vessel being sacrificed to the gods, in this case given the appearance of fire damage, perhaps to Teranis (*132*). The find is recorded as follows:

About half a mile [0.8km] from the town head, in the year 1774, was found in digging peats, two foot [0.60m] below the surface, a copper vessel, sound and entire, the diameter whereof at the bottom is 8 inches [20cm], at the top 14 inches [35cm], in the widest part just under the neck 16 inches [40cm], the depth 18inches [45cm]; it contains about 8 gallons and half [*c*.38.5l]. It is made of three plates of copper, neatly joined together, and hath been pretty much used as a fire vessel. It is very slender, and therefore there are fixed six fillets of copper at equal distances, which reach up the sides two inches and a half, and are turned down about as much upon the bottom. That part of the fillets turned over the bottom, is a good deal thicker than the other extremities which go up the sides, and are ornamented with ridges, somewhat in the manner of fluting. The vessel, when set down, rests on the thicker part of these fillets, which keeps it steady, and the bottom from any wear or bulging. There is no iron in any part of it. Two ears or handles are fixed on the inside, the tops of which are on a level with the edge of the vessel; in each of which is a moveable ring. These ears or rings are pretty strong and massy, but of baser metal. The whole is of excellent workmanship, and very elegantly finished.

Nicolson and Burn 1777 vol. I, 529

The Ravenstonedale bucket is one of a small group of Irish-British buckets clustered in the northern Pennine area dated to the transition between the Bronze and Iron Ages, and closely parallels buckets found in the Heathery Burn cave in Weardale and at Gilmonby in Teesdale (Turnbull 1995). The latter two are so similar that they may have been made by the same local craftsman somewhere in the Pennine region. A repeated pattern of deposition in wet places tends to reinforce the impression of the buckets as ceremonial paraphernalia. The Heathery Burn material also, with its gold ornaments and the iron rings that fitted around the wheel hubs of an elaborate vehicle, best makes sense as a ritual deposit.

This grouping may be indicative of links between Britain and Ireland at this time for, although small, it represents the densest distribution of buckets outside Ireland. What is more both the Ravenstonedale and Gilmonby find-spots lie on the communication route between the Yorkshire Dales and the Stainmore corridor which link the north-east of England with Cumbria and the Irish Sea. This calls to mind Clare Fell's remarks about the importance of the Stainmore and Tyne routes in the reorientation of Cumbria away from Ireland and towards England, particularly Yorkshire, in the Late Bronze Age (Chapter 9; Fell 1940, 118-130).

Comparison between hoards from northern England and Scotland during the Iron Age demonstrate clear regional variations in practices of deposition (Hunter 1997, 108-133). A study undertaken by Fraser Hunter (Hunter 1997, 111 and fig 12.1) demonstrated the regionality of the hoards (*133*). The west of Scotland has very few hoards, while the lowland belt between Glasgow and Edinburgh, and the north-east corner both have a substantial number. In contrast to the position in Scotland, within northern England the distribution is biased towards the west, in modern-day Lancashire and Cumbria, with relatively few hoards in the east, modern-day Yorkshire and Northumbria. As Hunter pointed out, it may be significant

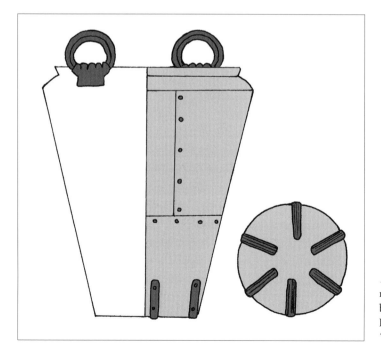

132 Hypothetical reconstruction of the bronze bucket found at Ravenstonedale. *After Turnbull 1995, fig. 1*

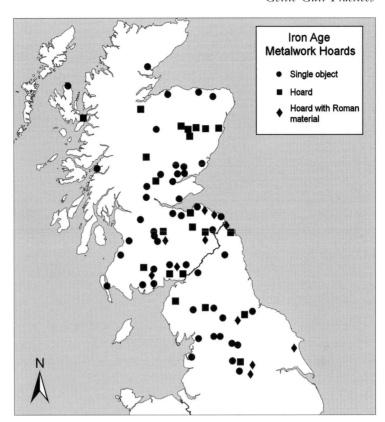

133 Distribution of Iron Age metalwork hoards in northern England and Scotland. *After Hunter 1997, 110 fig. 12.1*

that the absence of hoards in Yorkshire corresponds with the area occupied by the Arras and Parisi groups. Although the Arras burial tradition appears to die out by the first century BC (Stead 1991, 184), the apparent non-participation in hoarding in the first century BC and first century AD suggests continuing differences in ritual focus. The fact that elaborate metalwork tends to be found in graves in the area associated with the Parisi also suggests that the ritual activities of this group differ from those in the west and north (Hunter 1997, 111). Further regional differences have been detected between those areas in which hoarding did occur (Hunter 1997, 113-116). Hoards in southern Scotland are more diverse in both the range and number of objects found within them than those in the north-west of England where there is a focus on weapons deposited in small numbers (*134*). There is also a difference in location chosen for the act of deposition: in Scotland the focus is on wet and other marginal locations, whilst in the north-west they tend to be found in 'off-site' locations. In contrast to both the north-west of England and southern Scotland, Iron Age hoards found in north-east Scotland tend to contain personal ornaments deposited in pairs or as single objects, often within or close to settlements.

The Iron Age practice of deposition builds on the Late Bronze Age tradition and shares with it regional variation. Understanding what the deposits represented to those making them is difficult, they were most likely made by people of high status, if the contents can be taken as a reliable indicator (personal ornament and weapons). The hoards in the north-west

	Northern England	**Southern Scotland**	**North-East Scotland**
Contents	Weaponry common	Wide range of objects	Personal ornaments dominant; vessels rare in most of area
	Narrow range of associations	Wide range of associations	Narrow range of associations
	Some non-local material included	Inclusion of Roman and non-local Iron Age material	Distinctive local material
Size	Small deposits most common	Wide range of hoard sizes	Primarily small deposits (1–2 objects)
Context	Off-site location most common	Close association with settlements uncommon	Frequent close association with settlements
		Wet locations and other luminal locations typical	Vessels often from wet contexts; otherwise, luminal contexts less common

134 Summary of regional differences in Iron Age metalwork hoarding patterns between northern England, southern and north-east Scotland. *After Hunter 1997, table 12.6*

and southern Scotland show an emphasis on boundary locations, particularly wet places, which seems to represent a belief that via these places the otherworld could be contacted. The focus in the north-west on weaponry, generally of Brigantian type, is interesting and may represent a ritual response to the military threat posed by Roman expansion (Hunter 1997, 121). The strong regionality seen in votive traditions is also evident in other aspects of the archaeological record. The settlement evidence in the west of Scotland, where brochs dominate and hoards are virtually absent, is characterised by a stress on the household with ritual deposits of animal bone in house floors and walls (Hingley 1992, 12-17, 23-4). In areas where hoarding prevailed the north-east of Scotland is dominated by unenclosed house clusters and a scatter of hillforts, the south of Scotland by enclosed settlements of varying sizes (Ralston 1979, 449-58; Hingley 1992, 27-34) with some hierarchical organisation (Hingley 1992, 34). In the north-west of England there are few large enclosed sites, with the settlement record dominated by small enclosed farmsteads (Haselgrove 1984; Higham 1986, 119-35). This is matched by the generally smaller scale and less varied hoards which are likely to represent deposition by smaller social groups, perhaps fitting Ferrell's (1995, 135) suggestion that shared beliefs may have integrated the disparate site-communities, where powerful individuals, representatives from a number of local settlements, come together to make deposits which would serve to integrate the community (Hunter 1997, 122).

Conclusion

The evidence points to a considerable degree of continuity between the Late Bronze Age and Iron Age in Cumbria. Even the arrival of the Romans appears to have left the rural settlement pattern unaltered. Ritual and beliefs show similar continuity: offerings – not just of bodies and human heads, but also of precious metalwork such as weapons and bronze cauldrons – continued to be deposited in bogs, pools and rivers as they had been in the Late Bronze Age. With the benefit of Classical texts we can add to the archaeological evidence of deposition something of the belief system that lay behind these activities, associated with the Druid ritual practitioners, who by inference were probably also present, in some from, during at least the Late Bronze Age. Many of these deposits may be interpreted as sacrificial offerings to the gods, whose names, like the details of the calendar, are known at this time from a combination of archaeological and textual sources. In the case of the excellently preserved Lindow Man scientific analysis has revealed his threefold death, and the presence of mistletoe sacred to the Druids; both are pointers to the ritual nature of his death, which in turn may also shed light on the bodies, cauldrons and buckets found in the Cumbrian bogs. The original name for Carlisle, Luguvallum, and the presence of a range of bog deposits suggest that the place may have had a much greater sanctity than is at present demonstrable. The naming of the city after Lugh suggests that he may have been the local tribal god and perhaps suggests that the sacrifices took place on 1 August, the festival of Lugnasad.

CHAPTER 9

CONCLUSION:

UNDERSTANDING SOCIAL
REPRODUCTION IN CUMBRIA

Those who know the Lake counties well will realise how very close together the lands around the north of the Irish Sea are. On any fairly clear day the Isle of Man can be seen from the West Cumberland coast, while the hills from Dumfries to Galloway stand out clear and enticing across the Solway. Even Ireland itself may sometimes be seen by those who choose to climb Black Combe, or other hills on the western fringe of the Lake District. It is only, therefore, to be expected that contact, from early times, was maintained between these various shores of the Irish Sea, which are all within sight of one another.

Throughout the chapters of this book we have seen how the relationship between long-term continuity across archaeological periods, on the one hand, and technological innovation on the other was articulated. Continuity was particularly clear between the Late Upper Palaeolithic, Mesolithic and Early Neolithic when a high degree of mobility characterised the population. In coastal areas, much evidence for Mesolithic occupation has been obscured by later sea-level rise. Evidence for Early Mesolithic occupation is therefore confined to caves. For the Late Mesolithic there is radiocarbon-dated evidence from pits at Monk Moors, and evidence of the burning of heathland on the Eden valley floodplain. The earliest evidence for management of the woodland, in the form of small-scale woodland clearances, also dates from this period. There is nothing to distinguish Late Mesolithic lithic assemblages of 'mixed' scatters from those of the Early Neolithic, which when taken with the evidence from pollen cores, confirms a continuity of both technology and place over the Mesolithic-Neolithic transition (*colour plates 25 & 26*). This reflects a continuation of established seasonal patterns of life, which exploited wild plants and animals for food from the Mesolithic into the Neolithic. This may be suggested by the presence of blackberry and elderberry seeds in the Early Neolithic tree throw pit at Holbeck, together with carbonised wheat and burnt hazelnuts.

The earliest dated evidence for cultivation, at around 4000 BC, lies close to the coast and in the Eden valley. It was once thought that the introduction of domesticated plants and animals would have brought about significant changes in the ways people related to the land, reducing their mobility as they became fixed to farmsteads. The evidence now suggests that the predictable routines that came with domesticates were incorporated within existing traditions of behaviour, allowing them to maintain a degree of flexibility in their occupation and exploitation of the landscape. Analysis of the stone implements from coastal and other lowland sites reveals that people were moving around the landscape in the Mesolithic and into the Neolithic. Tools have been found around estuaries and along ridges above mosses close to the sea, on floodplains and in sheltered valley bottoms, and around lowland tarns. This pattern of movement implies that the population were moving to take advantage of a range of different resources including shellfish, waterfowl, game and wild berries.

Evidence for occupation inland from the coast is more limited, but points towards the habitual use of valleys as important routeways. Of particular importance were sites where valleys meet each other, as at Gleaston and Breastmill Beck in Furness, where the evidence suggests repetitive movement up and down valleys, with occupation focused on sources of fresh water (Evans 2008, 125). Upland areas were exploited for their summer pasture, with both wild and domesticated animals retreating to more sheltered areas in the autumn months. The ripening of crops and fruits probably influenced the timing of these movements.

In Chapter 2 the notion of a particular North Western Culture was introduced (Bu'Lock 1961); it is now time to revisit the theory in the context of the identity of the later prehistoric inhabitants of Cumbria, and to propose a new, diachronic, model for this small-scale society. In the preceding chapters we have seen that features of the archaeological record, as elsewhere in Britain and beyond, were the construction of ceremonial circles, the burial of individuals in funerary monuments and the deposition of metalwork in natural places. It was through those acts that the identity of places in the landscape was constructed. We also saw that the particular form of monuments and burials, and the particular metalwork types selected for deposition had a distinctly regional flavour. It was in the selection and performance of those acts that the participants defined themselves, through practices, as a community with its own identity. This is how the small-scale prehistoric society of Cumbria reproduced itself as a community with a distinct regional identity, whilst at the same time being recognisable as part of the wider Neolithic, Bronze and Iron Ages.

A number of recent archaeological studies (see papers in Canuto and Yaeger 2000) have demonstrated that an individual can be, simultaneously, a member of different communities: a household, an age group spanning several households, a burial community, and a sacrificial community. This is because a community is a symbolic construction: it is about differentiating between 'us' and 'them'. Membership is based on practices, knowledge and symbols, by which a group distinguishes itself from others (Canuto and Yaeger 2000, 1-15). In a study of later prehistoric society in the southern Netherlands, Gerritsen (2001) showed how different practices, carried out in the landscape, were related to the construction of communities. Similarly, in the case of Cumbria, the siting of particular practices in the landscape can be linked to the construction and maintenance of communal identities.

As the relationship between people and domestic animals changed and developed, so did relationships between people. On a day-to-day level domestic and agricultural practices often required collaborative working, and beyond this, wider encounters occurred at more specialised locations, often at prescribed times. In some cases long cairns were constructed in established places, such as prominent outcrops and watercourses in the cases of Heathwaite, Raiset Pike and Samson's Bratful, along known routes connecting the lowlands and uplands

(Evans 2008). These, and other features, the natural 'monuments' of the Mesolithic, were probably drawn on by the community to reinforce a sense of continuity between them and their ancestors. The construction of monuments can also be understood to reflect a growing concern with 'ownership' of land, albeit at the level of the group rather than the individual. With the introduction of domesticated animals, rights over grazing land became important with ancestral monuments serving to mark out the connections between groups of people and areas of land or grazing for their stock.

Moving beyond the scale of the local community, seasonal movements brought groups of people together, meeting at enclosures. As with long cairns, the specific chronologies of these monuments are unknown. Their location, at the heads of valley systems, and their large size, suggest that they were the result of collaboration between several different communities. There is also a strong association between enclosures and long cairns, as at Skelmore Heads and Howe Robin, and also with stone axes, as at Carrock Fell. Together these associations connect the local Early Neolithic communities of Cumbria with national networks of exchange.

Not all of the places where people gathered were marked by monumental constructions. On the coast, at the confluences of rivers and at the central Lakeland axe quarries, communities from different areas came into contact, perhaps as they brought their animals down from the fells. Meeting at monuments, and at particular natural places, axes may have been exchanged, perhaps for things brought from the wider world. As the Neolithic progressed, the venues for such meetings became institutionalised through the construction of henges and large stone circles characteristic of the Late Neolithic. These sites formalised the earlier use of natural places such as estuaries or the meetings of valley systems, or were built close to earlier monuments. Across Cumbria these monuments occur in different configurations, indicating the unfolding of localised sequences. As with other monument types, their chronology is problematic, however they appear to represent a point in a process which began with the construction of low-lying enclosures, such as those at Long Meg and Summer Hill, in the Middle Neolithic (Evans 2008, 141).

The evidence from the pattern of distribution, settings and dimensions suggests that henges and stone circles operated at overlapping scales (Evans 2008, 81). The larger monuments may even have taken over the roles of the earlier enclosures, whilst others may have been similar in scale to long cairns. Developing this idea, first proposed by Helen Evans (Evans 2008, ch. 7), the smaller, more 'localised' stone circles may represent continuity in the use of the landscape, marking places of physical, social and seasonal transition between the lowlands and fells. Compared to the numbers of known long cairns, the proliferation of stone circles suggests that the communities, which came together at the ceremonial complexes, had split off into more discrete areas of the landscape in the Late Neolithic. At this time distinctions were made both between landscape zones and between individual valley systems.

As Helen Evans has noted, the distribution of stone circles reflects an important point in a process of increasingly structured movement and settlement that took place between the Late Neolithic and Early Bronze Age. Along with their smaller physical scale, the proliferation of monuments across the landscape reflects an increasingly localised focus. The variety of settings in which they occur – along established pathways, on ridges and scarps, overlooking watersheds and close to earlier monuments – suggests that increasingly it was the practice to mark important places on routeways. Together with the erection and decoration of standing stones (*colour plate 27*) and prominent outcrops, these monuments drew on and referenced the pasts of individual communities, and suggest structured and formalised movement through the Cumbrian landscape. The construction and embellishment of these monuments connected local communities with particular places providing important foci in the processes leading to a shift in 'tenurial focus' into the Bronze Age (Evans 2008, ch. 7).

In both lowland and upland contexts, pollen evidence shows that places that had first been farmed in the Neolithic continued to be exploited in the Early Bronze Age, only in more intensive form, and that it was from these areas that agriculture spread into other areas of the landscape. In the uplands, as land was cleared of surface stones, clusters of cairnfields grew up between becks and rivers. Many of these cairnfields were associated with their own ring cairns and funerary monuments, suggesting that the monuments served as family burial plots, reflecting an increasingly localised domestic focus. In lowland areas similar themes were played out. Burials were placed in earlier funerary cairns and in natural features close to occupation areas, reflecting concerns with appropriating places of past significance.

At the local level, individual parcels of land and the monuments with which they were associated were often situated immediately adjacent to others. Working in these places would have involved daily encounters and shared practical activity. Members of co-resident communities, or parts of them, continued to move on a structured seasonal basis – journeys that involved planning and collaboration. People and their animals followed established routeways between the lowlands and uplands, camping in places that had been occupied for generations. In some contexts these journeys were carried out for specific purposes. These involved the exploitation of localised upland stone sources, and in coastal and riverine contexts occupation occurred where flint and other resources were available. As in earlier periods, these were the places where people came into contact with others and in some cases were marked by major ceremonial monuments.

Whilst the evidence from prehistoric monuments suggests that individual co-resident communities may be viewed as small groups tied to particular places, they were, at the same time, also located within wider social worlds. The tension between 'local' and 'regional' identities is reflected in both the settings and scales of Early Bronze Age monuments. These were often sited on rivers, which had both ritual meaning and also served as routeways. In other cases monuments were constructed in association with pre-existing henges, stone circles and ringcairns, where they established links with ancestral occupants and also marked routes through the landscape. One way to understand these different settings (Evans 2008, 81) is as a metaphor for the different scales at which these communities operated. The association of monuments with springs, becks, rivers, estuaries and the sea is one found elsewhere in north-west England (Barrowclough 2008) and beyond. The configuration had ritual meaning probably tied to beliefs about the cosmos and their own mortality.

If the small monuments close to springs and becks focused on the expression of localised – even personal – identities, then ceremonial complexes placed at the confluences of major rivers represented the concerns of larger communities. It was at these monuments that whole communities could gather and meet to affirm ties between groups of people and place. These larger sites were also a venue for people to negotiate the changes in social, temporal and geographical scale that are associated with the Bronze Age. One way in which these changes were manifest was through reworking old monuments (as was the case at Oddendale) together

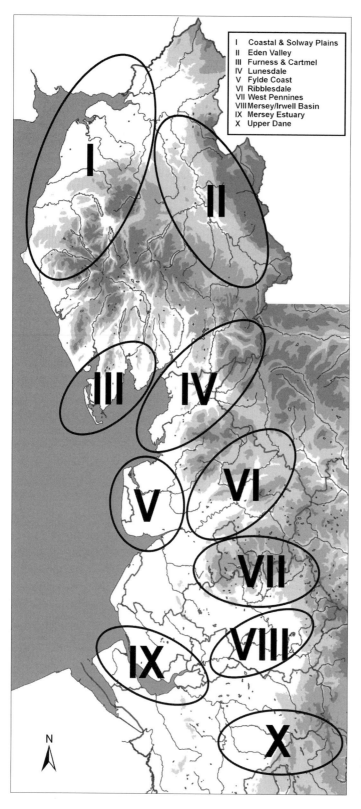

I   Coastal & Solway Plains
II Eden Valley
III Furness & Cartmel
IV Lunesdale
V   Fylde Coast
VI Ribblesdale
VII West Pennines
VIII Mersey/Irwell Basin
IX Mersey Estuary
X   Upper Dane

135 Ten areas of Late
Bronze Age occupation
in north-west England
identified on the basis of
metalwork distributions.
North-west England
covers Cumbria,
Lancashire, Merseyside,
Greater Manchester and
Cheshire

with the deposition of token remains, sometimes in ceremonial contexts and at other times in domestic ones. These actions suggest that the living were drawing on both the dead and the past in the negotiation of social tensions.

In the Middle and Late Bronze Ages a different type of community was constructed, a sacrificial community centred on bronze deposition in natural places (Chapter 7). In this case special practices of deposition were performed in particular, often wet, places in the landscape. These, too, may have resulted in the construction and maintenance of community affiliation. This process continued into the Iron Age and beyond, as attested by the human bodies and cauldrons that have been recovered from wetland sites around the Solway Firth and the west coast of Cumbria (Chapter 8).

Davey (1976), studying the distribution of Bronze Age metalwork in Lancashire, identified eight areas with statistically significant concentrations of finds. Adding the data from Cumbria, it is now possible to identify 10 groups of Late Bronze Age occupation within the north-west of England, from Solway to the Upper Dane (*135*).

The areas are: (1) the West Cumbrian Coastal, Solway and Carlisle Plains; (2) the Eden valley; (3) the northern coast of Morecambe Bay from Furness to Cartmel; (4) Lunesdale; (5) the Fylde Coast and Over Wyre districts; (6) Ribblesdale; (7) the West Pennines; (8) the Mersey-Irwell Basin; (9) the Mersey estuary; (10) the Upper Dane. In Cumbria, areas 1, 2 and 3 have been identified in previous chapters as important areas of human activity throughout prehistory. Similarly, the area of the Over Wyre mosses (5) on the south shore of Morecambe Bay has been identified as an important area of settlement in antiquity (Barrowclough 2008). Taken with Lunesdale (4), where there is a less dense concentration of artefacts around Lancaster, the three areas of Furness, Lunesdale and the Fylde Coast have an affinity. This is seen in the distribution of certain types, such as the Bandon sub-type of flat axe (*136*) which is locally confined to this area (*137*), and in the practice of hoarding which is also locally largely confined to this area, with the

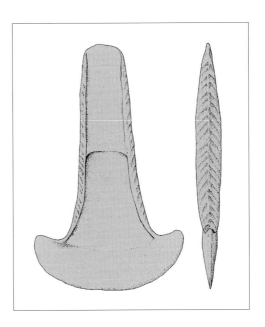

136 An example of a Bandon-type flat axe dated to Period 3, Overton. *After Middleton, Wells and Huckerby 1995*

No	Morecambe Bay Association	Place	Township	County
1	No	Fender Valley	Oxton	Merseyside
2	No	Ickornshaw Moor	Cowling	North Yorkshire
3	Yes	Mossfield, Roose	Barrow-in-Furness	Cumbria
4	Yes	New Barns	Arnside	Cumbria
5	Yes	Pilling Moss	Pilling	Lancashire
6	Yes	Pilling Moss	Pilling	Lancashire
7	Yes	Pilling Moss	Pilling	Lancashire
8	Yes	Pilling Moss	Pilling	Lancashire
9	No	Risley, Croft	Warrington	Cheshire
10	No	Turton	Turton	Lancashire
11	No	Whoop Hall	Burrow-with-Burrow	Lancashire

137 Table showing the occurrence of Bandon-type flat axes in north-west England. Of 11 Bandon axes found in the north-west of England six are associated with Morecambe Bay. Of the remainder at least two of these, the finds from the Fender Valley and Risley, are also associated with wetland landscapes

relatively large Urswick, Ambleside and Winmarleigh hoards. This has led me to argue elsewhere that there was a wider community focused on Morecambe Bay which may, along with the Ribblesdale group (6), have been the origin for the Setantii tribe in the Iron Age (Chapter 8).

Possible confirmation of this Morecambe Bay community is provided by the distribution of perforated stone axe-hammers. At least 85 examples are known from Furness and Cartmel where they are confined to low ground and the valleys leading up from them, whilst elsewhere in Cumbria perforated stone axe-hammers are rare (Collingwood 1933, 181). The distribution continues around the coastal area from the Lune south to Pilling Moss on the southern shore of Morecambe Bay. The pattern of distribution points toward occupation around the shores of Morecambe Bay. The bay and its adjacent wetlands would have provided opportunities for the collection of shellfish, birds' eggs and the hunting of wildfowl, whilst the light soils of the coast would have been more easily worked than those further inland. Rather than a barrier, the bay may have acted as a communication route connecting the people who lived around it. These people may have shared not only technology but also perhaps a common identity focused around the shared concerns and preoccupations of coastal communities.

Although there are stark differences between burial and sacrificial communities, particularly in the types of places selected as significant locations, there are also important similarities. Whilst expressing wider, national, cultural traits, both articulate these in a distinctive manner. This gives the assemblages of material culture a regional identity, implying the existence of a community, not just of people who co-existed but also of shared ideology. This is rendered visible to archaeologists in the selection and adoption of particular local forms of burial urn, the North Western Style Collared Urn, and the choice of some metalwork types, spears and axes, and not of others, particularly the absence of swords. Regional identity in Cumbria was therefore constructed in opposition to supra-regional Bronze Age identities.

Understanding Regional Identity

The difference between local and non-local identity mattered in Cumbria and had implications for the way in which objects were treated. Regionality was important, and as one of the 'ties that bind', was inextricably linked to the diachronic reproduction of society. The reality of a community firmly rooted in a specific environment, and the ensuing sense of belonging, seems to have been at odds with another reality, that of participation in long-distance, supra-regional exchange networks. Evidence for Cumbria's participation in wider networks of exchange date to at least the Neolithic, and possibly the Mesolithic, during which flint was being imported from two sources. To the west, Antrim flint was being imported along the West Cumbrian coast from Ireland, whilst to the east Yorkshire flint was being imported into the Eden valley. Although examples of each type are found in both areas, implying contact between the two, the predominance of each in its own areas points to the presence of two sub-regional groups at this point in Cumbria's prehistory (*138*). That notwithstanding, the primary position occupied by polished stone axes derived from the Langdales must have given Cumbria's Neolithic inhabitants a strong sense of regional identity, because exchange networks were not just about acquiring access to non-local materials, but also about sharing cultural knowledge of the supra-regionally acknowledged categories that give each archaeological period its distinct character.

By the Bronze Age Cumbria's dominant supra-regional identity had come to an end. Although the region contains raw materials, copper and lead, which were perhaps exploited, the inhabitants of Cumbria chose, in the main, to import their bronze from elsewhere. In this sense it became, to adopt Fontijn's terminology, an 'importing community' (Fontijn 2002, 273). Those imports followed the exchange routes established in the Neolithic (*139*). In the west metalwork was imported from Ireland following a coastal route via the Solway down to Maryport and thus inland via the River Ellen. Imports into Furness came either along the coast from Maryport or via the Isle of Man (Fell 1940, 121-122).

Examples of Early Bronze Age metalwork from Ireland include an axe found at Gleaston Castle, Furness, and flanged axes from Roose, near Barrow-in-Furness, and from Whittington, South Cumbria. These axes appear to be local copies of Irish types such as the decorated flanged axe from Brough-under-Stainmore in the Eden valley (Fell 1940, 121). Beaker-type burials are found only infrequently in the west of Cumbria; the predominant distribution is in the Eden valley, with a smaller number on the Cumbria-Lancashire border. This pattern reflects contacts with Yorkshire across the Tyne Gap over Stainmore to the Eden valley and its tributary the Irthing where a Beaker flint dagger was found (Evans 1897, 353).

As the Bronze Age progressed these two exchange routes continued to connect Cumbria with the outside world. Of particular interest are two halberds (*140*) the only examples known

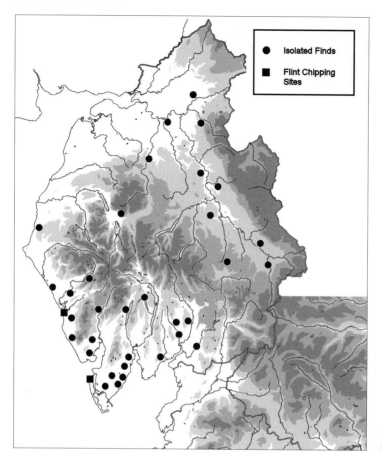

138 Distribution of
flint sites in Cumbria

from the north-west of England. The first comes from Haberwyn Rigg, Crosby Ravensworth and the second Maryport, which is of O' Riordain's Type 4, which he described as being 'sufficiently Irish in type to cause one to think of it as being an Irish specimen' (O' Riordain 1936, 272 and 312).

Other weapons of supposed Irish origin include a looped spearhead from Blindbothel near Cockermouth and a similar one from Whinfell Tarn near Kendal, which demonstrate the continued connection with Ireland. A connection reinforced by examples of Irish goldwork in the form of two twisted gold armlets found at Winton near Kirkby Stephen and Eaglesfield near Cockermouth. As the Bronze Age drew to a close connections with Ireland focused more on the Eden valley, reached via the Solway and the north-west Cumberland coast, for example a pennanular armlet found at Aspatria in 1828. Connections between Ireland and the Cumbrian coast south of St Bees seemed to cease; the area from St Bees to the Mersey is devoid of Late Bronze Age Irish finds. Instead contacts between Furness and Yorkshire seemed to intensify at this time as demonstrated by a square socketed axe from Urswick and the potential Late Bronze Age warrior burial at Butts Beck and the Iron Age burials of Nelson Square (Chapter 8). This north-south rather than east-west divide may be an archaeological reflection of historical accounts of tribal areas, with the Carvetii in the north and the Setantii around Morecambe Bay.

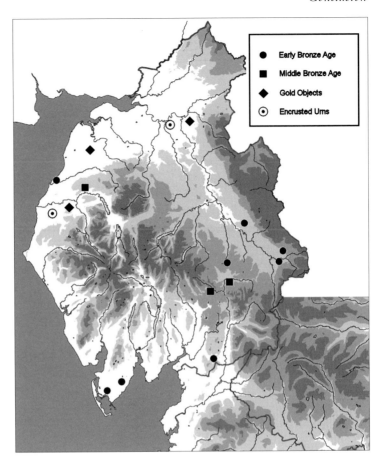

139 Distribution
of Bronze Age
metalwork in
Cumbria

In both the cases of Neolithic axes and Bronze Age metalwork the necessity to partici-
pate in exchange networks spanning vast areas was an essential characteristic of the *longue
durée* of prehistoric communities in Cumbria. This has consequences for the way Cumbrians
perceived themselves as part of the wider world. Helms (1988, 22) showed that all social
groups recognise spatial and cosmological frames, within which they occupy the central position. However, such frames were conceptualised, they are essentially about the identity of
the group as constructed in opposition to the world beyond. We know that at different times
Cumbrians systematically both contributed (axes) and derived (bronze) via long-distance
contact networks, so it may be assumed that there must always have been a tension between
two different kinds of social reality. First, the reality of the 'regional' community rooted in a
sense of belonging to a specific locality. This is the reality of daily life and feelings of belonging. It is also about feeling attached to the area in which one lives: the specific environment,
the buildings, the monuments and its idiosyncratic local history (Gerritsen 2001). For the
small-scale society that we are studying this local identity must have been the most important
and pervasive social reality (Chapman 1998, 110).

Secondly, there is also a reality that is detached from locality. This is the reality of the society
engaged in 'trade and exchange', in which one's own group is perceived as being part of a

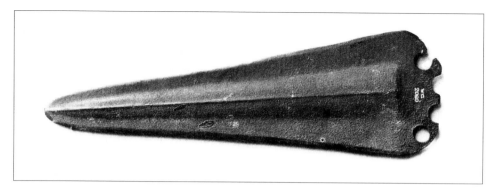

140 Bronze halberd of probable Irish origin found at Maryport on the West Cumbrian coast

wider social network (Barth 1992, 29). Here people saw themselves as necessarily linked to a more encompassing social world, acknowledging that the cycles by which a social unit reproduces itself both contribute to and draw upon resources derived from a wider geographical and social world (see Barrett 1998, 19).

These two realities need to co-exist. For a local group to reproduce itself, the world beyond that group is vital, if only for the exchange of marriage partners and of crucial non-local materials, for example stone axes and bronze. At the same time, the outside world is potentially ambiguous and dangerous. A sense of belonging to a wider social world denotes the dependency of the local group on others for the reproduction of the local group. It emphasises dependency on factors beyond one's own control. Crucial is the realisation that what effectively links both realities is the traded or exchanged object or material or individual (marriage partner). Helms shows how foreign things for that reason alone tend to be seen as imbued with meaning. They are the objectification of the reach of the local group upon resources beyond their existence as determined locally (Helms 1993, 99).

The Significance of Non-Local Identity

In the Bronze Age non-local materials were of importance; for example, even when a local industry existed bronze continued to be imported. Bradley has shown that one of the characteristic features of the European Bronze Age is the enormous distance travelled by some types of artefacts. He makes the argument that it must have been the foreignness of the metal itself which mattered. There must have been a cultural preference for non-local material (Bradley 1990, 131-5). Such a preference has wider implications than just the objects themselves. By adopting supra-regional artefacts, membership was claimed of distant non-local communities in, for example, Ireland and Yorkshire. Following Isbell (2000, 243-66), we may perhaps speak of membership of 'imagined' communities.

The point is that within Cumbria there was a concern with concepts of identity in which the links with the world beyond were emphasised from the Neolithic through the Bronze Age to the Iron Age. In the Neolithic the identity of the population was tied to the biography of stone axes, which foregrounded the importance of Cumbria as a production site for an arte-fact highly prized supra-regionally. In the Bronze Age the links with the outside world ran in the other direction as objects were imported into, rather than exported from, the region. As Barrett (1998, 23) puts it: 'In such cases the biographical histories of objects and of the body itself may have converged in such a way as to ensure that the body's identity was expressed in terms of distances travelled and of absent origins'. The significance of adopting such non-local identities seems to have been a feature that emerged in the Bronze Age in Cumbria. When local bronze industries emerged there never seem to have been attempts to make tools or ornaments that primarily emphasised locally or regionally specific identities, in contrast to the Neolithic, when local identity had been strongly associated with the production of stone axes.

Inherent in this situation, where the world beyond daily existence mattered considerably, was a tension between the significance of local and non-local identities, which had to be managed and resolved. It is argued that practices of deposition, associated with burial and also with metalwork, were related to this. The deliberate giving up of apparently valuable weapons was a culturally prescribed and meaningful way to deal with objects in the Late Neolithic and Bronze Ages (Fontijn 2002, 275). Whether placed in a grave, singly or in hoards, we are dealing with biographies of objects in which a life of circulation ended in deliberate deposition, where a useable object was sacrificed. This focus on identity intensified in the Late Bronze Age and Iron Age of Furness and the particular form of the Butts Beck and Nelson Square burials that seem to deliberately reference contacts with a particular non-local identity of East Yorkshire.

Time and Continuity of Deposition

Focusing on the Middle Bronze Age, metalwork deposits were structured: specific object types ended-up in specific places (Chapter 7). There appears to have been general agreement amongst the population that the landscape was structured in such a way that certain kinds of places were appropriate for depositing particular types of object. This implies that other environmental ele-ments, for example clay soils, were not considered the right place to deposit objects. The system of selective deposition seems to have been based on a shared, cultural understanding of the land-scape. Every new deposit reproduced this understanding. The system must therefore have been profoundly traditional. People repeatedly visited specific types of places in the landscape in order to carry out specific types of deposition. Throwing a spear into a bog leaves nothing but a memory in the mind of the observer. In the absence of permanent markers, for which there is no archaeological evidence, there existed a collective memory for the traditional location of deposition. To an outsider there would be nothing to indicate the long-term history of deposition in a moss or river. Yet par-ticular locations were selected time after time for such actions, in the case of the Furness Peninsula from the Neolithic through to the end of the Bronze Age. The repeated use of the same places must have been deliberate: such places were meaningful and historical, and imbued with memory.

It is impossible to recapture archaeologically what it was that made some places culturally appropriate locations for deposition. But, we may attempt to understand the mechanism by which knowledge was transmitted through the generations within the community by way of ethnographic analogy. These sources confirm the existence of comparable natural sacrificial sites, with usage over equally large spans of time as those in prehistory (Mulk 1997). Küchler (1987) and Rowlands (1993) both make the point that in the transmission of cultural knowledge there is a tension between continuity and change. In order to memorise particular mosses and rivers as historical locations for deposition people must have drawn upon mental templates to create a mental map (Rowlands 1993, 141; see also Gell 1992, 190-205).

In the case of bronze deposition in Cumbria we see evidence for the interplay between continuity and change. On the Furness Peninsula of Cumbria deposition of metalwork took place throughout the whole of the Bronze Age. The historical practice of deposition defines this context as a particular zone in the landscape. This continuity is set against changes that took place during the period. In particular, one can point to the shift from burial deposition to metal deposition in natural places dated to the Middle Bronze Age. This seems to have been associated with the acquisition of new forms of martial identity perhaps linked to a strengthening relationship with Yorkshire. On the Furness Peninsula the response was seen in the increased number of artefacts deposited during this period.

Continuity and change were in tension. In this context the Ambleside hoard may be re-interpreted as an attempt to break with the past. It reflects, in both its structure and components, a deliberate attempt to differentiate past from present as a way of claiming new status positions. These went hand in hand with attempts at naturalising these new positions by claiming bonds with former occupiers of the land. This is most clear on the Furness Peninsula where the large quantity of Middle Bronze Age metalwork continues an earlier tradition of deposition begun in the Late Neolithic.

The Reproduction of Cumbrian Society Through Deposition

We have seen that depositional practices were conceptually linked to imported objects. The strangeness and foreignness of the import is something that required a response among the people who acquired it; the object needed to be recontextualised. This required practices suppressing strangeness, relocating the artefact within Cumbrian society enabling its comprehension (see Barrett 1999, 23). These might involve practices that ignored the dependency to which the imported object testified, and realigned the object with the moral order at home (Bloch and Parry 1989). Metal artefacts, as carriers of histories of long-distance exchange, so often ended up in deposition, that we may assume that deposition was one way to achieve this.

The particular way in which deposition achieved this is unclear from the archaeology. The local landscape is the most conspicuous environment from which local communities can derive a sense of belonging (Gerritsen 2001, 125-6). Placing imported objects in this landscape might therefore be considered a compelling way to realign a foreign idea, symbolised by the object selected for deposition, with the local order at home. Bloch and Parry (1989) state that such practices were widespread. On the basis of ethnographic examples they point out how sacrifice, or transformation, of some representative item was a way to make alien, ambiguous items derived from beyond, morally acceptable at home.

Deposition was about much more than simply recontextualising foreign items. Rather it was about the recontextualisation or ordering of specific ideas and values. Many of the objects deposited have far more meanings and qualities than just being exotic. They are about personal statuses and identities, related to life cycles, social power and special activity (such as participating in long-distance exchange and warfare). They are about communal practices and identities: cutting down forest, building barrows, or highly specific ideas and values celebrated in ceremonial items, for example the Sompting-type socketed axes found at Skelmore Heads (*108*).

Many of the identities are charged, ambiguous and dangerous. Evidence for warrior identity is provided by the conspicuous ritual deposits of weapons. It is argued that this is in line with situations in which small-scale warfare is endemic, taking place as part of the life cycle of individuals. Warfare is, therefore, primarily of ideological importance. In such circumstances, aggression is something that requires a ritually transformed self. Following the anthropologist Harrison (1995, 87, 91) martial identities are essentially temporary ones. They are something on the outer surface that can be worn or shed by wearing or laying down the appropriate paraphernalia in ritualised circumstances.

It is argued, following Fontijn (2002, ch. 11), that the practice of weapon deposition in special places and circumstances may well be understood as the reflection of the ritual laying down of such roles. Supra-regional *personas* that were constructed through foreign, or foreign-styled, objects may also have been charged, confined ones, at odds with the reality of the local group, who defined itself as belonging to the people they live and work with on a daily basis and their attachment to the local environment.

Deposition, by its very nature, has the quality of coping with ambiguous and circumscribed identities and the values they represent. The meanings of the objects are celebrated and magnified in front of onlookers but deconstructed as well. The ritual ends up in their definite disappearance. Particularly in the case of weapons, the paraphernalia signalling it are laid down, making the elements of deconstruction almost tangible. It may be no coincidence that depositional locations were themselves often ambiguous in nature as were the objects which were placed in them.

Selective deposition, whether in burials or more clearly so in the case of metalwork deposition, is a system of maintaining regional identity whilst articulating change. As such it is a system for resolving ideological and political tensions stemming from different ideas and values that exist within every society. It is through this mechanism that we can see, in part at least, how small-scale society in Cumbria was reproduced throughout the prehistoric period.

Individual and social identities are fluid, learnt and cross cut gender, age and status identity. They are dependent on constant reiteration through both everyday actions and discursive practice that continually recreate and define the boundaries of those groups. Archaeologists should no longer see a direct link between the artefacts that people use, the way they dress, the monuments they bury their dead in, and their 'identity'. Nor should they see 'societies' or 'cultures' as static, isolated and homogenous, when they are in reality constantly in flux, characterised by ambiguity and complexity. Society in general, and identity in particular, are much more complex phenomena that have to be studied with greater subtlety, and with a greater regard for issues of action, interaction and practice. In order to study aspects of communal, *regional*, identity, archaeologists need to pay more attention to the diachronic contexts in which things are used and the ways in which people use them across different scales of analysis. It is these differences in practice that may serve as the locus for emphasising communal distinctions.

BIBLIOGRAPHY

Anon. 1884. *Transactions of the Cumberland and Westmorland Antiquarian Society* VII, 279

Anon. 1889. Report on ancient monuments in Cumberland and Westmorland. *Transactions of the Cumberland and Westmorland Antiquarian and Archaeological Society* (1) x, 272

Anon. 1903. Stone implements. In Addenda Antiquaria. *Transactions of the Cumberland and Westmorland Antiquarian and Archaeological Society* (2) 410-420

Anon. 1917. Axe hammer found near Silloth. *Transactions of the Cumberland and Westmorland Antiquarian and Archaeological Society* (2) 17, 254

Anon. 1955. In Memorium. *Transactions of the Cumberland and Westmorland Antiquarian and Archaeological Society* (2) 54, 305-307

Annable, R. 1987. *The Later Prehistory of Northern England.* Oxford: British Archaeological Reports British Series 160

Ashbee, P. 1970. *The Earthern Long Barrow in Britain.* London: Dent

Ashmead, P. and Wood, R. 1974. Second report on the archaeological excavations at Kirkhead Cavern. *North West Speleology* 2, 24-33

Atkinson, R. 1951. The henge monuments of Great Britain. In R. Atkinson, C. Piggott and N. Sandars. *Excavations at Dorchester.* Oxford: Ashmoleum Museum, 87-107

Atkyns, Sir R. 1712. *The Ancient and Present State of Glostershire.* London: Robert Gosling

Barber, H. 1869. Prehistoric Remains of Furness and Cartmel, 30

Barber, K.E. 1981. *Peat stratigraphy and climatic change: a palaeoecological test of the theory of cyclic peat bog regeneration.* Rotterdam: Balkema

Barnes, B. 1975. *Palaeoecologial Studies of the Late Quaternary Period in the North West Lancashire Lowlands.* Lancaster: University of Lancaster

Barnes, B. 1982. *Man and the Changing Landscape.* Liverpool: University of Liverpool, Department of Prehistoric Archaeology, Work Notes 3, 39-40

Barnes, B., Edwards, B.J.N., Hallam, J.S. and Stuart, A.J. 1971. The skeleton of a Late-Glacial elk associated with barbed points from Poulton-le-Fylde, Lancashire. *Nature* 232, 488-9

Barnes, F. 1956. Pottery from prehistoric sites, North End, Walney Island. *Transactions of the Cumberland and Westmorland Antiquarian and Archaeological Society* (2) 56: 1-16

Barnes, F. 1955. Pottery from prehistoric sites, North End, Walney. *Transactions of the Cumberland and Westmorland Antiquarian and Archaeological Society* (2) 55: 1-16

Barnes, F. 1970a. Microlithic sites on Walney Island. *Transactions of the Cumberland and Westmorland Antiquarian and Archaeological Society* (2) 70: 277-280

Barnes, F. 1970b. Prehistoric pottery from Furness. *Transactions of the Cumberland and Westmorland Antiquarian and Archaeological Society* (2) 70: 1-8

Barrett, J.C. 1998. The politics of scale and the experience of distance: the Bronze Age world system. In L. Larsson and B. Stjernquist (eds) *The World View of Prehistoric Man.* Stockholm: KVHAA Konferenser, 40, 13-25

Barrett, J.C. 1999. The mythical landscapes of the British Iron Age. In W. Ashmore and A.B. Knapp (eds) *Archaeologies of Landscape: Contemporary Perspectives.* Oxford: Blackwell, 253-65

Barrowclough, D.A. 2005. Dancing in time: activating the prehistoric landscape. In M.E. Chester-Kadwell (ed.) Active landscapes, *Archaeological Review from Cambridge* 20.1: 39-54

Barrowclough, D.A. 2007. *Multi-Temporality and Material Culture: An Investigation of Continuity and Change in Later Prehistoric Lancashire.* Oxford: British Archaeological Reports British Series 436

Barrowclough, D.A. 2008. *Prehistoric Lancashire*. Stroud: The History Press

Barrowclough, D.A. and Malone, C.A.T. 2007. *Cult in Context: Reconsidering Ritual in Archaeology*. Oxford: Oxbow Books

Barth, F. 1992. Towards greater naturalism in conceptualising societies. In A. Kuper (ed.) *Conceptualising Society*. London, 17-33

Beckensall, S. 2002. *Prehistoric Rock Art in Cumbria*. Stroud: Tempus

Bell, M. and Walker, M.J.C. 1992. *Late Quaternary Environmental Change: Physical and Human Perspectives*. Harlow: Longman

Bellhouse, R.L. 1984. Roman sites on the Cumberland coast: the new tower on Rise How. *Transactions of the Cumberland and Westmorland Antiquarian and Archaeological Society* (2) 41-59

Bergh, S. 1995. *Landscape of the Monuments*. Stockholm: Riksantikvarieämbet Arkeologiska Undersöknigar

Bersu, G. 1940. King Arthur's Round Table. Final report, including the excavations of 1939 with an appendix on the Little Round Table. *Transactions of the Cumberland and Westmorland Antiquarian and Archaeological Society* (2) 40: 169-206

Bewley, R.H. 1992. Excavation of two cropmark sites in the Solway Plain, Cumbria: Ewanrigg Settlement and Swarthy Hill 1986-1988. *Transactions of the Cumberland and Westmorland Antiquarian and Archaeological Society* (2) 23-47

Bewley, R. 1993. Survey and excavation at a crop-mark enclosure, Plasketlands, Cumbria. *Transactions of the Cumberland and Westmorland Antiquarian and Archaeological Society* (2) 93: 1-18

Bewley, R. 1994. *Prehistoric and Romano British Settlement in the Solway Plain, Cumbria*. Oxford: Oxbow Monograph 36

Bewley, R., Longworth, I., Browne, S., Huntley, J. and Varndell, G. 1992. Excavation of a Bronze Age cemetery at Ewanrigg, Maryport, Cumbria. *Proceedings of the Prehistoric Society* 58: 325-354

Birks, H. 1982. Mid-Flandrian forest history of Roundsea Wood National Nature Reserve, Cumbria. *New Phytologist* 90, 339-354

Bloch, M. and Parry, J. 1989. Introduction: Money and the morality of exchange. In J. Parry and M. Bloch (eds) *Money and the Morality of Exchange*. Cambridge: Cambridge University Press, 1-31

Blok, A. 1994. Zinloos en zinvol geweld. In H. Driessen and H. de Jonge (eds) *In de Ban van Betekenis. Proeven van Symbolische antropologie*. Nijmegen, 27-45

Boast, R. 1997. A small company of actors: a critique of style. *Journal of Material Culture* 2(2): 181-2

Bonsall, C. 1981. The Coastal Factor in the Mesolithic Settlement of North West England. In B. Gramsch (ed.) *Mesolithikum in Europa*. Postdam: Veröffentlichungen des museums fur Ur-und Frühgeschite, 451-452

Bonsall, C. 1983. Appendix: Trial Excavations at St Bees Site VIII (Golf-Course Field). In J. Cherry and P.J. Cherry, Prehistoric Habitation Sites in West Cumbria: Part 1, The St. Bees Area and North to the Solway. *Transactions of the Cumberland and Westmorland Antiquarian and Archaeological Society* (2) 83: 13-14

Bonsall, C., Sutherland, D.G., Tipping, R.M. and Cherry, J. 1991. The Eskmeals Project: Late Mesolithic Settlement and Environment in North-West England. In C. Bonsall (ed.) *The Mesolithic in Europe*. Edinburgh: John Donald, 175-205

Bonsall, C., Sutherland, D. and Payton, R. 1994. The Eskmeals coastal foreland: archaeology and shore-line development. In J. Boardman and J. Walden (eds) *Cumbria Field Guide*. Oxford: Quaternary Research Association, 90-103

Borlase, W. 1769. *Antiquities Historical and Monumental of the County of Cornwall* (2nd edn). London: S. Baker and G. Leigh

Bradley, R. 1978. *The Prehistoric Settlement of Britain*. London: Routledge

Bradley, R. 1984. *The Social Foundations of Prehistoric Britain*. London: Longman

Bradley, R. 1990. *The Passage of Arms: an archaeological analysis of prehistoric hoard and votive deposits*. Cambridge: Cambridge University Press

Bradley, R. 2000. *An Archaeology of Natural Places*. London: Routledge, 56

Bradley, R. 2000. *The Good Stones: a New Investigation of the Clava Cairns*. Edinburgh: Society of Antiquaries of Scotland (Monograph 17)

Bradley, R. 2005. *The Moon and the Bonfire: An Investigation of Three Stone Circles in North-East Scotland.* Edinburgh: Society of Antiquaries of Scotland, 99-115

Bradley, R. and Edmonds, M. 1993. *Interpreting the Axe Trade: Production and Exchange in Neolithic Britain.* Cambridge: Cambridge University Press

Brennand, M. (ed.) 2006. *The Archaeology of North West England: An Archaeological Research Framework for North West England: Volume 1 resource assessment.* CBA North West

Breuil, H.P.E. 1926. Preface. In D.A.E. Garrod, D.A.E. *The Upper Palaeolithic Age in Britain.* Oxford: Clarendon Press, 7

Briard, J. 1965. L'Age du bronze. In P-R. Giot, J. Briard and L. Pape. *Protohistoire de la Bretagne.* Rennes, 153

Bu'Lock, J.D. 1961. The Bronze Age in the North-West. *Transactions of the Lancashire and Cheshire Antiquarian Society* 71, 1-42

Burgess, C.B. 1968. *Bronze Age Metalwork in Northern England c. 1000 to 700 BC.* Newcastle-upon-Tyne: Oriel Press

Burgess, C.B. 1970. The Bronze Age, *Current Archaeology* 19, 208-15

Burgess, C.B. 1976. Britain and Ireland in the Third and Second Millenia BC: A Preface. In C. Burgess and R. Miket (eds) *Settlement and Economy in the Third and Second Millenia B.C.* Oxford: British Archaeological Reports 33

Burgess, C.B. 1979. The background of early metalworking in Ireland and Britain. In M. Ryan (ed.) *The Origins of Metallurgy in Atlantic Europe: proceedings of the fifth Atlantic Colloquium.* Dublin: Stationery Office, 207-14

Burgess, C. 1980. *The Age of Stonehenge.* London: Dent

Burgess, C.B. 1988. Britain at the time of the Rhine-Swiss group. In P. Brun and C. Mordant (eds) *Le Groupe Rhin-Suisse-France-Orientale et la Notion de Civilisation des Champs d'Urnes.* Nemours: Mémoires du Musée de Préhistoire d'Ile-de-France No. 1, 559-73

Burl, A. 1976. *The Stone Circles of the British Isles.* New Haven: Yale University Press

Burl, A. 1981. By the light of the cinerary moon: chambered tombs and the astronomy of death. In C. Ruggles and A. Whittle (eds) *Astronomy and Society in Britain during the Period 4000-1500 BC.* Oxford: British Archaeological Reports 88, 243-74

Burleigh, R. and Matthews, K. 1982. British Museum natural radiocarbon measurements XIII. *Radiocarbon* 24, 198-205

Camden, W. 1971 [1586]. Britannia: or, a chorographical description of the flourishing kingdoms of England, Scotland and Ireland, and the islands adjacent, from the earliest antiquity. Newton Abbott: David and Charles, 'Cumberland', paragraph 18

Canuto, M.A. and Yaeger, J. 2000. *The Archaeology of Communities, a New World Perspective.* London: Routledge

Caruana, I. 1989. Fieldwalking in the Solway Plain, 1983-4. *Transactions of the Cumberland and Westmorland Antiquarian and Archaeological Society* (2) 89: 51-68

Casedine, C. and Hatton, J. 1993. The development of high moorland on Dartmoor: fire and the influence of Mesolithic activity on vegetation change. In F. Chambers (ed.) *Climate Change and Human Impact.* London: Chapman and Hall, 11-131

CFA. 1993. Archaeological Excavations and Watching brief within the Roman Vicas at Ambleside: interim report. Centre for Field Archaeology report 121. Unpublished report

Challis, A. and Harding, D.W. 1975. *Later Prehistory from the Trent to the Tyne.* Oxford: British Archaeological Reports British Series 20

Chambers, F.M. and Elliott, L. 1989. Spread and expansion of Alnus Mill. In the British Isles: timing, agencies and possible vectors. *Journal of Biogeography* 16, 541-50

Champion, S. 1998. Women in British Archaeology, Visible and Invisible. In M. Diaz-Andrew and M.L.S. Sørensen (eds) *Excavating Women. A History of Women in European Archaeology.* London: Routledge, 175-197

Chaplin, R.R. 1975. The ecology and behaviour of deer in relation to their impact on the environment of prehistoric Britain. In J.G. Evans, S. Limbrey and H. Cleere (eds) *The Effect of Man on the Landscape: the Highland Zone.* Council for British Archaeology Research Report 11, 40-2

Chapman, J. 1998. Objectification, embodiment and the value of places and things. In D. Bailey and S. Mills (eds) *The Archaeology of Value, Essays on prestige and the process of valuation*. Oxford: British Archaeological Reports International Series 730, 106-30

Chapman, J. 2000. *Fragmentation in Archaeology: people, places and broken objects in the prehistory of south-eastern Europe*. London: Routledge

Cherry, J. 1963. Eskmeals sand dunes occupation sites. *Transactions of the Cumberland and Westmorland Antiquarian and Archaeological Society* (2) 63: 31-52

Cherry, J. 1965. Flint chipping sites at Drigg. *Transactions of the Cumberland and Westmorland Antiquarian and Archaeological Society* (2) 65

Cherry, J. 1966. Four stone axes and a macehead from SW Cumberland. *Transactions of the Cumberland and Westmorland Antiquarian and Archaeological Society* (2) 66

Cherry, J. 1967. Prehistoric habitation sites at Seascale. *Transactions of the Cumberland and Westmorland Antiquarian and Archaeological Society* (2) 67: 1-16

Cherry, J. 1969. Early Neolithic sites at Eskmeals. *Transactions of the Cumberland and Westmorland Antiquarian and Archaeological Society* (2) 69: 40-53

Cherry, J. 1982. Sea cliff erosion at Drigg, Cumbria: evidence of prehistoric habitation. *Transactions of the Cumberland and Westmorland Antiquarian and Archaeological Society* (2) 82: 1-6

Cherry, J. and Cherry P.J. 1973. Mesolithic Habitation Sites at St Bees. *Transactions of the Cumberland and Westmorland Antiquarian and Archaeological Society* (2) 73: 47

Cherry, J. and Cherry, P.J. 1983. Prehistoric Habitation Sites in West Cumbria: Part I, The St. Bees Area and North to the Solway. *Transactions of the Cumberland and Westmorland Antiquarian and Archaeological Society* (2) 83: 1-14

Cherry, J. and Cherry, P.J. 1984. Prehistoric habitation sites in west Cumbria: part II, Nethertown to Seascale. *Transactions of the Cumberland and Westmorland Antiquarian and Archaeological Society* (2) 84: 1-18

Cherry, J. and Cherry, P.J. 1985. Prehistoric habitation sites in west Cumbria: part III, Drigg to Ravenglass. *Transactions of the Cumberland and Westmorland Antiquarian and Archaeological Society* (2) 85: 1-10

Cherry, J. and Cherry, P.J. 1987a. *Prehistoric Habitation Sites on the Limestone Uplands of Eastern Cumbria*. Kendal: Cumberland and Westmorland Antiquarian and Archaeological Society Research (2)

Cherry, J. and Cherry, P.J. 1987b. Prehistoric habitation sites in west Cumbria: part V: Eskmeals to Haverigg. *Transactions of the Cumberland and Westmorland Antiquarian and Archaeological Society* (2) 87: 1-10

Cherry, J. and Cherry, P.J. 1996. Coastline and upland in the Cumbrian Neolithic. In P. Frodsham (ed.) *Neolithic Studies in No-Mans Land*. Northern Archaeology 13/14, 63-66

Cherry, J. and Cherry, P.J. 2000. A Late Mesolithic assemblage from Levens Park. *Transactions of the Cumberland and Westmorland Antiquarian and Archaeological Society* (2) 100: 25-32

Cherry, J. and Cherry, P.J. 2002. Coastline and upland in Cumbrian prehistory – a retrospective. *Transactions of the Cumberland and Westmorland Antiquarian and Archaeological Society* (3) 2: 1-21

Cherry, P.J. and Cherry, J. 2007. The Other Side of the Coin, Yorkshire Flint in Prehistoric Cumbria. In P. Cherry (ed.) *Studies in Northern Prehistory: essays in memory of Clare Fell*. Kendal: Cumberland and Westmorland Antiquarian and Archaeological Society, Record Series 33: 173-182

Childe, V.G. 1925. *The Dawn of European Civilisation*. London: Kegan Paul

Childe, V.G. 1930. *The Bronze Age*. Cambridge: Cambridge University Press

Claessen, H.J.M. 1988. *Over de politiek denkende en handelende mens*. Een inleiding tot de politieke antropologie. Assen/Maastricht

Clare, T. 1979. Rayset Pike Long Cairn in the Machell MSS. *Transactions of the Cumberland and Westmorland Antiquarian and Archaeological Society* (2) 79: 144-146

Clare, T. 1999. The environs of Castlerigg stone circle: an analysis of the landscape of the Naddle valley near Keswick. *Transactions of the Cumberland and Westmorland Antiquarian and Archaeological Society* (2) 67-87

Clare, T. 2000. The distribution of some archaeological sites in relation to features of Holocene coastal change. *Transactions of the Cumberland and Westmorland Antiquarian and Archaeological Society* (2)100: 1-24

Clare, T. 2003. A case of one or two stone axes? *Transactions of the Cumberland and Westmorland Antiquarian and Archaeological Society* (3) 213-214

Clare, T. 2007. *Prehistoric Monuments of the Lake District*. Stroud: Tempus

Clare, T., Clapham, A.J., Wilkinson, D.M. and Taylor, J.J. 2002. The context of stone axes found at Portinscale and in the vicinity of the Castlerigg stone circle. Neolithic settlement sites or a case of votive offerings? *Archaeological Journal* 159: 242-265

Clarke, D.L. 1973. Archaeology: the loss of innocence. *Antiquity* 47, 6-18

Clough, T. 1973. Excavations on a Langdale axe chipping site in 1969 and 1970. *Transactions of the Cumberland and Westmorland Antiquarian and Archaeological Society* (2) 73: 25-46

Collingwood, R.G. 1933. An introduction to the Prehistory of Cumberland, Westmorland and Lancashire-north-of-the-Sands. *Transactions of the Cumberland and Westmorland Antiquarian and Archaeological Society* (2) 33: 163-200

Collingwood, R.G. 1938. King Arthur's Round Table. Interim Report on the Excavations of 1937. *Transactions of the Cumberland and Westmorland Antiquarian and Archaeological Society* (2) 38: 1-31

Collingwood, R.G. 1946. *The Idea of History*. Oxford: Clarendon

Collingwood, R.G. 1933. An introduction to the prehistory of Cumberland, Westmorland and Lancashire-north-of-the-Sands. *Transactions of the Cumberland and Westmorland Antiquarian and Archaeological Society* (2) 33: 163-200

Collingwood, R.G. and Wright, R.P. 1965. *The Roman inscriptions of Britain. I: Inscriptions on stone*. Oxford: Oxford University Press

Collingwood, W.G. 1932. *The Lake Counties*. London: Dent

Conkey, M.W. 1990. Experimenting with style in archaeology: some historical and theoretical issues. In M.W. Conkey and C. Hastorf (eds) *The Uses of Style in Archaeology*. Cambridge: Cambridge University Press, 5-17

Cooney, G. 2000. *Landscapes of Neolithic Ireland*. London, Routledge, 135-138

Cooney, G. 2002. So many shades of rock: colour symbolism and Irish stone axeheads. In A. Jones and G. MacGregor *Colouring the Past: the significance of colour in archaeological research*. Oxford: Berg, 93-107

Coope, G.R. 1994. The late glacial coleopteran from St Bees, Cumbria. In J. Boardman and J. Walden (eds) *Cumbria Field Guide*. Oxford: Quaternary Research Association, 86-89

Coope, G.R. and Joachim, M.J. 1980. Late glacial environmental chanes interpreted from fossil Coleoptera from St Bees, Cumbria, North West England. In J.J. Lowe, J.M. Gray and J.E. Robinson (eds) *Studies in the Late Glacial of North-West Europe*. Oxford, 55-68

Cowell, R.W. 1996. The Upper Palaeolithic and Mesolithic in Newman, R. (ed.) *The Archaeology of Lancashire: Present State and Future Priorities*. Lancaster: Lancaster University Archaeological Unit

Cowell, R.W. 2000. The late prehistoric period in the north west. In R.W. Cowell and R.A. Philpott *Prehistoric, Romano-British and Medieval Settlement in Lowland North West England: Archaeological Excavations Along the A5300 Road Corridor in Merseyside*. Liverpool: National Museums and Galleries on Merseyside, 169-174

Cowper, H.S. and Ferguson, C. 1893. *Archaeological Survey of Cumberland, Westmorland and Lancashire North-of-the-Sands*. Westminster: Society of Antiquaries

Cowper, H.S. 1899. *Hawkshead, its History, Archaeology, Industries, Folklore, Dialect etc*. London: Bemrose and Sons

Cross, M. 1938. A prehistoric settlement on Walney. *Transactions of the Cumberland and Westmorland Antiquarian and Archaeological Society* (2) 38: 160

Cross, M. 1939. A prehistoric settlement on Walney Island, Part II. *Transactions of the Cumberland and Westmorland Antiquarian and Archaeological Society* (2) 39: 262-283

Cross, M. 1942. A prehistoric settlement on Walney Island, Part III. *Transactions of the Cumberland and Westmorland Antiquarian and Archaeological Society* (2) 42: 11-19

Cross, M. 1946. A prehistoric settlement on Walney Island, Part IV. *Transactions of the Cumberland and Westmorland Antiquarian and Archaeological Society* (2) 46: 67-76

Cross, M. 1949. A prehistoric settlement on Walney Island, Part VI. *Transactions of the Cumberland and Westmorland Antiquarian and Archaeological Society* (2) 49: 1-9

Cross, M. 1950. A prehistoric settlement on Walney Island, Part VII. *Transactions of the Cumberland and Westmorland Antiquarian and Archaeological Society* (2) 50: 15-19

Cummins, W. 1980. Stone axes as a guide to Neolithic communications in England and Wales. *Proceedings of the Prehistoric Society* 46: 4-60

Cundhill, P.R. 1981. The history of vegetation and land use of two peat mosses in south-west Lancashire. *The Manchester Geographer*, new series, 2(2), 35-44

Cunliffe, B.W. 1997. *The Ancient Celts*. Oxford: Oxford University Press, 192

Curwen, J.F. 1933. 'Notes of the Early History of the Society'. *Transactions of the Cumberland and Westmorland Antiquarian and Archaeological Society* 2 1933: 1-6

Darbishire, R. 1873. Notes on discoveries at Ehenside Tarn, Cumberland. *Archaeologia* 44: 273-292

Darvill, T. 2007. Towards the within: Stonehenge and its purpose. In D.A. Barrowclough and C. Malone *Cult in Context*. Oxford: Oxbow Books, 148-157

Darvill, T. 2007. Research frameworks for World Heritage Sites and the conceptualization of archaeological knowledge. *World Archaeology* 39 (3), 436-457

Davenport, J. 1996. The Bewcastle cauldron. *Transactions of the Cumberland and Westmorland Antiquarian and Archaeological Society* XCVI, 228-230

Davis, S.R., Wilkinson, D.M. and Clare, T. 2007. Putative ritual deposition of Neolithic stone axes in a wetland context in Cumbria: refining the narrative using beetle remains. *Journal of Wetland Archaeology* 7, 73-81

Davies, W. 1999. Dorothy Annie Elizabeth Garrod: A Short Biography. In W. Davies and R. Charles. (eds) *Dorothy Garrod and the Progress of the Palaeolithic*. Oxford: Oxbow Books, 1-14

Defoe, D. 1927 [1727] *A tour thro' the whole island of Great Britain, divided into circuits of journies.* London: J.M. Dent and Co. Letter X, Lancashire, Westmorland and Cumberland

Dickinson, W. 1975. Recurrence surfaces in Rusland Moss, Cumbria. *Journal of Ecology* 63, 913-993

Dietler, M. and Herbich, I. 1998. Habitus, techniques, style: an integrated approach to the social understanding of material culture and boundaries. In M.T. Stark (ed.) *The Archaeology of Social Boundaries.* Washington: Smithsonian Books, 232-63

Douglas, M. 1966. *Purity and Danger. An analysis of concepts of pollution and taboo.* London: Routledge

Douglas, M. 1973. *Natural Symbols: explorations in cosmology.* Harmondsworth: Penguin

Dresser, Q. 1985. University College Cardiff radiocarbon dates 1. *Radiocarbon* 27(2B) 338-385

Dugdale, Sir W. 1981 [c.1664] in John Aubrey *Monumenta Britannica*, 113-14

Dumayne, L. and Barber, K.E. 1994. The effect of the Romans on the environment of northern Britain: pollen data from three sites close to Hadrian's Wall. *Holocene* 4(2) 165-173

Durden, T. 1996. Lithics in the north of England: production and consumption on the Yorkshire Wolds. In P. Frodsham (ed.) Neolithic Studies in No-Man's Land. *Northern Archaeology* 13/14: 79-86

Dymond, C.W. 1880. Gunnerkeld Stone Circle. *Transactions of the Cumberland and Westmorland Antiquarian and Archaeological Society* (1) iv, 537-545

Dymond, C.W. 1881. A Group of Cumberland Megaliths. *Transactions of the Cumberland and Westmorland Antiquarian and Archaeological Society* (1) v, 39-57

Dymond, C. 1889. Mayburgh and King Arthur's Round Table. *Transactions of the Cumberland and Westmorland Antiquarian and Archaeological Society* (1) 11: 187-219

Dymond, C.W. 1891. 'Mayburgh and King Arthur's Round Table' *Transactions of the Cumberland and Westmorland Antiquarian and Archaeological Society* (1) 11: 187-219

Dymond, C.W. 1893. An Ancient Village near Yanwath. *Transactions of the Cumberland and Westmorland Antiquarian and Archaeological Society* (1) 12: i

Dymond, C.W. 1893. An Ancient Village in Hugill. *Transactions of the Cumberland and Westmorland Antiquarian and Archaeological Society* (1) 12: 6

Dymond, C.W. 1893. Barnscar: an ancient settlement in Cumberland. *Transactions of the Cumberland and Westmorland Antiquarian and Archaeological Society* (1) 12: 179

Dymond, C.W. and Cowper, H..S. 1897. 'Notes on an Ancient Village in Hugill' *Transactions of the Cumberland and Westmorland Antiquarian and Archaeological Society* (1) 14: 460

Dymond, C.W. 1897. 'The Ancient Village near Threlkeld' *Transactions of the Cumberland and Westmorland Antiquarian and Archaeological Society* (1) 14: 309

Dymond, C.W. and Collingwood, W.G. 1876. 'An Exploration of Sunken Kirk, Swinside, Cumberland' *Transactions of the Cumberland and Westmorland Antiquarian and Archaeological Society* (1) 2: 53

Dymond, C.W. 1876. 'Note on Sunkenkirk' *Transactions of the Cumberland and Westmorland Antiquarian and Archaeological Society* (1) 2: 354

Edmonds, M. 1990. Description, understanding and the Chaîne Opératoire. *Archaeological Review from Cambridge* 9(1): 55-70

Edmonds, M. 2004. *The Langdales: Landscape and Prehistory in a Lakeland Valley.* Stroud: Tempus

Edmonds, M., Evans, H., Lund, J., Maxwell, R. and Start, M. 2002. Evaluation of landscape features on Sizergh Fell. *Archaeology North* winter 2002, 13-15

Edwards, B.J.N. 1969. Lancashire Archaeological Notes, Prehistoric and Roman. *Transactions of the Historical Society of Lancashire and Cheshire* 121, 99-108

Edwards, K.J. and Hirons, K.R. 1984. Cereal pollen grains in pre elm decline deposits: implications for the earliest agriculture in Britain and Ireland. *Journal of Archaeological Science* 11, 71-80

Ehrenreich, B. 1997. *Blood Rites: Origins and History of the Passions for War.* London: Virago

Eogan, G. 1964. The later Bronze Age in Ireland in the light of recent research. *Proceedings of the Prehistoric Society.* 30, 277

Eogan, G. 1986. *Knowth and the Passage-Tombs of Ireland.* London: Thames and Hudson

Evans, Sir J. 1872. *The Ancient Stone Implements, Weapons and Ornaments of Great Britain.* London: Longmans, Green and Co.

Evans, Sir J. 1881. *The Ancient Bronze Implements, Weapons and Ornaments of Great Britain and Ireland.* London: Longmans, Green and Co.

Evans, Sir J. 1897. *The Ancient Stone Implements, Weapons and Ornaments of Britain* (second edition). London: Longmans, Green and Co., 353

Evans, H. 2004. Where is the Cumbrian Neolithic? In V. Cummings and C. Fowler (eds) *Neolithic Traditions of the Irish Sea: Materiality and Traditions of Practice.* Oxford: Oxbow, 123-128

Evans, H. 2008. *Neolithic and Bronze Age Landscapes of Cumbria.* Oxford: British Archaeological Reports British Series 463

Evans, Sir J. 1897. *The Ancient Stone Implements, Weapons and Ornaments of Britain* (second edition). London: Longmans, Green and Co., 353

Evans, H. and Edmonds, M. 2003. Interim report on archaeological fieldwork undertaken on Sizergh Fell, South Cumbria, July 2003. Unpublished report

Evans, H. and Coward, D. 2004. A prehistoric occupation site at Sandscale Haws, Barrow-in-Furness. *CBA North* Winter 2004

Fair, M.C. 1932. A reconsideration of the lakeside site at Ehenside Tarn. *Transactions of the Cumberland and Westmorland Antiquarian and Archaeological Society* (2) xxxii 57-62

Fair, M.C. 1935. A note on some West Cumberland stone axes. *Transactions of the Cumberland and Westmorland Antiquarian and Archaeological Society* (2) 35: 259-261

Fair, M.C. 1936. A sandhill site at Eskmeals. *Transactions of the Cumberland and Westmorland Antiquarian and Archaeological Society* (2) 36: 20-23

Fair, M.C. 1943. The Gosforth area in Prehistory. *Transactions of the Cumberland and Westmorland Antiquarian and Archaeological Society* (2) 43: 50-54

Fair, M.C. 1946. Bronze Age swords and daggers of Cumberland, Westmorland and Lancashire North of the Sands. *Transactions of the Cumberland and Westmorland Antiquarian and Archaeological Society* (2) 45: 34-38

Fair M.C. 1946. An interim review of types of Bronze spearheads and axes of Cumberland, Westmorland and Lancashire North of the Sands. *Transactions of the Cumberland and Westmorland Antiquarian and Archaeological Society* (2) 35: 172-178

Farrer, W. 1923-4. Records relating to the Barony of Kendale II. *Cumberland and Westmorland Antiquarian and Archaeological Society Record Series* (ed. J. Curwen), 126

Feeley-Harnik, G. 1989. Cloth and the creation of ancestors in Madagascar. In J. Schneider and A.B. Weiner (eds) *Cloth and Human Experience.* Washington DC: Smithsonian Institution Press, 73-116

Fell, C. 1940. Bronze Age connections between the Lake District and Ireland. *Transactions of the Cumberland and Westmorland Antiquarian and Archaeological Society* (2) 40: 118-130

Fell, C. 1953. A beaker burial on Sizergh Fell, near Kendal. *Transactions of the Cumberland and Westmorland Antiquarian and Archaeological Society* (2) 53: 1-5

Fell, C. 1971. Committee for Prehistoric Studies-unpublished records for Westmorland and Lancashire-north-of-the-Sands. *Transactions of the Cumberland and Westmorland Antiquarian and Archaeological Society* (2) 71: 1-11

Fell, C. and Davis, V. 1988. The petrological identification of stone implements from Cumbria. In T. Clough and W. Cummins (eds) *Stone Axe Studies*. London: CBA Research Report 67, 71-77 & table 29

Ferguson, R.S. 1894. On a Tumulus at Old Parks, Kirkoswald. *Transactions of the Cumberland and Westmorland Antiquarian and Archaeological Society* OS xiii, 389-99

Ferrell, G. 1995. Space and society: new perspectives on the Iron Age of North-East England. In J.D. Hill and C. Cumberpatch (eds) *Different Iron Ages:studies on the iron age in temperate Europe*. Oxford: British Archaeological Reports S-602, 129-147

Fiennes, C. 1888. *Through England on a Side Saddle in the Time of William and Mary*. London: Field and Tuer, The Leadenhall Press

Fischer, Chr., 1979. Moseligene fra Bjaeldskoval, *kuml*, 7-44

Fontijn, D.R. 2002. Sacrificial landscapes: cultural biographies of persons, objects and 'natural' places in the Bronze Age of the southern Netherlands c. 2300-600 BC. *Analecta Praehistorica Leidensia* 33/34

Fowler, C. and Cummings, V. 2003. Places of transformation: building monuments from water and stone in the Neolithic of the Irish Sea. *Journal of the Royal Anthropological Institute* 9, 1-20

Fox, C. 1932. *The Personality of Britain*. Cardiff: National Museum of Wales

Fraser, D. 1983. *Land and Society in Neolithic Orkney*. Oxford: British Archaeological Reports British Series 117

Gale, S. and Hunt, C. 1985. The stratigraphy of Kirkhead Cave an Upper Palaeolithic site in northern England. *Proceedings of the Prehistoric Society* 51, 283-304

Gale, S. and Hunt, C. 1990. The stratigraphy of Kirkhead Cave an Upper Palaeolithic site in northern England: a discussion. *Proceedings of the Prehistoric Society* 56, 51-6

Gaythorpe, H. 1897. Prehistoric Implements in Furness. *Transactions of the Cumberland and Westmorland Antiquarian and Archaeological Society* (1) xiv 442-447

Gaythorpe, H. 1899. *Transactions of the Cumberland and Westmorland Antiquarian and Archaeological Society* (1) xv 161-171

Gaythorpe, H. 1900. Prehistoric implements in Furness and Cartmel. *Transactions of the Cumberland and Westmorland Antiquarian and Archaeological Society* (1) xvi 152-156

Gaythorpe, H. 1903. Notes on the Bronze Celts from Urswick and Bronze Spearhead from Piel Castle. *Transactions of the Cumberland and Westmorland Antiquarian and Archaeological Society* (2) iii, 373

Gaythorpe, H. 1904. Prehistoric Implements from Furness. *Transactions of the Cumberland and Westmorland Antiquarian and Archaeological Society* (2) 4: 325-329

Gaythorpe, H. 1904. Notes on Stone Implements at Stainton-in-Furness. *Transactions of the Cumberland and Westmorland Antiquarian and Archaeological Society* (2) 4: 352

Gaythorpe, H. 1906. Prehistoric Implements in Furness. *Transactions of the Cumberland and Westmorland Antiquarian and Archaeological Society* (2) 6: 128

Gaythorpe, H. 1907. Note on a Stone Celt from Urswick. *Transactions of the Cumberland and Westmorland Antiquarian and Archaeological Society* (2) 7: 269

Garwood, P. 1999. Grooved ware in Southern Britain: chronology and interpretation. In R. Cleal and A. MacSween (eds) *Grooved Ware in Britain and Ireland*. Oxford: Oxbow Books, 145-176

Gelderd, C., Randall, J. and Dobson, J. 1914. Some Birkrigg barrows. *Transactions of the Cumberland and Westmorland Antiquarian and Archaeological Society* (2) 14: 466-479

Gell, A. 1992. *The Anthropology of Time: cultural constructions of temporal maps and images*. Oxford: Berg

Gerritsen, F.A. 2001. *Local Identities. Landscape and community in the late Prehistoric Meuse-Demer-Scheldt Region*. Amsterdam: Free University of Amsterdam

Gibson, A. and Kinnes, I. 1997. On the urns of a dilemma: radiocarbon and the Peterborough problem, *Oxford Journal of Archaeology* 16, 65-72

Glob, P.V. 1977. *The Bog People*. London: Faber and Faber

Godelier, M. 1999. *The Enigma of the Gift*. Cambridge: Polity Press

Godwin, H. and Willis, E.H. 1959. Cambridge University natural radiocarbon measurements I. *Radiocarbon* 1: 63-65

Gosden, C. and Marshall, Y. 1999. The cultural biography of objects. *World Archaeology* 31, 169-78

Greenwell, W. 1874. Tumuli of Cumberland and Westmorland. *Transactions of the Cumberland and Westmorland Antiquarian and Archaeological Society* 1, 19-26

Greenwell, W. 1877. *British Barrows.* Oxford: Clarendon Press

Hall. 1844. *Gentleman's Magazine.* London

Hallam, A.M. 1990. *The Bronze Age Pottery of North-West England and its Social Context.* Unpublished MPhil dissertation, University of Liverpool

Hallam, A.M. 1993. Irish food bowl vessel from the Netherby Hall collection. *Transactions of the Cumberland and Westmorland Archaeological and Antiquarian Society* (2) 43-50

Hallam, J.S., Edwards, B.J.N., and Stuart, A.J. 1973. A late glacial elk with associated barbed points from High Furlong, Lancashire. *Proceedings of the Prehistoric Society* 39, 100-128

Harding, A.F. 1981. Excavations near Milfield, Northumberland. *Proceedings of the Prehistoric Society* 47, 87-135

Harding, A. and Lee, G. 1987. *Henges and Related Monuments in Britain.* Oxford: British Archaeological Reports 190, 65

Harrison, S. 1995. Transformation of identity in Sepik warfare. In M. Strathern (ed.) *Shifting Contexts, Transformations in Anthropological Knowledge.* London, 81-97

Harrison, W. 1910. Leland's itinerary. Transactions of the Lancashire and Cheshire Antiquarian Society, 28, 40-57

Haselgrove, C.C. 1984. The later pre-Roman Iron Age between the Humber and the Tyne. In P.R. Wilson, R.F.J. Jones and D.M. Evans (eds) *Settlement and Society in the Roman North.* Bradford, School of Archaeological Sciences, 9-25

Hearne, T. (ed.) 1710. *The Itinerary of John Leland the Antiquary.* Oxford: Thomas Hearne

Helms, M.W. 1993. *Craft and the Kingly Ideal: art, trade and Power.* Austin: University of Texas Press

Hibbert, F.A., Switsur, V.R. and West, R.G. 1971. Radiocarbon dating of Flandrian pollen zones at Red Moss, Lancashire. *Proceedings of the Royal Society of London B* 177, 161-76

Higham, N.J. 1979. An aerial survey of the upper Lune Valley. In Higham, N.J. (ed.) *The Changing Past: some recent work in the archaeology of northern England.* Manchester: University of Manchester, 31-38

Higham, N.J. 1986. *The Northern Counties to AD 1000.* London: Longman 119-35

Higham, N.J. and Jones, G.D.B. 1975. Frontiers, forts and farmers, Cumbrian aerial survey, 1974-75. *Archaeological Journal,* 132: 16-53

Hingley, R. 1992. Society in Scotland from 700 BC to AD 200, *Proceedings of the Society of Antiquaries of Scotland* 122, 7-53

Hoaen, A.W. and Loney, H.L. 2003. Later prehistoric settlement in Matterdale and Hutton parishes: recent survey results. *Transactions of the Cumberland and Westmorland Antiquarian and Archaeological Society* (3) 3: 51-65

Hoaen, A.W. and Loney, H.L. 2004. Bronze Age and Iron Age connections: memory and persistence in Matterdale, Cumbria. *Transactions of the Cumberland and Westmorland Antiquarian and Archaeological Society* (3) 4: 39-54

Hodgkinson, D., Huckerby, E., Middleton, R. and Wells, C. 2000. *The Lowland Wetlands of Cumbria.* North West Wetlands Survey 6. Lancaster: Lancaster University Press

Hodgson, T.H. 1895. Bone spear or harpoon head from Terra del Fuego, found on peat near Crosby-on-Eden. *Transactions of the Cumberland and Westmorland Antiquarian and Archaeological Society* (1) 13, 402, pl 1 and 2

Hodgson, T.H. 1904. An ancient palisade on Bowness Common. *Transactions of the Cumberland and Westmorland Antiquarian and Archaeological Society* (2) 4: 211-212

Hodgson, J. and Brennan, M. 2006. The prehistoric period resource assessment. In M. Brennand (ed.) *The Archaeology of North West England: An Archaeolgical Research Framework for North West England: Volume 1 resource assessment.* CBA North West

Hogg, R. 1972. Factors which have affected the spread of early settlement in the Lake Counties. *Transactions of the Cumberland and Westmorland Antiquarian and Archaeological Society* (2) 72: 1-35

Hood, S. 2004. Cumbrian stone circles, the calendar and the issue of the Druids. *Transactions of the Cumberland and Westmorland Antiquarian and Archaeological Society* (3) 4: 1-25

Horne, P. 2000. A Neolithic causewayed enclosure in Cumbria. *Archaeology North* 17: 13

Howard, H. 1983. The Bronze Casting Industry in Later Prehistoric Southern Britain. University of Southampton, unpublished PhD thesis

Huckerby, E. and Wells, C. 1993. Recent work at Solway Moss, Cumbria. In R. Middleton *North West Wetlands Survey annual report 1993*. Lancaster: University of Lancaster Press

Huddart, D., Tooley, M.J. and Carter, P.A. 1977. The coasts of North-West England. In C. Kidson and M.J. Tooley (eds) The Quaternary History of the Irish Sea. *Geological Journal* Special Issue, 7, Liverpool, 119-154

Hunter, F. 1997. 'Iron Age hoarding in Scotland and northern England' in A. Gwilt and C. Haselgrove *Reconstructing Iron Age Societies*. Oxford: Oxbow, Oxbow Monograph 71, 108-133.

Hutchinson, William. 1794-1797. *The History of the County of Cumberland and some adjacent places*, vols 1 and 2. Carlisle, F. Jollie

Isbell, W.H. 2000. What we should be studying: the 'imagined community' and the 'natural community'. In M.A. Canuto and J. Yaeger *The Archaeology of Communities, a New World Perspective*. London: Routledge, 243-66

Jackson, E. 1906. On a stone celt found near Cockermouth. *Transactions of the Cumberland and Westmorland Antiquarian and Archaeological Society* (2), 149-150

Jacobi, R.M. 1978. Northern England in the eighth millennium BC: an essay. In P. Mellars (ed.) *The Early Postglacial Settlement of Northern Europe*. London: Duckworth, 295-332

Jacobi, R.M. 1980. The early Holocene settlement of Wales. In A.J. Taylor (ed.) *Culture and Environment in Prehistoric Wales*. Oxford: British Archaeological Reports 76, 131-206

Jacobi, R.M., Tallis, J.H. and Mellars, P.A. 1976. The southern Pennine Mesolithic and the ecological record. *Journal of Archaeological Science* 3, 307-20

Jankuhn, H. 1938. *Haithabu eine germanische Stadt der Frühzcit*. Neümunster, 89-137

Jollie, F. 1795. In Hutchinson, William. 1794-1797. *The History of the County of Cumberland*, vols 1 and 2. Carlisle, F. Jollie, ix

Jones, A. 1999. Local colour: megalithic architecture and colour symbolism in Neolithic Arran. *Oxford Journal of Archaeology* 18(4): 339-350

Jones, A. 2006. Animated Images: Images, Agency and Landscape in Kilmartin, Argyll, Scotland. *Journal of Material Culture* 11, 211-225

Jones, A. and Bradley, R. 1999. The significance of colour in European archaeology. *Cambridge Archaeological Journal* 9, 114

Kaul, F. 1997. Skibet og solhesten. Om nye fund af bronzealderens religiøse kunst. *Nationalmuseets Arbejdsmark*, 101-14

Kendall, M.B. 1880. Archaeological discovery in Chapel Meadow, Park, Dalton-in-Furness. *Proceedings of the Barrow Naturalists Field Club* 3, 37-40

Kendall, W.B. 1900. Submerged peat mosses, forest remains and post glacial deposits in Barrow harbour. *Proceedings of the Barrow Naturalists Field Club* 3, 55-62

Kenworthy, Rev. J.W. 1870. 'Remains of Ancient British Dwellings at Ehenside Tarn, near Egremont' *Whitehaven Herald*, 19 November 1870

Kidson, C. and Tooley, M.J. (eds) The Quaternary History of the Irish Sea. *Geological Journal* Special Issue, 7, Liverpool, 139, 142

Kinnes, I. 1979. *Round Barrows and Ring Ditches in the British Neolithic*. London: British Museum (Occasional Paper 7)

Kinnes, I. and Longworth, I. 1985. *Catalogue of Excavated Prehistoric and Romano-British Material in the Greenwell Collection*. London: British Museum

Kopytoff, I. 1986. The cultural biography of things: commoditisation as process. In A. Appadurai (ed.) *The Social Life of Things*. Cambridge: Cambridge University Press, 64-91

Kristeva, J. 1982. *Powers of Horror: an essay on abjection*. New York: Columbia University Press

Kristiansen, K. 1985. *Archaeological Formation Processes. The Representativity of Archaeological Remains from Danish Prehistory*. Københaven: Nationalsmuseets Forlag

Küchler, S. 1987. Malangan: art and memory in a Melanesian society. *Man* (N.S.) 22, 238-55

Leach, E. 1976. *Culture and Communication: the logic by which symbols are connected*. Cambridge: Cambridge University Press

Leach, E. 1977. A view from the bridge. In M. Spriggs (ed.) *Archaeology and Anthropology: areas of mutual interest*. Oxford: British Archaeological Reports Supplementary Series 19, 161-76

Lemonnier, P. 1993. Introduction. In P. Lemonnier (ed.) *Technological Choices: Transformation in Material Cultures since the Neolithic*. London: Routledge, 1-35

Lewis, G.D. 1970. The Bronze Age in the Southern Pennines. Unpublished M.A. thesis, University of Liverpool

Lort, Rev. 1779. Observations on Celts. *Archaeologia* 5, 106-18

LUAU. 1995. Field Survey 1980-1994. Lancaster University Archaeological Unit, unpublished report

Lucy, S.J. 1994. Children in early medieval cemeteries. *Archaeological Review from Cambridge* 13: 21-34

Lucy, S.J. 1997. Housewives, warriors and slaves? Sex and gender in Anglo-Saxon burials. In J. Moore and E. Scott (eds) *Invisible People and Processes: writing gender and childhood into European archaeology*. Leicester: Leicester University Press, 150-68

Lukis, W.C. (ed.) 1883. *Family memoirs of William Stukeley* vol ii, Surtees Society, p73. Rev. Mr Patten to Roger Gale 30 January 1730/1

Lynch, F. 1997. *Megalithic Tombs and Long Barrows*. Princes Risborough: Shire

Lynch, F. 1998. Colour in prehistoric architecture. In A. Gibson and D. Simpson (eds) *Prehistoric Ritual and Religion*. Stroud: Tempus, 68-79

MacAdam, R. 1861-62. Ancient leather cloak. *Ulster Journal of Archaeology* (9) 294-300

Malinowski 1922. *Argonauts of the Western Pacific*. London: Routledge

Manby, T. 1965. The distribution of rough-out 'Cumbrian' and related axes of Lake District origin in Northern England. *Transactions of the Cumberland and Westmorland Antiquarian and Archaeological Society* (2) 65: 1-37

Manby, T. 1970. Long barrows of Northern England: structural and dating evidence. *Scottish Archaeological Forum* 2: 1-27

Manby, T.G. and Turnbull, P. 1986. *The Bronze Age in Western Yorkshire*. Oxford: British Archaeological Reports British Series 158, 55-82

Manning, S. and Dunwell, A. 1995. An interim note on further discoveries in the Roman vicas at Ambleside, 1992-93. *Transactions of the Cumberland and Westmorland Antiquarian and Archaeological Society* (2) 95, 79-83

Mauss, M. 1979 [1950]. Body techniques. In G. Gurwich (ed.) *Sociology and Anthropology*. London: Routledge, 97-123

Mauss, M. 1993 [1923/1924]. *The Gift. The form and reason for exchange in archaic societies*. London: Routledge

Marsden, B.M. 1999. *The Early Barrow Diggers*. Stroud: Tempus

Masters, L. 1984. The Neolithic long cairns of Cumbria and Northumberland. In R. Miket and C. Burgess (eds) *Between and Beyond the Walls*. Edinburgh: John Donald, 52-73

Matthews, K.J. 2001. The Iron Age of North-West England. *Journal of the Chester Archaeological Society* 76, 1-51

McCarthy, M.R. 1995. Archaeological and environmental evidence for the Roman impact on vegetation near Carlisle, Cumbria. *Holocene* 5(4) 491-495

McK. Clough, T.H. 1969. Bronze Age metalwork in Cumbria. *Transactions of the Cumberland and Westmorland Antiquarian and Archaeological Society* (2) 69: 1-39

McKenny Hughes, T. 1904. Some Notes on Mound Opening, with a description of one recently explored on Sizergh Fell, Westmorland. *Transactions of the Cumberland and Westmorland Archaeological and Antiquarian Society* (2) 4: 71

McKenny Hughes, T. 1904. On another Tumulus on Sizergh Fell. *Transactions of the Cumberland and Westmorland Archaeological and Antiquarian Society* (2) 4: 201

McKenny Hughes, T. 1904. Note on the supposed 'burn' near Sizergh. *Transactions of the Cumberland and Westmorland Archaeological and Antiquarian Society* (2) 4: 338

McKenny Hughes, T. 1912. On an Ancient Enclosure and Interment on Heaves Fell. *Transactions of the Cumberland and Westmorland Archaeological and Antiquarian Society* (2) 12: 397

McKenny Hughes, T. 1912. On some Interments near Hyning, Westmorland. *Transactions of the Cumberland and Westmorland Archaeological and Antiquarian Society* (2) 12: 403

McKenny Hughes, T. 1913. On the occurrence of a portion of the Skull and Antlers of Red-deer of exceptionally large size in the Estuary of the Gilpin. *Transactions of the Cumberland and Westmorland Archaeological and Antiquarian Society* (2) 13:59

Mellars, P. 1976. Settlement patterns and industrial variability in the British Mesolithic. In G. Sieveking, I. Longworth and K. Wilson (eds) *Problems in Economic and Social Archaeology*. London: Duckworth, 375-399

Middleton, R. 1993. Landscape archaeology in North West England and the definition of surface lithic scatter sites. In R. Middleton *North West Wetlands Survey Annual Report 1992*. Lancaster: Lancaster University Press, 1-8

Middleton, R., Wells, C.E. and Huckerby, E. 1995. *The Wetlands of North Lancashire, North West Wetlands Survey 3*. Lancaster: Lancaster Imprints

Middleton, R. and Tooley, M.J. in prep. *The Wetlands of West Lancashire*. North West Wetland Survey. Lancaster: Lancaster University Archaeological Unit

Moore, P. 1988. The development of moorlands and upland mires. In M. Jones (ed.) *Archaeology and the Flora of the British Isles*. Oxford: Oxford University Committee for Archaeology

Moore, P. 1993. The origin of blanket mire, revisited. In F. Chambers (ed.) *Climate Change and Human Impact*. London: Chapman and Hall, 217-224

Needham, S. 1996. Chronology and periodisation in the British Bronze Age. *Acta Archaeologica* 67: 121-40

Mulk, I.M. 1997. Sacrificial places and their meaning in Saami society. In D.L. Carmichael, J. Hubert, B. Reeves and A. Schanche (eds) *Sacred Sites, Sacred Places*. London: One World Archaeology 23, 121-31

Munn, N.D. 1986. *The Fame of Gawa: a symbolic study of value transformation in a Massim (Papua New Guinea) society*. Cambridge: Cambridge University Press

Needham, S. 1996. Chronology and periodisation in the British Bronze Age. *Acta Archaeologica* 67: 121-40

Needham, S., Bronk Ramsay, C., Coombs, D., Cartwright, C. and Pettitt, P. 1997. An independent chronology for British Bronze Age metalwork: the results of the Oxford radiocarbon accelerator programme. *Archaeological Journal* 154, 55-107

North, O.H. 1934. Some recent finds of stone implements. *Transactions of the Cumberland and Westmorland Archaeological and Antiquarian Society* (2) 34: 113-115

North, O.H. and Spence, J.E. 1936. Stone circle, Summerhouse Hill, Yealand Conyers. *Transactions of the Cumberland and Westmorland Archaeological and Antiquarian Society* (2) 36: 69-70

North, O.H. 1936. Local stone implements. *Transactions of the Cumberland and Westmorland Archaeological and Antiquarian Society* (2) 36: 129-131

North, O.H. 1936. Two recently discovered bronze Celts. *Transactions of the Cumberland and Westmorland Archaeological and Antiquarian Society* (2) 36: 142-143

North, O.H. 1938. Local stone and bronze implements. *Transactions of the Cumberland and Westmorland Archaeological and Antiquarian Society* (2) 38: 155-156

North, O.H. 1942. A bronze axe and other local finds. *Transactions of the Cumberland and Westmorland Archaeological and Antiquarian Society* (2) 42: 232-233

North, O.H. 1943a. A Bronze Age spearhead. *Transactions of the Cumberland and Westmorland Archaeological and Antiquarian Society* (2) 43: 70

North, O.H. 1943b. A stone axe-hammer from Threlkeld. *Transactions of the Cumberland and Westmorland Archaeological and Antiquarian Society* (2) 43: 161 and 200

North, O.H. 1948. A polished stone axe from. Holme, Westmorland. *Transactions of the Cumberland and Westmorland Archaeological and Antiquarian Society* (2) 48: 217

O'Ríordáin 1936. *Archaeologia* 86, 276 and 312

Oldfield, F. 1960. Pollen analysis and man's role in the ecological history of the south east Lake District. *Geografiska Annaler* 45 (1): 23-40

Oldfield, F. 1963. Studies in the Post Glacial history of British vegetation: lowland Lonsdale. *New Phytologist* 59: 192-217

Oldfield, F. 1965. Problems of mid-post-glacial pollen zonation in parts of north-west England. *Journal of Ecology*, 53: 247-260

Oldfield, F. 1971. Appendix on the results of pollen analytical studies on the foreshore of South Walney, *Proceedings of the Barrow Naturalists Field Club*, X, 20-23

Oldfield, F. and Statham, D.C. 1963. Pollen-analytical data from Urswick Tarn and Ellerside Moss, North Lancashire. *New Phytologist*, 62: 53-66

Olivier, A. 1987. Excavation of a Bronze Age funerary cairn at Manor Park, near Borwick, North Lancashire. *Proceedings of the Prehistoric Society* 53: 129-186

Parker Pearson, M. and Ramilisonina 1998. Stonehenge for the ancestors: the stones pass on the message. *Antiquity* 72, 308-26

Parker Pearson, M. 1999. *The Archaeology of Death and Burial*. Stroud: Sutton

Pennant, T. 1790 [1769]. *A Tour of Scotland*. London: Benjamin White

Pennington, W. 1964. Pollen analyses from the deposits of six upland tarns in the Lake District. *Proceedings of the Royal Society* B 248: 205-44

Pennington, W. 1970. Vegetational history of north-west England: a regional study. In D. Walker and R. West (eds) *Studies in the Vegetational History of the British Isles*. Cambridge: Cambridge University Press, 41-80

Pennington, W. 1975. The effect of Neolithic Man on the environments of north west England: the use of absolute pollen diagrams. In J. Evans, S. Limbrey and H. Cleere (eds) *The Effect of Man on the Landscape: the Highland Zone*. CBA Research Report 11: 74-86

Pennington, W. 1997. Vegetational history. In G. Halliday (ed.) *A Flora of Cumbria*. Centre for north west regional studies, University of Lancaster. Bolton: Shanleys, 43-50

Petch, D.F. 1987. The Roman Period. In B. Harris (ed.) *A History of the County of Chester*. Oxford: Oxford University Press, 115-236

Pigott, C.D. and Pigott, M.E. 1963. Late-glacial and post-glacial deposits at Malham, Yorkshire. *New Phytologist* 62: 317-334

Pitts, M. 2000. *Hengeworld*. London: Arrow Books, 272-274

Powell, T. 1963. Excavations at Skelmore Heads near Ulverston, 1957 and 1959. *Transactions of the Cumberland and Westmorland Antiquarian and Archaeological Society* (2) 63: 1-30

Powell, T. 1972. The Tumulus at Skelmore Heads near Ulverston. *Transactions of the Cumberland and Westmorland Antiquarian and Archaeological Society* (2) 72: 53-56

Pryor, F. 1982. *Fengate*. Aylesbury: Quartermaine

Quartermaine J. and Leech, R. forthcoming. *The Later Prehistory of the Lake District: Results of Recent Surveys*

Raftery, J. 1972. Iron Age and Irish Sea: problems for research. CBA Research Report 9

Ralston, I.B.M. 1979. The Iron Age (c.600BC-AD200): Northern Britain. In J.V.S. Megaw and D.D.A. Simpson (eds) *Introduction to British Prehistory*. Leicester, Leicester University Press, 449-58

Renfrew, A.C. 1979. Discontinuities in the endogenous change of settlement pattern. In C. Renfrew and K.L. Cooke (eds) *Transformations, Mathematical Approaches to Culture*. London: Academic Press, 437-61

Richardson, J. 1880. *Furness: Past and Present its History and Antiquities*. Barrow

Robinson, J. 2009. *Blue Stockings: the remarkable story of the first women to fight for an education*. London: Penguin, 46

Ross, A. 1986. Lindow Man and the Celtic tradition. In I.M. Stead, J.B. Bourke and D. Brothwell (eds) *Lindow Man: The Body in the Bog*. New York: Cornell University Press, 162-169

Royal Commission for Historical Monuments of England survey of Westmorland 1936

Royal Commission for Historical Monuments of England. 1996a. *Carrock Fell, Caldbeck and Mungrisdale, Cumbria*. Unpublished survey report

Royal Commission for Historical Monuments of England. 1996b. *Howe Robin, Crosby Ravensworth, Cumbria*. Unpublished survey report

Royal Commission for Historical Monuments of England. 1996c. *Skelmore Heads, Urswick, Cumbria*. Unpublished survey report

Rowlands, M.J. 1993. The role of memory in the transmission of culture. *World Archaeology* 25, 141-51

Roymans, N. 1996. The sword or the plough. Regional dynamics in the romanisation of Belgic Gaul and the Rhineland area. In N. Roymans (ed.) *From the sword to the Plough. Three Studies on the Earliest Romanisation of Northern Gaul*. Amsterdam: Amsterdam Archaeological Studies 1, 9-126

Salisbury, C. 1986. Comments on Kirkhead Cave an Upper Palaeolithic site in northern England. *Proceedings of the Prehistoric Society* 52, 321-3

Salisbury, C. 1988. Late Upper Palaeolithic artefacts from Lindale Low cave, Cumbria. *Antiquity* 62, 510-13

Salisbury, C. 1992. The Pleistocene exploitation of Cumbria: a review of the evidence. *Transactions of the Cumberland and Westmorland Antiquarian and Archaeological Society* (2) 92: 1-7

Salisbury, C. 1997. The Prehistoric occupation of Blenkett Wood, near Allithwaite. *Transactions of the Cumberland and Westmorland Antiquarian and Archaeological Society* (2) 97: 1-10

Salisbury, C.R. and Coupe, J. 1995. The Mesolithic occupation of Mill Dam Meadow, Gleaston, Cumbria, *Contrebis* 20: 4-8

Salisbury, C.R. and Sheppard, D. 1994. The Mesolithic occupation of Heysham Head, Lancashire. *Transactions of the Cumberland and Westmorland Antiquarian and Archaeological Society* (2) 141-147

Sayce, R.U. 1956. The Celtic Iron Age. *Transactions of the Lancashire and Cheshire Antiquarian Society* 66, 1-21

Schneider, J. and Weiner, A. (eds) 1989. *Cloth and Human Experience.* Washington DC: Smithsonian Institution Press

Shee Twohig, E. 1981. *The Megalithic Art of Western Europe.* Oxford: Clarendon Press, 114

Sheridan, A. and Davis, M. 1998. The Welsh 'jet set' in prehistory: a case of keeping up with the Joneses? in A. Gibson and D. Simpson (eds) *Prehistoric Ritual and Religion: essays in honour of Aubrey Burl.* Stroud: Sutton, 148-62

Sharpe, K.E. 2007. The Lady of the Lakes in P.J. Cherry (ed.) *Studies in Northern Prehistory, Essays in Memory of Clare Fell.* Cumberland and Westmorland Antiquarian and Archaeological Society, extra series vol. xxxiii, 1-24

Simmons, I. 1993. Vegetation change during the Mesolithic in the British Isles: some amplifications. In F. Chambers (ed.) *Climate Change and Human Impact.* London: Chapman and Hall, 109-118

Simmons, I. 1996. *The Environmental Impact of Later Mesolithic Cultures.* Edinburgh: Edinburgh University Press

Simmons, I.G. and Innes, J.B. 1987. Mid Holocene adaptations and later Mesolithic forest disturbance in northern England. *Journal of Archaeological Science* 14, 385-403

Skinner, C. 2000. Recognising and reconstructing prehistoric landscapes: a new case study from eastern Cumbria. Unpublished PhD thesis, University of Leicester

Smith, A. 1958. Two Lacustrine deposits in the south of the English Lake District. *New Phytologist* 57: 363-386

Smith, P.J. 2000. Dorothy Garrod as the first woman Professor at Cambridge University. *Antiquity* 74: 131-136

Smith, R.A. 1907. A bronze fragment of late-Keltic engraving. *Transactions of the Cumberland and Westmorland Antiquarian and Archaeological Society* (2) 7: 95-99

Soffe, G. and Clare, T. 1988. New evidence of ritual monuments at Long Meg and Her Daughters, Cumbria. *Antiquity* 62, 552-557

Sørensen, M.L.S. 1998. The Atlantic Bronze Age and the construction of meaning. In S. Oliveira Jorge (ed.) *Existe uma Idade do Bronze Atlântico?* Lisboa: Trabalhos de Arqueologia 10, 255-66

Spence, J. 1939. Ancient remains in Ennerdale and Kinneside parish. *Transactions of the Cumberland and Westmorland Antiquarian and Archaeological Society* (2) 39: 31-34

Stead I.M. 1991. *Iron Age cemeteries in East Yorkshire.* English Heritage Archaeological Report 22. London

Stead, I.M., Bourke, J.B. And Brothwell, D. (eds) 1986. *Lindow Man.* London

Stockdale, J. 1978 [1872]. *Annales Caermoelenses.* Ulverston, 250

Stukeley, W. 1740. *Stonehenge, a temple restor'd to the British druids.* London: W. Innys and R. Monby

Stukeley, W. 1743 *Abury: A Temple of the British Druids.* London: Printed for the author

Stukeley, W. 1776. *Itinerarium Curiosum.* London: Baker and Leigh

Sturdy, D. 1976. A ring cairn in Levens Park, *Scottish Archaeological Forum* 4, 52-61

Sweet, R. 2004. *Antiquaries: The Discovery of the Past in Eighteenth-Century Britain.* London: Hambledon and London

Tauber, H. 1979. Kulsoff-14 datering af moselig. *Kuml* 73-8

Turnbull, P. 1995. A lost bronze bucket from Westmorland. *Transactions of the Cumberland and Westmorland Antiquarian and Archaeological Society* (2) 95: 55-59

Turner, R.C. 1988. Cumbrian body from Scaleby. *Transactions of the Cumberland and Westmorland Antiquarian and Archaeological Society* 1-7

Turner, R.C. 1989. Another Cumbrian bog body found in Seascale Moss in 1834. *Transactions of the Cumberland and Westmorland Antiquarian and Archaeological Society* (2) 89: 21-23

Turner, R.C. and Scaife, R.G. 1995. *Bog Bodies: New Discoveries and New Perspectives*. London: British Museum Press

Taylor, M. 1881. On the discovery of prehistoric remains at Clifton, Westmorland. *Transactions of the Cumberland and Westmorland Antiquarian and Archaeological Society* (1) 5: 79-97

Taylor, M.W. 1884. On the discovery of stone moulds for spearheads at Croglin, Cumberland, and on the process of casting in bronze. *Transactions of the Cumberland and Westmorland Antiquarian and Archaeological Society* (1) 7: 279-288

Taylor, J.J., Innes, J.B. and Jones, M.D.H. 1994. Locating prehistoric wetland sites by an integrated palaeoenvironmental/geophysical survey strategy at Little Hawes Water, Lancashire. In R. Luff and P. Rowley-Conwy (eds) *Whither Environmental Archaeology*. Oxford: Oxbow Monograph 38, 18-23

Thomas, N. 1955. The Thornborough Circles, near Ripon, North Riding. *Yorkshire Archaeological Journal* 38, 436

Thomas, J. 1999. *Understanding the Neolithic*. London: Routledge

Tilley, C. 1996. The powers of rocks: topography and monuments construction on Bodmin Moor. *World Archaeology* 28, 161-76

Tipping, R. 1994. Williamsons Moss: palynological evidence for the Mesolithic-Neolithic transition in Cumbria. In J. Boardman and J. Walden (eds) *Cumbria Field Guide*. Oxford: Quaternary Research Association, 104-127

Tooley, M.J. 1974. Sea-Level Changes During the Last 9000 Years in North-West England. *Geographical Journal* 140, 18-42

Tooley, M.J. 1978. *Sea Level Changes: The Coast of North West England during the Flandrian Stage*. Oxford: Oxford University Press

Tooley, M.J. 1985. Climate, sea-level and coastal changes. In M.J. Tooley and G.M. Sheail (eds) *The Climatic Scene*. London 206-30

Tooley, M.J. 1990. The chronology of coastal dune development in the United Kingdom. *Catena Supplement* 18: 81-88

Tooley, M.J. and Shennan, I. (eds) 1987. *Sea-level*. London: Basil Blackwell

Topping, P. 1992. The Penrith Henges: A Survey by the Royal Commission on the Historic Monuments of England. *Proceedings of the Prehistoric Society* 58, 249-264

Treherne, P. 1995. The warrior's beauty: the masculine body and self-identity in Bronze Age Europe. *Journal of European Archaeology* 3 (1) 105-44

Turnbull, P. and Walsh, D. 1996. A beaker burial in Levens Park. *Transactions of the Cumberland and Westmorland Antiquarian and Archaeological Society* (2) 96: 13-26

Turnbull, P. and Walsh, D. 1997. A prehistoric ritual sequence at Oddendale, near Shap. *Transactions of the Cumberland and Westmorland Antiquarian and Archaeological Society* (2) 97: 11-44

Turner, R.C. 1988. A Cumbrian bog body from Scaleby. *Transactions of the Cumberland and Westmorland Antiquarian and Archaeological Society* (2) 88: 1-7

Turner, R.C. 1989. Another Cumbrian bog body, found in Seascale Moss in 1834. *Transactions of the Cumberland and Westmorland Antiquarian and Archaeological Society* (2) 88: 1-7

Uchibori, M. 1978. *The Leaving of this Transient World: a study of Iban eschatology and mortuary practices*. Canberra: Australian National University

Ucko, P.J. 1969. Ethnography and the archaeological interpretation of funerary remains. *World Archaeology* 1, 262-90

van der Sanden, W. 1996. *Through Nature to Eternity: the bog bodies of Northwest Europe*. Amsterdam: Batavian Lion International

Vandkilde, H. 1996. *From Stone to Bronze, the Metalwork of the late Neolithic and Earliest Bronze Age in Denmark*. Aarhus: Jutland Archaeological Society Publications XXXII

Walker, D. 1965. The Postglacial period in the Langdale Fells, English Lake District. *New Phytologist* 64: 488-510

Walker, D. 1966a. The Late Quaternary history of the Cumberland lowland. *Transactions of the Royal Society B* 251: 1-210

Ward, G.K. and Wilson, S.R. 1978. Procedures for comparing and combining radiocarbon age determinations: a critique. *Archaeometry* 20: 19-31

Warmenbol, E. 1996. L'or, la mort et les Hyperboréens. La bouche des Enfers ou le Trou de Han à Han-sur-Lesse. In Archäologische Forschungen zum Kultgeschehen in der jüngeren Bronzezeit und frühen Eisenzeit Alteuropas. *Ergebnisse eines Kolloquiums in Regensburg* 4. 7 October 1993, 203-235

Watson, A. 2001. Composing Avebury. *World Archaeology* 33: 296-314

Wegner, G. 1976. Die vorgeschichtlichen Flußfunde aus dem Main und aus dem Rhein bei Mainz. Kallmünz

Weiner, A.B. 1992. *Inalienable possessions: the paradox of keeping-while-giving.* Oxford: University of California Press

Wells, C. 1991. The environmental history of part of South Cumbria (High Furness, Duddon and Lyth Valleys) from the Early Bronze Age to Historic times. In R. Middleton *North West Wetlands Survey annual report 1991.* Lancaster: University of Lancaster Press, 38-9

Wells, C., Huckerby, E. and Hall, V. 1997. Mid- and late-Holocene vegetation history and tephra studies at Fenton Cottage, Lancashire, UK. *Vegetation History and Archaeobotany* 6(3) 153-166

Wimble, G.A. 1986. The palaeoecology of Lowland Coastal Raised Mires of South Cumbria. Unpublished thesis, University of Wales

Wild, C. 2003. A Bronze Age cremation cemetery at Allithwaite, Cumbria. *Transactions of the Cumberland and Westmorland Antiquarian and Archaeological Society* (3) 3: 23-50

Williams, J. 1986. *A prehistoric cairn on Hardendale Nab.* Unpublished report referred to in Turnbull, P. and Walsh, D. 1997

Williams, D.J., Richardson, J.A. and Richardson, R.S. 1987. Mesolithic sites at Malham Tarn and Great Close Mire, North Yorkshire. *Proceedings of the Prehistoric Society* 53: 362-383

Wilson, Rev. Canon J. 1901. *Victoria County History of Cumberland.* The Victoria County History of the Counties of England. London: University of London, Institute for Historical Research

Wimble, G., Wells, C. and Hodgkinson, D. 2000. Human impact on mid and late Holocene vegetation in south Cumbria, UK. *Vegetation History and Archaeobotany* 9 (1): 17-30

Wordsworth, W. 1906 [1810]. *Guide to the Lakes.* London: Francis Lincoln Ltd

Wymer, J.J. (ed.) 1977. *Gazetteer of Mesolithic sites in England and Wales.* Norwich: CBA Research Report 20, 162

Wymer, J.J. 1981. The Palaeolithic. In I. Simmons and M.J. Tooley (eds) *The Environment in British Prehistory.* London: Duckworth, 77

Yeager, J. and Canuto, M.A. 2000. Introducing an archaeology of communities. In M.A. Canuto and J. Yaeger *The Archaeology of Communities, a New World Perspective.* London: Routledge, 1-15

Young, R. 2002. The Palaeolithic and Mesolithic periods in Northern England: An overview. In C. Brooks, R. Daniels and A. Harding (eds) *Past, Present and Future: the archaeology of Northern England.* Durham: Architectural and Archaeological Society of Durham and Northumberland Research Report 5: 19-36

Zong, Y. 1993. Flandrian sea level changes and impacts of projected sea level rise on the coastal lowlands of Morecambe Bay and the Thames estuary, UK. Unpublished PhD thesis, University of Durham

Zong, Y. 1997. Mid and Late Holocene sea-level changes in Roudsea Marsh, northwest England: a diatom biostratigraphical investigation. *The Holocene,* 7(3): 311-323

Zong, Y. and Tooley, M.J. 1996. Holocene sea-level changes and crustal movements in Morecambe Bay, northwest England. *Journal of Quaternary Science,* 11(1) 43-58

INDEX